Biological Threats in the 21st Century

The Politics, People, Science and Historical Roots

Biological Threats in the 21st Century

The Politics, People, Science and Historical Roots

Editor

Filippa Lentzos

King's College London, UK

ICP

Imperial College Press

Published by

Imperial College Press
57 Shelton Street
Covent Garden
London WC2H 9HE

Distributed by

World Scientific Publishing Co. Pte. Ltd.
5 Toh Tuck Link, Singapore 596224
USA office: 27 Warren Street, Suite 401-402, Hackensack, NJ 07601
UK office: 57 Shelton Street, Covent Garden, London WC2H 9HE

Library of Congress Cataloging-in-Publication Data
Names: Lentzos, Filippa.
Title: Biological threats in the 21st century / Filippa Lentzos.
Description: New Jersey : Imperial College Press, [2016]
Identifiers: LCCN 2015050736 | ISBN 9781783269471 (hc : alk. paper)
Subjects: LCSH: Biological warfare. | Biological warfare--Prevention. |
Biological weapons. | Bioterrorism--Prevention.
Classification: LCC UG447.8 .L46 2016 | DDC 358/.38--dc23
LC record available at http://lccn.loc.gov/2015050736

British Library Cataloguing-in-Publication Data
A catalogue record for this book is available from the British Library.

First published 2016 (Hardcover)
Reprinted 2017 (in paperback edition)
ISBN 978-1-911299-82-0 (pbk)

Desk Editors: Chandrima Maitra/Mary Simpson

Typeset by Stallion Press
Email: enquiries@stallionpress.com

for

Elena & Maia
Cameron
Casper & Felix
Kai & Evan
Gabriel & Esmé
Mathilde
Mara & Lea
Felix & Ursula
Holly & Grace
Loui, Zino & Elia

and other inquisitive minds of the next generation

Contents

Preface

An excerpt from my fieldnotes reads:

> *The men and women who built the United Nations understood that peace is more than just the absence of war. A lasting peace, for nations and for individuals, depends on a sense of justice and opportunity, of dignity and freedom. It depends on struggle and sacrifice, on compromise, and on a sense of common humanity.*

It is a quote from President Barack Obama's first address to United Nations (UN) member states in 2011. His message, in plain English, was that peace is hard.

It was a moving speech, and my notes of it are riddled with checks, underlined words and exclamation marks. Obama brought the national representatives, sitting behind their country name plates in the General Assembly Hall on East 42nd Street, back to first principles, to the intention of the founders of the United Nations, in the wake of the horror and staggering scale of death in the world wars, to make "not merely peace, but a peace that will last."

Obama's words on the pursuit of peace in an imperfect world resonated with words I was reading in a very different aspect of my life. Earlier in 2011, I had given birth to my second daughter and I had become very interested in children's learning and development.

The pursuit of peace, I found, was also something that occupied one of the great leaders in this field. Maria Montessori, whose writings and lectures in the first half of the 20th century increasingly linked societal problems with inappropriate educational systems, and who was nominated for the Nobel Peace Prize for furthering international understanding through her educational work, wrote:

> *Establishing lasting peace is the work of education; all politics can do is keep us out of war.*
>
> (Montessori, 1992: viii)

Like her contemporaries who founded the United Nations, Maria Montessori believed peace was more than just avoiding war. For her, peace was primarily about restructuring society through education. She worked with very young children to develop a pedagogy for peace that teaches values such as global citizenship, personal responsibility and respect for diversity on an equal footing with maths, language and science. It is by fostering these values, alongside the intellectual skills of critical thinking, analysis and problem-solving, that we nurture a culture of peace and non-violence.

The driving force behind this book has been a desire to develop the next generation's understanding of the social contexts of biological threats and our responses to them, and, through this, to strengthen its resolve that biological weapons are not developed or used. By critically engaging with the personal, political and historical dimensions of biological weapons, the book highlights how these weapons are not merely the products of particular historical intersections and of technological, political and cultural conjunctures, but also of individual choices and values. The message is that individuals and their moral frameworks matter, not just in the conception, development and use of biological weapons, but in efforts to create a lasting ban and to sustain the moral abhorrence against these weapons.

My own journey into the biological weapons world began when I was still an undergraduate student at University College London. It was inspired by Brian Balmer, my personal tutor at the time, and his wonderful course "Science, Warfare & Peace". Brian has continued as a mentor to me over the last 20 years and has grown to become a dear colleague. My initial engagement with the Biological Weapons Convention (BWC) and the disarmament diplomacy community was encouraged by Nicholas Sims during my time at the London School of Economics & Political Science. A decade has already passed since we first sat down in the Senior Dining Room to discuss how we could best support the treaty and to draft the first of what has become an extensive series of joint statements to BWC meetings. I treasure his mentorship. My sincere thanks to both Nicholas and Brian for their guidance and continual encouragement over the years.

Also formative in my early years were Jeanne Guillemin, Julian Perry Robinson, Matt Meselson, Malcolm Dando, Alastair Hay and Graham Pearson who all deserve a special mention for their inspiration and support.

This book has been a collective effort, and my deep appreciation goes first and foremost to the set of outstanding contributors who have generously shared their research, perspectives and experiences through the chapters and point of views. It is their contributions that make this book, and it has been a real pleasure to work with each and every one of them.

I am also grateful to Amy Smithson for her encouragement and substantive contributions at the inception of this project. I fondly remember long late night phone calls across the Atlantic and a walk on the Wilton Park grounds as we thought about different approaches to tell the story of biological weapons and who the right people were to tell those stories. Amy suggested combining some chapters, adding new topics and shorter companion pieces for certain chapters to highlight events or factors of particular note, and the concluding roundtable to expose the breadth of opinion on issues in the field. Amy was also instrumental in getting some of the contributors on board.

A warm thank you to Andy Weber and Ray Zilinskas for use of their photographs of the Soviet BW program and to artist Kathryn Smith for use of her photographs of the South African BW program on the front cover.

Laurent Chaminade first suggested the idea of an edited book like this. I thank him for his gentle persistence, without which the book would not have happened. Thank you too to the rest of the helpful team at Imperial College Press for their excellent support through the publication process.

Finally, a very special thanks to my family for their love and unfailing support.

Reference

Montessori, M (1992) *Education and Peace.* CLIO Montessori.

About the Authors

Brian Balmer is professor in science policy studies in the Department of Science & Technology Studies at University College London. His research interests combine historical and sociological approaches and include military technology and arms limitation, particularly the history of chemical and biological warfare. His books include *Secrecy and Science: A Historical Sociology of Biological and Chemical Warfare* (Ashgate, 2012) and *Britain and Biological Warfare: Expert Advice and Science Policy 1935–65* (Palgrave, 2001).

Sonia Ben Ouagrham-Gormley is an associate professor in the School of Policy, Government & International Affairs at George Mason University (GMU). She holds affiliations with GMU's Biodefense Program, Center for Global Studies, and the Department of History and Art History. She received her PhD in development economics from the Ecoles des Hautes Etudes en Sciences Sociales (EHESS) in Paris; and a graduate degree in strategy and defense policy from the Ecoles des Hautes Etudes Internationales in Paris. Ben Ouagrham-Gormley is the author of *Barriers to Bioweapons: The Challenges of Expertise and Organization for Weapons Development* (Cornell University Press, 2014).

Seth Carus is a distinguished research fellow at the Center for the Study of Weapons of Mass Destruction at the National Defense University (NDU). A Johns Hopkins University PhD in political science, his research focuses on issues related to biological warfare, including threat assessment, biodefense and the history of biological warfare. He has written a monograph — *Bioterrorism and Biocrimes: The Illicit Use of Biological Agents in the 20th Century* — and several articles on allegations of biological agent use. Carus has been at NDU since 1997.

Marie Chevrier is professor of public policy and chair of the Department of Public Policy and Administration at Rutgers University, Camden, NJ. Her research focuses on analysis of arms control negotiations and implementation, in particular on negotiations to control chemical and biological weapons. She has written widely on the Biological Weapons Convention, and is author of *Arms Control Policy: A Guide to the Issues* (Praeger, 2012) and coeditor of *Incapacitating Biochemical Weapons: Promise or Peril?* (Lexington Books, 2007).

Jacob Cohn is vice president of governmental affairs (Europe and MENA) at Bavarian Nordic, where he has been for 7 years. An international biotech company developing and manufacturing novel cancer immunotherapies and vaccines for infectious diseases, Bavarian Nordic has through extensive and long-term partnerships with various governments established a unique knowledge of global preparedness in the biodefence space. During his time at the company, Cohn has strengthened Bavarian Nordic's links with a range of national governments as well as the Biological Weapons Convention, the World Health Organization, NATO, the EU Commission and the Directorate-General for Health, among others. Before joining Bavarian Nordic, Cohn had 10 years hands-on experience supplying medicine in disaster or war zones and in developing areas, including dealing with Ebola and Marburg virus disease that Bavarian Nordic is now working to develop vaccines against.

Leonard A. Cole is an adjunct professor of emergency medicine at the Rutgers New Jersey Medical School, where he directs the program on terror medicine and security. A Columbia University PhD in political science, Cole has researched, taught and written extensively on biowarfare- and bioterrorism-related issues, and is the author of *Clouds of Secrecy: The Army's Germ Warfare Tests over Populated Areas* (1988), *The Eleventh Plague: The Politics of Biological and Chemical Warfare* (1997) and *The Anthrax Letters* (2003) — which was named an Honor Book by the New Jersey Council for the Humanities. Trained in both the health sciences and public policy, Cole has testified before congressional committees and made invited presentations to the U.S. Department of Energy, U.S. Department of Defense, the Centers for Disease Control and Prevention, and the Office of Technology Assessment. He is on the Advisory Board of the International Institute for Counter-Terrorism.

Nancy D. Connell is professor and vice-chair for research in the Division of Infectious Disease in the Department of Medicine at Rutgers New Jersey Medical School and the Rutgers Biomedical Health Sciences. A Harvard University PhD in microbiology, Connell's major research focus is antibacterial drug discovery in respiratory pathogens such as *M. tuberculosis* and *B. anthracis*; recent work focuses on the use of predatory bacteria as novel therapeutics for bacterial infections. She is Director of the BSL3 facility of Rutgers' Center for the Study of Emerging and Re-emerging Pathogens, and chairs the university's Institutional Biosafety Committee. Connell is a member of the Board on Life Sciences of the National Academies of Sciences (NAS). She has served on a number of NAS committees including the *Committee on Advances in Technology and the Prevention of their Application to Next Generation Biowarfare Agents* (2004), *Trends in Science and Technology Relevant to the Biological Weapons Convention* (2010), and the *Committee to Review the Scientific Approaches used in the FBI's Investigation of the 2001 Bacillus anthracis mailings* (2011). Connell is currently chairing the *Standing committee for Faculty Development for Education About Research with Dual Use Issues in the Context of Responsible Science and Research*

Integrity, which has directed a series of workshops held in Jordan (2012), Malaysia (2013), Trieste (2014), India, Istanbul and Egypt (2015).

John Ellis van Courtland Moon is emeritus professor of history at Fitchburg State University. He has written widely on chemical and biological weapons, arms control and war, including *Confines of Concept: American Strategy in World War II* (1988) and, with Erhard Geissler, the SIPRI volume *Biological and Toxin Weapons: Research, Development and Use from the Middle Ages to 1945* (Oxford University Press, 1999). He is a member of the extended arms control community and a participant in Harvard University's Kennedy School international security seminar.

Nicholas G. Evans is a postdoctoral fellow in biomedical ethics at the Department of Medical Ethics and Health Policy at the University of Pennsylvania, and a 2015 Emerging Leaders in Biosecurity fellow at the UPMC Center for Health Security, Baltimore. His research focuses on dual-use research of concern in the life sciences, and in particular the ethics of liberty-limiting measures to prevent the misuse of life sciences research and technology. His edited collection (with Tara C. Smith and Maimuna S. Majumder), *Ebola's Message: Public Health and Medicine in the 21st Century*, will be published with MIT Press in 2016.

A Cambridge graduate, **Toby Ewin** worked at the Ministry of Defence, Cabinet Office and Joint Terrorism Analysis Centre from 1980–2010. In 2009–2010, he was a visiting scholar at the Centre for the Study of Terrorism & Political Violence at the University of St. Andrews. He is currently a visiting senior research fellow at the Centre for Science and Security Studies at King's College London. Ewin was appointed an Order of the British Empire (OBE) in 2002.

Melissa Finley is a principal member of the International Biological and Chemical Threat Reduction (IBCTR) program at Sandia National Laboratories. With expertise in infectious diseases of livestock, laboratory diagnostics, disease control and laboratory proliferation risk assessments, she contributes extensively to assessments of biological threats. She leads the team's engagement work in Iraq and Afghanistan, and she has conducted laboratory biorisk assessments there as well as visited numerous bioscience facilities internationally. Finley received her D.V.M. from Colorado State University, and continued her clinical training with a residency in large animal medicine at Cornell University. She received a PhD in pharmacology from Kansas State University, and was a post-doctoral fellow at the Salk Institute from 2001 until she started working at Sandia in 2005.

David R. Franz served as Commander of the U.S. Army Medical Research Institute of Infectious Diseases (USAMRIID) and as Deputy Commander of the US Army Medical Research and Materiel Command. He retired as Colonel after 27 years on active duty. Prior to joining the Command, he served as group veterinarian for the 10th Special Forces Group (Airborne). He served as a committee member for the National Academy of Sciences study *Biotechnology Research in an Age of Terrorism*, and as a charter member of the National Science Advisory Board for Biological Security (NSABB). A Kansas State University D.V.M. and Baylor College of Medicine PhD in physiology, he currently holds an adjunct professorship in the Department of Diagnostic Medicine and Pathobiology in the College of Veterinary Medicine at Kansas State University. His current research interests focus on the role of international engagement in public health and the life sciences as a component of global biosecurity policy. Domestically he continues to encourage thoughtfulness when regulating research in the name of security to minimize negative impact on progress in the life sciences.

Jennifer Gaudioso leads the International Biological and Chemical Threat Reduction (IBCTR) program at Sandia National Laboratories. IBCTR aims to enhance United States and international security by promoting safe, secure and responsible use of dangerous biological and chemical agents, and the program has organized many international conferences, trainings and workshops to build local capacity to address these issues. In the last 5 years, the team has visited facilities in more than 40 countries specifically to consult on biosecurity and chemical security issues. A Cornell University PhD in chemistry, Gaudioso has served on the National Academy of Sciences' *Committee on Education on Dual Use Issues in the Life Sciences* and is currently on the *Anticipating Biosecurity Challenges of the Global Expansion of High Containment Biological Laboratories* committee. She has also served on Sandia's Institutional Biosafety Committee, is coeditor of *Laboratory Biorisk Management* and *Laboratory Biosecurity Handbook*, and is an active member of the American Biological Safety Association.

Chandré Gould is a senior research fellow in the Governance, Crime and Justice Division of the Institute for Security Studies and editor of the journal *South African Crime Quarterly*. Between 1996 and 1999 she was an investigator and evidence analyst for the South African Truth and Reconciliation Commission, where she was involved in the investigation of Project Coast — the chemical and biological weapons program of the apartheid government. After 1999 Gould continued research into Project Coast. She coauthored a monograph with Peter Folb — *Project Coast: South Africa's Chemical and Biological Warfare Programme* — published by the United Nations Institute for Disarmament Research, and numerous papers and articles. She also coauthored *Secrets and Lies: Wouter Basson and the Chemical and Biological Warfare Programme* (Zebra Press, 2002) about the trial of Dr Wouter Basson. Gould has been a member of South Africa's Council for the Non-Proliferation of Weapons of Mass Destruction (NPC) (2007–2010), and a member of the Biological Weapons Working Group of the NPC for the past 6 years. She is a member of the Standing Committee on Biosafety and Biosecurity of the Academy of Science of South Africa, and was a member of the consensus study panel that produced the report titled *The State of biosafety and biosecurity in South Africa* in 2015. A Rhodes University PhD in history, Gould's current work is focused on violence prevention and criminal justice issues in South Africa.

Gigi Kwik Gronvall is a senior associate at the UPMC Center for Health Security and an associate professor at the University of

Pittsburgh School of Medicine and Graduate School of Public Health. A Johns Hopkins University PhD in immunology, her work addresses the role of scientists in biosecurity — how they can diminish the threat of biological weapons and how they can contribute to an effective technical response against a biological weapon or a natural epidemic. She has published and lectured extensively on issues that affect scientists and the practice of science, including laboratory security and personnel security, the need for and process of procuring medical countermeasures, the management and governance of dual-use biological advances, and the approach the U.S. should take to ensure national security while promoting new advances in biotechnology. Gronvall is the author of *Preparing for Bioterrorism: The Alfred P. Sloan Foundation's Leadership in Biosecurity*, in which she describes the major grants that represented Sloan's investments in civilian preparedness, public health law, law enforcement, air filtering in buildings, influenza preparedness and business preparedness, and constructs a chronicle of early gains in U.S. efforts to confront the threat of bioterrorism. She is currently working on a second book about the governance and risks of synthetic biology.

A professor of sociology at Boston College for 25 years, **Jeanne Guillemin** has for the last 10 years been a senior fellow in the security studies program at Massachusetts Institute of Technology. Trained as a medical anthropologist at Harvard and Brandeis Universities, she became engaged in research in the 1980s on two Cold War controversies involving potential violation of the Biological Weapons Convention. One was the U.S. allegation that the Soviet Union had been complicit in using mycotoxins as weapons in Southeast Asia (the "yellow rain" controversy), with the implication that it possessed an offensive capability. The 1979 anthrax outbreak in Sverdlovsk, USSR, precipitated further questions about the Soviet Union's possible pathogen production at the city's military base. In both cases, Guillemin's work focused on victim accounts as a means of verifying actual events. Since then, she has written on the history of biological weapons, including post-WWII proliferation and President Nixon's 1969 decision to abolish the U.S. offensive program, which promoted momentum for the 1972 creation of the BWC. Her books include *Anthrax: The Investigation of a Deadly Outbreak* (University of California Press, 1999) and *Biological Weapons: From the Invention of State-Sponsored Programs to Contemporary Bioterrorism* (Columbia University Press, 2005). Her most recent book — *American Anthrax* (2011) — on the 2001 anthrax letter attacks in the United States, explored the subject of bioterrorism, non-state actors and criminal justice.

Alastair Hay is emeritus professor of environmental toxicology at the University of Leeds, where for most of his research career he has worked on biological markers of exposure to chemicals. For the last half of his career, he has been involved in setting standards for occupational exposure to chemicals for the U.K. Government and latterly for the EU. In parallel with his scientific interests, Hay has had a near 40-year involvement with chemicals weapons issues. He has conducted six investigations of allegations of use of chemical weapons in a range of countries. With a particular interest in education, Hay has worked for many years with the U.K. Royal Society, U.S. National Academy of Sciences, and the Organization for the Prohibition of Chemical Weapons to develop teaching material on chemical and biological weapons. He currently helps train academics and students to use innovative and engaging approaches to promote the responsible conduct of science. Hay was recognized for his distinguished service to science through an Order of the British Empire (OBE) award.

Iris Hunger works at the Federal Information Centre for Biological Threats and Special Pathogens (IBBS) of the Robert Koch Institute in Berlin, Germany. The responsibility of IBBS is to strengthen national public health preparedness and response capabilities to biological threats caused by highly pathogenic or bioterrorism-related agents. From 2006 to 2011, Hunger headed the Hamburg Research Group for Biological Arms Control at the University of Hamburg, where her work focused on bioweapons non-proliferation and arms control, security aspects of the life sciences, and the role of civil society in preventing the (re)emergence of biological weapons. She has also held positions at the Office for Disarmament at the United Nations in Geneva and the Planning Staff of the Federal Foreign Office in Berlin. She holds an MSc in biochemistry and a PhD in international relations, and is author of *Biowaffenkontrolle in Einer Multipolaren Welt. Zur Funktion von Vertrauen in Internationalen Beziehungen* (Bioweapons control in a multipolar world: The role of trust in international relations) (2005) and coeditor of *Biopreparedness and Public Health: Exploring Synergies* (2013).

Jo L. Husbands is a senior project director with the Board on Life Sciences of the National Academies of Sciences, Engineering & Medicine, where she manages studies and projects related to biosecurity and dual use issues, with a specific focus on education and outreach in the broader context of responsible science and on the implications of continuing advances in the life sciences for efforts to mitigate the risks of misuse. She represents the National Academies on the Biosecurity Working Group of IAP: The Global Network of Science Academies, which also includes the academies of Australia, China, Cuba, Egypt, India, Nigeria, Pakistan, Poland, Russia and the United Kingdom. From 1991 to 2005, Husbands was director of the NAS Committee on International Security and Arms Control (CISAC) and its working group on biological weapons control. In parallel to her National Academies work, Husbands, who holds a PhD in political science from the University of Minnesota, worked as adjunct professor in the Security Studies Program at Georgetown University from 2001–2012.

Gregory D. Koblentz is an associate professor and director of the Biodefense Graduate Program in the School of Policy, Government & International Affairs at George Mason University. The Biodefense Graduate Program is a multidisciplinary research and education program designed to bridge the gap between the public health, life sciences and national security communities. Koblentz is also a research affiliate with the Security Studies Program at the Massachusetts Institute of Technology and a member of the Scientists Working

Group on Chemical and Biological Weapons at the Center for Arms Control and Non-Proliferation in Washington, DC. He is the author of *Living Weapons: Biological Warfare and International Security* (Cornell University Press, 2009).

Gabriele Kraatz-Wadsack served for 8 years as head of the Weapons of Mass Destruction Branch in the United Nations Office for Disarmament Affairs in New York (2006–2014). She served as the interim head of the BWC Implementation Support Unit in Geneva for seven months before being appointed Chief of the Regional Disarmament Branch, where she served until retirement in August 2015. Trained in veterinary medicine and microbiology, Kraatz-Wadsack served in different functions as a weapons inspector in Iraq on 26 inspection missions, including as Chief Inspector of the biological weapons inspections.

Jens H. Kuhn specializes in highly virulent viral pathogens and is a Principal at Tunnell Government Services (TGS) tasked as the Virology Lead at the new BSL4 lab at the Integrated Research Facility (IRF) at Fort Detrick. Kuhn was the first western scientist with permission to work in a former Soviet biological warfare facility — SRCVB "Vector" in Siberia, Russia — within the U.S. Department of Defense's Cooperative Threat Reduction (CTR) Program. He was a member of the National Academies of Sciences' committee on *Animal Models for Assessing Countermeasures to Bioterrorism Agents*; and is continuously involved with AAAS's and the U.S. State Department's bioengagement efforts in the BMENA Region, Turkey, and the NIS countries. Kuhn is also a member of the Scientists Working Group on Chemical and Biological Weapons at the Center for Arms Control and Non-Proliferation in Washington, DC. Kuhn is the author of *Filoviruses: A Compendium of 40 Years of Epidemiological, Clinical, and Laboratory Studies* (Springer, 2008) and coauthor of *The Soviet Biological Weapons Program: A History* (Harvard University Press, 2012).

Milton Leitenberg is a senior research scholar at the Center for International Security Studies at the University of Maryland. Originally trained in biochemistry, Leitenberg entered the field of arms control in the late 1960s and was recruited to join the initial staff of the Stockholm International Peace Research Institute (SIPRI) in 1968. Although his primary research and writing responsibilities at SIPRI concerned nuclear weapons-related subjects, he was also one of the team, along with Julian Perry-Robinson, that produced the six-volume study *The Problem of Chemical and Biological Weapons.* He has continued to published extensively on biological weapons, including *The Problem of Biological Weapons* (Swedish National Defence College, 2004), *Assessing the Biological Weapons and Bioterrorism Threat* (U.S Army War College, 2005), and, most recently, *The Soviet Biological Weapons Program: A History* (with Raymond A. Zilinskas, Harvard University Press, 2012).

Filippa Lentzos is a senior research fellow in the Department of Global Health & Social Medicine at King's College London. Her work focuses on social, political and security aspects of the life sciences, and she is particularly interested in contemporary and historical understandings of the threat of biological weapons and bioterrorism. Originally trained in human sciences before obtaining her sociology doctorate, Lentzos spent the first 10 years of her career at the London School of Economics and Political Science (LSE). In 2012, she moved with her research group to King's College London to establish the Department of Global Health & Social Medicine, a unique interdisciplinary social science department aiming to provide international leadership for the social studies of health, medicine and the life sciences. Lentzos' work is theoretically driven, empirically informed and policy-relevant. It draws on a range of methods from participant observation, interviews and documentary analysis, to archival research, database searches and statistical analysis. She is committed to rigorous and responsible research that contributes to addressing the significant social, political and security challenges of developments in the life sciences. Responding to these challenges rarely involve simple, reductive or straightforward answers; and she embraces interdisciplinary perspectives and learning, as well as collaborative research, like that embodied in *Biological Threats in the 21st Century.*

Jez Littlewood is an assistant professor of international affairs at the Norman Paterson School of International Affairs (NPSIA), Carleton University, Canada. His research interests include proliferation and counter-proliferation of WMD, terrorism and counter-terrorism, international security and intelligence. He has written extensively on biological weapons, including *The Biological Weapons Convention: A Failed Revolution* (Ashgate Publishers 2005). He previously served as an advisor to the Counter-Proliferation Department of the U.K. Foreign and Commonwealth Office, the United Nations Department for Disarmament Affairs in Geneva, and with HM Forces (Army) of the U.K.

Caitríona McLeish is a senior fellow at the Science Policy Research Unit (SPRU) at the University of Sussex, and the Sussex Director of the Harvard-Sussex Program on CBW arms and arms limitation. Her research interests are focused on the dual use problem in both the chemical and biological warfare environments. This includes how dual use technologies have been exploited in past offensive and defensive programmes so as to better understand how they might be exploited in the future, and the methods and mechanisms by which different elements of the CBW governance framework try to accommodate scientific and technical change.

Matthew Meselson is professor in the Department of Molecular and Cellular Biology at Harvard University, which he joined in 1960. Early on in his career, he served as resident summer consultant in the U.S. Arms Control and Disarmament Agency, and has, since then, continued his interest in arms control aspects of biological and chemical weapons and in anti-CBW protection, acting as an advisor to various government agencies on the subjects. During August and September 1970, on behalf of the American Association for the Advancement of Science, he led a team to study the ecological and health effects of military use of herbicides in the Republic of Vietnam, and, upon returning to Cambridge, he and his students developed an advanced mass-spectrometric method for the analysis of the toxic herbicide contaminant TCDD and applied it to environmental and biomedical samples from Vietnam and the U.S. In 1983, Meselson and Thomas Seeley, then at Yale, went to Thailand to conduct a field study of the so-called "yellow rain," initially feared to be a toxic weapon but shown by Meselson and his colleagues to be non-toxic feces dropped by large swarms of the giant Asian honeybee *Apis dorsata*. More recently, in 2002 and again in 2003, Meselson led a team to Yeketerinburg (formerly Sverdlovsk), Russia to investigate an outbreak of human and animal anthrax that occurred there in 1979 and had been a subject of international dispute, conclusively demonstrating that it was caused by an airborne release of the pathogen from a closed military biological facility located in the city. In 1990, Meselson and Julian Perry Robinson established the Harvard-Sussex Program on CBW arms and arms limitation, based at the University of Sussex and at Harvard.

Piers D. Millett is principal of Biosecure Ltd., a company dedicated to safeguarding the bioeconomy. He currently consults for the World Health Organization supporting their R&D efforts on Ebola, and he also holds a global fellowship at the Woodrow Wilson Center for International Scholars in Washington DC, where he focuses on the implications of, and responses to, the security considerations of modern biology and biotechnology. Until June 2014, he was deputy head of the Implementation Support Unit for the Biological Weapons Convention, a treaty for which he worked for over a decade. Trained originally as a microbiologist, Millett is a Chartered Biologist and works closely with the citizen science movement, synthetic biologists, the biotechnology industry as well as governments. His efforts have seen him collaborate with a range of intergovernmental organizations spanning health (human and animal), humanitarian law, disarmament, security, border control, law enforcement, and weapons of mass destruction — both inside and out of the United Nations system.

Julian Perry-Robinson is emeritus professor at the University of Sussex Science Policy Research Unit, which he joined in the early 1970s. Prior to joining the Science Policy Research Unit, Perry-Robinson worked at the Stockholm International Peace Research

Institute where, along with Milton Leitenberg, he was part of the team producing the six-volume study *The Problem of Chemical and Biological Weapons.* He continued his engagement with non-governmental, intergovernmental and governmental bodies on CBW-related matters throughout his career, maintaining particularly close links with Pugwash and its specialist international study groups on CBW. In 1990, Perry Robinson and Matthew Meselson established the Harvard-Sussex Program on CBW arms and arms limitation, based at the University of Sussex and at Harvard.

Brian Rappert is a professor of science, technology and public affairs at the University of Exeter. His long-term interest has been the examination of the strategic management of information; particularly in the relation to armed conflict. His books include *Controlling the Weapons of War: Politics, Persuasion, and the Prohibition of Inhumanity* (Taylor and Francis, 2013); *Biotechnology, Security and the Search for Limits* (Palgrave, 2007); and *Education and Ethics in the Life Sciences* (Australian National University Press, 2011). More recently he has been interested in the social, ethical and political issues associated with researching and writing about secrets, as in his book *Experimental Secrets* (University Press of American, 2009) and *How to Look Good in a War* (Pluto Press, 2012).

Following a degree in biochemistry at Cambridge, a PhD in neurochemistry in London and post doc periods in Oxford, Rome and London, **Steven Rose** was appointed professor of biology and director of the brain and behavior research group at the Open University in 1969 at the age of 30, where he is now emeritus professor. His research centered on the neurobiology of learning and memory, on which he has published more than 300 papers and reviews. Most recently his research has been focused on developing a therapy for Alzheimer's disease. Throughout his career he has also been actively concerned with the ethical, legal and social aspects of developments in science, especially genetics and neuroscience. He was a regular panel member of Radio 4's *The Moral Maze* for 5 years, and he has written or edited 15 books including *Chemical and Biological*

Warfare (1968), *Not in Our Genes* (1984, with Richard Lewontin and Leon Kamin), *No Fire, No Thunder: Threat of Chemical and Biological Weapons* (1968, with Sean Murphy and Alastair Hay), *The Making of Memory* (science book prize 1993, new edition 2003), *Lifelines: Life beyond the Gene* (2005), *Alas Poor Darwin* (2000; with feminist sociologist Hilary Rose), and *The 21st Century Brain: Explaining Mending and Manipulating the Mind* (2005). Hilary Rose's and his most recent book *Genes, Cells and Brains: Bioscience's Promethean Promises* was published in 2012, and they are currently working on a critique of the political economy of neuroscience to be published next year. Rose has been politically active throughout his career, founding, with Hillary Rose, the British Society for Social Responsibility in Science already in 1969. In 2002, the two Roses initiated a call for a moratorium on European research collaboration with Israel whilst that country was in breach of the EU Charter of Human Rights and until a just peace was negotiated with the Palestinians. This call led to the creation of the British Committee for the Universities of Palestine. Steven Rose has received a variety of medals and international awards, and BBC4 transmitted a filmed profile of him in 2003.

Nicholas A. Sims holds an emeritus readership in international relations from the London School of Economics & Political Science (LSE) in the University of London. He taught in the LSE Department of International Relations from 1968 until retirement in 2010, specializing in disarmament and arms limitation treaties, verification and international organizations. He has written on the BWC ever since it was under negotiation, with particular reference to its review and reinforcement. He witnessed its entry into force in 1975, participated in its first review conference in 1980, and was an invited speaker at the 40th anniversary event held in 2015 in the Council Chamber of the Palais des Nations at Geneva in which it had been negotiated. Sims' involvement with the BWC derives from a life-long commitment to the enterprise of disarmament and a continuing interest in the interaction of science, law and diplomacy to strengthen the BWC treaty regime. His books include

The Diplomacy of Biological Disarmament (1988), *The Evolution of Biological Disarmament* (2001) and *The Future of Biological Disarmament* (2009).

Alex Spelling is a research fellow in the Science & Technology Studies Department at University College London. A Nottingham University PhD in history, his research interests lie in Cold War history from a transatlantic perspective, with special reference to the U.S.–U.K. relationship and arms control issues relating to chemical and biological weapons. He is currently working on the AHRC-funded project *Understanding Biological Disarmament: The Historical Context of the Origins of the Biological Weapons Convention* with Brian Balmer and Caitriona McLeish.

Ralf Trapp is an independent consultant providing technical, legal and policy advice in the fields of chemical and biological disarmament and non-proliferation. He specializes in analysing the impact of advances in science and technology on the Chemical Weapons Convention and the Biological Weapons Convention, and he provides advice on preparedness and consequence management.

Tim Trevan is an expert on biosecurity and health security, and on assessing and mitigating biological risks arising from nature, accidents and deliberate misuse of biology. Previously, Trevan was a British diplomat, serving in Yemen and at the United Nations Conference on Disarmament. While at the U.K. Foreign and Commonwealth Office, he dealt with weapons of mass destruction and later with the rules of war, refugees and human rights issues. He also acted as the political advisor to the United Nations Special Commission for Iraq and Trevan's book — *Saddam's Secrets* (1998) — details Iraq's weapons of mass destruction programs. Most recently, Trevan was the Executive Director of the International Council for the Life Sciences.

Kathleen M. Vogel is an associate professor in the Department of Political Science at North Carolina State University. She also serves as director of the Science, Technology and Society Program. Vogel holds a PhD in biological chemistry from Princeton University. Prior to joining the NC State faculty, Vogel was an associate professor at Cornell University with a joint appointment in the Department of Science and Technology Studies and in the Judith Reppy Institute for Peace and Conflict Studies. Previously, she has been appointed as a William C. Foster Fellow in the U.S. Department of State's Office of Proliferation Threat Reduction in the Bureau of Nonproliferation. Vogel studies the production of knowledge on technical security issues. Her book *Phantom Menace or Looming Danger? A New Framework for Assessing Bioweapons Threats* (Johns Hopkins University Press, 2013) examines the social context and processes of how U.S. governmental and non-governmental analysts produce knowledge about contemporary biological weapons threats.

List of Common Abbreviations

BSL	Biosafety Level
BW	biological warfare
BWC	Biological and Toxin Weapons Convention
CBW	chemical and biological warfare
CTR	Cooperative Threat Reduction
CW	chemical warfare
CWC	Chemical Weapons Convention
DURC	dual use research of concern
IBC	Institutional Biosafety Committee
U.K.	United Kingdom
U.S.	United States
USA	United States of America
USSR	Union of Soviet Socialist Republics
UN	United Nations
WHO	World Health Organisation
WMD	Weapons of Mass Destruction

Photograph Sources and Descriptions

The photographs on the front and back cover are modified versions of the originals specified below. The photographs are listed from the top down, left to right.

Front cover:

1. Nuclear, biological and chemical (NBC) field exercise, 1981, United Kingdom. Photo courtesy of Imperial War Museum (HU 102377).
2. United Nations Security Council discussion of germ warfare, 1952. Photo by MB courtesy of the United Nations.
3. H1N1 influenza virus. Shutterstock photo 41099986.
4. BSL 4 lab at the Scientific-Production Association "Vektor" in Koltsovo, Novosibirsk, a key site of Biopreparat and the Soviet biowarfare program. Photo courtesy of Raymond A. Zilinskas.
5. Pipetting. iStock photo 18306342.
6. Demonstration by Soviet soldiers during a 1988 visit by Porton Down scientists, part of an exchange during negotiations in Geneva for a comprehensive global ban on chemical weapons. Photo courtesy of Imperial War Museum (HU 102374).
7. U.S. President Richard Nixon at United Nations headquarters, late 1960s. Photo by Yutaka Nagata courtesy of the United Nations.

8. A bioweapons inspector taking a sample from a fermentor at Al Hakam, a key site of the Iraqi bioweapons program, 1991. Photo by H Arvidsson courtesy of the United Nations.
9. Bacterial colonies in a Petri dish. iStock photo 11861847.
10. Nuclear, Biological and Chemical (NBC) field exercise, Saudi Arabia, 1990. Photo courtesy of Imperial War Museum (GLF 400).
11. Vaccine production. Photo courtesy of Bavarian Nordic.
12. Plan of the Roodeplaat Research Laboratories, the main site of Project Coast and the South African bioweapons program. Photo courtesy of Kathryn Smith.
13. "Amerithrax" envelope containing anthrax spores sent to Senator Daschle in October 2001 shortly following 9/11. Photo courtesy of the U.S. Federal Bureau of Intelligence.
14. Monkey cages at the Roodeplaat Research Laboratories, South Africa. Photo courtesy of Kathryn Smith.
15. Row of 20,000-liter fermenters in Building 221 at Stepnogorsk Progress Scientific and Production Base. Photo courtesy of Andy Weber.
16. The Stepnogorsk Progress Scientific and Production Base, a key site of Biopreparat and the Soviet bioweapons program. Photo courtesy of Andy Weber.
17. The Experimental Pathology Section at Porton Down, late 1960s. Photo courtesy of Imperial War Museum (HU 102378).

Back cover:

1. Demonstration by Soviet soldiers during a 1988 visit by Porton Down scientists, part of an exchange during negotiations in Geneva for a comprehensive global ban on chemical weapons. Photo courtesy of Imperial War Museum (HU 102374).
2. USSR cluster bomb, Photo courtesy of Raymond A. Zilinskas.

Chapter 1

Editor's Introduction: The Politics, People, Science and Historical Roots

Filippa Lentzos

Biological weapons

This volume explores biological threats in the 21st century through the lens of biological weapons. It tells the story of how we have come to view contemporary biological threats through the politics, people, science and historical roots of biological warfare (BW).

It is a story suffused by secrecy. Most of us are familiar with chemical and nuclear weapons in the sense that they conjure images in our mind's eye: gas clouds wafting over WWI trenches, nuclear missiles displayed in military parades and the mushroom cloud. But it is hard to imagine what biological weapons look like. This is partly because we know so little about them. Biological weapons were researched and developed in the utmost secrecy. The programs were concealed in labs at military sites not listed on ordinary maps; special code names and exceptionally high classification categories were assigned to biological agents and the projects devised to weaponize them; and bioweaponeers were sworn to secrecy and under constant surveillance. Mistakes were costly — one bioweaponeer caught peddling bioweapons-related information to the Soviets was secretly trialled under a news blackout and spent a decade of his 20-year sentence in solitary confinement in an Israeli high security prison under a fake name and a fabricated profession. Much of the documentation and other evidence of past programs has been destroyed. Where there were concerted efforts to bring war crimes and human rights abuses to public light, information about BW programs was suppressed. In the post-WWII Tokyo war crimes trials, similar to the Nuremberg trials in Germany, immunity was traded for lab notebooks and the results of experiments, and the trials concluded without revelations about the atrocities committed by Japan's medical and biological scientists. When the Truth and Reconciliation Commission hearings in South Africa began to uncover details of the BW program "Project Coast" they were faced with delays and legal challenges, and eventually shut down before the investigators could complete their work; the head of the program was never brought to justice and remains a practising medical doctor to this day. What has not been destroyed, concealed or silenced from these programs, often remains highly classified.

The secrecy surrounding past programs have made them difficult to research. Yet, a small group of leading academics has carefully collated documents, interviewed the scientists and others involved in the programs, and visited the labs, facilities and testing grounds in an effort to analyze and piece-together the open-source material available. The efforts to suppress information about biological weapons have also meant that they have rarely been discussed in public forums; BW programs have to a large extent been insulated from outside criticism and open debate about their ethical, social and political aspects. Biological weapons have never aroused the international outcries and protests we are so familiar with from the nuclear field. Yet, in spite of this, the international community has laid down very clear red lines about BW. The preamble to the Biological Weapons Convention (BWC), the treaty banning biological weapons and now signed by over 170 countries, sets out an exceptionally strong normative frame, stating that states party are:

> "Determined for the sake of all mankind, to exclude completely the possibility of bacteriological (biological) agents and toxins being used as weapons, Convinced that such use would be repugnant to the conscience of mankind and that no effort should be spared to minimize this risk"

The efforts and narratives of the people involved in advocating, negotiating and sustaining biological disarmament, and of those who analyze, manage and limit contemporary biological proliferation risks also, therefore, form a crucial element of the story of biological weapons. *Biological Threats in the 21st Century* brings together the accounts of academics and policymakers, diplomats and biosecurity experts, bioweaponeers and activist scientists, in a unique, rigorous and authoritative volume.

Early history

Biological weapons are complex systems that disseminate disease-causing organisms or toxins to harm or kill humans, animals or plants. They can take many different forms, but generally consist of two parts: a weaponized biological agent and a delivery mechanism. For most of human history, attempts to transmit infections were rare and clumsy; they probably seldom worked out and, when they did, they were in all likelihood redundant with natural routes of transmission (Wheelis 1999). Among the older military techniques that can be considered BW is the use of corpses of humans or animals to contaminate wells and other sources of drinking water. While the principal objective was thought to be the denial of clean water to the enemy, a secondary effect was to spread disease among people and animals that consumed the contaminated water.

The earliest recorded account of armies using infectious disease as a weapon is the 1346 siege of the heavily fortified Crimean city of Kaffa, an important trading hub on the Black Sea between Europe and the Far East controlled by the Maritime Republic of Genoa (Wheelis 2002). The Mongol forces besieging Kaffa suffered a severe natural outbreak of bubonic plague that was killing "thousands upon thousands every day" (Horrox 1994: 17). A contemporary Arabic source estimates 85,000 plague fatalities among the Mongol forces in the Kaffa region during this epidemic (Wheelis 1999). But the Mongols turned this to their advantage and catapulted the plague-infected corpses of their dead comrades over the city walls to spread the disease to the European traders taking refuge in Kaffa. The Mongols were skilled siege warriors, and their artillery at Kaffa was likely numerous and sophisticated. The numbers of cadavers hurled into the city could well have been in the thousands. The Mongol's tactic finally broke the 3-year stalemate; the Genoese were crippled by the plague and fled Kaffa by sea back to Europe.

A second well-documented account comes from North America and the wars against the Native Americans. Of the many new diseases that the Europeans brought with them to the New World in the 1700s and 1800s, smallpox was the most feared. Among Europeans, smallpox epidemics typically had a case fatality rate of 20–40 percent; but among Native Americans, who had not previously been exposed to smallpox and who had not built up immunity towards the disease, fatality rates of 90 percent or higher were common (Wheelis 1999). In the late 1700s, at Fort Pitt on the Ohio River — in present day Pittsburg — conditions were extremely crowded. Traders and settlers had been driven in by the hostilities, and smallpox had just broken out. Journal entries, ledgers and other documents from the time indicate that the ranking British officers at the fort met with a delegation from the native Delaware tribe, and handed over smallpox-contaminated sheets and linens from the Fort's hospital under the false pretence of a gift (Wheelis 1999). A smallpox epidemic is reported to have broken out in the Delaware tribe at this time. Of course, the extent to which the spreading epidemic can be attributed to the blankets is impossible to determine, but the incident is indicative of what appears to be a history of sporadic British and American efforts to infect North American tribes with smallpox (Wheelis 1999).

Rational design and industrial scale

Lack of knowledge about infectious disease and how they are transmitted prevented rational design of methods of biological attack. This changed in the 20th century. The revolution in microbiology transformed ignorance about infection into sophisticated understanding. Over the period 1880–1900, the microbial basis of infectious disease was proven, the pathogens causing virtually every common bacterial disease of importance were identified and studied, and their mechanisms of transmission worked out. Coupled with new organizational links between the military and sciences, this paved the way for manipulating infection and for the systematic design and improvement of biological weapons.

Advances in science were applied to unconventional weapons at an industrial scale for the first time in World War I, and the horrors of gas warfare led to several arms limitation treaties. A key treaty was the League of Nations' 1925 Geneva Protocol prohibiting the use of chemical weapons in international armed conflicts. Unlike chemistry, there were no indications at the time that biology was being militarized, but a prohibition on the use of "bacteriological methods of warfare" was added to the treaty late in the negotiations. Yet shortly after the treaty was signed, the Japanese did exactly that. They developed a biological weapons program on a significant scale that included the most atrocious human-subjects experiments on thousands of Chinese prisoners of war and attacks on civilians with biological agents. These actions, unique in military history, crossed a normative and legal barrier that other military powers avoided breaching, and are detailed by anthropologist and sociologist Jeanne Guillemin in Chapter 2.

Most major World War II combatants conducted research on biological weapons, but none of these programs were on the scale of the Japanese program. The post-war nuclear age set a high standard for the next 20 years of biological weapons development; they made it imperative for bioweaponeers to show how pathogens could devastate populations at the same enormous scale as the bombs dropped on Hiroshima and Nagasaki (Guillemin 2005). The post-war Allied efforts of the United Kingdom (U.K.), United States (U.S.) and Canada to show that BW could rival nuclear warfare were extensive, and, as described by historians Brian Balmer and John Moon in Chapter 3, involved laboratory and human subjects research into potential pathogens, the industrial production and stockpiling of agents, the manufacture of bombs and spray generators, fitting of airplanes and ships for dispersal, the indoctrination of troops, and large-scale field trials. Yet, despite the intensive development and testing of these programs, elaborated by political scientist Lenny Cole in his Point of View contribution, and which eventually demonstrated that biological weapons could be as great a threat to large populations as nuclear weapons, biological weapons were not assimilated into the thinking and planning of the regular military. In a political move that caught the bioweaponeers off-guard, the newly-elected President Richard Nixon unilaterally renounced biological weapons in 1969, paving the way for the multilateral BWC. The U.S. bioweapon program was dismantled in the early 1970s, the considerable stockpiles destroyed and the facilities converted.

Ironically, it was only after signing the BWC that the Soviet program began its incredible expansion. The expansion and redirection of the program was proposed by a small but very influential group of scientists arguing for exploiting the new field of genetic engineering that was just beginning to emerge in the West. As virologist Jens Kuhn and arms control expert Milton Leitenberg describe in Chapter 4, new pathogen properties, such as increased virulence, antibiotic resistance and enhanced stability, were to be engineered directly into pathogens, including agents not on classical bioweapons agent lists. These altered pathogens formed a novel arsenal of weapons that could not be predicted by western intelligence. The tightly controlled program was even more secret than the USSR's efforts in the realm of nuclear weapons. Rather than expanding the Soviet military biological institutions, the new offensive program was established in the civilian sphere. Western intelligence services most likely knew about the military biological institutions and kept them under observation, so the better option was to "hide" the new institutions in plain sight. An entirely new, ostensibly commercial, network of institutes, production plants and storage facilities was constructed. Collectively known as Biopreparat, it worked both sides of the street: it cured diseases and invented new ones. In the years following the USSR's collapse, the Cooperative Threat Reduction (CTR) program decommissioned the main production plant and testing site, and transformed the majority of the Biopreparat facilities into more open research facilities some of which began international collaborations on peaceful microbial research, including international scientist exchanges. The three key military institutes involved in the BW program remain closed to outsiders, and it is not possible to ascertain whether the biological weapons program has been terminated in its entirety. Russia's current official position is that no offensive BW program ever existed in the Soviet Union.

In her Point of View contribution, Sonia Ben Ouagrham-Gormley presents a 4-year oral history project on the former Soviet and American bioweapons programs. She introduces two scientists from the former Soviet program — one defector living in the U.S. and one practising scientist still working in Russia — and provides a snapshot of what it was like inside the highly secretive program, what motivated their work, how they felt about it and how they grappled with the ethical dilemmas raised by their research.

There were also other 20th century efforts by nations to add biological weapons to their arsenals. In Chapter 5, political advisor and former diplomat Tim Trevan describes the origins, expansion and eventual demise of the Iraqi program through United Nations (UN) intervention following the first Gulf war "Desert Storm". UN bioweapons inspector Gabriele Kraatz-Wadsack details the Iraqi leadership's tactics to undermine the UN inspectors, with her Point of View contribution describing her experiences of cutting through the Iraqi lies, half truths, intimidation and deceptions. In Chapter 6, toxicologist and activist scientist Alastair Hay describes another of the smaller BW programs, that of Apartheid-era South Africa, which came to light during the public hearings of the Truth and Reconciliation Commission held as the 20th century was drawing to a close. His research gives insight into the motivations of the scientists behind the program, and is complemented by Truth and Reconciliation Commission investigator Chandré Gould's Point of View examining transitional justice institutions as a means of revealing otherwise hidden weapons programs.

What stands out in the accounts of historical BW programs is the different ways in which they conceived of biological weapons — another factor complicating what biological weapons look like in our mind's eye. The major Allied powers predominantly saw biological weapons as strategic weapons comparable to the atomic bomb. Biological agents were researched for militarily useful criteria — dispersible as an aerosol, economically scalable, stable in the air, high virulence and so on — and their delivery systems took the form of missiles, cluster bombs and drones, or sprayers and spray tanks fitted to aircraft, cars, trucks and boats. The later, smaller programs viewed biological weapons differently. The South African program focused on assassinations, sabotage operations and the development of a "vaccine" to limit the fertility of black women, and on developing injection systems and concealed delivery devices like sugar cubes, chocolates and cigarettes, seeing biological weapons more as tactical weapons. The Iraqis conceived of biological weapons in yet another way. They focused on their psychological impact, viewing biological weapons more as weapons of terror, where it did not matter if the weapons were poorly designed and ineffective as long as they instilled exceptionally high levels of fear and dread in their enemies.

Bioterrorism

The fear biological weapons can elicit has also appealed to non-state actors. In Chapter 7, political scientist Seth Carus, from the U.S. National Defense University, describes four historical cases where individuals or small groups have attempted to use biological agents as weapons of terror, and he draws out suggestive features that can enrich assessments of the current and future threat. Former British security services analyst Toby Ewin further elaborates what makes terrorists choose, or avoid, biological weapons in his Point of View, reminding us that the terrorism threat is not "a static subject to be 'uncovered' like an archaeological find" but constantly evolving.

Bioterrorism first emerged as a political concept during the early 1990s in the United States. As the Cold War faded, the threat of terrorists armed with biological weapons and other "weapons of mass destruction" (WMD) began to replace the Soviet threat. Different assessments of the importance, urgency and scale of the newly perceived threat were present in the early political debates on bioterrorism (Wright 2007). "Alarmists," who included prominent scientific and technical advisers, tended to emphasize the possibility of "apocalyptic" attacks with natural pathogens and genetically engineered hybrids, and the vulnerability of the civilian population. They were less focused on the identities of "bioterrorists," and in their interests in pursuing such attacks or in their capacities to do so. "Sceptics," on the other hand, tended to have backgrounds and training in the history, politics and culture of terrorism, and for them, question of identity, interests and details of past attackers were the primary questions to ask. Although little credible evidence existed at the time that terrorists would, or even could, resort to biological weapons, alarmism ultimately trumped scepticism and federal funds poured into new U.S. preparedness and civilian biodefense programs of considerable institutional proportions (Guillemin 2005; Wright 2007).

The "Amerithrax" attacks — as the FBI code-named the series of anonymous letters containing anthrax sent to media outlets and the U.S. Senate within weeks of the "9/11" terrorist attacks on New York and Washington on September 11, 2001 — revealed serious shortcomings in U.S. biosecurity. They also raised fears about the growing potential for bioterrorism on American soil. The threat of bioterrorism became one of the Bush administration's key security concerns during its two terms in office, and, as described by science and technology studies scholar Kathleen Vogel in Chapter 8, initiated a series of new regulations, policies and programs to further strengthen U.S. preparedness and defense against a bioweapon attack.

Concern about the threat of international terrorism coupled with WMD proliferation was also exported from the United States to international security forums and back to capitals around the world. "Bioterrorism" became an international problem requiring a policy response, and counteroffensives materialized in international risk and security strategies. In Europe, the European Commission launched a program to respond to the consequences of WMD attacks, and particularly bioterrorism attacks, already within a few weeks of 9/11 and Amerithrax. The European security strategy, drawn up for the first time in 2003, focused heavily on the new threat from WMD and "terrorists committed to maximum violence."[1] In parallel, the European Union also adopted a strategy against proliferation of WMD.[2]

Dual use research of concern

The global political focus on the bioterrorism threat has been sustained since 2001 by the perception that biological weapons are increasingly becoming accessible through scientific advances.

The BWC prohibits the development, production and stockpiling of biological weapons, but it does not prevent states conducting research activities for peaceful and defensive purposes. However, distinguishing between permitted and prohibited activities is difficult at the level of basic biological research where the same techniques used to gain insight and understanding about fundamental life processes for the benefit of human health and welfare may also be used for the development of BW agents, as biosecurity expert Gigi Kwik Gronvall elaborates in her Point of View contribution.

A set of high profile scientific experiments in the early 2000s added to the growing political concerns about bioterrorism. These aimed to make mousepox more deadly, synthesize poliovirus from scratch, and reconstruct the extinct 1918 flu virus. Experiments aiming to make flu viruses more easily able to spread first attracted attention in 2011. Many scientists and others worried that if the potent new lab strain was accidentally or deliberately released, it could result in a deadly pandemic. By 2012, leading influenza virologists agreed to a voluntary moratorium on these so-called gain-of-function studies, but the work resumed in 2013. New experiments on dangerous flu strains like H5N1, H1N1, H7N9 and H7N1 rekindled concerns — in part because a series of lab accidents and breaches at the Centers for Disease Control and Prevention and the National Institutes of Health had heightened concerns about safety at high-containment labs. In October 2014, the U.S. government stepped in, imposing a federal funding pause on the most dangerous gain-of-function experiments and announcing an extended deliberative process, analyzed by microbiologist Nancy Connell and sociologist Brian Rappert in Chapter 9.

The seminal report framing current discussions about dual use research of concern is the U.S. National Academies of Sciences report *Biotechnology Research in an Age of Terrorism*. In his Point of View,

Dave Franz, a member of the committee behind the report and previous Commander of the U.S. Army Medical Research Institute of Infectious Diseases (USAMRIID) at Fort Detrick, reflects on how thinking about dangerous life sciences research has developed over the last 15 years.

Global health security

The World Health Organization (WHO), which has traditionally been reluctant to address security-related issues for fear that its public health mission would be compromised, has increasingly been gaining a profile as a key actor in the security world, and it has exerted significant influence on how the perception of biological threats has evolved. From the outset, its overriding message has been that, whatever the cause of epidemics or emerging infectious diseases, the response to them will initially be the same: "In most situations, the public health system will be the first to detect cases and raise the alarm."[3] In other words, the threat of deliberate use of biological weapons should be thought of as part of a wider spectrum of threats that also includes the threat of disease from natural outbreaks and accidental releases, and the most effective response to these threats is to bolster public health measures.

Following this lead, the Obama administration ushered in an evolution in U.S. thinking about its response to bioterrorism. The administration's first major policy initiative on biosecurity was the *National Strategy for Countering Biological Threats*. While the Bush Administration's efforts had been focused on biodefense, this strategy was focused on prevention. It emphasized linking deliberate disease outbreaks from bioterrorism attacks with naturally occurring disease outbreaks, to create a more "seamless" and "integrated" link across all types of biological threats — echoing what the WHO had been pushing multilaterally for years. In his 2011 speech to the UN General Assembly, President Obama called upon all countries to "come together to prevent, and detect, and fight every kind of biological danger — whether it's a pandemic like H1N1, or a terrorist threat, or a treatable disease."[4] In February 2014, the U.S. spearheaded the Global Health Security

Agenda to establish global capacity to prevent, detect and rapidly respond to biological threats. A test case was brewing even as the initiative was getting off the ground. By August 2014, the WHO declared the Ebola epidemic in Western Africa a "Public Health Emergency of International Concern." But as Margaret Chan, the Director-General of the WHO, explained to the international community's premier security forum, the Security Council of the UN, this Ebola epidemic was very different to the many big infectious disease outbreaks managed by the WHO in recent years: "This is likely the greatest peacetime challenge that the UN and its agencies have ever faced. None of us experienced in containing outbreaks has ever seen, in our lifetimes, an emergency on this scale, with this degree of suffering, and with this magnitude of cascading consequences."[5] The Ebola outbreak was characterized not merely as a public health crisis, but as "a threat to national security well beyond the outbreak zones." In Chapter 10, bioethicist Nick Evans considers the international response to the Ebola outbreak and some of the larger implications of securitizing public health.

The lack of vaccines and treatments for Ebola was one of the overriding challenges of the outbreak, and the key lesson coming out was the need to pool risks and share responsibilities in private–public partnerships for medical countermeasure development. The emerging biodefense industry, which often has an unusual disease focus and where there is little to no commercial market, has had years of experience with this. One company, Bavarian Nordic, has demonstrated how private–public partnerships can be successful in the biodefense area. It developed a novel smallpox vaccine and secured a series of contracts to supply the vaccine to the U.S. government stockpile, all the while reinvesting the profits into its cancer and infectious disease research. In his Point of View contribution, Jacob Cohn, Vice President of governmental affairs at Bavarian Nordic, reflects on the company's experiences, and outlines how to nurture the emerging biodefense industry to become not only a vital part of national security but also an asset to global health in the battle against emerging diseases. In Chapter 11, political scientist Greg Koblentz continues the focus on biodefense, and explores how governments can develop defenses against biological threats securely, responsibly, safely, legally, transparently and in alignment with public health priorities — bringing together some of the key themes raised in earlier chapters of the "Biological weapons in today's context" section.

Governance and responsible research

The normative and legal framework against the use of disease as a weapon is exceptionally strong; yet, as political scientist Marie Chevrier and historian Alex Spelling detail in Chapter 12, the enforcement mechanism remains weak. Unusually for an arms control treaty, the BWC was agreed without routine on-site verification mechanisms to enhance assurance of compliance. Some states argued that the nature of biological weapons is such that they are inherently impossible to verify: not only can significant quantities of biological agents be produced in small and readily concealable facilities, but most of the equipment required — the fermenters, centrifuges and freeze-dryers — is ubiquitous in public, private and commercial laboratories. Other states argued that, while the same level of accuracy and reliability as the verification of, for example, nuclear arms control treaties is unattainable, it is possible to build a satisfactory level of confidence that biology is only used for peaceful purposes.

In the Witness Seminar, Jeanne Guillemin, Matt Meselson, Julian Robinson and Nicholas Sims provide first-hand insights into the delicate treaty negotiation process in the late 1960s, early 1970s. Their narratives highlight the significant role played by life scientists, as political advisors, technical experts and advocates, in getting biological weapons on the international disarmament agenda, in building support for a treaty and pushing it through to agreement. The Interview with biologist and activist scientist Steven Rose focuses on the political role of scientists in the 1960s and 1970s, the revulsion they felt about the military misuse of their science, and their efforts to sound the alarm. The life science community continues to play a crucial role in sustaining biological disarmament and non-proliferation, and political scientist Jo Husbands' Point of View makes the case for framing scientist engagement in terms of professional ethics and the responsible conduct of science, rather than in terms of legal obligations.

The responsible conduct of science is also one of the core ambitions of the biological CTR initiative of the Global Partnership Against the Spread of Weapons and Materials of Mass Destruction. Originally focused on former Soviet Union states, and on destroying stockpiles of biological weapons, dismantling production facilities, redirecting research to peaceful purposes, and reemploying former weapons scientists, the initiative now emphasizes biosafety and biosecurity, disease detection and control, and scientist engagement — in line with changing political conceptions of the biological threat and the Global Health Security Agenda, as described in the Interview with Trevor Smith from Canada's Global Partnership Program. In their Point of View contribution, Melissa Finley and Jen Gaudioso, from Sandia National Laboratories, provide examples of the frontline work of biological CTR demonstrating the diversity and complexity of their programs, which have expanded beyond former Soviet Union states into Africa, the Middle East and Asia.

The final contribution of the volume is a Roundtable with five of today's foremost experts on biological disarmament and non-proliferation: Iris Hunger, Jez Littlewood, Caitríona McLeish, Piers Millett and Ralf Trapp. They discuss and reflect on contemporary biological weapons threats, the management of misuse risks and the shifting nature of biological threats.

Editor's note: All contributions to this volume are in a personal capacity; the views expressed are those of the authors and do not necessarily represent the views of the organizations where they are or were employed. The witness seminar, interviews and roundtable are all edited versions, where the contributors were provided with the opportunity to comment on and amend the text.

References

Guillemin J (2005) 'Secret sharing and the Japanese Biological Weapons Program', in J. Guillemin (Ed.) *Biological Weapons: From the Invention of State-Sponsored Programs to Contemporary Bioterrorism*. New York: Columbia University Press.

Horrox R (1994) *The Black Death*. Manchester: Manchester University Press.

Wheelis M (1999) 'Biological warfare before 1914', in E. Geissler and J. E. van Courtland Moon (Eds.) *Biological and Toxin Weapons: Research, Development and Use from the Middle Ages to 1945*. Oxford: Oxford University Press.

Wheelis M (2002) 'Biological warfare at the 1346 siege of Caffa', *Emerging Infectious Diseases* Vol. 8(9): 971–975.

Wright S (2007) 'Terrorists and biological weapons: Forging the linkage in the Clinton Administration', *Politics and the Life Sciences* Vol. 25(1–2): 57–115.

Notes

[1] European Council (2003) *European Security Strategy: A Secure Europe in a Better world*, adopted December 12, 2003, Brussels.

[2] European Council (2003) EU Strategy Against the Proliferation of Weapons of Mass Destruction, adopted December 12, 2003, Brussels.

[3] World Health Organization (2002) 'Preparedness for the deliberate use of biological agents: A rational approach to the unthinkable' WHO/CDS/CSR/EPH/2002.16.

[4] https://www.whitehouse.gov/the-press-office/2011/09/21/remarks-president-obama-address-united-nations-general-assembly (accessed March 17, 2016).

[5] http://www.who.int/dg/speeches/2014/security-council-ebola/en/ (accessed March 17, 2016).

Chapter 2

Crossing the Normative Barrier: Japan's Biological Warfare in China in World War II

Jeanne Guillemin

Introduction

Imperial Japan's use of biological weapons in China during World War II was unique in military history. Surrounded by secrecy long after the war ended, the phenomenon still remains to be fully understood. How was it that the Japanese chose to attack Chinese civilians with plague, cholera, anthrax, glanders and other diseases, killing thousands and terrorizing entire cities and regions? The British and Americans achieved a biological warfare (BW) capacity during the same war and planned strategic attacks on their enemies, Germany and Japan, but they never followed through. In contrast, in 1940–1942, the Japanese went from intensive preparations for BW to BW itself and crossed a normative and legal barrier that other military powers avoided breaching. Unlike the other major powers, Japan also chose to use chemical weapons, again, in its efforts to conquer China. Japan's actions defied the 1925 Geneva Protocol, which banned the use of chemical and bacteriological weapons in war. Yet, Japan began the century as a modernizing nation willing to participate in international arm control agreements and after World War I was a signatory to major peace-keeping accords. Its radical shift towards war in the

1930s is historically documented, but what were the circumstances that propelled Japan towards the use of biological weapons?

One way to begin to answer this question is to consider the political restraints on military decisions that arguably prevented the use of chemical weapons, the other pre-1945 unconventional innovation, in World War II, and which might have affected Japan. The substantive differences between chemical and biological weapons and their diverging histories limit easy comparison, but the two weapons types have points in common, such as their origins in basic science, their indiscriminate impact and their ultimate reliance on air warfare. According to one analysis (Brown 2006), three factors worked against chemical weapons use: (1) moral objections from the government and the public; (2) fear of reprisals in kind and (3) technical drawbacks compared to other munitions.

None of these restraints seemed to have influenced Japan in China. In the West, chemical weapons, used pervasively throughout World War I, became reviled for their impact on defenseless troops. But this was not true for the Japanese, who did not have the World War I experience of battlefield chemical weapons; Japan, in fact, became interested in chemical weapons because of their widespread use in Europe. In contrast, moral objections to germ weapons were based on the imaginings of their gruesome consequences, rather than their demonstrated harm. U.S. Admiral William Leahy, head of the Joint Chiefs of Staff under Roosevelt and Truman famously declared that using "germs" in war "would violate every Christian ethic I have ever heard of and all of the known laws of war" (Leahy 1950: 440). When state programs were first developed, by France starting in 1922 and then by Japan a decade later, the secrecy surrounding them protected them from moral debate. Within state governments, it took just a few visionaries to start and run such ventures, which were kept hidden within the larger military bureaucracy.

Fear of Allied reprisals in kind restrained German plans to use their new nerve agents in 1944 and ultimately had the same effect on the Japanese in the Pacific theater. In the history of biological weapons, deterrence appears nearly irrelevant. To the contrary, the perceived threat of an enemy's arsenal was often enough to spark an arsenal build-up that served self-perpetuating institutional interests (Guillemin 2005). The French in the 1920s and later were convinced that the Germans were preparing to bombard them with diseases, the same misapprehension that spurred the British in 1940 to embark on their BW venture. In the 1930s, the Japanese were concerned that Soviet troops in Siberia would launch germ attacks on Japanese-occupied Manchuria. That trepidation helps explain why Japan began its BW program in that place at that time, but not how its germ weapons were later developed on a large and lavish scale and then used.

For the Allied powers, technical drawbacks restrained the use in war of both chemical and biological arms. In the major battles of World War II, conventional arms and aerial bombing more efficiently met the strategic designs of the Allied and Axis powers. In comparison to incendiary munitions, for example, chemical bombs were heavy and not sufficiently destructive in target areas, while the effects of biological weapons — at least by American reckonings — were unpredictable and slow; even though the British seemed ready to use U.S. anthrax bombs on Germany, they were technically limited by delayed U.S. production. In contrast, in its war with China, the Japanese military seemed somewhat naive about these calculations.

Rules of war and imperial Japan

Although the histories of chemical and biological weapons diverge, they also cross. For centuries, noxious chemicals and diseases were categorically grouped as "poisons." The norms against chemical weapons and germ weapons were often twinned, as in the 1925 Geneva Protocol (see Chapter 12). When weapons of mass destruction were defined after World War II, chemical and biological weapons were added to nuclear arms as the most dangerous strategic threats.

The moral qualms about both chemicals and biologicals have their roots in 19th century humanitarian concerns. With Napoleon, the rise of national armies, coupled with mechanized warfare produced a certain normlessness; militaries lacked the proper rules of conduct — how to treat the battlefield wounded, how to take prisoners, how to protect civilians in war zones. In the years prior to World War I, major world powers were already confronting the human destruction in war that technological progress (for example, more efficient rifles, mobile heavy artillery, and the invention of machine guns) was causing. The battlefield carnage in the Crimean War (1853–1856) and the American Civil War (1861–1865) in particular demonstrated the need to safeguard wounded soldiers and those taken captive. This humanitarian awareness had institutional consequences. In 1862, the suffering and neglect of injured soldiers in the Battle of Solferino during the 1859 Franco-Austrian War were widely publicized (Dunant 1986) and led to the creation of the International Committee of the Red Cross.

Military commanders and civilian recruits alike were baffled by the new scale of battlefield horrors. In the United States, in 1863, a draft of laws of land warfare, written by Francis Lieber, a professor of law at Columbia University, was adopted as General Orders No. 100 (Witt 2012: 375–396). The Lieber Code, as it became known, laid out the morally acceptable rules for treating prisoners and civilians in war zones.

As for arms innovations, the role of chemicals in the industrial production of munitions was well understood. References to dangerous chemical substances and poisons were commonplace and even appear in the Lieber Code. Gun powder produced noxious sulfur fumes; sulfuric acid was used to make nitric acid, which was then used to make mercury fulminate for percussion caps; ideas to use chloroform, hydrochloric acid, cyanide, arsenic, and nauseating smokes and stink bombs in war were circulating in the late 19th century (Smart 2004). As part of the industrial exploration of chemistry, other substances were researched for their potential; chlorine, hydrogen cyanide, cyanogen chloride, phosgene and mustard agent had been discovered or synthesized in the late 18th and early 19th centuries (Sartori 1943).

In 1874, the Brussels Conference added to the movement to put limits on war; it, too, banned the use of "poison or poisoned weapons."

The Brussels Conference, in turn, led to the *Manual of the Laws and Customs of War* adopted by the Institute of International Law at Oxford.

The Lieber Code, the St. Petersburg Declaration and the Brussels Conference informed the 1899 Hague Convention, a major breakthrough in articulating new norms in warfare. It, too, asserted that it was forbidden to employ poison or poisoned weapons. The 1907 Hague Convention reiterated the 1899 principles and bans, including those on balloon attacks and expanding bullets (also called Dum Dum bullets after the British arsenal in India that produced them), and it extended these bans beyond the original 5-year limit. Together the conventions reinforced the concept that the "right of belligerents to adopt means of injuring the enemy is not unlimited" (Boserup 1973: 151–154).

Imperial Japan was a signatory to The Hague Conventions. At the time, it was the only Asian nation recognized as modern by the West. The other possible contender, China, was still geographically fractured by 19th century "free trade" agreements with Western powers and had nothing like Japan's strong central government or industrial resources.

The high estimation of Japan was based primarily on the power of its military, which (assisted by U.S. loans) had defeated the Russians in the 1905 war in Manchuria. That same year, the British raised the status of its legation in Tokyo to that of an embassy, and other major powers followed suit. On its way to becoming a regional power, in 1879, Japan took control over the Ryukyu Islands; then, after its victory in the 1895 Sino-Japanese War, it acquired Taiwan. In 1910, when it annexed Korea, its replication of Western colonizers of Asia passed almost unnoticed.

Part of Japan's rapid modernization, in addition to its growing industrialization, drew on German medicine; its best students were sent to German capitals to study and medical textbooks were in German or translated from German. By 1905, the Japanese, who vaccinated their troops against smallpox and plague and imposed sanitary standards on its military, were revolted by the squalid conditions tolerated in the Russian army. Japan's superior Western-based public health protections were extended to the Japanese living outside the Home Islands, for example, to those who worked for the South Manchurian Railway and in the Liaotung Peninsula, given to Japan in the Treaty of Portsmith as part of the settlement of the 1905 Russo-Japanese War. The Hague Conventions and other accords failed to keep Europe from blundering into World War I in 1914 nor did they prevent the ensuing 4 years of all-out warfare. The war's mechanical innovations (long-range mortar, air power, tanks and submarines with torpedoes) and its scale of destruction outstripped anything that had come before.

Despite the banning of poisons, in April 1915, at Ypres in Belgium, the Germans had introduced chemical weapons to break the stalemate of trench warfare. Directed by scientist Fritz Haber, the German military released 167 tons of chlorine gas that, carried by the wind, passed in minutes into the French and British trenches, killing 1,000 soldiers and injuring another 4,000. This surprise attack signaled the beginning of an arms race among all the involved nations, Germany, France, Great Britain, Italy, Russia and the United States (Lepick 1998). Phosgene munitions, then mustard gas, and an assortment of tear gases and blistering agents were soon widely in use, causing death, burns, blindness, and other injuries and an abiding terror of the "killing clouds."

Imperial Japan and the 1925 Geneva Protocol

In the aftermath of World War I, the major powers were seized by an urgency to unite in order to prevent another such disaster. Millions of lives had been lost, environments were destroyed and political instability was worldwide. Supported by a range of visionaries, the official 1920 creation of the League of Nations heralded a new, institutional approach to peace centered on the political resolution of conflicts (Kennedy 1987). Members would submit to arbitration rather than take up arms and they would act in each other's defense in the event of unprovoked aggression. The 1922 establishment of the Permanent Court of International Justice at The Hague gave member states the option to settle their disputes through legal hearings.[1] The court heard 50 cases between 1922 and 1932, the height of its activity and the League's influence.

The League also promised a vigorous new era of arms control. By Article 8 of its Covenant, members affirmed that "the maintenance of peace requires the reduction of national armaments to the lowest point consistent with national safety and the enforcement by common action of international obligations." Member states agreed to "full and frank information as the scale of their armaments, their military, naval and air programs and the condition of such of their industries as are adaptable to warlike purposes." In addition to the League's active agenda of conflict arbitration and conferences on armaments, the international community began building on the Hague Conventions of 1899 and 1907 and other accords on the rules of war: that attacks on undefended nations must be banned, that prisoners of war had rights to fair treatment, that zeppelin raids and expanding bullets must be prohibited, that the laws of the sea forbade attacks on civilian and commercial vessels.

At the time, Japan, which largely sat out the war, was still seeking an international role and initially signed every significant peace and arms control accord. Its representatives participated in the Paris meetings where the Treaty of Versailles was arbitrated and signed. To their dismay, the Japanese request to have a racial equality clause inserted in the treaty was refused by the Western powers. The rebuff rankled, but Japan nonetheless joined the League of Nations. The League then awarded it the mandate to administer the former German colonies in the Pacific — the Caroline, Mariana and Marshall Islands. Yet Japan's spirit of internationalism was being challenged by national problems. To protect its enlarged empire, its government was incurring increasing defense expenditures and rising debt; at the same time, its population was fast growing and the need for citizens to immigrate was publicly discussed (Jansen 2000: 445–449). Japan's challenge was to balance national interests against the practical benefits of international agreements, and appear sensitive to humanitarian concerns.

After the Americans took the lead in assembling the 1922 Washington Conference on the Limitation of Armaments, Japan joined with the United States, the United Kingdom, France and Italy in signing the resulting treaty, which banned the use in war of noxious gases and submarines (Goldblat 1971: 46–47). The Washington Treaty never came into force due to French objections to its provisions about submarines. Still, it demonstrated a consensus on chemical weapons and paved the way for the 1925 Geneva Protocol that banned the use of chemical weapons in war. As a precautionary measure, the Geneva Protocol also prohibited the use of bacteriological weapons. At the time, no major power had attempted to wage germ warfare, but during World War I Germany had used anthrax and glanders to sabotage pack animals. Should Germany rearm, which seemed likely, its preeminence in microbiology could create a BW threat.

The Geneva Protocol was embraced with enthusiasm. In the interwar years, 43 nations became parties, with the British, French, the Soviet Union, Italy and Germany leading the way. The Protocol could not, however, offer a full guarantee against proliferation. Instead, it allowed a provision for retaliation in kind, an option for defensive weapons development in anticipation of enemy attack. The difference between defensive and offensive capability was left undefined, leaving the option of proliferation even to adherents to the treaty. Nor was the treaty universally supported. In an isolationist phase, the United States Senate failed to ratify the Protocol, although anti-chemical warfare (CW) sentiments were strong in America and the U.S. Army had little inclination to build up its stockpile or reenact the excesses of World War I.

Japan also refused to become a party, for different reasons. After its participation in the 1922 Washington Conference, when its relations with the great European powers and the United States had been reaffirmed, factions within its government began promoting militaristic ultra-nationalism. This movement was fueled in part by Western racism. Despite its modernity, Japan suffered from incidents of “yellow peril” discrimination by the United States. In 1924, the Americans used a new Immigration Act to block all Asian immigrants; the Japanese, who had been exempted in previous legislation, were incensed. Later, to justify its regional dominance, Japanese propaganda would itself turn racist, emphasizing the purity of the Japanese versus other inferior races and also other Asians.

Japan signed the 1928 Kellogg–Briand Pact, which condemned the use of war "as an instrument of national policy" and pledged instead recourse to "pacific means." So, too, did Germany and Italy. But by the early 1930s, each of these three nations envisioned forcibly conquering new dominions. In 1931, militarists in the Japanese government gained popular support by a blatant show of force against China, which some had begun representing as its enemy, along with the Soviet Union and the United States. In September of that year, Japanese troops staged an explosion on the rail line north of Mukden, Manchuria's capital, and blamed the Chinese for provoking aggression. Japan's Kwantung Army units quickly overwhelmed Manchuria and installed a puppet government, making Henry Pu-yi, the last Manchu emperor, its executive leader.

At a February 1933 meeting in Geneva, in a belated defense of China, the League unanimously voted for Japan's withdrawal. The Japanese delegate resigned on the spot, arguing that Manchuria was vital to Japan's existence; in his parting speech, he observed that the United States would be just as unwilling to give up control of the Panama Canal or the British to relinquish Egypt (Brown 1933). The decision to leave had, in fact, been decided well in advance (Bix 2000: 261). The League could do little more than chide the Japanese, still Asia's strongest nation.

In 1933, Nazi-controlled Germany also quit the League, claiming that the World Disarmament Conference it sponsored had unfairly denied Germany arms parity with France. Italy was next to go. In 1934–1936, under Prime Minister Benito Mussolini, it engaged in a war with Ethiopia patently aimed at colonial expansion in Africa. Both nations were members of the League, which attempted reconciliation, but to no avail. Starting in December, 1935, Italy violated the Geneva Protocol by using asphyxiating and poisonous gases on undefended Ethiopian troops and civilians. According to Article 10 of the League's Covenant, its members ought to have rushed to Ethiopia's defense, but their response was uneven and tepid. Despite complaints from Emperor Haile Selassie of Ethiopia and proof of gas casualties from Red Cross physicians, the League failed to implement effective military and trade sanctions against Italy or to deter further gas attacks and the continuation of the war. After Mussolini defeated Ethiopia in May 1936, it became part of Italian East Africa. Soon after Italy exited the League. The example was set of a major power using chemical weapons in a colonial war and doing so with impunity.

Japanese germ weapons

In this period of the early 1930s, on the initiative of just a few advocates, the Japanese Imperial Army began its support of a biological weapons enterprise, located in Manchuria. The venture's prime mover was Ishii Shiro, a military physician trained in infectious diseases and microbiology who achieved the rank of Lieutenant General. Ishii's vision of state-sponsored BW based on medical science dated back to the mid-1920s, but it was disregarded until 1930 when Japan's government began to turn to militarism and aggressive regional dominance. Ishii's supporters were the nationalist Koizumi Chikahiko, once the army's surgeon general and later Japan's minister of health, War Minister Araki Sadao, and General Nagata Tetsuzan, also influential in the military. Masked as an initiative to combat infectious disease, Ishii's research was put under the direct administration of the Kwantung Army, whose leaders were often promoted to high positions in Tokyo. Among the best known of these was General Umezu Yoshijiro, who in 1944 left Manchuria (or Manchukuo, as the Japanese renamed it) to become Japan's Chief of the General Staff.

The colonization of Manchuria offered Ishii ample funds and open territory for his vision of biological weapons. In 1932, he began his research in a guarded encampment built for him in a village called Beiyinhe 70 kilometers outside the city of Harbin (Harris 2002: 31–37). Experiments on plague and cholera, along with others on phosgene gas, potassium cyanide and frostbite, were conducted with captives (referred to as Chinese bandits). Experiments were carried out on artillery shells that were modeled on chemical munitions. Ishii's request for a larger facility, to be built in another village closer to Harbin, was granted and, in 1937, Unit 731, the size of a small town, became the center of the Japanese BW program. In addition, a testing field northwest of Harbin, called Anda, was opened for experiments on bacteriological bombs and sprays. Meanwhile, a new center for veterinary medicine was established near Changchun, the new capital of Manchukuo. Called the Kwantung Army Antiepizootic Protection Unit, it was later designated as Unit 100. Unit 100 became an active center for animal and plant disease research that, perhaps even more than Ishii's unit, relied on Chinese, Russian and other captives as test subjects. Although it was independent of Unit 731, the two centers often cooperated.

With plans to push into Mongolia, the Kwantung Army foresaw a use for Ishii's biological weapons. In the spring of 1939, to contest the Mongolian–Manchurian border, in the Nomonhan district east of Lake Buir, Japanese troops aggressed beyond Khalkin Gol River and quickly met opposition. Since the Soviet Union had signed a mutual assistance pact with Mongolia, its military led the fighting against the Japanese and, armed with tanks and planes, routed the Kwantung Army. Before the September truce, with Japan in retreat, Ishii provided a team of 22 men to contaminate the river with typhus, paratyphus and cholera (Williams and Wallace 1989: 64). It was understood as a suicide mission, due to the danger of the diseases, but the team returned safely. The consequences for the enemy troops were unclear and, since Japan and the Soviet Union soon entered into a 5-year neutrality pact, that frontier for aggressive expansion closed. The idea of leaving an enemy territory lethally contaminated, though, would occur again to Ishii and the Japanese military.

Ishii's major opportunities to organize biological attacks would come from conflict to the south. In July 1937, the Japanese initiated war against China, using a conflict on the rail line near Beijing as a pretext for retaliation. Known as the Marco Polo or Lugao Bridge incident, it marked the beginning of the Second Sino-Japanese War. League members were outraged at the aggression but none dared to act openly against belligerent Japan in China's defense. After quickly taking control of Beijing, Japanese troops battled for Shanghai. There the fighting was bitter and the Chinese army resisted for 3 months before being defeated and fleeing the city.

Unexpected Chinese resistance likely prompted the Japanese Imperial Army's turn to chemical weapons, which began with the battle for Shanghai. As they fought westward to capture Nanking, China's capital, the Japanese continued with aerial chemical attacks. Its military had prepared for this innovation. The Western use of chemicals in World War I had earlier mobilized Japan, its scientists trained in German and British chemistry, to create a research institute. There they conducted experiments on mustard gas, hydrogen cyanide and other agents, testing them on captive Chinese in cooperation with Unit 731 (Williams and Wallace 1989: 44–46). The Imperial Army built a large chemical weapons factory on Okuno Island south of Hiroshima, where mustard gas and other CW agents and a variety of munitions were produced and then shipped to China. Aware that its violation of the Geneva Protocol would count against it in the West, Japan kept secret the Okuno Island facility and its chemical attacks in China (Grunden 2005: 178–183).

In October 1937, China's delegates went to the League of Nations with complaints about Japan's use of what appeared to be mustard and tear gases on defenseless Chinese troops, along with the indiscriminate bombing of cities and towns on the way from Shanghai to Nanking (Goldblat 1971: 175–190). The use of expanding bullets was soon added to the list. The League, its peace-keeping influence gone, could only express sympathy for the Chinese and remind its members that "the civilized world" had rejected chemical weapons. The League also encouraged the sharing of any investigative reports members might have concerning China's claims — as if some future legal forum might adjudicate Japan's violations of the rules of law.

On December 13, 1937, the Japanese conquered Nanking and in its first 9 weeks of occupation slaughtered some 200,000 soldiers and civilians, raped hundreds of women of all ages, looted shops and homes, and randomly burned down buildings (Brook 1999). The scale of destruction was enormous, even though its exact dimensions continue to be debated (Fogel 2000). American embassy officials, allowed to return to Nanking later that winter, were fully advised about the travesties through a city committee of concerned Americans and Europeans. Although the U.S. diplomats relayed their concerns to the Japanese Foreign Office in Tokyo, the "Rape of Nanking," as it was soon labeled in the press, provoked no overt international intervention. Instead, China's allies in the west began covertly funding its army and air force and helping it with building roads for transporting munitions.

Japan continued chemical attacks on the nearly defenseless Chinese troops, seemingly with little fear of an Allied response (Brown 2006: 245–246). But Japan's strength was in conventional air and land warfare, which, in the first 16 months of the war, overwhelmed General Chiang Kai-shek's ill-equipped army. By the autumn of 1938, the Japanese military had "consolidated control over the cities of northeast China, advanced up the Yangtze River to seize the Wuhan tri-cities, and occupied Guangzhou" (Spence 1981: 311). China's General Chiang Kai-shek had lost more than a million men in those battles and the territory of his Kuomintang government was limited to Sichuan Province, with Chungking (Chongqing) as the provisional capital.

The war on China proved a boon for General Ishii, who was allowed to create subdivisions of Unit 731 elsewhere in Manchuria and in occupied China. In Nanking (Nanjing), where a puppet government ruled, he established Ei1644, a garrison in the center of the city equipped with laboratories, rooms to propagate fleas, operating theaters, barracks for soldiers and a prison for captives used in human experimentation.

After the first 16 months, though, Japan's attempt to conquer China began going more slowly than anticipated and it was proving costly. By 1940, over 200,000 of its troops had been sent to fight in China and more were needed; popular discontent was rising because of a shortage of goods, labor and food and "belt-tightening" policies (Yoshimi 2015: 58–59). Outside Beijing and Nanking, the Japanese were attacking cities that were key to its total conquest of China, but the sieges seemed without end. An increase in chemical weapons capability was ordered. Having started in 1937 with a token CW detachment in China, in 1941–1942 Japan increased its CW units to three battalions and five separate companies (Brown 2006: 255).

For Major General Ishii, the continued resistance of certain key Chinese cities offered a golden opportunity for germ warfare. He was able to persuade army command that he could mount surprise disease attacks that would kill and demoralize civilian populations from within. The attacks had to be secret; if warned in advance, public health and hospital assistance could ruin the impact. The disease agent should be one to which the targeted civilians had not been exposed or developed a natural immunity. Ishii proposed a stratagem to which he held consistently. Combined with conventional bombing, biological weapons should disappear in the "fog of war," with their source obscured by the broader chaos in which communication and intelligence were disrupted.

The plague attacks

Ishii's choice of weapon was plague, a disease with special significance in both Chinese and Japanese history. Plague had long been associated with China as the source of the 14th century "Black Death" that traveled from central China via shipping routes to European ports, carried by plague-infected rats. In more recent times, the 1894 Hong Kong outbreak had killed thousands but also allowed the Swiss microbiologist Alphonse Yersin, a protégé of Louis Pasteur, to discover the microbe that caused the disease (now known as *Yersinia pestis*) and pave the way to vaccines and antisera to prevent future outbreaks (Perrot and Schwartz 2013: 181–191). Also in Hong Kong investigating the outbreak was a well-known Japanese scientist, Kitasato Shibasaburo, a former student of Robert Koch in Berlin. Kitasato claimed it was he who had discovered the bacillus, although it is more likely that he later learned about and copied Yersin's methods.

At the same time as their Western colleagues, Japanese microbiologists early on understood the plague bacillus and how it was transmitted by fleas, usually by the species *Xphylla cheopsis.* As carriers, fleas are unaffected by the disease. When they bite their animal hosts, usually rats, they inject them with the bacilli they have in their stomachs. When the rats die, the fleas leave the rats' nests for human bedding and, by biting humans, infect them. Understanding this cycle, Ishii had his scientists at Unit 731 develop a method for propagating thousands of fleas in glass jars with the object of infecting them with plague and spreading them in habitats where rats would be either the primary hosts or the fleas would find their human hosts directly. It took 2 or 3 months to produce around 45 kilograms of fleas (Materials 1950: 255–256).

Ishii's choice of plague was probably related to its being endemic in Manchuria. There he had easy access to the microbe and, at Unit 731, he could measure the progression of the disease in inoculated captives compared to the sick outside its walls. Excellent research had been done on plague in Harbin, where a legendary figure in Chinese public health, Dr Wu Lien-teh, successfully had contained two enormous outbreaks, one in 1910 and another in 1921–1922. Wu used a combination of public education, laboratory analyses and rapid vaccinations that became China's public health response model (Wu *et al.* 1923). In 1928, Harbin became the site of the League of Nations Plague Prevention Laboratory, which was run by Dr Wu and his assistant, the Austrian-born Dr Robert Pollitzer, later known as a world authority on the disease. Both physicians fled Harbin in 1932 and abandoned the laboratory to the Japanese. Ishii's other decision was to target cities where plague was not endemic, places where the population would be especially susceptible, not only through a lack of natural immunity but by the likely absence of vaccines or antisera stocked in cities like Harbin and in Hong Kong by public health departments. The targets should also already be under aerial attack. The plan, which had been tested on Chinese captives in Manchuria, was to bundle the plague-infected fleas with grain to attract rats, which were more or less prevalent in Chinese cities. Low-flying airplanes would dump kilograms of the fleas on city centers with high population density. Three eastern cities which met these criteria were selected: the inland city of Chu-hsiang, the ancient port city of Ningpo (Ningbo) and Kingwa, an important commercial center between these two cities.

On October 4, Japanese planes dropped wheat and rice grains mixed with fleas in the western part of Chu-hsiang. For more than a week, there were no results. Undeterred, on October 27, 1940, Ishii sent a low-flying Japanese airplane to attack the city of Ningpo with a mix of fleas and wheat. This time, Ishii confidently had the expedition filmed for a later showing to his army superiors. On October 29, physicians in Ningpo clinically diagnosed the first case. For centuries, the disease had been recognized by its symptoms: painful swellings in the groin (called buboes), skin lesions, and intense fever and vomiting. After a week, laboratory tests confirmed that the plague bacterium, then called *Bacillus pestis*, had caused the disease. Nothing could be traced to the Japanese. About 100 people died. The number would surely have been higher, save for the rapid cooperation between public health and citizens to disinfect bedding and clothes, keep patients in quarantine, and cordon off and burn buildings in the section of the city where the outbreak emerged. As Ishii predicted, vaccines were not immediately available, only less effective antisera. To his delight, although there were rumors and suspicions, the Chinese press could not identify the outbreak with any unusual Japanese overflight.

On November 12, bubonic plague finally erupted in Chu-hsiang, in the western part of the city, as intended. A gradual spread of the disease as fleas migrated from dead rats to humans might have caused the 38-day delay. The epidemic lasted 24 days and caused 21 deaths. This city, like Ningpo, had never experienced a plague outbreak before. But explicit proof of Japanese culpability was lacking. A local man brought a sample of grains and dead fleas to air raid officials who passed them on to the province's public health laboratory. Due to war time conditions, tests were delayed and no sign of the plague bacteria was found.

On November 26, 1940, while epidemics in Ningpo and Chu-Hsiang were afflicting inhabitants there, three Japanese planes flew over Kingwa. According to residents, the planes dropped a large quantity of small granules, about the size of shrimp eggs. Examined in the local health laboratory, the strange material yielded gram-negative bacilli that resembled *Bacillus pestis*, but, again, due to the privations of war, the laboratory was not equipped to perform more accurate tests. More than a month later, in January 1941, a team of scientists arrived at Kingwa to test the microbes on rodents. No infection was produced, nor did anyone in Kingwa contract the plague. Perhaps the virulence of the bacteria had been impaired. This experimental attack had to be counted as a dud.

The final plague attack organized by Ishii came nearly a year later and yielded the results he wanted. The target was Changteh (Changde) in Hunan Province where the Japanese were without success attempting to reach Chungking. At about 5 a.m. on November 4, 1941, an airplane flew low over the city and scattered wheat and rice grains, pieces of paper, cotton wadding and some unidentified particles. A few city residents brought samples of the dropped material to the local Presbyterian Hospital, where tests revealed microorganisms resembling *Bacillus pestis*. Seven days later, on November 11, the first plague victim was diagnosed, followed by five more the same month. There were two more cases in December and a final one on January 13, 1942. The public health system was mobilized: rats were hunted and killed, victims' homes were disinfected, and, eventually, vaccines were made available. Still, the death count was over 100, a victory for General Ishii.

Whether the plague attacks broke the stalemate or contributed to Japan's overall mission to conquer China is debatable. Ningpo fell to the Japanese about 6 months later; Chu-hsiang and Kingwa remained caught in the contested eastern war zone. Japanese–Chinese battles for Changteh, with one side winning and then the other, continued for three more years, destroying the city and forcing tens of thousands to migrate.

Despite the disruptions of war, China's central public health ministry, based in Chungking, was able to send plague experts to the affected cities, even to Kingwa, to investigate. Robert Pollitzer, dispatched to Changteh, contributed greatly to the summary report on all the attacks, which he rightly surmised were caused by the Japanese recourse to plague-infected fleas (King, 1942). Although the report was distributed to the Allied embassies in Chungking in late 1941 and publicized at a press conference in early 1942, it was dismissed by American and British BW experts as "inconclusive." To them and to government officials, it seemed logistically incredible that the Japanese army could mount such attacks.

The relative success of the plague attacks — perhaps primarily the fact that Japan could not be associated with them — poised Ishii to do more. In early 1942, he was called on to participate in a prolonged series of regional strikes against Chinese civilians called the Zhejiang-Jiangxi Campaign. After the June 1942 Doolittle bombing raid on Tokyo in retaliation for Pearl Harbor, the United States relied on the region southwest of Hangzhou as an escape route for dozens of downed pilots. Protected by locals, many of these pilots made their way to safe havens. That summer and into the fall, Japan took its revenge for this complicity. Its troops assaulted the area by destroying air fields that might serve in future Allied raids, conducting public executions of the Chinese who had assisted the pilots, razing villages and city neighborhoods, and destroying air railroads in a "scorched earth" campaign that would leave little behind for General Chiang Kai-shek's army.

As part of this punitive campaign, General Ishii and 300 of his trained staff assisted in dispersing disease agents by aerial spraying, bombing and sabotage. The diseases were anthrax, cholera, dysentery, glanders, plague, typhoid and paratyphoid. While it is difficult to separate the numbers of people who died from conventional warfare from those who died of these intentionally-spread infectious diseases, estimates run to the many thousands (Williams and Wallace 1989: 69; Harris 2002: 147). Post-war testimony from victims also attest to many casualties and to the decimation of entire villages and city neighborhoods (Li 2005). Indicative perhaps of the severity of these intentional outbreaks is the large number of Japanese soldiers, around 10,000, who accidentally contracted cholera during the campaign raids, of whom 2,000 died. If this many troops were vulnerable, the Chinese population could have been infected on a similar scale.

The cholera casualties among Japanese soldiers were Ishii's great failure and perhaps one reason why the Japanese command, instead of cooperating with him on another significant campaign, relied on conventional weapons. They also ceased using chemical weapons at this time, after a warning by President Roosevelt that the United States would "retaliate in kind and in full measure" if it persisted in using poisonous or noxious gases on China (Brown 2006: 200–201).

In 1945, as Japan was losing the war, Ishii escaped from Manchuria with several dozen of his scientists and found refuge in Japan, which was soon under the Allied Occupation. In early 1946, he was discovered in Tokyo by U.S. military intelligence and, with others from Unit 731, he began the lengthy process of recounting its exploits, including human experimentation, in return for protection from war crimes prosecution.

Conclusion

The epoch in which Imperial Japan developed and used biological weapons was one in which the idea of total war — the legitimate targeting of enemy urban and manufacturing centers — gained great currency (Buckley 1999). As early as 1927, the idea's main proponent, Giulio Douhet foretold that aeronautics would open up a revolutionary new way to make war. "Air power makes it possible," he wrote, "not only to make high explosive bombing raids over any sector of the enemy's territory, but also to ravage his whole country by chemical and bacteriological warfare" (Douhet 1942: 6–7). Of the major powers, only Japan attempted aerial attacks with chemicals and biologicals and, fortunately, not on the scale Douhet predicted.

The concept of total war justified the invention of atomic bombs and their use on Japan in 1945. After Hiroshima, international relations were redefined. Nuclear weapons introduced the potential of a state inflicting instantaneous annihilating harm on an enemy, more than the world had ever known, and of its civilians being exposed to the same threat of mass killing. Foregoing outright military victory as a goal, the major nuclear powers had to rely on the art of coercion, intimidation and deterrence — "the diplomacy of violence" (Schelling 1966: 1–34) — to protect their national and regional interests. As wars continued, in Korea, Vietnam, Afghanistan and elsewhere, the major powers, emulated by minor ones, justified the build-up of their strategic biological and chemical arsenals even as the norms against these weapons strengthened (Robinson 1998) (see Chapters 3 and 4). With the end of the Cold War, the rationales for superpower nuclear and chemical stockpiles broke down, and with them Russian support for the enormous biological weapons program it had inherited from the Soviet Union. While far from perfect, the atmosphere for arms control among the great industrial powers and many developing nations improved greatly over what it had ever been.

In the more than 70 years since Japan used biological and also chemical weapons in China, the idealistic legal restraints promoted in the interwar years — specifically the 1925 Geneva Protocol — have been reinforced by nearly universal acceptance and by two important treaties, the 1972 Biological Weapons Convention and the 1993 Chemical Weapons Convention (see Chapter 12). Not only is the state use of these weapons against the law, but so too are any state programs to develop or add to the proliferation of these arms.

International arms control cooperation, if also imperfect, has improved. Unlike the League of Nations, the United Nations, created in 1945, requires its members to support cooperative armed intervention if necessary. In the difficult process of having Syria become a party to the Chemical Weapons Convention, UN personnel worked on site with teams from the convention's monitoring organisation, Organization for the Prohibition of Chemical Weapons (OPCW). Like the League of Nations, the United Nations supports judicial recourse for disputes, at the International Court of Justice at The Hague. The International Criminal Court, an independent forum also at The Hague, has in its statute the provision for prosecuting those who violate the restrictions of the Geneva Protocol.

Although much is different, the case of Imperial Japan's biological weapons adventure reminds us of important political constants. Historically, ultra-nationalism and militarism, combined with scientific and technological prowess, can provoke war without limits; this was the great lesson of World War II. But the lesson can be forgotten as regimes are overturned or rigidly hold on, and as shifting regional politics pose existential threats that increase the allure of banned weapons. These patterns, obvious in Imperial Japan's wartime history, can be seen repeated in the Middle East and parts of Asia.

What, too, should we be thinking about the pace at which the life sciences and the study of human physiology are rapidly advancing? Research in industrial chemistry that laid the path to Ypres developed over the course of a century. Essential discoveries in the study of infectious diseases predate the Japanese plague attacks by 50 years. Breakthroughs in contemporary genetics and molecular and cellular biology, and the mix of physics, chemistry and mathematics that fuel them, are counted in months and weeks. Are the rules of research sufficient to the challenge? (see Chapters 9 and 12, Point of View).

In addition, one cannot ignore the problem of prejudice in waging limitless wars with unconventional weapons. In the 1930s, Imperial Japan considered China and the Chinese as ripe for colonialization, if not enslavement; when the Chinese resisted, the Japanese saw every reason to treat their already devalued lives as expendable, whether the intent was to break a stalemate or take wholesale revenge. The Imperial Japanese replicated every colonial war of the previous century and presaged contemporary conflicts in which great powers are unrestrained in war precisely because the enemy is considered "backward" and foreign, and yet strangely obstinate. The war deaths of millions of foreign "others" — notably, Koreans, Vietnamese and Iraqis — have counted little to Americans whose much fewer casualties have been carefully counted and memorialized (Tirman 2011).

We can also ask whether germ weapons lend themselves to contemporary terrorism, the kind of indiscriminate targeting of civilians that arose after World War II and shatters the conventions of war (Walzer 1977: 197–206). The 1995 sarin nerve gas attacks on the Tokyo subway by the Aum Shinrikyo cult sounded an alarm about a possible new age of terrorism. Simultaneously, fears of bioterrorism became pervasive, especially in the United States. Then, in 2001, the U.S. anthrax letter attacks (timed to follow the 9/11 attacks on New York and Washington) caused 11 deaths and precipitated a national emergency. That crisis, in turn, generated an enormous biodefense industry (Guillemin 2011) (see Chapter 10, Point of View). Since 2001, though, terrorists have routinely relied on explosives, in somewhat the same way that the Japanese army fought through its war with China without Ishii's plague, anthrax or cholera weapons. Disabling the enemy by simple and dramatic violence has had a lasting appeal, greater than confronting the uncertainties of human infection.

The essential danger surrounding biological weapons remains state secrecy or, more accurately, a failure to achieve international transparency. Without openness, no end of malice is possible with indiscriminate weapons. Ishii's stratagem, the masking of germ weapons in the chaos of conventional war, resonates with the use of nerve gas and other chemical weapons in Syria that started in 2013. With such ambiguity, the question becomes whether it is possible to find evidence that would stand up in court — an obfuscation Ishii would have relished. Most serious are the possible hidden laboratories and testing sites where, as in Manchuria in the 1930s and 1940s, germ weapons can be pursued without restraint. As Japan's BW program and others have shown — one can think of the 1990s revelations about South Africa and Iraq — it takes only a few entrepreneurs with the right connections to carve a secret military niche (see Chapters 5 and 6).

The reasons for optimism rest in the constant endeavors of committed nations and non-governmental organizations to promote cooperation and openness. At our most optimistic, we might also believe that the contemporary online, open-source world in which almost nothing remains secret for long will both discourage treaty violations and terrorism, and quickly bring to justice those criminals who break international law and target civilians.

References

Bix HP (2000) *Hirohito and the Making of Modern Japan.* New York: HarperCollins.

Boserup A (1973) *The Problem of Chemical and Biological Warfare. Volume III. CBW and the Law of War.* New York: Humanities Press.

Brook T (Ed.)(1999) *Documents on the Rape of Nanking.* Ann Arbor: University of Michigan Press.

Brown S (1933) 'Japan stuns world, withdraws from league,' UPI Archives, http://100years.upi.com/sta_1933-02-24.html.

Brown FJ (2006) *Chemical Warfare: A Study in Restraints.* New Brunswick, NJ: Transaction Books.

Buckley J (1999) *Air Power in the Age of Total War.* Bloomington: Indiana University Press.

Douhet G (1942) *Command of the Air.* New York: Coward-McCann, Inc. Dino Ferrari (trans.)

Dunant H (1986) *A Memory of Solferino.* Geneva: International Committee of the Red Cross.

Fogel JA (Ed.) (2000) *The Nanjing Massacre in History and Historiography.* Berkeley: University of California Press.

Goldblat J (1971) *The Problem of Chemical and Biological Warfare.* Volume IV. CB Disarmament Negotiations, 1920–1970. New York: Humanities Press.

Grunden, WE (2005) *Secret Weapons and World War II: Japan in the Shadow of Big Science.* Lawrence, KS: University Press of Kansas.

Guillemin J (2005) *Biological Weapons: From State-sponsored Programs to Contemporary Bioterrorism.* New York: Columbia University Press.

Guillemin J (2011) *American Anthrax: Fear, Crime, and the Investigation of the Nation's Deadliest Bioterror Attack.* New York: Times Books.

Harris SH (2002) *Factories of Death: Japanese Biological Warfare 1932–45 and the American Cover-Up.* New York: Routledge.

Jansen MB (2000) *The Making of Modern Japan.* Cambridge, MA: Harvard University Press.

Kennedy D (1987) 'The Move to Institutions,' *Cardozo Law Review* Vol. 8(5): 841–988.

King PZ (1942) 'Japanese attempt at bacterial warfare in China,' Sheldon H. Harris Papers, Hoover Institution Archives, Stanford University, Box 1, folder 1CC.

Leahy WD (1950) *I Was There.* New York: McGraw-Hill.

Lepick O (1998) *La Grande Guerre Chimique.* Paris: Presses Universitaires de France.

Li X (2005) *Blood-Weeping Accusations: Records of Anthrax Victims.* Beijing: CCP Press; *Materials on the Trial of Former Servicemen of the Japanese Army Charged with Manufacturing and Employing Bacteriological Weapons* (1950) Moscow: Foreign Languages Press.

Perrot A and Schwartz M (2013) *Pasteur et ses Lieutenants: Roux, Yersin et les Autres.* Paris: Odile Jacob.

Robinson JP (1998) 'The impact of pugwash on the debates over chemical and biological weapons,' in LC de Cerreño A and Kaynan (Eds.) *Scientific Cooperation, State Conflict: The Role of Scientists in Mitigating International Discord.* New York: New York Academy of Sciences.

Sartori M (1943) *The War Gases.* New York: D. Van Nostrand Company, Inc.

Schelling TC (1966) *Arms and Influence.* New Haven, CN: Yale University Press.

Smart JK (2004) 'History notes: Chemical and biological research and development during the Civil War,' *CBIAC Newsletter* Vol. 5(2): 3–11.
Spence JD (1981) *The Gate of Heavenly Peace: The Chinese ad Their Revolution*. New York: Viking Penguin.
Tirman J (2011) *The Deaths of Others: The Fate of Civilians in America's Wars*. New York: Oxford University Press.
Walzer M (1977) *Just and Unjust Wars: A Moral Argument with Historical Illustrations*. New York: Basic Books.
Williams P and Wallace D (1989) *Unit 731: Japan's Secret Biological Warfare in World War II*. New York: Free Press.
Witt JF (2012) *Lincoln's Code: The Laws of War in American History*. New York: Free Press.
Wu LT, Chun WH, and Pollitzer R (1923) 'Plague in Manchuria,' *Journal of Hygiene* Vol. 21(3): 307–358.
Yoshimi Y (2015) *Grassroots Fascism: The War Experience of the Japanese People*. Cambridge, MA: Weatherhead Books on Asia, Harvard University Press. Ethan Mark (trans.)

Notes

[1] International Court of Justice (ICJ) The website of the International Court of Justice offers documentation on the history of the PCIJ, including a 2012 commemorative volume, http://www.icj-cij.org/pcij/?p1=9.

Section I: Past Proliferators

Chapter 3

The British, United States and Canadian Biological Warfare Programs

Brian Balmer & John Ellis van Courtland Moon

Introduction

This chapter considers the history of three of the most noteworthy biological warfare (BW) programs of the 20th century: The U.K., U.S.A. and Canada. They are considered together here because of the close collaborative links that existed between the three programs. Moreover, this close collaboration persisted even at times when scientific cooperation in other areas was threatened, such when the U.S. shut the U.K. out of atomic collaboration in the years following the McMahon Act of 1946. The chapter focuses largely on the Second World War and Cold War periods but, because a defensive program continues within each country, we have made some connections to the present in our historical narrative.

In all three countries significant resources were, at particular times, devoted to their programs and — again, at times — all three countries seriously considered biological weapons to possess enormous potential. Yet, all three countries abandoned their offensive programs. Any study of the American, British and Canadian BW programs therefore evokes recurring questions: Why did these countries pursue biological weapons programs? What types of bioweapons were envisaged? Given the initial ambitious aims of the BW programs, what progress had they made by the time they were closed down and how can this be explained? Why did the British and American governments abandon the policy of retaliation in kind and adopt BW disarmament and defensive research?

With respect to the U.K. program, we argue that changes in the perception of the U.K. independent nuclear deterrent, coupled with defense cuts led to a downgrading of the potential of biological weapons in military thinking. The thesis with respect to the American program is direct: the American offensive BW program failed to achieve its goals because it did not reconcile its contradictory objectives, because it did not receive the persistent support necessary to its success, and because it was based on speculative anticipation rather than experience.

Although there are significant differences as well as similarities between the U.S. and U.K. programs, we have structured the sections that describe them along broadly similar lines. For both, we discuss policy, organizational structure and defense priorities, research and development including agent and weapon choice, and envisioned use. Because the U.S. military standardized agents into their arsenal, we have also included a discussion of preparedness in that section. We finish with a brief historical overview of the Canadian program so as to include this third member of the ongoing Tripartite Collaboration that existed for much of the period we discuss.

A. The British program

Policy

The British program of research into BW, like the U.S. and Canadian programs, went through a primarily offensive and then defensive phase. Although the boundary between offensive and defensive research is blurred (King and Strauss 1990), in the context of this chapter we refer to the stated policy objectives of each research program.[1]

The first signs of governmental concern about BW can be found in the 1930s, when the journalist Wickham Steed published claims that German spies had been experimenting with bacteriological aerosols on the London Underground and Paris Metro. While the authorities eventually dismissed this so-called "Wickham Steed Affair," it prompted them to establish the Imperial Defence Subcommittee on Bacteriological Warfare, which first advised on the threat and eventually arranged for the stockpiling of vaccines and sera as part of Britain's general preparations for war.

Once war was declared, Prime Minister Neville Chamberlain sanctioned some defensively orientated microbiological research at the prestigious National Institute of Medical Research, but there was no concerted effort to produce a biological weapon. With the change to a coalition government led by Winston Churchill in May 1940, followed by the rapid and unexpected fall of France to German invasion, the new Prime Minister approved a dedicated program of research based at Porton Down, Wiltshire. In this decision, Churchill was closely advised by Lord Maurice Hankey, a highly experienced civil servant and member of the War Cabinet, who took care of bringing a team of biologists, led by Dr Paul Fildes, an expert on bacterial nutrition, in secret to the Porton site. Hankey, later in the war, described policy in the following terms:

> It was finally agreed that we should press out work in all directions to produce a weapon and that the power of retaliation was the best means of defence. We were specifically instructed to produce a weapon which should be available at short notice for retaliation.[2]

In relation to the notion of retaliation in kind, Hankey — and so too presumably Churchill — was fully aware of Britain's obligations under the 1925 Protocol for the Prohibition of the Use in War of Asphyxiating, Poisonous or Other Gases, and of Bacteriological Methods of Warfare (usually abbreviated to the 1925 Geneva Protocol). While ostensibly a ban on the use of chemical and biological weapons, the number of reservations tabled by different states parties to the protocol rendered it effectively a "no first use" agreement between nations.

The policy of retaliation in kind persisted into the Cold War, but now with biological weapons taking a place alongside chemical, nuclear and (in some archival sources) radiological weapons as "Weapons of Mass Destruction." Indeed, the Deputy Chiefs of Staff sub-committee, in January 1947, noted that: "research on BW [biological warfare] is of the highest category of research as atomic energy and policy."[3] And later that year the Chiefs of Staff, referring to atomic, chemical and biological weapons, stated that it was "a cardinal principle of policy to be prepared to use weapons of mass destruction."[4]

By the mid-1950s the status of BW in defense and research policy had changed. Following the explosion of the first Soviet atomic bomb in 1949 and the emergence of the U.K.'s own nuclear deterrent in the 1950s, the attention of the Armed Forces increasingly shifted away from BW. This downgrading was further propelled, in the aftermath of the Korean War, by the U.K.'s abandonment of plans for rapid rearmament. In 1953, the committee of independent scientists who advised on research at Porton Down complained that, in a new directive from the Minister of Supply, "priority appeared to be given to the defensive and research aspects rather than to the building up of BW offensive potential by weapon development and production investigations."[5] The same directive also made it clear that with regard to offensive aspects of BW research, the U.K. would have to rely on close collaboration with the U.S.A. Indeed, this close collaboration, together with the Canadian program, had continued and would continue into the Cold War with exchanges of information and personnel, and annual Tripartite Conferences.

By 1956, BW research at Porton was generally referred to in classified government papers as defensive. Moreover, in terms of research priority grading relative to its perceived use in a global war, the Chief Scientist at the Ministry of Supply, Owen Wansborough-Jones, pointed out that the ambitious series of open air biological weapons trials, discussed later in this chapter, ought to rank as priority number six, which meant no effort should be allocated to it. At Cabinet level, the decisions to move to a wholly defensive research policy were simply assumed by many to be covered by a July 1956 secret decision to abandon a chemical weapons capability.

Although the aim of producing a biological weapon had been abandoned, a series of reviews in the early 1960s reported on chemical and biological warfare from both operational and research perspectives. In the context of nuclear stalemate, this re-visiting of the role of chemical and biological weapons resulted in a series of recommendations that were approved by the MacMillan Cabinet in 1963. One recommendation was to provide a budget for work on "offensive aspects" of BW, not with the aim of producing a weapon, but to assess the credibility of the threat to the U.K. But, apart from this decision, Britain had moved towards a policy of undertaking defensively orientated research. This stance was reinforced in the late 1960s and early 1970s as the U.K. took a leading role in the negotiations that led up to the 1972 Biological Weapons Convention, the treaty that placed an international ban on such weapons (Spelling *et al.* 2015).

Organization and priorities

When the Biology Department Porton (BDP) was secretly established in 1940, it was little more than a series of huts and fewer than 12 staff. The site in Wiltshire was already the focus of Britain's chemical warfare research effort. The department grew throughout the war, although never to more than 50 staff (Carter 2000). As mentioned, the priority was to produce a biological weapon for use in retaliation. Some research was also undertaken at the behest of the Special Operations Executive (SOE), the highly secretive organization charged with carrying out sabotage operations. Much of the research was aimed at an anti-personnel weapon, but work also took place on anti-livestock and anti-crop warfare. During the war very close relationships were established between the U.K., U.S.A. and Canadian chemical and biological warfare research efforts, and as already mentioned, this tripartite collaboration continued on an equally close basis into the Cold War.

Porton continued as the site for the British program accompanied by a huge investment in facilities in the late 1940s. The BDP became the Microbiological Research Department (MRD) (1946) and then the Microbiological Research Establishment (MRE) (1957). Throughout the 1970s the MRE came under increasing pressure to "civilianize" its work and undertake industrial contracts. Eventually, this led to its closure in 1979 and a small Defence Microbiology Division was created within the Chemical Defence Establishment. In 1991, the establishment broadened its title to the Chemical and Biological Defence Establishment, and 4 years later became part of an umbrella organization, the Defence Evaluation and Research Agency (DERA). DERA split in 2001 into one publicly and one privately-owned organization, with the work of the Chemical and Biological Defence Establishment, later renamed Dstl Porton Down, being subsumed into the public organization, the Defence Science and Technology Laboratory (Dstl).

Alongside the research, a network of advisory committees was established on BW matters. These included a technical advisory board comprising of independent scientists (the Biological Research Advisory Board, BRAB) and, until the mid-1950s, a Chiefs of Staff sub-committee on BW. Responsibility for the Porton establishments lay with the Ministry of Supply until its dissolution in 1959, when it passed briefly to the War Office and finally to the Ministry of Defence in 1964.

This shift from a fairly extensive program of research accompanied by a hierarchy of advisory committees, through to the closure of the MRE, reflects, to some extent, the changing policy priorities outlined in the earlier section. In the early years of the Cold War, the MRD had been working under an expectation that it would produce a biological weapon comparable to the atomic bomb by 1957. An Air Staff Target for an anti-personnel biological bomb was cancelled in 1954 and, as described, policy shifted to defensive research. The priority at the MRE shifted to threat assessment, particularly as research indicated that, unlike the U.S.A. or USSR, it might be possible to cover Great Britain with a single attack. But, successive reviews of the MRE throughout the 1970s, which indicated that its high containment facilities for working with micro-organisms might be opened up so that the U.K. could benefit more widely from the emerging field of biotechnology, led to the closure and move to Chemical Defence

Establishment (CDE) (Hammond and Carter 2001; Agar and Balmer 2015).

Research and development

During the World War II, the BDP scientists considered a range of possible agents for a biological weapon. A 1941 list of possible agents includes the diseases: typhoid, para-typhoid, dystentery, cholera and anthrax for use against humans, and anthrax, foot-and-mouth disease, rinderpest, glanders, and swine fever for use against livestock. In relation to policy, the report accompanying this list included a consideration of whether or not the "retaliation in kind" instruction that animated the work of the BDP should be broad (germ warfare with any germ warfare) or specific (disease with same disease). In order to deliver and disseminate the agent, the scientists considered both bursting munitions and sprays. Much of the focus of work, alongside the American effort, came to rest on anthrax and also Botulinum toxin.

In 1942, the work moved beyond Porton for trials of an anthrax weapon on Gruinard Island, a small island off the west coast of Scotland. Scientists and technicians used modified chemical bombs, now filled with a liquid suspension of anthrax, as their test weapon. These bombs were detonated at various distances from tethered sheep and the effects on the animals were monitored. The Gruinard trials were followed up with a trial at a firing range on Penclawdd beach, Wales, using a bomb dropped from an aeroplane. Reports of the success of these trials were eventually passed to Churchill. His close adviser, physicist Lord Cherwell, urged the Prime Minister to include them in the U.K. armory noting that N-bombs (the code-word for the anthrax bomb) would be easier to make than "tube alloys" (the code-word for the atomic bomb). Porton also came up with an interim measure, using cattle-feed cakes made of anthrax-laced linseed. If Germany had initiated BW, the plan was to drop the 5 million stockpiled cakes on to fields of German livestock to disrupt its agricultural sector. With the N-bomb, an arrangement was made for the U.S.A. to mass-produce anthrax and for Canada to test the bombs, but after several delays, the war ended before the plan could be put into action.

After the War, the high priority accorded by the Chiefs of Staff to biological weapons ensured the broadening of the scope and scale of research at the newly renamed MRD. By 1946, plans were mapped out to develop research on both offensive and defensive aspects of BW, including agent dissemination, effectiveness of new agents, large-scale production, preparation and storage problems, sabotage methods to initiate epizootics and increasing the efficiency of known agents. On the defensive side, future directions included research on immunization, new antibiotics, large-scale antibiotic production, physical protection and disease control.[6] Research on bomb design was passed to the Chemical Defence Experimental Establishment.

By 1948, work at the MRE had progressed to include a series of outdoor trials of various pathogenic organisms, each lasting several months (see Chapter 3, Point of View). Operation Harness was the code name for the first trial, an elaborate exercise undertaken off the coast of Antigua. Although the U.K. scientists carried out the exercise, the U.S.A. and Canada supplied some additional personnel. The trials involved the experimenters placing animals in crates, placed on a small "island" of 35 floating dinghies. Each metal crate held cages that could accommodate one sheep, one monkey in a separate compartment and side arms for holding guinea-pigs. Each crate was attached to a sampling device. This island, known as the "trot," was then towed out into the open water and a nearby bomb charged with live agent was detonated by remote control. Two ships, known as the clean and dirty ship, accompanied the trial with animals and equipment starting in the clean ship but then being sent after the experiment to the dirty ship, which contained laboratories for monitoring the effects on the animals. Both lethal (*Bacillus anthracis*) and incapacitating (*Brucella abortus*, *Brucella suis* and *Franciscella tularensis*) agents were tested in Operation Harness.

Harness was succeeded by two tests off Lewis, in the Scottish Outer Hebrides. Code-named Cauldron (1952) and Hesperus (1953), they also involved animals exposed to live pathogens, but by this time much had been simplified, for example, only one ship was used and a purpose-built wooden pontoon had replaced the less reliable dinghies (which had frequently attracted shark attacks). Cauldron once again used the bacteria responsible for brucellosis — *Brucella suis* — in the tests, and also tried out *Pasturella pestis*, the cause of plague, as a potential agent; Hesperus used *Brucella suis* and *Francisella tularensis*. Operation Ozone was carried out off Nassau in 1954 with the aim of finding out how agents survived after being spread by various dispersal methods including high explosive propellant explosive, and spraying. Scientists used the bacteria *Brucella suis* and *Francisella tularensis* and also tested a virus, Venezuelan Equine Encephalitis (VEE). Finally, Operation Negation started in 1954 but approval was accompanied by hints from the Chiefs of Staff that it would be the last one. Again in the Bahamas, Negation employed *Brucella suis* and *Franciscella tularensis* as well as vaccina virus which acted as a simulant for smallpox. One of the key findings from this series of trials was quite how vulnerable micro-organisms were to conditions such as sunlight, humidity and temperature.

Once U.K. policy shifted from offensive and defensive to defensive-only research, the emphasis of the scientists and their advisors also shifted. Now with a remit primarily to assess the threat to the U.K., scientists at the MRE revisited the idea that, rather than using a bomb, an aircraft might spray an aerosol of BW agent across a whole region or even country. Testing this "Large Area Concept" became a key rationale for continuing the biological weapons defense program in the late 1950s and into the 1960s. It also marked a conceptual divergence from the U.S. program which, much to the dismay of David Henderson, head of the MRE, continued to emphasize bombs and, later, missiles.

The Large Area Concept was tested in 1957 using a fluorescent tracer particle, zinc cadmium sulfide, which was sprayed from an airplane in a 300 mile line across large parts of the U.K. Scientists estimated that, had the trial used pathogenic agent such as tularemia or Q-Fever, around 28 million people would have received an infective dose. The Large Area Concept also served to keep biological weapons on the military agenda. The various reviews of chemical and biological weapons in the early 1960s, mentioned earlier, kept returning to the fact that the U.K. could potentially be covered in a single attack and therefore some research into the nature of the threat would be likely to aid defense.

Once these warnings had translated into the MacMillan Cabinet's award of £470,000 over 5 years for assessing the threat, part of this budget was spent on further open air trials. Between 1963 and 1965, 23 trials were carried out from the English Channel, off the coast of Dorset county. Scientists and naval personnel were involved in spraying and tracing the progress of a cloud of non-pathogenic bacteria from its source on a ship and across land. Trials continued into the late 1960s and early 1970s, but now focused on the vulnerability of ship's crews to a biological weapon attack. During the 1970s, the focus of the work was increasingly on diseases with wider public health implications, while the rise of the new "genetic engineering" and biotechnology raised the prospect of putting the MRE's high containment facilities to wider civil use (Agar and Balmer 2015).

Envisioned use

During the Second World War, it is clear from archival sources that the Porton scientists were instructed to produce a biological weapon as quickly as possible in case of the need to retaliate in kind against a similar German attack (Balmer 2001). Indeed, after the war scientists on the BRAB described the cattle cake and N-bomb as mere wartime expedients.

At the end of the war, a draft version of the 1949 Chiefs of Staff report on Biological Warfare noted:

> We assume that, as a party to the Geneva Protocol of 1925, this country will not initiate biological warfare but will resort to its use only as a retaliatory measure... It should therefore be regarded not as a competitor with the other types of weapon in our armoury, but as a complementary weapon to be used when its peculiar characteristics can be fully exploited.[7]

And, 2 years earlier, in their written Air Staff Requirement for a biological bomb it was envisaged as a strategic weapon that would inflict "widespread incapacitation of the workers" and produce "maximum adverse effects on morale."[8]

Once the U.K. shifted to defensive research only, it is interesting that envisioned use by the enemy or the U.K.'s allies also changed in the minds of research scientists. In one case for further sea trials, it was noted that:

> It was plainly stated by UK representatives at the 10th Tripartite Conference that the present emphasis (especially in American work) on overt on-target attack with conventional aircraft BW cluster bombs was, in their opinion quite wrong and was missing the whole point of the covert potential of BW.[9]

The author continued, defining covert use twice: as conventional sabotage, but also as the Large Area Concept. It is also interesting that by the mid-1970s the terminology had shifted from a concern about sabotage to the threat from terrorism, possibly reflecting a change in the thinking about the nature of the threat and not merely a change of label.

B. The American program

The American BW program went through two major phases: an offensive and defensive period (1942–1969), which was terminated by President Richard Nixon; a defensive phase (1970 to the present). The first phase, however, divides into a wartime program (1942–1945) and a peacetime program (roughly 1946–1969). The first was focused on the production of a weapon as rapidly as possible; the second explored the multiple possibilities of offensive BW before settling down on a few weapon/agent combinations. In the post-1970 phase, the American defensive program struggled with the challenges posed by BW proliferation and terrorism. In particular, following the anthrax attacks in the wake of the September 11, 2001 terrorist attacks on the

World Trade Center, the George W. Bush administration struggled with the specter of a 9/11 BW catastrophe.[10]

Policy

Influencing American policy on biological weapons was the hostile public opinion regarding the warfare use of germs or gas, commonly bound together in the acronym chemical and biological warfare (CBW). Especially during the Cold War, this hostility was reflected in the correspondence between members of Congress and U.S. administrations. Most frequently, Congressmen cited the declarations of Presidents Roosevelt and Eisenhower on the abhorrent nature of these weapons.

American BW policy emerged during World War II as an unwritten assumption tagged on to President Franklin D. Roosevelt's policy on chemical weapons. Responding to reports that the Japanese were using poison gas against the Chinese and that the Germans were threatening to unleash chemical warfare against the Soviets, Roosevelt issued a pledge that the U.S. would treat such an attack as if it were against itself. Although the United States would "under no circumstances resort to the use of such weapons unless they are first used by our enemies," he warned that: "We promise to any perpetrators of such crimes full and swift retaliation in kind" (Roosevelt 1950).

Roosevelt made no similar pledge regarding biological weapons. But the association between chemical and biological weapons was so close that subsequent policymakers assumed that the Roosevelt pledge held for both weapon systems. Although the U.S. had never ratified the Geneva Protocol of 1925, which as already mentioned, prohibited "first use" of biological and chemical weapons, the Roosevelt policy was in conformity with the protocol.

The policy of "no first use" and its corollary, "retaliation in kind," held until 1956 when a policy change was adopted by the National Security Council: "To the extent that the military effectiveness of the armed forces will be enhanced by their use, the United States will be prepared to use chemical and bacteriological weapons in general war.

The decision as to their use will be made by the President."[11] This new CBW policy, NSC 5602/1, which kept all options open, was the preferred choice of the Joint Chiefs of Staff (JCS) throughout the offensive phase of the BW program. But it was either ignored or forgotten by succeeding presidents. And, on January 22, 1975, on signing the instrument of ratification for the Geneva Protocol and the Biological Weapons Convention, President Gerald Ford could state: "The United States...has always observed the principles and objectives of the protocol" (Ford 1977). The United States government had, indeed, gone even further: for the first time, it had renounced the principle of retaliation in kind, and the option of preparedness for retaliation in kind.

During the offensive phase of the BW program, three separate positions criss-crossed one another over the value of BW weapons and the options for its use. The first reiterated the Roosevelt policy of "no first use." The second position consisted in "true believers," especially within the Chemical Warfare Service and its successor, the Chemical Corps, who stressed the strategic offensive potential of both lethal and incapacitating biological weapons. The third position was voiced by the JCS, especially during the 1969 debate within the Interdepartmental Political Military Group, which was then reviewing the options regarding BW policy. The JCS argued that BW preparedness should be pushed to strengthen deterrence and to preserve the option of retaliation in kind. By 1969, NSC 5602/1, still classified, seems to have disappeared from official cognizance. Recognizing the BW policy chaos, the JCS called for a "coherent U.S. policy."[12]

In May 1969, President Richard Nixon initiated National Security Studies Memorandum (NSSM) 59, a multi-agency review of U.S. chemical and BW policy. This had been prompted largely by chemical weapons concerns — on the international front, the use of herbicides and tear gas in Vietnam, and on the domestic front a highly publicized escape of VX nerve gas from an open-air trial, which killed around 6,000 sheep, at Dugway Proving Ground (Tucker and Mahan 2009). The review led to a public announcement by the President in November that the U.S. would unilaterally abandon production of biological weapons and destroy its existing stockpiles.

Intelligence

Throughout most of the Cold War, it was axiomatic that the U.S. should seek to match, or preferably to surpass, the USSR in every weapon challenge. Although the United States could measure the size of Soviet conventional forces or, once the U-2 flights commenced, count missiles and planes deployed by its adversary, it could not estimate the extent of the Soviet BW program, which was being carried out in the multiple laboratories of a closed society. National Intelligence estimates were mostly limited to an evaluation of Soviet BW capabilities. It was what they could do, not what they were doing. American decision makers were faced with the intelligence dilemma. Unable to see what was taking place, they had to plan on the basis of worst case scenarios, assuming that what the U.S. was pursuing in its BW program, the USSR was also pursuing. Mirror imaging replaced reality checks.

Organization and defense priorities

In the early decades of the Cold War, the United States faced a formidable military challenge: to rebuild its conventional forces, quickly demobilized at the close of the Second World War, and now faced with a numerically superior Soviet ground army positioned in central Europe and a hostile China in Asia; and to build a nuclear arsenal of air, sea and ground weapons, maintaining its atomic supremacy against all challengers.

The BW program was only one competitor among many claimants who pushed their weapon systems. It was not well positioned to do so. It was a subordinate unit within the Chemical Corps, in an Army that was often lukewarm, if not hostile, to the Corps' mission. And even within the Chemical Corps, the BW program was competing with the favored chemical weapons program. In this multi-leveled competitive atmosphere, it was difficult for the BW program to gain the priority it needed to push its program forward.

It received strong support only twice within the offensive planning period (1946–1969). The first surge took place during the

Korean War, when Communist allegations that the U.S. was waging BW against North Korea and China, prompted fears that the Soviets were preparing themselves to launch biological war. The second surge came during the Kennedy years when military leaders were being pressured to devise alternative strategies to all-out nuclear war. But these surges were momentary, followed by cut-backs as emergencies faded or changed direction.

Research and development

Despite its budgetary restrictions, the scientists within the biological research and development program pursued multiple projects throughout the offensive period: anti-personnel, anti-animal, anti-plant. The annual project lists formed a veritable cornucopia: screening and development of viruses, rickettsia, bacteria and fungi; arthropod dissemination; decontamination; rapid warning and detection; special operations; physical protection; cloud meteorology; occupational safety; aerobiological research; bio-engineering; stability and virulence of BW aerosols.

Research, development and limited testing of biological agents was largely carried out during and after World War II at the Camp Detrick facilities (1943–1969). Open air testing of BW agents was centered at Dugway Proving Ground. Established in 1954, Pine Bluff Arsenal, Arkansas, produced a limited amount of biological agents and munitions. In an emergency, it could launch full production within 72 hours (Moon 2006).

Agent and weapons choices

Two arguments have been put forth to soften the image of the U.S. biological weapons program: the agents of choice were incapacitating rather than lethal; they were infective but not contagious. Neither of these arguments is convincing given the available record.

During World War II, the American BW program, like the U.K. program, focused on two agents: *Bacillus anthracis* and Botulinum toxin. In 1951, the early days of the Cold War, the priority list had shifted: *Pestis, Brucella melitensis, Malleomyces, Tularense, Brucella Suis, Burnetii,* Anthrax, Psittacosis and Botulinum toxin.[13] The stockpiling of biological agents was limited compared to either chemical or nuclear weapons. With the exception of anthrax spores, BW agents are highly vulnerable to environmental degradation. Given the difficulties of storing them, the practice was to keep a small pile for immediate use; and then, in case of a military emergency, mass-produce them as the occasion warranted. Nevertheless the following agents were in stock when their destruction was ordered in the early 1970s:

- Lethal: *Bacillus anthracis*; *Francisella tularensis*; Botulinum toxin; Saxitoxin.
- Incapacitating: *Coxiella burnetii*; Venezuelan equine encephalitis; *Staphylococcal enterotoxin* Type B.
- Crop agents: *Puccinia graminis*: stem rust of wheat and *Piricularia oryzae*: rice blast disease (Moon 2006).

In addition, the Detrick laboratories had standardized the yellow fever virus; and their entomological facility was successfully breeding mosquito vectors. With regard to the claimed emphasis on non-contagious agents, the research records show protracted research stretching into the 1960s on smallpox and plague, although neither of these lethal agents was successfully weaponized by the U.S.

The probable explanation for the divergence of available agents is that different agencies were interested in the type of biological agent they wanted. The Army favored incapacitating brucellosis; the Air Force, which was interested in combining biological attacks with nuclear attacks, favored a killing weapon and settled upon anthrax when it became evident that plague would not be immediately available. The policy makers on the National Security Council (NSC), who were more conscious of public opinion, favored the development of incapacitants. A secondary factor, especially during the Vietnam War, was the need to convince the public that the U.S. was not using poisonous weapons, by differentiating riot control agents from lethal CBW weapons. The main points, however, are that all toxic agents are fatal under certain circumstances and that research and development work of the U.S. resulted in the development of several options, which competed with one another.

Several delivery systems were devised for the dissemination of biological weapons: cluster bombs, rockets, balloons, generators, mines, spray tanks and feathers. Warheads for a short-range missile (Sergeant) were programmed, but in 1968 the program was rescinded. The available record, however, does not indicate that BW agents were ever loaded into missile carriers. Since explosive bombs would destroy a large portion of its toxic load, it is most likely that spray would have served as the chief disseminator if these weapons had been used (Moon 2006).

Envisioned use

Although some tactical possibilities were envisioned for biological weapons (elimination of strong points, interdiction of terrain), they were seen largely as strategic weapons, useful for city-busting operations. Tactically, they posed the problem of blow-back. During the Kennedy/Johnson era, some attention was given to the use of CBW as an alternative to nuclear weapons in limited war situations, but the idea was ultimately scrapped by Secretary of Defense McNamara. Throughout the Cold War, the shadow of nuclear weapons fell over all weapons systems. Planners asked themselves whether the use of CBW would cross the threshold into nuclear war, and whether nuclear-armed nations needed any other weapon of mass destruction.

Preparedness

Was the United States ready to defend itself against biological weapons? Was the United States ready to wage offensive BW? Several assumptions steered the development of weapons of mass destruction: (1) to assure deterrence, the United States had to match the Soviets weapon system by weapon system; (2) if attacked, the U.S. should respond in kind, so if the Soviets used BW, the U.S. should strike back with BW weapons.

Throughout the Cold War, repeated alarms were sounded that the U.S. was *not* ready, that it must make a greater effort in CBW preparedness. The Earl Stevenson report (1950) led to the revision of stated CBW policy in 1956 referred to above. It led to a temporary hiking of funding during the Korean War. But it did not quell the repeated warnings that the USSR was surging ahead of the U.S. in the CBW arms race, a warning nourished by the failure of American intelligence to produce firm intelligence regarding the Russian program.[14]

But what is preparedness? The United States could have waged a biological attack against the USSR, which would have caused horrific casualties in an unprotected civilian population. The U.S.A., by at least 1965, had the weapons, and the production facilities. Its Project 112 tests in the Pacific had demonstrated that the dissemination of agents, downwind in large area attacks, was feasible and would be effective (see Chapter 3, Point of View). Preparedness, however, must balance defense against offense. The U.S. never solved the problem of real time agent detection and identification; a problem magnified by the difficulty of differentiating BW agents from pollutants and other elements in the environment. The sword was sharp but the shield was rusty. So it would not be able to protect its own terrain from a major biological attack. As a 1964 study pointed out "practically total unpreparedness is revealed for each and every element in the civil defense chair: detection, warning, masks, shelters, immunization, and (except for limited stockpiles of atropine syrettes) therapy."[15]

C. The Canadian program

The third member of the tripartite BW program was Canada. It worked closely with Britain and the United States in both the Second World War and Cold War on BW preparedness. The Canadian program, under the ultimate authority of the War Cabinet, was directed by the National Research Council and the Canadian Army's Directorate of Chemical Warfare and Smoke (DCW&S). However, because the Army was not especially concerned with BW, the major Canadian BW decisions were made by a triumvirate of scientists: Dr Otto Maass,

Chairman of the DCW&S, Dr. Everitt Murray of McGill University and Dr. Guilford Reed of Queen's University (Avery 2013).

The government had ratified the 1925 Geneva Protocol in 1930. It had strong Commonwealth ties with the United Kingdom and developed a close alliance with the United States during the war. However, as historian Donald Avery notes: "Canada was a junior partner in the Anglo-American BW alliance, and had neither the capability nor the responsibility of deploying these weapons in a retaliatory attack. This heavy burden rested with Canada's allies-the governments of the United States and Great Britain" (Avery 2013).

The first Canadian scientist to push for the development of a BW program was Sir Frederick Banting, the coinventor of insulin. Banting was convinced that Germany was forging ahead with its biological weapons program, which constituted a major threat to the U.K., U.S. and Canada. With the encouragement of General A.L.G. McNaughton, Chair of the National Research Council, tentative and limited steps were taken in 1939 and 1940. McNaughton encouraged Banting to draw up a study of the offensive potentialities of BW. Banting's death, in an aircraft crash on February 20, 1941, put a temporary halt to preliminary government discussion of the envisioned program. But on November 16, 1941, the secret Committee M. 1000 was established. Professor E.G.D. Murray served as its chairman.

American BW collaboration led to the Grosse Isle project. In July 1942, initial contacts led to the creation of a Joint U.S.–Canadian Commission. Its top priority was rinderpest, "cattle plague," a disease unknown in the North American continent. Grosse Isle, an island in the St. Lawrence River, was chosen as "eminently qualified" for joint study of this dangerous animal disease, which if introduced, "would spread rapidly and would have a most disastrous result."[16] Joint experiments with rinderpest were carried out at the War Disease Control Station on Grosse Isle. They resulted in the production of over 1,000,000 doses of the vaccine, which was successfully tested in East Africa after the war. Another joint Grosse Isle project included a limited manufacture of anthrax, which ended after producing around 400 liters of a heavy suspension of anthrax spores.[17]

In May 1945, British, American and Canadian BW officials, meeting at Camp Detrick, decided to continue the wartime BW collaboration into the post-war period.[18] Next year, at the first meeting of the Tripartite Conference, the Canadian delegation announced that its basic BW research would take place at the Kingston Testing Laboratory, Ontario; and its testing at the Suffield Experimental Station, Alberta whose trial grounds were open to all three parties. Subsequently, the weaponized agents of *brucella* and tularemia were tested at Suffield. The Grosse Isle Project, again prompted by fears of rinderpest and other agricultural threats was reactivated.

From 1953 to 1958, the Canadian government vigorously pursued BW anti-animal programs, developing a number of offensive biological agents, among them: "1. Cattle (Rinderpest); 2. Swine (African Wart Hog disease (African swine fever); 3. Chicken (Fowl Plague). Despite these successes, 4 years later the Grosse Isle program was cancelled" (Avery 2006).

The Cuban Missile Crisis heightened Canada's sense of vulnerability to biological attack. And, in January 1963, GR Vavasour, Secretary of the Defence Research Board (DRB) outlined two Soviet BW attacks against the North American continent. The first scenario envisioned a first use biological attack launched by the Soviet Union against U.S. metropolitan centers, "designed solely to kill inhabitants of large cities." The second scenario centered on a covert attack delivered by advanced aircraft or submarines. Vavasour warned that neither the U.S. or Canada were prepared to defend themselves against such attack since they possessed neither the verification nor warning systems to defend themselves against biological weapons (Avery 2013). Other scenarios centered on subversive attacks against Canadian targets. JF Currie of the Kingston Laboratory described four scenarios: "(a) a release in Montreal Forum with 14,000 persons present; (b) release at Malton Airport during a rush hour; (c) release in the Toronto subway; (d) release at railroad stations in large, intermediate and small cities." The September draft of the report envisioned a Large Area Coverage attack launched from an enemy trawler operating off the coast of Nova Scotia. The BW attack would contaminate around 25 square miles, causing approximately 115,000 casualties (Avery 2013).

Throughout the Cold War, Canada stuck to its commitment to the "no first use" policy of the Geneva Protocol. However, it continued to feel seriously unprepared — defensively and offensively for BW.

Conclusions

The U.K., U.S. and Canadian programs — and moreover, the three together as a tripartite collaboration — stand as the sum of the most significant in scale and scope of efforts, by various nations in 20th century, to add biological weapons to their arsenals. While the concept of a biological weapon did not appear *ex nihilo*, all three programs were initiated in wartime as a response to a perceived imminent threat. Of course, as Guillemin (2005) has argued, we should also not ignore the role of key "product champions" pushing the idea towards reality, including figures such as Banting in Canada and Hankey in the U.K. Military use of these weapons was envisioned as primarily strategic and came to rest on delivery by bomb, missile or large area spray. That said, beneath this broad brush picture we should not forget that scientists and military planners seriously entertained other ideas — such as tactical use and sabotage. Much of the archival material on the British program suggests that — beyond the war-time N-bomb — only faltering progress had been made towards an anti-personnel weapon by the time the Air Staff Requirement for such a weapon was cancelled in July 1954. The U.S. had moved significantly further, having established a limited stockpile of lethal and incapacitating BW agents and weapons, and having carried out extensive dispersion testing in the Pacific during the early 1960s, by the time of the 1969 Nixon decision to cease production and destroy stockpiles of biological weapons.

In both the U.K. and U.S. programs many factors combined to shift them to defensive programs. In the U.K., the increasing significance of an independent nuclear deterrent combined with cuts to the defense budget stand out as the most apparent influences on policy. The goals of the U.S. research program were thwarted by conflicting and contradictory demands from different branches of the armed services, coupled with inconsistent support over time. However, unlike the drift of U.K. policy where no Cabinet level decision appears to have been made to abandon offensive research, the 1969 Nixon decision marks a turning point for the U.S. program. It is also worth pointing out that in the U.K., U.S. and Canadian programs much depended on what might be called the "imaginaries" surrounding each program. Although history is strewn with examples of biological incidents — the hurtling of infected bodies over city walls in the 14th century siege of Kaffa, the use of smallpox blankets against Indians in the late 18th century — there was no example of full-scale BW on which to evolve preparedness out of experience. The term imaginaries does not imply that all research was speculative, rather it highlights this lack of historical precedent for those devising the weapons and their envisaged uses.

A broad consideration of the main features of the U.K., U.S. and Canadian programs should convince readers that we must not think about any weapons program as a single thing or entity. A biological weapons program amounts to far more than scientific and other technical capability. Indeed, as we have shown in this chapter, such capability is but one element of an intersecting network of technical, logistical, political and military considerations that encompass both capability and intent. Moreover, it is a network that shifts and reconfigures over time. This complexity does not make contemporary biological arms control any easier, but as it is likely to be an enduring feature of any organized state program, it is important to recognize and so avoid oversimplifying the very thing we are trying to control.

References

Agar J and Balmer B (2015) 'Defence research and genetic engineering: Fears and dissociation in the 1970s', in C Sleigh and D Leggett (Eds.) *Scientific Governance in Britain, 1914–1979.* Manchester: Manchester University Press.

Avery D (2006) 'The Canadian biological weapons program', in M Wheelis, L Rósa and M Dando (Eds.) *Deadly Cultures: Biological Warfare Since*

1945. Cambridge, Massachusetts and London, England: Harvard University Press, pp. 88, 93–94.

Avery D (2013) *Pathogens for War: Biological Weapons, Canadian Life Scientists and North American Biodefence*. Toronto: University of Toronto Press, pp. 1, 16, 103.

Balmer B (2001) *Britain and Biological Warfare: Expert Advice and Science Policy, 1935–1965*. Basingstoke: Palgrave.

Balmer B (2006) 'The British program', in M Wheelis, L Rósa and M Dando (Eds.) *Deadly Cultures: Biological Warfare Since 1945*. Cambridge, Massachusetts and London, England: Harvard University Press.

Balmer B (2012) *Secrecy and Science: A Historical Sociology of Biological and Chemical Warfare*. Farnham: Ashgate.

Carter GB (2000) *Chemical and Biological Defence at Porton Down 1916–2000*. London: The Stationery Office.

Cole L (1990) *Clouds of Secrecy: The Army's Germ Warfare Test over Populated Areas*. Savage, Maryland: Rowman & Littlefield Publishers, Inc.

Ford G (1977) 'Remarks upon signing instruments of ratification of the Geneva Protocol of 1925 and the Biological Weapons Convention, 22 January 1975', in *Public Papers of the Presidents of the United States: Gerald R. Ford: Containing the Public Messages, Speeches, and Statements of the President: 1975*, 2 books. Book I-January 1 to July 17, 1975. Washington, DC: United States Government Printing Office, pp. 72–73.

Guillemin J (2005) *Biological Weapons: From the Invention of State Sponsored Programs to Contemporary Bioterrorism*. New York: Columbia University Press.

Guillemin J (2011) *American Anthrax: Fear, Crime, and the Investigation of the Nation's Deadliest Bioterror Attack*. New York: Times Books: Henry Holt and Company, 2011.

Hammond P and Carter GB (2001) *From Biological Warfare to Healthcare: Porton Down, 1940–2000*. Basingstoke: Palgrave.

King J and Strauss H (1990) 'The hazards of defensive biological weapons research', in S Wright (Ed.) *Preventing a Biological Arms Race*. Cambridge, MA: MIT Press.

Moon JEvC (1999) 'US biological warfare planning and preparedness: The dilemmas of policy', in E Geissler and JEvC Moon (Eds.) *Biological and Toxin Weapons: Research, Development and Use from the Middle Ages to 1945*. No. 18 in SIPRI (Stockholm International Peace Institute) Series on Chemical and Biological Warfare. Oxford: Oxford University Press.

Moon JEvC (2006) 'The US biological warfare program', in M Wheelis L Rozsa and M Dando (Eds.) *Deadly Cultures: Biological Weapons Since 1945*. Cambridge, Massachusetts and London, England: Harvard University Press.

Moon JEvC (forthcoming) *The American Biological Warfare Program: A History*. Cambridge, MA: Harvard University Press.

Roosevelt FD (1950) Public Papers. Compiled by SI Rosenman, *1943 Volume: The Tide Turns*. New York: Harper & Brothers Publishers, p. 243.

Schmidt U (2015) *Secret Science: A Century of Poison Warfare and Human Experiments*. Oxford: Oxford University Press.

Spelling A, McLeish C and Balmer B (2015) *Briefing Note: Where Did The Biological Weapons Convention Come From? Indicative Timeline and Key Events, 1925–75*, www.ucl.ac.uk/sts/cbw (accessed June 26, 2015).

Tucker J and Mahan (2009) *President Nixon's Decision to Renounce the US Biological Weapons Program*. Center for the Study of Weapons of Mass Destruction. Washington: National Defense University.

Notes

1 Key secondary sources on the history of the British Program are Balmer, (2001, 2006, 2012); Carter (2000); Guillemin (2005); Hammond and Carter (2001); Schmidt (2015).

2 UK The National Archives, Kew (hereafter TNA) WO 188/654. Letter Fildes to Rt. Hon. Mr Earnest Brown (January 8, 1944).

3 TNA WO 188/660. ISSBW. Shortage of Scientific Staff for Research in Biological Warfare (January 30, 1947).

4 TNA DEFE 10/19. DRPC. Final Version of Paper on the Future of Defence Policy (July 30, 1947).

5 TNA WO 188/668. BRAB 30th Meeting (November 6, 1953).

6 TNA WO 188/667 Future Development of Biological Warfare Research (April 30, 1946).

7 TNA AIR 20/11355 1949 Report on Biological Warfare. Section V. The Practical Requirements for Offence and Defence. Air Ministry Draft Contribution (November 1949).

8 TNA AIR 20/8727. Air Staff Requirement No. OR/1065 (November 12, 1947).

9 TNA WO 286/78. Ministry of Supply, Research and Development Board. Requirement for Further Sea Trials in 1957/58 (Note by C.M. and Chief Scientist) (August 24, 1956).

[10] Key secondary sources on the U.S. program are Cole (1990); Guillemin (2005, 2011); Moon (1999, 2006, *forthcoming*).

[11] National Archives and Records Administration (hereafter NARA), NSC 5602/1: Basic National Security Policy, March 15, 1956, RG 273, NARA.

[12] Interdepartmental Political-Military Group, U.S. Policies on Chemical and Biological Warfare and Agents, November 10, 1969 in AJ Mauroni, *U.S. Chemical and Biological Warfare Policy Strategic Deterrents during the Cold War* (U.S. Air Force Center of Unconventional Weapons Studies, Maxwell Air Force Base, Alabama, August 2014). Thanks to Greg Koblenz for an electronic copy of this collection.

[13] NARA, Joint Chiefs of Staff, Memorandum for the Chairman, Research and Development Board, Subject: Military-Priority Rating for Development of BW Agents, September 13, 1951, RG 218, NARA.

[14] NARA, *Stevenson Report: Report of the Secretary of Defense's Ad Hoc Committee on Chemical, Biological, and Radiological Warfare*, June 30, 1950, RG 330, NARA.

[15] PROJECT SUMMIT (1964): "The Development and Use of Biological and Chemical Weapons", Vol. 1: 128. A syrette is a device with a closed flexile tube, which injects drugs like atropine through a needle.

[16] NARA, *Historical Report*, pp. 27–28, NARA.

[17] NARA, British and U.S. BW Officials Meeting, December 28, 1944, RG 160, NARA.

[18] TNA WO 188/654. British Inter-Services Sub-Committee Memorandum, United Kingdom; Subject: Proposal for a Cooperative Research Policy in Biological Warfare in the United States, United Kingdom and Canada, (May 31, 1945).

Point of View

Open-Air Biowarfare Testing: American and British Experiences

Leonard A. Cole

Experiments involving select agents — potential biological weapons — are conducted in high containment laboratories. Thus, bacteria such as *Bacillus anthracis* and *Yersinia pestis* (causes of anthrax and plague) are managed in laboratories with airlock access rooms, reduced inside pressure to prevent outward airflow, and filtration of exhaust air. These requirements began during the latter part of the 20th century.

Still, dangerous biological agents have long received special handling. During World War II, safety measures for British workers developing anthrax weapons included protective outerwear and "meticulous technique." Structural protection consisted of a glass screen near the production machinery "to prevent gross splashing" (Carter and Pearson 1999: 183). Protection at America's military biological research facility at Fort Detrick included newly developed laboratory cabinets. Investigators would slip their hands into long rubber gloves affixed to portals, which enabled them to reach the work area (Covert 1993: 23).

When an agent is released outdoors, containment precautions are, self-evidently, non-existent. Apart from operators in protective suits an exposed population may be subject to health risks. Yet several countries have engaged in extensive field-testing: Japan in the 1930s and 1940s (including torturous killing of human subjects) (Harris 1994: 113–114), and the Soviet Union through the 1980s (Miller *et al.* 2001: 176; Leitenberg *et al.* 2012: 121–137).

Open-air experiments by the U.K. and U.S. began during World War II and continued for decades, many in collaboration with each other and with Canada. By the late 1950s, the U.K. had largely ended its offensive biological program and in 1969 the U.S. abruptly renounced its own offensive program. Both countries helped establish the 1972 Biological Weapons Convention, which aims to universalize the ban on such weaponry. But defensive measures are permitted and Dugway Proving Ground in Utah remains a principal field-testing location for the U.S. and its allies.[1] Before the late 1970s, the U.S. and U.K. had conducted numerous open-air tests in other settings as well.

The first test sites

British and American research during World War II explored the efficacy of dozens of pathogens to cause illness and death, among them the causative agents of anthrax, brucellosis, plague, tularemia, Q fever and botulism. By the war's end the only biological weapon produced in quantity was the U.K.'s arsenal of five million anthrax-laced cattle cakes. The plan was to drop them over Germany's pastures to infect livestock (Harris and Paxman 1982: 86–88). Although never implemented, the idea was based on field tests on the shore of Penclawdd, Wales, and on Gruinard Island, a small landmass off the Northwest coast of Scotland (Carter and Pearson 1999: 179).

When the Gruinard testing ended, scientists sought to decontaminate the island by setting it on fire. Upon returning to the charred remains they were stunned to find the anthrax spore count unaffected and for nearly a half-century people were forbidden to land there. In the mid-1980s scientists found that only three of Gruinard's 522 acres were heavily contaminated. After soaking the suspect areas with massive quantities of seawater and formaldehyde, in 1990

Gruinard was deemed safe for human return.[2] Meanwhile, the durability and lethality of anthrax bacilli had been firmly established.

American field-testing during the war was limited. The main intended test location, Horn Island off the Mississippi Gulf coast, opened in October 1943. It closed 9 months later because winds were predominantly blowing toward the mainland (Regis 1999: 76–77). In January 1945, the biological testing area at Dugway was completed but activity there was short lived. By the time the war ended, the British and American biological programs were reduced and Dugway was closed. In 1948, however, a presumed Soviet biological threat prompted reinvigoration of the American and British programs.

U.K. field-testing during the Cold War

The British response included a series of open-air tests with pathogens, at sea. Between 1948 and 1954, five trials — Operations Harness, Cauldron, Hesperus, Ozone, and Negation — were conducted in waterways around the U.K. and in the Caribbean region. Ships towed pontoons and dinghies that carried caged monkeys, sheep and guinea pigs. Personnel in protective outerwear sprayed select agents or detonated agent-filled bombs in the direction of the trailing animals. The released agents included *B. anthracis* and *Y. pestis* as well as *Brucella suis* and *Francisella tularensis* (causes of brucellosis and tularemia) (Balmer 2006: 54–58).

The purpose was to assess the effects of dispersal methods and durations of exposure on the animals. Technical details of the findings remain unavailable, though broad conclusions were mixed. Various trials were judged to be successful, partially successful or a failure (Balmer 2006: 56). Success, of course, meant that many animals had become infected.

Outdoor testing by the U.K. persisted even as the emphasis shifted from offensive to defensive design. By the late 1950s, rather than employing actual biological weapons, the British commonly used 'simulants' in what became known as large area coverage

(LAC) tests. The simulants were principally *Escherichia coli*, *Bacillus globigii* (*BG*), *Serratia marcescens* (*SM*), and the chemical Zinc Cadmium Sulfide (Balmer 2006: 66–67, 77–78).[3]

Trials with actual warfare agents had been conducted at some distance from population locations. But with a shift to large area testing, a simulant could blanket an inland area of more than 1,000 square miles. (Balmer 2006: 77–78).[4]

Between 1955 and 1977 simulants were repeatedly sprayed from aircraft, ships, and land generators. When released along the south coast of England these agents reached Swindon, Dorset and other population centers. Additional tests with simulants were conducted in variously located cities including London, Norwich, Southampton, and Salisbury. During the 22-year period, millions of Britons had been unwittingly exposed to the test agents, which demonstrated the country's vulnerability to a biological attack.[5]

U.S. field-testing during the Cold War

British and American open-air experiments were much alike. They tested the effects of the same pathogens, used the same simulants, and employed comparable scenarios. American scientists participated in the early British Caribbean trials in part to gain experience for future U.S. sea-based tests (Regis 1999: 122). Thus, shipboard activity was similar when, in 1964, five U.S. boats sailed in a 100 mile-long line off the Johnston Island atoll in the Pacific, carrying monkeys. With boat crews in sealed quarters, an airplane sprayed the sea path with the select agents *F tularensis* and *Coxiella burnetti* (the cause of Q fever). Four years later, in 1968, a similar U.S. test was conducted near Eniwetok, another Pacific atoll, using *Staphylococcal enterotoxin B*, a cause of debilitating illness. The tests were part of Project SHAD: Shipboard Hazards and Defenses.

From 1963 to 1973, SHAD included 52 sets of tests, many involving multiple releases of biological or chemical agents in locations as far ranging as the Deseret Test Center (80 miles from Dugway), Hawaii, the Panama Canal Zone, and off the coast of San Diego. Besides the three microbes cited above, open-air releases included the nerve agents sarin, tabun, soman and VX. One or more of these potential biological or chemical weapons were used in 26 SHAD tests. Biological simulants were also released: *BG* in 24 tests, *SM* in seven tests, and *E coli* in five tests (Regis 1999: 202–205).[6]

The public learned about Project SHAD at congressional hearings in 2002.[7] The belated disclosures were especially surprising because 25 years earlier the Army had acknowledged other 1950s–1960s germ warfare tests and had made no mention of SHAD. At 1977 Senate hearings, army witnesses disclosed that from 1949 to 1969, 239 open-air tests were conducted in populated areas throughout the U.S. Unlike SHAD, the previously revealed tests used only simulants, mainly SM, BG, and the chemical Zinc Cadmium Sulfide (FP, for Fluorescent Particles).[8]

Aims of the field tests

Reports about several of the U.K. and U.S. open-air tests eventually were declassified. The purpose of a test, stated or implied, was to assess any of the following:

- Effects of environmental conditions on released agents (over water versus land; daytime brightness versus night darkness; sunlight (ultraviolet) versus cloudy condition; weather variations including temperature, wind velocity and direction, humidity);
- Ability of specific agents to cause illness and death;
- Dispersion patterns of agents after release;
- Survivability of released microbes;
- Vulnerability of particular target areas — subways, city streets, open land;
- Effectiveness of various methods of delivery — munitions, air blowers/ generators, hand sprayers; and
- Effectiveness of various protective measures.

The tests expanded knowledge in all these areas. They demonstrated, for example, that *brucella* organisms packed in bomblets could survive a detonation and infect animals a mile from the point of release (Regis 1999: 140–142). Also, agents could spread over great distances. An airplane flying from South Dakota to Minnesota released FP later detected 1,200 miles away (Cole 1997: 20).[9] But even after years of research, few biological weapons had been produced and stockpiled. From a 1969 report, the year that the U.S. renounced its offensive program: "No large inventory of dry (powdered) anti-personnel lethal or incapacitating biological agents is maintained and only eight aircraft spray disseminators are in the inventory" (Moon 2006: 34). Historian John Moon concluded that a key reason for the meager stockpile was that the use of these weapons could result in "unpredictable consequences" (Moon 2006: 46).

The long-term contamination of Gruinard Island was a prime example of an unexpected consequence. Another occurred during a British sea operation in 1952, when a fishing vessel strayed into a cloud of plague bacteria near the northern Scottish island of Lewis. After no cases of infection were reported, most records of the incident were destroyed (Balmer 2006: 57).

In the U.S., after the secret spraying of San Francisco with SM in 1950, 11 patients at a city hospital contracted serratia infections, one of whom died. The army deemed the outbreak a coincidence and continued to use SM as a simulant in subsequent open-air tests (Cole 1990: 78–82).

Through the years the Americans and British explored numerous ways that a biological attack might be launched. A list of scenarios and simulants used in several U.S. tests is illustrative:

- **1950.** Release by seaborne generators blowing from a boat offshore toward San Francisco: SM, BG, FP (Cole, 1990: 78–81).[10]
- **1953.** Release by land-based and rooftop-based generators in Minneapolis: FP.[11]
- **1953.** Release from automobiles moving in traffic in Minneapolis and St. Louis: FP.[12]
- **1956.** Release of *Aedes aegypti* mosquitoes (vectors for the yellow fever virus) in

Savannah, Georgia. The test mosquitoes were uninfected females and the aim was to estimate "how many mosquitoes entered houses and bit people" (Cole 1997: 28–29).[13]

- **1957–1958.** Continuous release from airplanes during LAC flights "from the Rockies to the Atlantic, from Canada to the Gulf of Mexico": FP (Cole 1997: 19–21; Guillemin 2005: 108).[14]
- **1965.** Release by "minigenerators" hidden in briefcases at Washington DC National Airport and Greyhound Bus Terminals: BG. Previous tests in Washington, in 1949 and 1950, used SM.[15]
- **1966:** Release from light bulbs, filled with simulant, tossed on subway tracks as trains approached stations, New York City: BG (Cole 1990: 65–69).[16]

In addition to these scenarios, various explosive and other aerosol dissemination methods were investigated during the decades of American and British testing. But for all the inventiveness of the scenarios, none included widespread dispersal of an agent by mail. Which is how the only actual large-scale biological assault was launched in either country (Cole 2009; Cole *et al.* 2012: 25–26).

In the fall of 2001, about a half-dozen letters containing anthrax spores were mailed to American political and media figures. Spores leaking from the letters killed five people, sickened 17, and necessitated prophylactic antibiotics for 30,000 others. More than a month passed before recognition that scores of buildings had also been contaminated, some of which remained shut for years. Ironically a study of BG released from envelopes was conducted in a confined space months before the anthrax letters attack. But it did not foretell the massive cross-contamination by leaked spores that occurred during postal processing (Cole 2009: 93).[17] The many years of field-testing had done little to help prepare for an attack via the U.S. mail.

When the public found out

The belated disclosures about the open-air tests drew charges that simulants as well as select agents had caused previously unexplained illnesses. People from targeted areas — San Francisco, Minneapolis, St. Louis, Puerto Rico, Dorset (England) — sued the government or demanded investigations to validate their health claims (Cole 1990: 85–104).[18] Neither ensuing studies nor court cases confirmed that the tests had caused illness. In fact, establishing a correlation 30–50 years after an event complicates the search. The continued murkiness of the issue was evident in a 2004 study that found no patterns of ill health among 5,500 veterans involved in SHAD. The study warned that the "findings should not be misconstrued as clear evidence that there are no possible long-term health effects related to SHAD involvement."[19] In 2015, the Institute of Medicine was still assessing the long-term health effects of participation in Project SHAD.[20]

Conclusion

Available reports on the British and American open-air biological warfare tests are replete with data. Descriptions typically include details about how, when and where an agent was disseminated and about the results of the trial. But the open-air programs also left a legacy of unintended consequences including lawsuits against the government for concealing information about the tests and their possible dangers. Moreover, the simulants SM and BG, previously considered harmless, are now deemed human pathogens.[21]

Much has changed in western political culture since the early days of the American and British testing programs. People have become less reluctant to question authority and institutional review boards must now pre-approve research involving human subjects. Further, the heightened stringency of laboratory containment has accentuated the safety gap between a confined test space and one without physical boundaries. All this makes less likely that masses of people would again be unwittingly subjected to open-air biological warfare tests.

References

Balmer B (2006) 'The UK biological weapons program,' in M Wheelis L Rosza and M Dando (Eds.) *Deadly Cultures: Biological Weapons Since 1945*. Cambridge, MA: Harvard University Press.

Carter B and Pearson G (1999) 'British biological warfare and biological defense, 1925–45,' in E Geissler and Moon JEvC (Eds.) *Biological and Toxin Weapons: Research, Development and Use from the Middle Ages to 1945*. New York: Oxford University Press.

Cole LA (1990) *Clouds of Secrecy: The Army's Germ Warfare Tests Over Populated Areas*. Lanham, MD: Rowman and Littlefield.

Cole LA (1997) *The Eleventh Plague: The Politics of Biological and Chemical Warfare*. New York: WH Freeman.

Cole LA (2009) *The Anthrax Letters*. Washington DC: National Academies Press (2003)/New York: Skyhorse.

Cole LA, Kahn LH and Sandman PM (2012) 'Bioterrorism and the communication of uncertainty,' in LA Cole and ND Connell (Eds.) *Local Planning for Terror and Disaster: From Bioterrorism to Earthquakes*. Hoboken, NJ: Wiley-Blackwell.

Covert NM (1993) *Cutting Edge: A History of Fort Detrick, MD 1943–1993*. Fort Detrick, MD: Public Affair Office, Headquarters, US Army Garrison, Fort Detrick, MD.

Guillemin J (2005) *Biological Weapons: From the Invention of State-Sponsored Programs to Contemporary Bioterrorism*. New York: Columbia University Press.

Harris R and Paxman J (1982) *A Higher Form of Killing: The Secret Story of Chemical and Biological Warfare*. New York: Hill and Wang.

Harris SH (1994) *Factories of Death: Japanese Biological Warfare 1932–45 and the American Cover Up*. New York: Routledge.

Leitenberg M, Zilinskas RA and Kuhn JH (2012) *The Soviet Biological Weapons Program: A History*. Cambridge MA: Harvard University Press.

Miller J, Engelberg S and Broad W (2001) *Germs: Biological Weapons and America's Secret War*. New York: Simon and Schuster.

Moon JEvC (2006) 'The US biological weapons program,' in M, Wheelis L Rosza and M Dando (Eds.) *Deadly Cultures: Biological Weapons Since 1945*. Cambridge, MA: Harvard University Press.

Regis E (1999) *Biology of Doom: The History of America's Secret Germ Warfare Project*. New York: Henry Holt.

Notes

[1] Welcome to Dugway Proving Ground, Website. http://www.military.com/base-guide/dugway-proving-ground.

[2] Pearson GS (1990) 'Gruinard Island returns to civil use,' *ASA Newsletter*, No. 20, September. See http://www.asanltr.com/newsletter/01-5/articles/015c.htm.

[3] Barnett A, 'Millions were in Germ War Tests,' *The Guardian* April 21, 2002: http://www.theguardian.com/politics/2002/apr/21/uk.medicalscience.

[4] Norris KP (1966) 'Concentration, Viability, and Immunological Properties of Airborne Bacteria Released from a Massive Line Source.' U.K. Ministry of Defense, MRE Field Trial Report No. 3 (Trials conducted October 1963 to April 1964).

[5] Barnett 2002, as per note 3.

[6] U.S. Department of Defense (2003) Military Countermeasures, Project 112/SHAD Fact Sheets. http://mcm.fhpr.osd.mil/cb_exposures/project112_shad/shadfactSheets.aspx.

[7] U.S. Senate (2003). Committee on Armed Services. Subcommittee on Personnel, The Department of Defense's inquiry into Project 112/Shipboard Hazard and Defense (SHAD) tests. October 10, 2002. Government Printing Office.

U.S. House of Representatives (2003). Committee on Veterans' Affairs. Subcommittee on Health, Military operations aspects of SHAD and Project 112. October 9, 2002. Government Printing Office.

[8] U.S. Senate (1977) Committee on Human Resources. Subcommittee on Health and Scientific Research. Biological testing involving human subjects by the Department of Defense. March 8 and May 23, 1977. Government Printing Office. pp. 125–131.

[9] U.S. Army Chemical Corps (1958) *Summary of Major Events and Problems for 1958*, Historical Office Army Chemical Center, Maryland, annual reports, 1953–1962. pp. 108–109.

[10] U.S. Chemical Corps (1951) Biological Laboratories, Special Report No. 142, *Biological Warfare Trials at San Francisco, California, 20–27 September 1950.* Camp Detrick, Frederick, MD, January 22, 1951.

[11] U.S. Army Chemical Corps (1953) Behavior of Aerosol Clouds Within Cities, Joint Quarterly Report No. 3, January–March 1953. Submitted to the Chemical Corps by contractors Stanford University and the Parsons Co., Pasadena, CA. n.d.

[12] U.S. Army Chemical Corps (1953) Behavior of Aerosol Clouds Within Cities, Joint Quarterly Report No. 4, July–September 1953. Submitted to the Chemical Corps by contractors Stanford University and the Parsons Co., Pasadena, CA. n.d.

[13] U.S. Army Chemical Corps (1959) *Summary of Major Events and Problems for 1959*. Historical Office Army Chemical Center, Maryland, Annual Reports, 1953–1962.

[14] U.S. Army Chemical Corps 1958, as per note 5.

[15] U.S. Army Biological Laboratories (1965) Miscellaneous Publication 7, Study US65SP, Fort Detrick, Frederick, MD, July 1965; U.S. Senate 1977, as per note 6, pp. 125–126.

[16] U.S. Army (1968) 'A Study of the Vulnerability of Subway Passengers in New York City to Covert Action with Biological Agents,' Miscellaneous Publication 25, Fort Detrick, Frederick, MD, January 1968.

[17] Kournikakous B, Armour SJ, Boulet CA, *et al.* (2001) *Risk Assessment of Anthrax Threat Letters*, Canada Defense R&D, Technical Report DRES TR-2001-048 September.

[18] Barnett 2002, as per note 3; Boudreau A and Bronstein S 'Island Residents Sue U.S., Saying Military Made Them Sick,' *CNN*, February 1, 2010 http://www.cnn.com/2010/US/02/01/vieques.illness/; Mann J 'Suit filed over government test spraying in St. Louis during Cold War,' *St. Louis-Post Dispatch*, November 21, 2012 http://www.stltoday.com/news/local/crime-and-courts/suit-filed-over-government-test-spraying-in-st-louis-during/article_9bc1fc7d7093-58a3-b557-0cbac5dc38ab.html; Worthington R (1994) Army Test Raises Accusations. *Chicago Tribune*, June 15. http://articles.chicagotribune.com/1994-06-15/news/9406150171_1_zinc-cadmium-sulfide-tests-sen-paul-wellstone.

[19] Institute of Medicine (2004) Health effects of Project SHAD, biological agent: *Bacillus Globigii*, Prepared for the National Academies by The Center for Research Information, Inc., Silver Spring, MD. https://www.iom.edu/~/media/Files/Report%20Files/2007/Long-Term-Health-Effects-of-Participation-in-Project-SHAD-Shipboard-Hazard-and-Defense/BACILLUSGLOBIGII.pdf.

[20] Institute of Medicine (2015) National Academies Current Projects, Shipboard Hazard and Defense II (SHAD II). http://www8.nationalacademies.org/cp/projectview.aspx?key=IOM-BSP-10-08.

[21] Institute of Medicine 2004, as per note 5; Kurz CL, Chauvet S, Andrès E, *et al.* 'Virulence Factors of the Human Opportunistic Pathogen *Serratia marcescens* Identified by *in vivo* Screening,' EMBO J, (2003) http://www.ncbi.nlm.nih.gov/pubmed/12660152.

Chapter 4

The Soviet Biological Warfare Program

Jens H. Kuhn & Milton Leitenberg

Introduction

Following the end of World War I, the USSR appeared to have been the very first nation to initiate an offensive biological warfare (BW) program. Following the introduction of the Biological Weapon and Toxin Convention (BWC) signed by the USSR in 1972, a greatly expanded Soviet program grew into the largest that the world had ever witnessed. By 1972, there were no longer any British, United States or Canadian offensive BW programs (see Chapter 3).

Considerable progress has been made in understanding the Soviet BW program over the years,[1] culminating in an extensive historical treatise written in part by the authors of this chapter, titled *The Soviet Biological Weapons Program: A History* (Leitenberg *et al.* 2012). This chapter draws heavily from that treatise, and the many hundreds of references cited in it. However, despite all the efforts to understand the Soviet BW program, large parts of it remain shrouded in secrecy due in part to current Russian laws prohibiting any former participant from revealing its details. What is known about the program is therefore largely owed to information from defectors or former participants in the Soviet program that could legally leave the USSR or its successor countries, and information pieced together from extensive literature searches and interviews. This chapter describes that program.

The first major informant was microbiologist Vladimir Artemovich Pasechnik, director of the Institute of Highly Pure Biopreparations (IHPB), a major bioweapons facility in Leningrad (today St. Petersburg), who arrived in Great Britain at the end of October 1989. Pasechnik's revelations about an enormous Soviet secret BW program, employing tens of thousands of scientists and technicians and supporting vast research and production facilities entirely in violation of the BWC, came largely as a surprise to western academic arms control analysts and to some degree also to the Western intelligence community. These revelations were later confirmed by a junior informant code-named "Temple Fortune" from the same institute.

The second major informant was Kanatzhan Bayzakovich Alibekov, who left late in 1992. He had worked his way up in the secret program's hierarchy by working at various weapons research and development institutes. At the crown of his career, Alibekov was the First Deputy Director of "Biopreparat," a vast network of civilian institutes that performed the bulk of the research and development work that supported the second generation of the Soviet biological weapons program under the direction of the Ministry of Defense (see below). Together with the information by other major insiders like Igor V. Domaradsky, Sergei Popov and Vladimir P. Zaviyalov, Western analysts concluded that all other known efforts to acquire biological weapons paled in comparison to the Soviet system. The Soviet BW program was the world's oldest, largest and longest lasting program (1918–1993 or longer). It was the only known program that had ever developed a weapons-on-demand mobilization system focused massively on incorporating modern genetic techniques into weapons development.

The Soviet biological weapons program can be roughly divided into two generations. The first generation evolved from the Soviet chemical weapons program around 1918 and lasted until about 1971. The second generation began shortly after 1971 and lasted at least until it was nominally dismantled by official decree in 1993. However, it may have continued for several years longer, and there is no precise knowledge as to exactly when all offensive BW activities in Russia were terminated.

The first generation Soviet BW program

The first generation BW program was initiated in part because Imperial Russian armies had suffered tremendous losses during past military conflicts due to infectious diseases, and in part because of attacks waged against the Imperial Russian army with chemical weapons during World War I. Initial biological weapons efforts began as early as 1918 at a proving ground in Kuzminki, Moscow Oblast, where the People's Commissariat of Health initiated tests with anti-livestock agents. Subsequently, a two-pronged approach was initiated. First, a Soviet chemical weapons program was begun under Yakov Moiseyevich Fishman in the Military Chemical Agency (established in 1925) to develop future chemical deterrence or retaliation capabilities. Second, a biological defense program was begun under Ivan Velikanov at the Vaccine Serum Laboratory close to Moscow that aimed to develop vaccines, treatments and prophylactic measures for soldiers to withstand infectious agents naturally encountered in the theater of military operations. Several dozen institutes under the Soviet People's Commissariats of Health and Education, all managed overall by the Military Chemical Agency, were part of the biological program.

Very little is known about the first generation BW program, but with time it expanded to include dozens of small laboratories or institutes distributed over the USSR. The program transitioned from a defensive to an offensive nature in 1928 through a secret decree by the Revolutionary Military Council. For instance, the Zlatogorov-Maslokovich Laboratory began developing techniques to fill ammunitions with pathogen formulations. In addition, the Red Army's Veterinary Scientific-Research Institute in Leningrad began examining the effects of bioweapons on animals. Other major centers involved in the program were the Bacteriological Laboratory in the Pokrovskii Monastery in Suzdal, Vladimir Oblast, and the

Workers' and Peasants' Red Army Vaccine-Sera Laboratory in Vlasikha, Moscow Oblast.

Both the defensive and offensive arms of the program resembled similar programs that followed in other nations: Japan, France, Canada, U.K. and the U.S. These were initiated at different times in the 1930s, with the U.S. program being the last to begin, in 1942. The Soviet program focused primarily on bacteria known to have been scourges to mankind without easily applicable cures, (e.g., *Bacillus anthracis* [causing anthrax], *Brucella melitensis* [brucellosis], *Burkholderia mallei* [glanders], *Burkholderia pseudomallei* [melioidosis], *Clostridium botulinum* [botulism], *Coxiella burnetii* [Q fever], *Francisella tularensis* [tularemia], *Rickettsia prowazekii* [epidemic typhus], *Vibrio cholerae* [cholera], *Yersinia pestis* [plague]). Successful weapons development also included at least two viruses: variola virus (the cause of smallpox) and Venezuelan equine encephalitis virus. Limited efforts included agricultural pathogens. Candidate weapons were tested at at least three field sites: at the Tomka Central Army Chemical Proving Ground close to Shikhany, Saratov Oblast; on Gorodomlya Island in the Seliger Lake, Kalinin Oblast; and on Vozrozhdeniye, Komsomolskii, and Konstantin Islands in the Aral Sea (governed jointly by the Kazakh and Uzbek SSRs).

After World War II, the offensive program was heavily infused by knowledge and experience gathered by the Imperial Japanese Army, which had performed biological experiments with infectious disease-causing agents and toxins on Chinese and other prisoners of war (see Chapter 2). The program was also influenced substantially by two monographs published in 1947 and 1949 by Theodor Rosebury on the American biological weapons program (Rosebury 1949; Rosebury and Kabat 1947). The Soviet program was controlled by the Main Military Directorate under the lead of Yefim Smirnov for most of its history (code-named "Smirnov's System" or "P.O. Box A-1968"). This program expanded considerably and finally became organized under flagship Ministry of Defense institutes located in Kirov, Sverdlovsk (today Yekaterinburg), and Zagorsk (today Sergiyev Posad).

However, the first generation program did not transcend growth and direct use of the classical biological agents mentioned above as

Trofim Denisovich Lysenko, who did not believe in modern genetics, influenced the Soviet leadership. In addition, genetic techniques did not become available until the 1960s. The first generation program therefore focused on classical selection techniques to isolate microorganisms that were resistant to antibiotics and vaccines and that could evade then-current diagnostic systems.

The second generation Soviet BW program

By the late 1960s, Soviet military or military-associated scientists persuaded political leaders that modern biotechnology, including genetics, held substantial military potential. The era of "Lysenkoism" thereby came to a halt. At the end of 1971, shortly before the Soviet Union signed the BWC, the Central Committee of the Communist Party and the USSR Council of Ministers approved a massive expansion of the biological weapons program. The expansion and redirection of the program was proposed by a small but very influential group of scientists in the leadership of the USSR Academy of Sciences, in particular Yury A. Ovchinnikov. The 15th Directorate of the General Staff under General Smirnov until 1985, and senior officials of the Military Industrial Commission (VPK) were responsible for carrying out and administering the new program. The aim was to assimilate and exploit the new field of genetic engineering that was just beginning to emerge in the West. New pathogen properties, such as resistance to countermeasures or enhanced stability, were planned to be engineered directly into pathogens, including agents not on classical bioweapons agent lists. These altered pathogens formed a novel arsenal of weapons that could not be predicted by western intelligence. The tightly controlled program was more secret than the USSR's efforts in the realm of nuclear weapons.

While the U.S. was the principal adversary of the Soviet Union and therefore the primary envisioned target for an attack with biological weapons, other potential targets, the European North Atlantic Treaty Organization (NATO) allies of the U.S. and China might have played a role in the decision to expand the Soviet biological weapons program as well. Actual Soviet planning for the use of biological weapons is unknown. Inferences can only be made from the agents that the Soviet military chose to weaponize, notably contagious pathogens and even more, from the weapon platforms and delivery systems that the Soviet military procured to distribute its biological weapons. From these inferences it has been assumed that the Soviet leadership did not envision using biological weapons for tactical purposes. Their role was primarily strategic: to attack population centers, military bases, vital industrial hubs, and major agricultural targets. Such weapons are thought to have been intended for killing the remnants of populations that survived a preceding exchange of nuclear weapons between the Soviet Union and an adversary. Soviet doctrine for BW is, however, probably the area about which the least is known.

The second generation program, controlled by the 15th Directorate of the Ministry of Defense, can be divided roughly into five branches carried out by different government agencies: Ministry of Defense, Glavmikrobioprom/Biopreparat, Ministry of Health (2nd and 3rd Directorates), Ministry of Agriculture and Ministry of the Interior. Institutes affiliated with the USSR Academy of Sciences, such as the Institute of Protein Research, the Institute of Molecular Biology, the Institute of Biochemistry and Physiology of Microorganisms, the M. M. Shemyakin Institute of Bioorganic Chemistry (all in or close to Moscow) and the Pacific Ocean Institute of Bioorganic Chemistry in Vladivostok, became intricately involved as contributors and participants in the program.

Together, the second generation program involved some 40–50 research, development and production facilities; the Vozrozhdeniye Island testing site; and seven to eight mobilization-capacity production facilities. By 1990, the Soviet Union had approved at least 13 pathogen and delivery systems, all of which, however, were based on non-genetically modified classical bacteria and viruses. These pathogens were planned to be delivered by missiles, spray systems mounted on medium bombers or bomblets carried in air-delivered munitions. None of these weapons, as far as is known, could have reached the continental U.S. other than Alaska, suggesting that their primary targets would have been European NATO partners.

Ministry of Defense

This part of the second generation biological weapons program was a logical continuation of the first generation program, and it remained entirely under the Ministry of Defense's control since 1928. The S. M. Kirov Military Medical Academy in Leningrad provided basic training for the colonels and generals who headed or worked for military and "civilian" bioweapons facilities. The lead Ministry of Defense institutes established for the first generation program, located in Kirov, Sverdlovsk and Zagorsk, continued to focus most research efforts. Researchers from the institutes in Kirov and Sverdlovsk specialized in bacterial research, while the scientists from the institute in Zagorsk specialized in working with viruses and bacteria that were difficult to culture. The institute in Kirov possessed an extensive vivarium, a pilot plant, a small-size production plant including downstream processing equipment, chambers for aerosol testing, and an explosive test chamber.

The Sverdlovsk plant was located within a military cantonment named Compound 19. As far as is known, research and development almost exclusively focused on *Bacillus anthracis*, the principal Soviet biological weapons agent. In April 1979, an outbreak of anthrax occurred in Sverdlovsk in proximity to the Sverdlovsk plant. Civilians living in several villages adjacent to the city became sick and numerous people succumbed to infection. Using a disinformation campaign, the Soviet government was able to convince a number of prominent Western experts for years that the anthrax outbreak was due to contaminated meat products (Meselson *et al.* 1994; Leitenberg 1991, 1992). By 1990, the plant was supported by some 7,000 people, including scientists, guards and dependents.

Researchers from the Zagorsk institute focused on the weaponization of alphaviruses (Eastern and Venezuelan equine encephalitis viruses), viral hemorrhagic fever-causing agents (Junín virus, Lassa virus, Machupo virus, Rift Valley fever virus, Marburg virus and Ebola virus), and orthopoxviruses (monkeypox and variola viruses). Bacterial agents that were researched included rickettsiae, *Chlamydophila psittaci* (cause of psittacosis), *Coxiella burnetii* (Q fever) and *Orientia tsutsugamushi* (Tsutsugamushi disease). The institute possessed sufficient production and processing equipment for the pilot-scale production of agents, but not full industrial-scale production. The institute also had a vivarium housing the many hundreds of animals required for animal testing. Researchers from the Zagorsk institute were instrumental in developing new variola virus production methods that were based on cell-culture techniques rather than injected embryonated chicken eggs. The technique for growing variola virus in cell culture was completed at a Glavmikrobioprom/Biopreparat institute (Vektor, see later). This effort was but one example of how the various branches of the biological weapons program collaborated in a common weapon development effort across their respective institutional and ministerial boundaries.

The Ministry of Defense established the military city of Kantubek on Vozrozhdeniye Island in the early 1950s. The Aralsk-7 complex, as it became known, continued expanding and by 1990, soon before its life came to an end with the dissolution of the USSR, had about 90 structures, a central steam plant that provided heat for all buildings, and a large field laboratory facility. Its population during the test season ranged from 1,200 to 2,000 people, including more than 600 soldiers, but during the off-season, the population dwindled to a few hundred. Aralsk-7 was developed as the major Soviet biological weapons field-test site — the last step before a newly developed biological weapon was validated and taken up in the official arsenal. The field laboratory facility consisted of 50 to 60 buildings of various types and sizes that housed scientists and technicians temporarily dispatched from the Ministry of Defense institutes in Kirov, Sverdlovsk and Zagorsk.

A small ghost village was constructed to test the behavior of aerosolized pathogens in an urban setting, defensive measures, and newly developed personal and collective protection equipment. Field tests on Vozrozhdeniye Island were performed primarily at night to take advantage of the blanket of cool air covering the warmer layer over the ground (known as the inversion layer) and to avoid damaging UV radiation from sunlight. These tests would simulate how actual attacks would be performed. Various biological agents were dispersed by explosions or sprayers and would drift over caged-animals. Aerosol impactors used to analyze the number and size of aerosolized particles were spread out at pre-determined intervals. The animals were used to measure the direct effect of the tested aerosol, i.e., whether disease was induced and whether the induced disease resembled the expected/desired clinical signs and lethality. Conclusions could then be drawn as to which kind of aerosol had the greatest effects on the test animals and how to increase the effective radius of dispersion for the tested aerosols under various meteorological conditions.

At the end of 1971, an outbreak of smallpox was recorded in Aralsk, Kazakh SSR, despite the fact that smallpox had been eradicated from Soviet Territory since 1961. Ten people contracted the disease and three died. In addition, an unusually high incidence of *Yersinia pestis* infections was noted among rodents on Vozrozhdeniye Island throughout the 1970s and 1980s. Both human and rodent infections very likely occurred as a result of tests with aerosolized bioweapon candidates.

Glavmikrobioprom/Biopreparat

In their memorandum to the Soviet Politburo, Ovchinnikov and his colleagues proposed to extend the offensive BW program into research facilities that would appear to be in the civilian sphere to evade Western intelligence services. Rather than expanding the military branch, their proposal was to hide the new institutions "in plain sight" by masquerading them as large-scale pharmaceutical enterprises. The Politburo approved the proposal and ordered the construction of an entirely new network of ostensibly commercial institutes, production plants and storage facilities that were secretly dedicated to developing biological weapons. The entire complex was placed under the pharmaceutical-industrial department Glavmikrobioprom, and was known publicly as Biopreparat. Despite being a "civilian" enterprise, all weapons-related activities (code-named "Ogarkov's System," "P.O. Box A-1063," or "Ferment") were directed and funded by the Ministry of Defense's 15th

Directorate. The head of Biopreparat was Vsevolod Ivanovich Ogarkov until 1979, followed by Yury Tikhonovich Kalinin.

To keep its cover, Biopreparat did indeed develop products for commercial markets, including medical countermeasures against infectious diseases, while clandestinely pushing new avenues to develop biological weapons. Of course, this dichotomy posed challenges for maintaining secrecy. Legends, i.e., plausible but misleading cover stories, were created by the Committee for State Security (KGB) to explain ongoing activities to outsiders. A new classification level higher than "top secret," called "series F clearance," was established to keep activities partially or completely hidden. In Central Committee documents, the term "biological weapons" was never used; the program was referred to as "Special Problems." Importantly, the organization of Biopreparat facilities was such that most employees were unaware of ongoing secret activities performed by their colleagues. Some employees knew part of the activities; and only a very few of the most senior staff members knew about all the activities taking place in their own institute. All major Biopreparat institutes had specially constructed rooms within their (KGB-controlled) First Departments in which series F meetings could be held, and special archives within their Second Departments where series F documents could be stored. Employees with series F clearance ("List 1" persons) were under constant KGB surveillance and limited in their possibilities to change jobs, travel abroad or meet with foreigners.

Ferment was divided into numerous compartmentalized subprograms, of which only a few are known by name and of which even fewer are understood. Among those that have been revealed, the most important ones are "Bonfire/Metol," "Factor," "Hunter," and "Chimera." The goal of the Bonfire/Metol subprogram was to develop multidrug-resistant bacteria to evade common treatment regimens; bacteria and viruses with modified/unnatural antigenic structures to evade common antibody-based diagnostic tests; and bacteria and viruses more resistant to environmental pressures than wild-type microorganisms. Factor's aim was to increase the virulence and stability of pathogens, in particular by modifications that also changed the course of the disease induced upon infection.

The Hunter subprogram was more ambitious than Bonfire/Metol and Factor as it sought to develop bacteria that would release encoded viruses upon encountering antibiotics. Infected individuals who would not succumb to infection with the bacterium due to timely antibiotic treatment in a healthcare setting would then encounter a second potentially lethal viral infection. Similar in spirit to Bonfire/Metol, the goal of the Chimera subprogram was to investigate the possibility of creating orthopoxviruses (e.g., vaccinia virus) that would encode small RNA viruses such as Venezuelan equine encephalitis virus or Ebola virus. It is unknown whether any Hunter or Chimera projects were successful. None are known to have reached the stage of weaponization and testing.

At the peak of the Soviet BW effort at the end of the 1980s, Biopreparat included three dozen institutes as well as mobilization production plants that had been tested and approved, and were prepared to produce tens of tons of agent on notification of an anticipated prewar situation. These included the Berdsk Chemical Factory, the Omutninsk Chemical Factory, Combine "Sintez" in Kurgan, and Combine "Biosintez" in Penza. There were other types of facilities spread all over the Soviet Union that were involved in Ferment to produce equipment and reagents needed by the research and production institutes. Some 30,000 people are estimated to have worked for Biopreparat, though some argue that figure should be substantially higher.

All-Union Research Institute for Applied Microbiology

Biopreparat's flagship for weaponizing bacteria was a very large, high-security facility in Obolensk south of Moscow called the All-Union Research Institute for Applied Microbiology. Officially, its employees developed biological pesticides such as *Bacillus thuringiensis* for use in agriculture. Unofficially, the institute was the most militarized of all Biopreparat facilities and was referred to by the code name "PO Box V-8724." The institute consisted of 90–100 buildings spread over 250 hectares. The centerpiece was Korpus N1, a nine-story building with a floor area of 37,000 m^2. The first two floors of N1 housed the administration and control rooms. Floors three to eight contained laboratories, with each floor roughly dedicated to bacteria belonging to the same genus. Each of the six floors had its own aerosol chambers in which the effects of aerosolized formulations of pathogens could be tested on experimental animals. Two hundred laboratory rooms were supplied with filtered air and were run under negative air pressure to prevent escape of pathogens into the environment. The top floor of the building contained a small-scale production unit with fermenters up to 100-liter capacity. More than 4,000 people are estimated to have worked at the institute during the late 1980s.

The Obolensk institute focused primarily on developing *Francisella tularensis* and *Bacillus anthracis* strains resistant to current vaccines and multiple antibiotics. For instance, in 1986, scientists involved in the Bonfire/Metol subprogram developed a strain of *Bacillus anthracis* able to resist seven or eight antibiotics commonly used for cases with anthrax. During 1987–1988, similar multidrug-resistant strains were created for *Francisella tularensis, Burkholderia mallei,* and *Burkholderia pseudomallei.* Another Bonfire/Metol project was the successful transfer of a gene encoding the *Bacillus cereus* virulence factor cereolysin into the closely related *Bacillus anthracis.* This novel strain proved to be highly immunosuppressive and avoided anthrax vaccine-induced immune responses. Within the Factor subprogram, bacteria, such as *Legionella pneumophila*, were also manipulated to express fragments of myelin, the insulating substance surrounding neuronal axons. These fragments provoked an immune response in infected animals, thereby leading to an attack of the immune system against the animal's own myelin. In test animals, temporary pneumonia developed as expected for legionella infection, but in addition, the infection caused brain damage, paralysis and near lethality similar to the autoimmune disease multiple sclerosis. Another Factor project was the creation of a recombinant *Yersinia pestis* strain that expressed diphtheria toxin.

Scientific-Production Association "Vektor"

Biopreparat's primary institute for virology was the Scientific-Production Association "Vektor," which was built as a large, isolated research campus in Koltsovo outside of Novosibirsk, Novosibirsk Oblast. Similar to the facility in Obolensk, Vektor's cover was the development of biological pesticides for use in agriculture. In addition, the institute officially worked for the Ministry of Defense on developing medical countermeasures for military personnel, which is how Vektor's leadership could justify work on high-consequence pathogens in especially constructed biosafety level 3 and 4 laboratories. Code-named "PO Box V-8036," Vektor's classified mission was to research, develop and laboratory-test viruses for their ability to be used in biological weaponry. Reminiscent of the Obolensk facility, Vektor was highly secured with some buildings surrounded by secondary walls that had their own guarded entry points for added security. The floor area of buildings within these closed areas eventually totaled 200,000 m^2. The floor area of biosafety level 4 facilities, designated for work with the most lethal pathogens known to mankind, covered 1,440 m^2. These facilities included chambers for testing the aerosol characteristics of viruses and the efficacy of vaccines against specific viral pathogens in rodents and non-human primates.

Bioreactors and large egg incubators (capacity of up to 5,000 eggs) existed for the growth of viruses in both pilot plant-scale and industrial quantities. Vektor also included an open-air test site for testing non-infectious biological simulants and inert chemicals. Tests were performed at night. Using single-source dispersal from a land-based aerosol generator or line-source dispersal from aircraft carrying special canisters and spray equipment, scientists developed mathematical aerosol cloud dispersion models for viruses over open fields, urban areas and coastal areas. By 1990, Vektor employed almost 4,500 people. The primary pathogens that were researched and developed at the facility were variola virus and Marburg virus. At its top production capacity in December 1990, Vektor's maximum yield of weaponized variola virus from cell culture was estimated to have been about two tons annually.

Just like the institute in Obolensk, Vektor scientists experimented with the introduction of foreign genes, such as genes encoding myelin fragments, into viruses (Factor subprogram). The hosts were primarily orthopoxviruses, such as vaccinia virus, as surrogates for variola virus.

Vektor scientists also created recombinant viruses expressing heterotypic viral genes. The goal of these experiments, however, is still under debate among analysts. In 1990, Vektor scientists began developing recombinant strains of vaccinia virus and ectromelia viruses (another orthopoxvirus causing mousepox in laboratory mice) with improved abilities to defeat host immune systems compared to wild-type strains. Theoretical virology experts employed bioinformatics to guide laboratory scientists in constructing structural and functional maps of orthopoxvirus genomes to identify genes that could be removed or replaced with foreign immunoregulatory genes (e.g., encoding endorphins) without affecting pathogenicity. Vektor personnel also developed methods for the large-scale production of a dry Marburg virus formulation that was effective, i.e., lethal, when used as an aerosol on non-human primates in closed aerosol chambers. As these efforts led to Ministry of Defense awards presented to the head scientists of this project, one can only imagine that the program was successful.

Institute of Highly Pure Biopreparations

The official function of the IHPB in Leningrad was to develop human and animal vaccines against natural infectious pathogens and to protect crops from common scourges. The secret mission of the institute was to support the Obolensk and Vektor institutes by synthesizing peptides (to support the Factor subprogram) and developing formulations for bacteria and virus bioweapon candidates. Secret research activities took place in one of the institute's three buildings, which had five floors (10,000 m^2). In 1989, approximately 400 scientists and 200 support personnel were employed at the institute. Importantly, IHPB was also apparently the lead institute for developing a long-range cruise missile delivery system for biological weapons at the time that the USSR ceased to exist.

Engineering Immunology

The Institute of Engineering Immunology in Lyubuchany, Moscow Oblast, focused officially on the development of monoclonal antibodies, recombinant interferons and other cytokines, and recombinant vaccines as treatments for common infectious diseases. The secret program (code-named "P.O. Box G-4883") was to characterize the immune response of experimental animals to pathogens suitable for BW. The ultimate goal was to identify ways to overcome the immune response and to pinpoint weaknesses in the immune system that could be targeted by other pathogens. For instance, scientists at the institute managed to develop a *Francisella tularensis* formulation in which the bacteria were covered with Protein A to protect them from attack by the human immune system. In addition, another goal was to develop medical countermeasures to protect Soviet troops or the Soviet population from pathogens used in a Soviet bioweapons attack.

Stepnogorsk Progress Scientific and Production Base

The Stepnogorsk Progress Scientific and Production Base was located in the Kazakh SSR. Code-named "PO Box 2076," the compound was surrounded by high grey walls and an electric-wire fence. The surrounding land was stripped of all vegetation and motion sensors were ubiquitous. Inside the compound, dozens of buildings were arranged on a grid of narrow streets, with several buildings more than five stories high. Separate entrances with armed guards were available for the approximately 800 civilian and military employees working on the 200 hectare site.

The main pathogen production facility, Building 221, had six stories, two of which were located underground (total floor area of 35,000 m^2). The top floor held 20 1,000-liter fermenters, which were used as pilot plants for propagation of an agent. The harvest of one of these fermenters would be transferred to one of 10 20,000-liter fermenters on the lower floors. After fermentation was completed, the contents were transferred to one of seven underground centrifuges for separation of the agent from growth media and waste, followed by transfer into 50-liter or 250-liter stainless steel containers. The containers were moved to Building 231, where the agent was dried into "cakes," milled in industrial-sized milling machines to produce particles of a uniform size. The product was then transferred either to

Bunkers 241–244 for filling weapons (e.g., bomblets) or to Bunkers 251–252 for long-term storage. The milled product was tested in Building 600, which was the largest indoor testing facility constructed in the Soviet Union. Final open-air field testing was carried out at Vozrozhdeniye Island.

The Stepnogorsk Production Plant was just one of the mobilization capacity production facilities that were organized for immediate production cycles on short notice. Upon receiving a message from Moscow, the plant would begin producing agent and filling weapons. Approved agent seed strains would be seeded in the fermenters, and milled product would be filled into bomblets and spray tanks. Subsequently, filled munitions would have been loaded onto trucks and transported to a railroad station or an airfield for further transport to various military sites, such as airbases at which dedicated bomber forces were located. The primary agent produced at the Stepnogorsk plant was *Bacillus anthracis.* The plant's production capacity is estimated to have been about 300 tons of weaponized spores per 10-month production cycle.

Ministry of Health

The Ministry of Health was also deeply involved in the Soviet biological weapons system, but most activities were defensive in nature such as those of the Second Main Directorate, code-named "Problem No. 5." The program was deeply hidden in an official network of so-called anti-plague institutes that evolved from so-called Pasteur stations in the late 1800s. The normal peacetime function of these institutes was to protect the nation from endemic lethal diseases, first and foremost plague. By the end of 1970, the anti-Plague system consisted of the six Anti-Plague Institutes spread over the USSR (in Alma-Ata [today Almaty], Irkutsk, Minsk, Rostov-on-Don, Saratov and Volgograd). In addition, 29 Anti-Plague Stations with 53 subordinate Anti-Plague Departments, 198 Seasonal Epidemic Brigades (intervention teams that would attempt to terminate ongoing natural infectious disease outbreaks) and 31 Specialized Anti-Epidemic Teams were also involved. Little is known about the system's secret activities. As the various institutes, stations and departments were already focused on developing defenses against pathogens that were also part of the biological weapons program, it is reasonable to assume that they were also tasked to develop defenses against pathogens created in that program. These institutes also played a role in the collection of wild strains of pathogens that were then transferred to the BW program to see if they were better suited for BW purposes than those already standardized and approved.

The Third Main Directorate of the Ministry of Health was responsible for dealing with any medical emergency that occurred at any institute invloved in biological, chemical, nuclear, or radiological work. The Ministry was responsible for responding to any outbreak of disease within, or caused by, the BW program. Again, very little is known about the ministry's involvement in the biological weapons realm. At least one institute, the Severin Institute, housed inside an insane asylum in Moscow, played a part in the "Flute" subprogram by developing non-lethal and lethal psychotropic agents.

Ministry of Agriculture

The organized BW program of the Ministry of Agriculture, code-named "Ekologiya," grew out of the very first biological weapons experiments in 1918 in Kuzminki. This program was organized in the late 1940s to develop anti-animal and anti-plant weaponry. The program was very limited in scope, but it expanded considerably in 1958, when six major institutes with numerous affiliated sub-branches were created. The All-Union Scientific-Research Foot-And-Mouth Disease Institute in Yuryevets, Vladimir Oblast began research on African swine fever virus, foot-and-mouth disease virus and rinderpest virus. The All-Union Scientific Research Institute of Virology and Microbiology in Posyolok Volginskii, Vladimir Oblast focused on *Bacillus anthracis* and other anti-livestock weapons in general. The Scientific-Research Agricultural Institute in the Gvardeiskii Military Settlement in the suburbs of Otar, Dzhambul Oblast, Kazakh SSR, evaluated African swine fever virus, bluetongue virus, equine influenza A viruses, fowlpox virus, goatpox virus, Newcastle disease virus, rabbit hemorrhagic disease virus, rinderpest virus, sheeppox virus, suid herpesvirus 1 and cereal rust fungi. The Scientific Institute of Phytopathology in Bolshiye Vyazemy close to Golitsyno, Moscow Oblast; the Central Asian Scientific-Research Institute of Phytopathology in Durmen, Tashkent Oblast; Uzbek SSR, and North Caucasus Scientific-Research Institute of Phytopathology in Krasnodar Krai developed anti-crop weapons targeting corn, rice, rye and wheat. The program also included mobilization production plants located in Pokrov and Vladimir.

Ministry of Interior

Very little is known about the biological weapons activities of the KGB. In all likelihood, KGB scientists were involved in the production and evaluation of substances and microbes that could be used for assassinations. It is known that umbrellas, ballpoint pens and walking sticks were developed that could shoot pellets with holes filled with poison. The KGB was also most likely involved in the procurement of pathogens not endemic in the USSR, and of course, in the procurement of secret information regarding biological weapons from other nations.

Bomblets and spray systems

Two major types of biological weapon dispersion devices were developed in the USSR: bomblets and spray systems.

The biological bomblet *Gshch*-304 closely resembled the U.S. E-130R2 or E-120 BW bomblets designed during the American offensive biological weapons program, which was terminated in 1969. Cantaloupe-sized, *Gshch*-304 were round, their outer shells made of 3-mm thick aluminum with small aerodynamic vanes on the surface, and with a burster charge in the center. The bomblets, all tested on Vozrozhdeniye Island, could be used to fill cluster bombs or missile warheads and would explode on impact with the ground releasing their payloads of formulated pathogens.

At least two spray systems were developed for dispersing biological agents. Bombers would be fitted with large tanks containing liquid pathogen formulations to be sprayed across vast areas of territory. A second system was developed and tested in which a large number of 20-liter containers would be placed on a platform that could be lowered from the bomb bay of an aircraft. The platform would be lowered before the aircraft reached the target area; the top of the container would be removed by an automatic device, and the contents would be sucked out into the open air by the Venturi effect. Knowledge about this system is limited; the aircraft that served as the test bed was unlikely to have been able to survive over a battlefield.

The Soviets developed a short-range (43–135 kilometer range) ballistic missile with a warhead for delivery of biological weapons agents. This missile underwent extensive testing, but was never approved for production nor entered the Soviet arsenal. To the best of the authors' knowledge, intercontinental ballistic missiles (ICBM) for the delivery of biological weapons never reached an advanced stage of development and were never deployed by the USSR.

Pressure to terminate the BW program

After debriefing Pasechnik, the U.S. and the U.K. exerted pressure through joint high-level démarches to the Soviet government with a double purpose: to obtain an admission of the existence of an illegal Soviet offensive BW program, and to see that it was absolutely terminated. On at least 15 occasions between May 1990 and July 1991, U.S. President Bush, U.K. Prime Minister Thatcher and their most senior deputies exerted pressure on Gorbachev and USSR Foreign Minister Shevardnadze to close down the program. Although an initial group of site visits was negotiated, allowing U.S. and U.K. experts to visit four Biopreparat facilities, the overall effort to bring about the termination of the Soviet program failed. *The Soviet Biological Weapons Program: A History* (Leitenberg *et al.* 2012) includes approximately 350 pages of text concerning the arms-control history associated with the Soviet BW program. This includes a dozen Soviet Central Committee documents which provide valuable insight into the level of secrecy and deception regarding the BW program and its activities, even within the Central Committee itself. The documents also provide evidence of the degree of deception that the Soviet government used in dealing with its negotiating partners, the U.S. and the U.K., as well as with the international arms-control community in general.

Efforts were partially successful with Russian President Yeltsin, who took office in January 1992; or so it seemed at first. Yeltsin finally publicly admitted the existence of the program in January 1992. In April 1992, he issued Decree 390 of the Russian Federation "On Ensuring the Implementation of International Pledges in the Field of Chemical, Bacteriological (Biological) and Toxin Weapons," declaring the program to be terminated. In July of the same year, the Russian Supreme Soviet passed Resolution No. 3244-1, which reemphasized the statement. However, as during the Soviet era, decrees were often disregarded. In early 1992, the Russian government also submitted its first confidence-building measure admitting a past offensive BW program, as well as providing some of the particulars of that program. Previous iterations of this document by the USSR had denied the existence of an offensive BW program. The 1992 Russian confidence-building measure was totally deficient, and it has never been amended to this day. Yeltsin also issued a decree that prohibited Russian scientists and officials to speak about their secret past. During the first half of 1992, the BW program was actually continuing.

In September 1992, the U.S. and the U.K. obtained Russian government signature to the Trialateral Statement. Russia admitted in this document that the program had continued through the early months of 1992, and to the existence of "experimental lines of production." Russia promised to allow additional U.S. and U.K. on-site visits, eventually to include the major Ministry of Defense BW facilities. Nevertheless, 3 years of difficult and acrimonious negotiations ground to a halt by the end of 1996 due to Russian government intransigence. The Ministry of Defense was once again in charge of Russian BW policy. U.S. and U.K. access to the Ministry of Defense BW facilities was never obtained.

With the help of international grant assistance programs, the Stepnogorsk and Aralsk-7 sites were destroyed (see Chapter 12, Interview by Smith & Lentzos; Point of View by Finley & Gaudioso). The majority of (known) Biopreparat facilities were transformed into more open research facilities, some of which began international collaborations on peaceful microbial research, including international scientist exchanges. As indicated previously, the Ministry of Defense institutes in Kirov, Ekaterinburg and Sergiyev Posad remain closed to outsiders and are still operating today under the same veil of secrecy as they were during the Soviet offensive biological weapons program. It is therefore not possible to ascertain at this time whether the biological weapons program has been terminated in its entirety. It must be assumed that the body of knowledge (protocols, manufacturing plans, growth recipes, etc.) that accumulated during the program has not been destroyed, and remains in the hands of the Ministry of Defense. Russia's official position — despite the existence of its 1992 confidence-building submission — reverted to claims that no offensive BW program ever existed in the Soviet Union, that the Sverdlovsk anthrax outbreak was a natural event, and that no weapons or weaponized agents had been tested on Vozrozhdeniye Island. Fortunately, virtually no proliferation — the transfer of knowledge or technology from the Soviet BW program — before 1992 or after, took place.

In a somewhat bizarre development in February and March 2012, then-Prime Minister Putin and Russian Minister of Defense, Anatoly Serdyukov, publically referred to 28 tasks that Putin established for the Ministry of Defense "to prepare for threats of the future." Putin wrote that Russia needed to be prepared for "quick and effective responses to new challenges." One of the 28 tasks that Putin specified was "the development of weapons based on new physical principles: radiation, geophysical, wave, genetic, psychophysical, etc."[2] "Genetic" weapons would obviously be forbidden by the BWC, and the remainder are an arms-control nightmare that would explicitly contravene another multilateral arms-control treaty championed by the Brezhnev administration ("The Convention on the Prohibition of Military or Any Other Hostile Use of Environmental Modification Technologies", signed on May 18, 1977, and entered into force on October 5, 1978).

Acknowledgments

J.H.K. is grateful for the technical writing services offered by Laura Bollinger (IRF-Frederick). The content of this publication does not necessarily reflect the views or policies of the U.S. Department of Health and Human Services, or of the institutions and companies with which the authors are affiliated. The work of J.H.K. was funded in part through Battelle Memorial Institute's prime contract with the U.S. National Institute of Allergy and Infectious Diseases (NIAID) under Contract No. HHSN272200700016I. A subcontractor to Battelle Memorial Institute who performed this work is J.H.K., an employee of Tunnell Government Services, Inc.

References

Leitenberg M (1991) 'A return to Sverdlovsk: Allegations of Soviet Activities Related to Biological Weapons', *Arms Control Contemporary Security Policy* Vol. 12: 161–190.

Leitenberg M (1992) 'Anthrax in Sverdlovsk: New Pieces to the Puzzle', *Arms Control Today* Vol. 223: 10–13.

Leitenberg M, Zilinskas RA and Kuhn JH (2012) *The Soviet Biological Weapons Program: A History.* Cambridge, MA: Harvard University Press.

Meselson M, Guillemin J, Hugh-Jones M, Langmuir A, Popova I, Shelokov A and Yampolskaya O (1994) 'The Sverdlovsk Anthrax Outbreak of 1979', *Science* Vol. 266: 1202–1208.

Rosebury T (1949) *Peace or Pestilence. Biological Warfare and How to Avoid It.* New York: Whittlesey House, McGraw-Hill Book Company.

Rosebury T and Kabat EA (1947) 'Bacterial warfare: A Critical Analysis of the Available Agents, their Possible Military Applications, and the Means for Protection Against Them', *Journal of Immunology* Vol. 56: 7–96.

Notes

[1] Alibek K and Handelman S (1999) Biohazard. *The Chilling True Story of the Largest Covert Biological Weapons Program in the World. Told from the Inside by the Man Who Ran It.* New York: Random House; Birstein V (2001) *The Perversion of Knowledge: The True Story of Soviet Science.* Boulder: Westview Press; Bozheyeva G, Kunakbayev Y and Yeleukenov D (1999) *Former Soviet Biological Weapons Facilities in Kazakhstan: Past, Present, and Future.* Monterey, California: Monterey Institute of International Studies' Center for Nonproliferation Studies. Chemical and

Biological Weapons Nonproliferation Project Occasional Paper No. 1; Buder E (2000) 'Stand der Konversion ehemaliger Sowjetischer BTW-Einrichtungen,' in E Buder (Ed.) *Möglichkeiten und Grenzen der Konversion von B-Waffen-Einrichtungen.* Beiträge zur Konversionsforschung, Vol. 7. Münster, Germany: LIT-Verlag, pp. 211–243; Guillemin J (1999) *Anthrax: The Investigaton of a Deadly Outbreak.* Berkeley: University of California Press; Hart J (2006) 'The Soviet Biological Weapons Program,' in M Wheelis, L Rózsa and M Dando (Eds.) *Deadly Cultures. Biological Weapons Since 1945.* Cambridge, Massachusetts: Harvard University Press, pp. 132–156; Ouagrham SB and Vogel KM (2003) *Conversion at Stepnogorsk: What the Future Holds for Former Bioweapons Facilities.* Cornell University Peace Studies Program, Occasional Paper Nr. 28; Rimmington A (1996) 'From Military to Industrial Complex? The Conversion of Biological Weapons' Facilities in the Russian Federation,' *Contemporary Security Policy* Vol. 17: 80–112; Rimmington A (1998) 'Conversion of BW facilities in Kazakstan,' in E Geissler, L Gazsó and E Buder (Eds.) Conversion of BW Facilities in Kazakstan. NATO Science Series. London: Kluwer Academic Publishers, pp. 167–186; Rimmington A (1999) 'Fragmentation and Proliferation? The Fate of the Soviet Union's Offensive Biological Weapons Programme,' Contemporary Security Policy Vol. 20: 86–110; Rimmington A (2000) 'Invisible Weapons of Mass Destruction: The Soviet Union's BW programme and Its Implications for Contemporary Arms Control,' *Journal of Slavic Military Studies* Vol. 13: 1–46; Rimmington A (2000) 'The Soviet Union's Offensive Program — The Implications for Contemporary Arms Control,' in S Wright (Ed.) *Biological Warfare and Disarmament — New Problems/New Perspectives.* Lanham: Rowman and Littlefield, pp. 103–148; Rimmington A (2003) 'From Offence to Defence? Russia's Reform of its Biological Weapons Complex and the Implications for Western Security,' *Journal of Slavic Military Studies* Vol. 16:1–43; Smithson AE (1999) *Toxic Archipelago: Preventing Proliferation from the Former Soviet Chemical and Biological Weapons Complexes.* Washington: The Henry L. Stimson Center, Report No. 32; Tucker JB and Zilinskas RA (2002) *The 1971 Smallpox Epidemic in Aralsk, Kazakhstan, and the Soviet Biological Warfare Program.* Chemical and Biological Weapons Nonproliferation Project Occasional Paper No. 9. Monterey: Monterey Institute of International Studies, Center for Nonproliferation Studies, http://cns.miis.edu/opapers/op9/op9.pdf (accessed February 25, 2016); Ben Ouagrham-Gormley S, Melikishvili A and Zilinskas RA (2006) 'The Soviet Anti-Plague System: An Introduction,' *Critical Reviews in Microbiology* Vol. 32:15–17;

Zilinskas RA (2006) 'The Anti-Plague System and the Soviet Biological Warfare Program,' *Critical Reviews in Microbiology* Vol. 32:47–64; Ben Ouagrham-Gormley S. (2006) 'Growth of the Anti-Plague System During the Soviet period,' *Critical Reviews in Microbiology* Vol. 32:33–46; Hoffman D (2010) *The Dead Hand: The Untold Story of the Cold War Arms Race and Its Dangerous Legacy.* New York: Anchor; Domaradskij IV and Orent W (2003) *Biowarrior: Inside the Soviet/Russian Biological War Machine.* Amherst: Prometheus Books; Lukina RN, Lukin YP and Bulavko VK (2004) *The 50 Years of the Ministry of Defense's Virology Center Deserve Recognition.* Veterans Council of the Virology Center of the Russian Federation Ministry of Defense's Scientific Research Institute for Microbiology and the publishing house Ves Sergiyev Posad, Sergiyev Posad, Russia; Petra L, Roffey R and Westerdahl KS (2000) *Disarmament or Retention: Is the Soviet Biological Weapons Programme Continuing in Russia?* FOI Report FOA-R--99-01366-865, Umeå, Sweden; Lindblad A, Norlander L, Normark M, Rydqvist J, Unge W, Waldenström L and Westerdahl KS (2005) *Russian Biological and Chemical Weapons Capabilities: Future Scenarios and Alternatives of Actions.* Report 1. FOI Report FOI-R-1561-SE, Umeå, Sweden; Roffey R, Unge W, Clevström J and Westerdahl KS (2003) *Support to Threat Reduction of the Russian Biological Weapons Legacy — Conversion, Biodefence and the Role of Biopeparat.* FOI Report FOA-R-0841-SE, Umeå, Sweden; Roffey R and Westerdahl KS (2001) *Conversion of Former Biological Wepaons Facilities in Kazakhstan.* A Visit to Stepnogorsk, July 2000. FOI Report FOI-R-0082-SE, Umeå, Sweden; Häggström B, Forsberg A and Norlander L (2004) Conversion of a Former Biological Weapons Establishment. FOI Report FOI-R-1316-SE, Umeå, Sweden; Westerdahl K and Norlander L (2006) *The Role of New Russian Anti-Bioterrorism Centres.* FOI Report FOI-R-1971-SE, Umeå, Sweden.

2 Putin, V. (2012) 'Being strong: National security guarantees for Russia' *Rossiyskaya Gazeta et al.* February 20, 2012, https://www.rt.com/politics/official-word/strong-putin-military-russia-711/ (accessed February 25, 2016).

Point of View

Life Inside the Soviet Bioweapons Program

Sonia Ben Ouagrham-Gormley

The Soviet Bioweapons program was one of the most secretive the world has ever known. Although much information was revealed about the program's activities after the break-up of the Soviet Union, to this day very little is known about the men and women who contributed to the program. What motivated their engagement in the use of biology for harm rather than healing? What was life like inside this highly secretive program? How did they feel about their work? And how did they grapple with the ethical dilemmas raised by their research? A 4-year oral history project of the former Soviet and American bioweapons programs[1] has elicited important answers to these and other questions about the two largest bioweapons programs in the world.

This chapter provides snapshots of life within the Soviet bioweapons program viewed through the eyes of two scientists. The first is Colonel Guennady Lepioshkin, a former military scientist who worked at the Institute for Microbiology in Obolensk, a facility managed by the Ministry of Defense, and later at the anthrax production plant in Stepnogorsk, a facility managed by the ostensibly civilian organization called Biopreparat. The second is Sergei Popov, a civilian scientist who worked at two facilities managed by Biopreparat, the

State Research Center of Virology and Biotechnology ("Vektor") and the State Research Center for Applied Microbiology at Obolensk. Their testimonies show how varied and contrasted individual experiences can be in spite of the fact that they evolved in a common environment.

It is important to note upfront that working within the Soviet bioweapons program was for most of its personnel not a choice, but an obligation. In the Soviet system, people were allocated a job upon completion of their education, and had no say about where and what their job would entail. Scientists who showed promising talents that could be used in the bioweapons program were sent to bioweapons facilities, sometimes at the urging of their doctoral advisors who were already participating in the program, or while serving in the military. Typically, people were given very little information about what type of work they were about to undertake, and they did not have the option of rejecting the positions they were offered. Sergei Popov recalls that he became aware of his future bioweapons work when he was asked to sign non-disclosure papers. As Popov noted in an interview:

> No one explained what exactly my role would be or what was going to be developed... [the document indicated that] there were going to be new types of biological weapons developed... No one spoke to me about that. I took a look at that document, realized that I had really gotten myself into a mess, and things were left at that... There was no turning back. There was no chance to say, 'Pardon me, excuse me, I really don't feel like doing this.'[2]

Those who expressed their displeasure with their position faced stiff penalties, including the inability to get another job, or were a job conceivable it would be in a remote region of the Soviet Union with the possibly of no connection to one's training. Displeased individuals were also placed on the so-called "list no. 1" — the KGB's surveillance list, which precluded future career advancement.[3] Thus, unlike American scientists who could leave the program if they had moral qualms about their work and its objectives, Soviet scientists, generally, did not have that option.

Employment in the bioweapons field came with attractive benefits. Salaries were routinely double the salaries prevailing in non-weapons facilities. Salary increases were also higher than in other institutions. Bioweapons personnel had easier access to scarce goods, such as private apartments, while the norm in the Soviet Union was to share communal apartments. Bioweaponeers also had better access to food products, as well as the option to buy a car, which remained virtually unattainable for the general population. Such privileges in a society plagued with shortages surely must have helped suppress some of the misgivings individuals had about using science for harm. Bioweapons facilities also had more modern equipment, and offered the possibility to do cutting-edge research, which was appealing to many scientists. As Popov puts it:

> Many of us believed that if we were involved in classified work, then it must be very important for the country, and this helped us somehow to cope with the situation ... basically, we were proud, in a way, that we had been entrusted with this knowledge ... such interesting and very important work.[4]

It is remarkable that most scientists interviewed for the oral history project indicated that despite their personal misgivings about bioweapons, they found scientific work within the bioweapons program interesting and stimulating. The bioweapons program offered the ability to investigate new scientific problems, without concerns for cost or feasibility, which often limited exploration in the civilian sector. The bioweapons program always had ample money available, and the military were especially prone to sponsor the exploration of new weapon ideas. Many therefore felt that they were exploring new frontiers in science, which kept them interested in their work.

Aside from these common features, individuals experienced life within the bioweapons program in very different ways. Guennady Lepioshkin is prone to wax nostalgic about life within the program. Born within a military family, he graduated from the Nizhnii

Novgorod military medical school in 1969. After graduation, he was sent to the Institute of Microbiology in Kirov. When asked whether he would have liked to work in another field, he responds:

Since I was in the military, I did the work that was given me, the job where I was placed. And I found satisfaction in that work, even though it was hazardous. But it was very interesting… I never wanted to do anything else… [I] lived a life that pleased me.[5]

His recollections of life within the BW program emphasize the camaraderie and friendships born out of working and living in isolated areas of the Soviet Union, with scientists and technicians who were generally as young as he was. Of his time at Kirov as a young physician and microbiologist, he recollects the institute's choir and athletic teams that he had joined. At the anthrax plant in Stepnogorsk, which he joined in 1984 to help scale up production of the Soviet anthrax weapon, Lepioshkin recollects the fishing, hiking and hunting trips he organized with his colleagues in the steps of Kazakhstan. Promoting social life was a conscious policy of the plant's management to create a good working atmosphere. When Lepioshkin became deputy director in 1984 and later director between 1987 and 2001, he continued to promote the "work hard, play hard" mindset. As he notes,

We focused a great deal of attention on matters of recreation for our staff. We organized group outings to the country, mushroom picking and fishing expeditions and trips to the beach. We had a system in place where people both worked and played and it all worked out to be a very good combination. It was quite a diverse workforce. The people were generally young: there were both men and women. They had various interests, but overall, all of that fostered a good atmosphere... a good, friendly atmosphere for all the work to be done.[6]

Interviews with other former employees of the Stepnogorsk facility paint a similar picture of life at Stepnogorsk. One indicated that "life was full of interesting things…life was free and easy, then."[7] In spite of the close relationships created by this socialization, the staff never talked about bioweapons, or their potential use, nor did they discuss the risks associated with working with pathogenic agents. They usually blame this lack of concern to the fact that they were young and carefree. In their minds, they "were only doing science."[8] Lepioshkin, however, rationalizes the ethical underpinnings for the program more bluntly:

> It was politics: every country was developing [bio]weapons… bio-weapons would never have been used on a large scale… they were for intimidation purposes. A way of saying, 'OK guys, stop your bully-ing, we can hit back.'

The compartmentalization and rationalization of the Soviet program was not a self-delusion technique. The KGB's constant surveillance coupled with the persistent emphasis on non-dis-closure documents represented a powerful disincentive — still present today — to talk about their work among themselves and to others, including their families. To this day, Lepioshkin has not discussed his former work with his adult children, who still think he was simply a military physician.

Sergei Popov joined the Soviet Bioweapons program a few years after Lepioshkin. After receiving a PhD in biochemistry from the university of Novosibirsk in 1976, he worked at Vektor for 10 years. In 1986, he was transferred to the Obolensk facility, where he worked until 1992. Like Lepioshkin, Popov also believed that bioweapons would have never been used, either by the United States or the Soviet Union. Similarly, he was not worried about the risks of his profession:

> We weren't afraid that infection would spread, we weren't afraid that someone would be infected, that someone nearby would catch something… Although, of course, technically it was possible, that is, we always had to fear that infection might spread and that then an epidemic might rage out of control. But for some reason we felt very tranquil and protected. Why, I couldn't say. I couldn't say.[9]

Unlike Lepioshkin and his Stepnogorsk colleagues, how-ever, Popov found the scrutiny of the KGB and the intrusive role of political organizations in private and professional lives increasingly oppressive. Background checks before enrollment in the program went several generations back. Once in the program, personnel were carefully watched, their phones were tapped, and they had to speak in codes with their colleagues. They were banned from using the terms "virus" or "bacteria" especially over the phone. They had to use the code name developed for each agent, such as N1 for smallpox, and N2 for plague. Employees of the bioweapons program could not travel abroad, and were occasionally restricted from taking vacations. As department director, Popov had regular meetings with the head of the KGB in the facility, focused on discussing his staff and reporting any suspicious activity. Popov notes, however, that most of the time, people did not mind such scrutiny, because it was viewed as a normal part of Soviet society.[10]

KGB and Communist Party interventions in private lives, however, sometimes reached absurd levels. Popov for example, recalls that the deputy director of an important institute was once fired because he read books about yoga and stood on his head, two activities deemed highly suspicious. In another instance, the Communist Party prevented a scientist from marrying his secretary because she did not have the same security clearance. Popov himself experienced the absurd intrusion of the KGB in his own life. In the early 1980s, he was sent to the Laboratory for Molecular Biology in Cambridge, U.K., ostensibly as a scientist from the Russian Academy of Sciences to learn a new technique of automated DNA synthesis that the British had developed. Beforehand, however, KGB officials required that he stop smoking because, he was told, England had very bad weather. For someone living and working in frigid Siberia, the request seemed palpably absurd, but he complied nonetheless. While at Cambridge, Popov was shocked by the freedom he enjoyed, including being given a key to the laboratory and allowed to do whatever he wanted. However, as a result of his trip to England, Popov was not allowed to join the Communist Party until 1991, which meant that he had little hope of being promoted beyond the level of department head.

Tight security and secrecy at bioweapons facilities also had a pernicious effect on science. Popov himself found it very depressing that he could not publish his research. As he reports:

> The research itself was definitely interesting, because it provided mental nourishment and fuelled new scientific ideas… And then, well, it came to a standstill, it was as if there wasn't enough air, because you would work and work, you would do something and no one knew about it. And things started to seem almost like a dead end. You know, kind of, what is the point, ultimately?[11]

Other scientists exploited the secrecy surrounding their work to hide their inactivity or to report fake results, true to a Soviet saying that goes "The government pretends that they pay us, and we pretend to work." Some fabricated results or just copied research from foreign journals such as *Nature*, and presented it as their own. Access to foreign journals was limited, so the possibilities of discovery of the faked results were reduced. Overall, Popov indicates, the Soviet bioweapons program was designed to consume a lot of resources while producing very few results.[12]

The end of the Soviet bioweapons program in the early 1990s was a challenging time for both Popov and Lepioshkin, albeit for different reasons. For Popov, the abrupt drop in funding was another proof that Soviet society placed little value in its people. Suddenly, scientists were told,

> No one needs you, … you've outlived your usefulness, so to speak. You did your research back then… And no one can use it, and no one will ever hear of it, and don't speak to a soul about it. … And now, if you want to do science, please, be our guest, but, by the way, we have zero money for science.[13]

And as odd as it might seem, he also notes the cruelty of the system *vis-à-vis* laboratory animals:

> President Yeltsin decreed an end to the biological program [and] they stopped feeding all the animals ... Well, that was just horrible, it was

barbarous, really. We tried, you know, to collect a little bit of grass and things for the guinea pigs … the system was cruel in that regard.[14]

Left with little to live on and feed his family, Popov decided to defect to the U.K. in 1992 under the guise of a scientific visit to the British institute that hosted him in the early 1980s. His wife and children, barred by the KGB from joining him, eventually managed to bribe a government official to secure passports, and joined him in the United States.

For Lepioshkin, the challenge was to accept that Russia had abandoned the Stepnogorsk facility, which came under the authority of the newly independent republic of Kazakhstan. When Kazakhstan agreed to dismantle the facility with funding from the U.S. Department of Defense under the Cooperative Threat Reduction program (CTR) (see Chapter 12, Point of View by Finley & Gaudioso), Lepioshkin observes,

It was hard to accept for both me and the employees. After all, they had worked out all the bugs, they had whipped everything into shape … they had gotten all of it up and running. And now an American comes and says: 'All of this has to be destroyed, all of this has to be done.'[15]

Soon, however, Lepioshkin became a willing partner in the CTR program and oversaw the dismantlement of his facility until no sensitive building remained standing. In 2003, he moved back to Russia where he now heads the Scientific Research Institute for Environmental Monitoring at Kirov. To this day however, he still describes Building 221, the main anthrax production building at Stepnogorsk, as a "beautiful" building.

Editor's note: Audio and video interviews gathered under the oral history project, along with their transcripts in Russian and English, will be posted on a dedicated website — *The Anthrax Diaries: An Anthropology of Biological Warfare* — currently under construction. Partial data from the project can be found in two recent books: Sonia Ben Ouagrham-Gormley, *Barriers to Bioweapons: The Challenges of Expertise and Organization for Weapons Development* (Cornell University

Press 2014); and Kathleen Vogel, *Phantom Menace or Looming Danger? A New Framework for Assessing Bioweapons Threats* (Johns Hopkins University Press 2013).

Notes

1 "Living Legacy: An Oral History of U.S. and Soviet Bioweaponeers and Its Implications for Understanding Past, Present, and Future Biosecurity Threats", 2008–2012, with funding from the Carnegie Corporation of New York.

2 Interview with Sergei Popov, Manassas, Virginia, August 19, 2011.

3 Interview with Sergei Popov, Manassas, Virginia, August 19, 2011.

4 Interview with Sergei Popov, Manassas, Virginia, August 19, 2011.

5 Interview with Guennady Lepioshkin, Washington DC, October 7, 2011.

6 Interview with Guennady Lepioshkin, Almaty, Kazakhstan, November 7, 2011.

7 Interview with former Stepnogorsk female scientist, Almaty, Kazakhstan, November 2011.

8 Interview with several former Stepnogorsk scientists, Almaty Kazakhstan, November 2011.

9 Interview with Sergei Popov, Manassas, Virginia, August 19, 2011.

10 Sergei Popov, "Discussion With Bioweapons Scientists," George Mason University, Fairfax, Virginia, March 29, 2010.

11 Interview with Sergei Popov, Manassas, Virginia, August 19, 2011.

12 Sergei Popov, "Discussion With Bioweapons Scientists," George Mason University, Fairfax, Virginia, March 29, 2010.

13 Interview with Sergei Popov, Manassas, Virginia, August 19, 2011.

14 Interview with Sergei Popov, Manassas, Virginia, August 19, 2011.

15 Lepioshkin Washington Interview (19).

Chapter 5

The Iraqi Biological Warfare Program

Tim Trevan

Introduction

Iraq's invasion of Kuwait in 1990, the first Gulf War "Desert Storm" in 1991, and their aftermath turned the term "weapon of mass destruction" (WMD) from technical jargon used only in the global arms control and strategic military communities into a household phrase, even making it into popular music.[1]

Prior to the invasion of Kuwait, Western intelligence agencies knew Iraq had a functioning chemical weapons capability (which it had used against both Iran and its own Kurds) and a large and active nuclear program (part of which Israel bombed in 1981 with the raid on the Osirak nuclear reactor). They also presumed Iraq had an active biological weapons program, although relatively little was known about it. Iraq was also known to have a large number of Scud ballistic missiles and to be working on converting them into strategic delivery systems for their WMD.

These presumptions were baked into the United Nations (UN) ceasefire resolution, which called for the International Atomic Energy Agency (IAEA) and a Special Commission to oversee the dismantling of Iraq's nuclear, chemical and biological weapons programs and capabilities, and its long-range ballistic missiles.[2] That they were taken seriously by the U.S. and other UN coalition forces is reflected in

President Bush's letter to Saddam Hussein, delivered by Secretary of State James Baker to Foreign Minister Tariq Aziz on January 9, 1991, and which stated that:

> The United States will not tolerate the use of chemical or biological weapons or the destruction of Kuwait's oil fields and installations. … you will be held directly responsible for terrorist actions against any member of the coalition. The American people would demand the strongest possible response. You and your country will pay a terrible price if you order unconscionable acts of this sort.
>
> (Woods *et al.* 2011: 221)

Later, in private conversations with the Chairman of the UN Special Commission (UNSCOM), Tariq Aziz added some color, stating that Baker had told him that, if Iraq used WMD against the coalition, the U.S. would "respond massively and overwhelmingly in a manner from which it would take Iraq centuries to recover" (Trevan 1998: 45). This was interpreted by the Iraqi leadership to mean a retaliatory nuclear strike. Later versions of the story became more colorful still, with the threat being to "bomb Iraq back into the Middle Ages" or to "turn Baghdad into glass."

Iraq explicitly denied having an offensive bioweapons program in its 1991 declarations of WMD holdings required under the ceasefire following Desert Storm. Subsequent UN weapons inspections proved the intelligence agencies' presumption right. This chapter details the origins, evolution and, ultimately, demise of the Iraqi biological warfare (BW) program.

Saddam's conception of "special weapons"

The biological weapons program was the poor cousin of Iraq's WMD programs. It was the last to start, the least well-funded, the least well-staffed, the worst managed and the most covert.[3] In many ways, the biological weapons program was an amateurish home-grown effort.

There are few source materials on how Saddam Hussein and the Iraqi regime viewed biological weapons specifically. There are, however, a number of direct quotes indicating that Saddam appreciated that the psychological impact of merely possessing weapons of mass destruction — "special weapons" — could far outweigh the actual military or even strategic value of using them. For example, on July 7, 1984, Saddam Hussein stated:

> ... even the special weapon that the brothers have, if they use it, it will lose its value ... sometimes what you get out of a weapons is when you keep saying "I will bomb you." It is actually better than bombing him. It is possible that when you bomb him the material effect will be 40 percent, but if you stick it up to his face the material and the psychological effect will be 60 percent, so why hit him? Keep getting 60 percent![4]

Biological weapons were viewed as a component of a comprehensive WMD capability: the *perception* that Iraq possessed WMDs was more important than actual possession, and the threat of use was more effective than actual use. Thus, their value was threefold to achieve: deterrence of others from attacking Iraq; freedom to pursue Iraq's conventional military adventures by precluding Great Power intervention through deterrence; and compellence of smaller neighbors to its regional hegemonic ambitions, preferably before resort to force and without resort to use of WMD.

Origins and expansion of the BW program

Iraq's biological weapons ambitions pre-dated Saddam's ascension to power, dating to the 1960s. The rise of Arab nationalism at that time brought with it a desire within the new military leaderships to modernize their military capabilities. Iraq applied for and was granted U.S. military training in offensive and defensive CBW warfare, sending 19 officers to Fort McClellan during the period 1957–1967. This training ceased in 1967 with the severance of diplomatic relations between the two countries as a consequence of the Arab–Israeli war.[5] One of the officers receiving this training, Nizar Al Attar, ultimately became the head of Iraq's chemical weapons program; he also had a hand in introducing biological weapons to Iraq.[6]

However, while these events led to the establishment of a small chemical weapons program in Iraq in 1968, it was not until 1974 that the Iraqi Intelligence Services launched an exploratory, clandestine biological weapons research program under cover of the Al Hasan Ibn-al-Haytham Research Institute.[7] The aim of this program included mastering the technologies required to develop biological weapons. A purpose-built closed institute, the Ibn Sina Centre, was created at Salman Pak. Nine scientists conducted research into the production, pathogenicity, dissemination and storage of potential BW agents such as anthrax, Botulinum toxin, cholera, polio and influenza. In addition, the Institute paid for overseas doctoral study in disciplines relevant to the biological weapons program.[8]

The initial biological weapons program was shut down in 1979 without significant results and under a cloud of fraud allegations. While "dual-use" biological research continued, it was not until 1983 that a new, militarily-significant biological weapons program was created at the Al Muthanna State Establishment, home of Iraq's much more advanced chemical weapons program. The initiative for the renewed program reportedly came from the Director-General of the Al Muthanna, Lt-Gen Nizar al Attar, with the support of the Minister of Defence (MOD), General Adnan Khairallah, Saddam Hussein's brother-in-law.[9] Work started in 1984 under the technical direction of Dr Rihab Rashida Taha, who was to become intimately associated with Iraq's biological weapons program and attempts to conceal it from UN weapons inspectors. Lt-Gen Nizar gave Rihab explicit instructions that the program should result in a usable weapon, not in mere research papers.

The timing of the Iraqi biological weapons program's rebirth was significant. Iraq invaded Iran in 1980, making initial gains, but by 1982 Iran had regained virtually all of the territory and remained on the offensive until the end of the war in 1988. By the end of 1982, Iran was using "human wave" tactics to devastating effect against Iraqi forces, and Iraqi commanders were desperate for a solution. It came in the form of chemical weapons, deployed to cause mass casualties against unprotected Iranian troop concentrations. While unsuccessful at first, the tactics soon caused mass chemical casualties,[10] and the Iraqi leadership became convinced of the value of weapons of mass destruction to their war effort. Biological weapons were seen as another string to this bow; and by some as a more toxic version of chemical weapons, complementing chemical weapons with the potential to achieve great surprise. BW was also seen by the leadership as a strategic counterbalance to Israel's presumed nuclear capabilities.

Iraq already had available a strategic vision and an operational plan for BW. At the outbreak of the war with Iran in 1980, one of Iraq's preeminent microbiologists, Professor Nassir al Hindawi, had submitted a proposal for biological weapons research to the President's Office. The proposal suggested focusing on Botulinum toxin as a tactical weapon and anthrax as a strategic and tactical weapon. This proposal had been forwarded to Lt-Gen Nizar at Al Muthanna and formed the core of the BW program,[11] although other avenues were also explored and added at later stages.

What we now think of as Iraq's biological weapons program essentially took place from 1983 to 1991, effectively ending with Operation Desert Storm and the requirement for Iraq to dismantle all its WMD and long-range missile programs under the ceasefire resolution. Efforts to hide, retain and even develop the intellectual and physical capacity to produce biological weapons continued until the overthrow of Saddam's regime with Operation Iraqi Freedom in 2003, but no production of new biological weapons occurred after January 1991.

In 1983, most of the remnants of the earlier BW program were brought back together at Al Muthanna under the MOD and Lt-Gen Nizar's command, while a parallel smaller anti-crop program was conducted by the intelligence services at their Salman Pak facility. A formal research program was pursued and, within 3 years, expanded into a 5-year plan for the development and production of deployable weapons. The report of the Iraq Action Group of inspectors sent to Iraq after Operation Iraqi Freedom in 2003 to find any remaining WMD and investigate the past programs stated that Rihab and her group implemented this plan "with urgency, authority, and great secrecy demonstrating considerable planning."[12] The team started with extensive literature surveys and conducted toxicological investigations. According to the report, the program progressed as follows.

In 1985, the research phase began. Iraq initiated research into candidate BW agents. This was followed in 1986 with the ordering of multiple isolates of pathogens from foreign culture collections. In 1987, the program was relocated to Salman Pak, and control was transferred to the Military Industrialization Commission from the MOD (given the need to focus on weaponization issues). More scientists were recruited and the range of pathogens studied was broadened.

In 1988, the program expanded beyond basic research with the commissioning of the Al Hakam site for pilot-scale and later large-scale production of anthrax, Botulinum toxin and (starting in August 1990) *Clostridium perfringens* (the causal agent of gangrene). Al Hakam would also be the focal point for weapons development and testing. The facilities of the Foot-and-Mouth Disease Vaccine plant at al Dawrah were later used to supplement production of Botulinum toxin, and possibly anthrax, although this latter was denied by Iraq. In addition, 1988 also saw the start of parallel research into fungal toxins. 1989 saw a setback, with the failure to produce domestically or import spray dryers to dry the fermentation slurry into particulate matter optimal for weaponization.

On April 2, 1990, Saddam Hussein gave a speech identifying Israel as a threat to Iraq (Woods *et al.* 2011: 238). In response, the Minister for Military Industrialization, Hussein Kamal Hassan (Saddam's son-in-law), ordered the BW program to expedite weaponization efforts. This led to frantic efforts to increase agent production and to adapt existing weapons to the purpose of delivering and dispersing biological agent. During this period, laboratory and environmental static and dynamic field tests were conducted on anthrax simulants, Botulinum toxin, *Clostridium perfringens*, ricin, aflatoxin and wheat cover smut. July 1990 saw the addition of a viral agent program at al Dawrah, encompassing hemorrhagic conjunctivitis, human rotavirus and camelpox. This program, given its short period of operation, achieved little by the time Desert Storm effectively shut down Iraq's WMD programs.

Weaponization efforts were essentially limited to the period August 1990–January 1991. Hussein Kamal Hassan had final say on the weapons platforms and BW agents used. Given that the R-400 bomb and the Al Hussein ballistic missile warheads were already in use for chemical weapons, he mandated — without any discussion on optimal delivery systems for biological agents — that these systems also be used for the biological weapons. However, Al Muthanna State Establishment had already (successfully in their view) adapted aircraft auxiliary fuel tanks for spray delivery of chemical weapons, and started work in November 1990 on further adapting this mechanism for delivery of BW. Finally, the Iraqi Air Force also experimented with using a remotely controlled MiG-21 aircraft as the platform for the fuel tank dispersal method.

A program on hold: The UNSCOM years, 1991–1996

Following defeat and the imposition of the ceasefire terms in UN Security Council Resolution 687 of April 3, 1991, Iraq sought to save as much as possible of its biological weapons program infrastructure with a view to riding out sanctions and the weapons inspection regime, and resuscitating the program after they were lifted. The Iraqi leadership did not expect sanctions or inspections to be rigorous, nor to last longer than 3 years.

The waiting strategy entailed destroying its existing bulk agent and weapons stockpiles and hiding evidence of the program. Implementation started immediately. In his letter to the UN Secretary General of April 18, 1991, Tariz Aziz denied that Iraq had a BW program. Another component of the plan was the rapid conversion of the Al Hakam biological weapons facility (which had escaped Allied bombing as it was unknown to intelligence agencies) into a biopesticide production plant before UN inspectors arrived for their first visit. This enabled Iraq not only to keep its intellectual BW capital intact, but also to improve its ability to produce biological agents on an industrial scale, manufacture its own complex growth media using local waste products from food and agricultural businesses, and to make progress in creating dry formulations of agent. Simultaneously, Iraq sought to preserve equipment and facilities at other sites which had not suffered damage in the war, transferring assets to Al Hakam for use there in its new cover function of biopesticide production.

To keep the UN inspectors from divining the prior use of these facilities, Iraq undertook comprehensive countermeasures and disinformation, cleaning plants to remove all traces of BW activity, removing documents, destroying agents, developing cover stories for ongoing and past activities at each site, and threatening all involved in the BW program, on pain of death, against disclosure to the UN inspectors. As part of this operation, facilities at Salman Pak, Al Hakam, Al Manal and Al Safa'ah were sanitized.[13]

End game: The end of UNSCOM and the UNMOVIC years, 1996–2003

When the accumulation of evidence by UNSCOM finally forced Iraq in 1995 to admit to its past BW program, Iraq had no option but to admit Al Hakam's central role. This lead to UNSCOM's dramatic destruction of Al Hakam in June 1996, and shattered Iraq's attempt to keep, as much as possible, its BW assets intact. With its physical infrastructure destroyed, many of the scientists dispersed, although some continued small-scale BW-related research in various facilities under the aegis of the Iraqi intelligence services — the true nature and purpose of which remains unclear. Iraq's BW program finally ended with Operation Iraqi Freedom in March 2003 and the overthrow of Saddam's regime.

While Saddam Hussein personally sanctioned the launch of the BW program, he was not closely involved in the day-to-day development of it. He was in awe of science and respected scientists, keeping three scientific advisers in his inner circle.[14] This, coupled with his conception of the value of being perceived to possess WMD, probably explains his support for the biological weapons program. Where he *was* directly involved was in decisions on how biological agents should be weaponized, and he reserved decisions on when and how they should be used for himself (Woods *et al.* 2011: 246–250). Senior Iraqi insiders briefed on their BW capabilities were under no illusion as to the ineffectiveness of their biological weapons designs, but understood that being perceived as having the ability to deliver BW to battlefield and strategic targets, and being able to land a BW on enemy territory resulting in the delivery of detectable amounts of biological agents, would be sufficient to achieve the strategic objective, regardless of any actual damage incurred.

Achievements of the Iraqi BW program

Given that Iraq did not cooperate openly with UN weapons inspectors (see Chapter 5, Point of View), a definitive accounting of the "total quantities of bulk agents produced, weaponized and destroyed, and the disposition of all biological seed stocks, etc." has never been achieved.[15]

However, both UN weapons inspections and the Iraq Action Group reported that Iraq established a functioning infrastructure encompassing: the importation of materials and equipment necessary for the program; a dedicated facility for researching BW and agents; outreach to other research capabilities within national universities; bulk agent production facilities; in conjunction with the armed forces and Military Industrialization Commission, design and adaptation of munitions and delivery systems; and, in conjunction with the armed forces, field testing of the agents and the weapons. Table 1 summarizes best estimates for production and weaponization by agent. Research work progressed to different degrees on cholera, mycotoxins, shigella, camelpox, human enterovirus 70, infectious hemorrhagic conjunctivitis, rotavirus and smallpox.

The military asset as of January 1991 when Operation Desert Storm broke out was 180 poorly designed biological weapons of various types deployed in five hide sites, whose utility on the battlefield was suspect, but whose value as a weapon of terror would be achieved in the eyes of the Iraqi leadership if the enemy merely detected biological agents after their delivery.[16]

Limits and failures of the Iraqi BW program

The success of a program can be judged either by its achievements set against intended objectives, or against how its fruits could be used

Table 1: Best estimates for Iraq's production and weaponization of biological agents[17]

Agent	Quantity produced	Weaponization
Anthrax	up to 25,000 liters (8,500 liters declared)	Missile warheads; R-400 aerial bombs; aircraft fuel drop tanks adapted for spraying; the Zubaidy device; a helicopter-mounted sprayer
Botulinum toxin	20,000 liters	Missile warheads; R-400 aerial bombs
Clostridium perfringens	5,000 liters	Not weaponized
Aflatoxin	2,000 liters	Missile warheads; R-400 aerial bombs
Ricin	10 liters	Not weaponized, used in field trials
Wheat cover smut	"not quantifiable"	Not weaponized

regardless of original objective. In assessing BW programs, the water is muddied because there are different views of what "biological weapons" are. Interpretations include: a WMD, causing casualties at least on the scale of chemical weapons and potentially, with live agent, on a scale approaching or surpassing nuclear weapons; a military weapon of mass disruption and territorial denial to be used to undermine an enemy's behind-the-lines logistics and hence greatly diminish its battlefield capability; a terrorist weapon aimed primarily at societal disruption, regardless of the number of actual casualties or numbers of people put at risk; an assassination weapon; or a strategic psychological weapon, as Saddam envisaged, based more on one's enemies' beliefs and fears than on actual military effectiveness.

There is no evidence that Iraq sought to develop a terrorist weapon for use in terrorist attacks in other countries. And while the record shows that Iraq's intelligence service were interested in biological weapons for assassination purposes, little is reported about the objectives of that program and whether they were achieved. However, given that the program did successfully produce large quantities of toxins, it has to be assumed that Iraq achieved some degree of success in that field, having the ability to use these toxins for assassination. What benefit Saddam's regime deemed they would have had over other forms of assassination is unclear. However, for a republic based on fear (Makiya 1989), use of a weapon which induces terror, such as BW, would be a logical choice for political assassinations, particularly if the fact and means of assassination were intended to become public.

Iraq's BW program did achieve at least one of Saddam's strategic goals: other players believed him to be in possession of some BW capability and so adjusted their behaviors and plans. However, these adjustments were not all in the manner intended, with, for instance, the U.S. threatening disproportionate responses should Saddam use unconventional weapons. Certainly, judged against Saddam's own criteria — deterrence, compellence and freedom of action — Iraq's BW program could be deemed to have failed on all three accounts. It did not *deter* the U.S.-led UN coalition campaign against Iraq in 1991, nor even the regime overthrow in 2003. The BW program was not sufficiently advanced to impact the Iran–Iraq War; the CW program was, but while it was effective at a tactical level and potentially contributed to Iran's decision to accept a ceasefire, it did not deter Iran from taking and maintaining the offensive for 6 years (1982–1988), nor did it *compel* Iran to yield to Saddam's ambitions for regional hegemony — it did not even succeed in compelling Kuwait to bend to Iraq's will without invasion by conventional means. The subsequent liberation of Kuwait shows that neither did it *guarantee Iraq relief from regional military action* without major power intervention through its deterrent effect.

Low credibility of Iraq's claims or innuendos that it was in possession of effective biological weapons may have played a role in these strategic-level failures. Certainly, given Iraq's widespread use of chemical weapons in the Iran–Iraq War, Iran had no reason to believe Iraq would not have used biological weapons against it if it were in possession of them, and could assume that because biological weapons weren't deployed Saddam did not possess effective weapons. Indeed, a senior Iraqi military officer is on record as saying Iraq would have used BW against Iran had they been available. And Saddam made clear his intention to use BW if the regime's survival was placed under threat.[18]

Likewise, the U.S. was fully aware, from its own former offensive BW program, how difficult developing a true biological WMD was. Part of the reasoning behind the decision to discontinue the U.S. BW program in 1969 arose from the conclusion that biological weapons are extremely difficult to develop into predictable, reliable and effective weapons.[19] This may have led them to discount the threat to Allied troops from BW even if Iraq were assumed to have had a fully functional and weaponized BW program.

To be effective in the longer-term, Saddam's strategy of using the fear of his WMDs would need to be backed up with deployment of those weapons if his bluff was called. In the case of his BW program, despite bulk production of agent and rudimentary efforts at building delivery systems, he was unable to deploy BW as an effective WMD, or even as a weapon of territorial denial or public terror.

To deploy an effective biological weapon capable of mass destruction, a clandestine and indigenous program has to accomplish the following: Isolate or purchase pathogenic strains of agents suitable for weaponization; build or import biological agent production and weaponization equipment and facilities; successfully grow the pathogen on a large-scale (this, in turn, requires appropriate large fermenter vessels, stirring mechanisms and controls, appropriate complex growth media and additives, knowledge of fermentation, good production practices to ensure non-contamination of the product and compliance with operating procedures); dry the fermentation slurry (failing this, wet slurry can be used but has a much shorter shelf life, as the Iraqi scientists discovered); store the agent in conditions that maintain its viability; mill the agent to a size most effective for aerosol dispersal; design and manufacture a delivery and dispersal system that distributes a viable pathogen or toxin effectively and efficiently on the target; and train pilots and troops in the effective deployment of the weapon while protecting themselves.

Arguably, prior to 1991, Iraq had only successfully acquired suitable pathogenic strains and grown them on a large scale.

It subsequently also made progress on drying the slurry. However, its munitions were known to be ineffective, and the program had not even begun to refine either the agents or the munitions to optimize the weapons. Engineering effective products requires a design cycle which starts with investigation, and then proceeds to an iterative cycle of design, plan, create, evaluate. For its agents and munitions, the Iraqi BW program had barely completed one cycle of this, with evaluation still underway.

Why did Iraq's program fail?

Creating biological weapons is not like following a recipe out of a cookbook. To begin with, the genetic code of DNA is not a dry piece of computer code with a one-to-one translation. Some genes do in fact code for one phenotypic expression. But many features require combinations of genes to work together, and some genes play a role in coding for multiple features (known as pleiotropy). Second, when, how, and how strongly genes are expressed depends not just on the genome, but also on the environment and epigenetic factors. Third, even the simplest of bacteria are complicated, and their interactions with human bodies even more so. There are some 20,000–25,000 human genes coding for some 1,000,000 proteins in the human proteome. Many metabolites, enzymes and proteins are involved in multiple metabolic pathways within the same cell, so tweaking the expression of one gene can have completely unpredictable impacts on an organism. Fourth, pathogenicity is not a characteristic solely of the pathogen; rather it is the interaction of the pathogen with the host organism in a particular environment. Finally, evolution is about fitness of the organism within particular ecosystem, which ultimately is about the organism's energy management. When we genetically engineer a bacterium to do things for our purposes, rather than for its own fitness and survival, we are asking it to take away energy from what it has evolved to do to survive. Thus, there will be strong selective pressure for the bacterium to evolve out the features engineered into it. Engineering a stable organism is an incredibly complex undertaking.

The consequence of this is that, if a BW program has ambitions to go beyond using natural strains of bacteria and viruses as its warfare agents, and to engineer in as many "desirable" characteristics as possible, that program will need a vast array of different scientific and engineering expertise, from basic bacteriology and virology, through pathogenicity, genomics, proteomics, metabolomics, genetic engineering or synthetic biology, industrial fermentation, aerosolization, and into weapons and delivery system design and defences for one's own troops involving pharmacology, vaccine design, protective equipment and so on.

This is not your poor man's nuclear weapon, but a huge, multidisciplinary scientific endeavour. And since much of the required knowledge is either classified or unknown, it requires innovation across all these disciplines, strong management, consistent funding and firm project integration over a prolonged period until success has been achieved. Innovation requires cultivating the best and brightest, cross-fertilization of ideas from a free flow of information and sharing of results (including failures), the freedom to experiment, and access to outside expertise when in-house expertise on a particular issue is found lacking. The requirements of secrecy imposed by clandestine programs, and the autocratic leadership and management style of authoritarian regimes strongly mitigate against achieving the requirements of innovation and full project integration.

In her book *Barriers to Bioweapons: The Challenges of Expertise and Organization for Weapons Development* Sonia Ben Ouagrham-Gormley notes that:

> In spite of their vastly different circumstances, Iraq's, South Africa's, and Aum Shinrikyo's programs shared a number of important characteristics. ...the three programs:

- started with insufficient or non-existent bioweapons expertise and a low absorptive capacity, leading to a steep learning curve.
- selected organizational and managerial models similar to those of the Soviet Union, which optimized covertness at the expense of efficient use and transfer of knowledge. Structurally, they adopted

a vertical model based on hierarchy and rules. Work was organized along fragmented and compartmentalized lines, with little to no coordination or integrative mechanisms.
- From the managerial point of view, ... selected an autocratic system, in which the top echelon of the hierarchy made decisions, frequently with no regard to scientific or technical feasibility.
- employed negative incentive systems. Individuals were not motivated to do good work, by either monetary compensation or positive recognition. Instead, they avoided retribution and punishment by falsifying results. Although this feature was also present in the Soviet case, in these three smaller programs the repercussions for failure were of a different nature: because they often consisted of threats to individuals' lives, the incentive to fake results was greatly enhanced, as was the concurrent waste of resources.
- selected personnel based on political loyalty rather than competence, thus creating a largely incompetent staff.

As a result, these programs did not accumulate much knowledge.

(Ben Ouagrham-Gormley 2014, Loc. 2948–2459 in Kindle version)

The Duelfer Report echoes this, noting that Saddam's "chain of command for WMD was optimized for his control" rather than any other consideration, and that "at some point...in the mid-1980s, a shift in priorities occurred in which Iraqi BW personnel were selected for participation in the program more for their loyalty and dependability than for their technical skills, an approach that distorted the entire higher educational process and frequently ensured that the 'best and the brightest' were replaced by the loyal and reliable."[20]

Thus, while Iraq's BW program failures were on the face of it technical, probably the biggest contributor to the failure to make greater technical progress lay in the management style imposed by the requirement for secrecy and exacerbated by the authoritarian and brutal nature of the regime. Given the amount that is still unknown about gene expression, pathogenicity, metabolism and other fields of direct relevance to effective biological weapons design, it is doubtful that current technological advances would have guaranteed greater Iraqi success under the Ba'athist regime.

References

Ben Ouagrham-Gormley S (2014) *Barriers to Bioweapons: The Challenges of Expertise and Organization for Weapons Development.* Ithaca: Cornell University Press.

Makiya K (1989) *Republic of Fear: The Politics of Modern Iraq.* London: University of California Press.

Trevan T (1998) *Saddam's Secrets: The Hunt for Iraq's Hidden Weapons.* HarperCollins.

Woods KM, Palkki DD and Stout ME (Eds.) (2011) *The Saddam Tapes: The Inner Workings of a Tyrant's Regime, 1978–2001.* Cambridge: Cambridge University Press.

Notes

[1] Faithless 'Mass Destruction' on No Roots, (2004); Crystal Method 'Weapon of Mass Distortion' on Legion of Boom, (2004).

[2] United Nations Security Council Resolution 687 (1991) see. http://www.un.org/Depts/unmovic/documents/687.pdf (accessed September 17, 2015).

[3] Twenty-second quarterly report on the activities of the United Nations Monitoring, Verification and Inspection Commission (UNMOVIC), UN Document S/2005/545, August 30, 2005.

[4] Saddam and Air Force Officers discussing the movements and performance of the Iraqi Air force during the Iran–Iraq War, July 7, 1984 (Woods, Palkki and Stout 2011: 219) SH-SHTP-A-001-035.

[5] http://www.govexec.com/defense/2003/01/army-gave-chem-bio-warfare-training-to-iraqis/13329/ (accessed April 29, 2015).

[6] Duelfer C, *Comprehensive Report of the Special Advisor to the DCI on Iraq's WMD*, September 30, 2004, U.S. Government Publications Office, Volume 3, Biological Section see https://www.cia.gov/library/reports/general-reports-1/iraq_wmd_2004 (accessed September 17, 2015) pp. 5–6.

[7] UN Monitoring, Verification and Inspection Commission (UNMOVIC) (2007) *Compendium*, 'Chapter V: Biological Weapons Programme' see http://www.un.org/Depts/unmovic/new/documents/compendium/Chapter_V.pdf (accessed September 17, 2015) p. 768.

[8] As per note 6, p. 6.

[9] As per note 6, p. 6.

[10] Office of the Special Assistant of Gulf War Illnesses, Document af/19961205/120596, 1996 see http://www.gulflink.osd.mil/declassdocs/af/19961205/120596_aaday_01.html (accessed April 29, 2015).

[11] As per note 6, p. 8.

[12] As per note 6, pp. 8–9.

[13] As per note 6, p. 11.

[14] Duelfer C, *Comprehensive Report of the Special Advisor to the DCI on Iraq's WMD*, September 30, 2004, Volume 1, Regime Strategic Intent see http://www.foia.cia.gov/sites/default/files/document_conversions/89801/DOC_0001156395.pdf, p. 20.

[15] As per note 3, p. 15.

[16] Iraq's Biological Weapons Program, Iraq Watch see http://www.iraqwatch.org/profiles/biological.html (accessed April 30, 2015).

[17] As per note 6, pp. 10–11.

[18] As per note 6, p. 8 and p. 11.

[19] See, for instance, http://fas.org/nuke/guide/usa/cbw/bw.htm (accessed April 30, 2015).

[20] As per note 6, p. 19.

Point of View

Hunting Saddam's Biological Weapons: A First-Hand Account

Gabriele Kraatz-Wadsack

After accepting the United Nations request through the German government to go to Iraq on a 3-month assignment, in January 1995, I left behind my world of work in a laboratory for a stint with the United Nations Special Commission (UNSCOM), which the United Nations created as part of the ceasefire conditions for the 1991 Gulf War to disarm Iraq of its weapons of mass destruction, its related programs and long-range missiles. No one briefed me about what I would be doing, I learned only when I landed outside Baghdad that I would be the Chief Inspector setting up the interim monitoring of Iraq's biological facilities to ensure they were not covertly used to make biowarfare agents. There was no handbook on how to do biological inspections and I had to rely on my scientific knowledge and logic. I was briefed by the departing Chief Inspector that Iraq needed to declare their dual-use facilities, and that cameras and other sensors must be installed to ascertain a baseline of operation of some of the most important dual-use facilities with breakout capabilities. The job seemed reasonably straightforward; little did I know just how surreal my experience would be or that my tenure as an inspector would last years.

Uncovering an offensive program

Early in the inspections, UNSCOM headquarters in New York

asked me to examine the air handling system on the roof of the animal house at Al Hakam. I went there not knowing that the Iraqis secretly built Al Hakam to make biowarfare agents and were trying to pass the site off as a manufacturer of chicken feed and biopesticide. I nodded curtly to Dr Rihab Rasheed Taha, who ran Al Hakam (and Iraq's bioweapons program), and headed straight to the roof to photograph the separated plenum of the air handling system, which had no special air filters. From the roof, I could see that Al Hakam had an expansive layout, with anti-aircraft batteries, bunkers, and other features that would not be expected at a commercial facility. As we toured the site, I kept questioning Dr Taha, as the manager of the plant, but she was very evasive and seemed embarrassed to talk about the scientific aspects of making single cell protein. When I saw three chicken in the animal house atrium that showed signs of other chickens pecking on them, I wondered why the Iraqis would have three feather-picking chickens there if they were making feed to have healthy chickens and why these chicken showed behavioral anomalies, usually only found in caged animals. Dr Taha also said they were hauling the yeast extract for the single cell protein process from a brewery 60 kilometers away, and the plant had 5,000 liter fermenters, not the 500,000 liter ones for commercial-scale production of single cell proteins. Nothing was logical, and I left thinking the whole thing was a charade set up as a cover for a bioweapons plant.

I also went on an inspection to Al Daura Foot-and-Mouth Disease Vaccine Plant, which made 1.2 million vaccine doses per year before the war. The Iraqi declaration said Al Daura was currently only making 600,000 doses. When I got there, the lights were off and the equipment was not working. The director toured me through the ghost town. He shook as he explained the sanctions made it difficult to get spare parts but otherwise he could not explain the plant's status. He said the plant last produced vaccine in 1992 and that he had just copied the 1994 declaration for 1995. The director agreed to revise the declaration, but I left very concerned that Iraq purposefully submitted a false one.

UNSCOM headquarters instructed me to look for growth media but did not elaborate why I needed to track down Iraq's supplies of nutrients for the growth of microorganisms. The Al Adile medical warehouse that stored medical supplies seemed a logical starting point for an inspection. The normal police and "minders" escorted my car, but on the way there suddenly other cars appeared with guys in leather jackets and sunglasses — the secret police. At first, the Al Adile staff showed me exactly what they had declared, small amounts of growth media in small containers labeled to be sent to hospitals. But, the Iraqis claimed not to have the keys to a locked room, the one door they wanted me to ignore. They said the room contained expired media. I made them open the door and saw a room with huge containers of 10, 25, 50 and 100 kilograms literally stacked to the ceiling. That amount of media was excessive. Al Adile personnel said their Ministry of Health had ordered the growth media and had made a mistake and argued that the declaration was just a mistake of a decimal point in the wrong place. I told the Iraqis their declaration was false and insisted that they change it. I left knowing that these quantities and container sizes were way out of any proportion for the stated hospital use and that the media must have been a special order for a special purpose other than diagnostics — most likely for production purposes.

Over the next several days, I went to Al Hakam, Al Razi, Al Amiriyah, Al Kindi, finding and photographing a total of 22 tons of growth media. Still, 17 tons of growth media were unaccounted for since UNSCOM had data indicating Iraq imported 39 tons. In March 1995, I went to Al Hakam hoping to learn when the fermenters were installed, became functional, and needed maintenance or repairs. This data was critical to what Iraq did with the missing growth media. Treating the matter as nothing important, I handed Taha's assistant a table charting each fermenter and asked him to fill in the blanks. He did so in 15 minutes, not realizing what he revealed.

The fermenters were all working from the outset, which meant Iraq could have produced warfare agents *en masse*. When I briefed the fermenter data the next day to UNSCOM Executive Director Rolf Ekeus and very senior Iraqis, Dr Taha pitched a fit, claiming we were wrong. Another UNSCOM inspector showed the calculations about the fermenter capacity and growth media consumption and we underscored that Dr Taha's key aid provided the information on the fermenter operability that could not be rebutted.

UNSCOM had Iraq cornered. Before long, an international review panel confirmed that our evidence showed Iraq's biological declaration was inaccurate and incomplete and Rolf Ekeus briefed the Security Council. On July 1, 1995, Iraq admitted that they had produced two types of bio-warfare agents, but claimed they destroyed the bulk agent and never filled any weapons. UNSCOM already had evidence that Iraq had loaded biological warfare agents into weapons and immediately pressed Iraq to amend this declaration.

Special munitions

Much of my time as an inspector was filled with different and multidisciplinary tasks. In July 1997, I led a 44-person chemical team to several facilities, including the headquarters of Iraq's Air Force. The Iraqis declared the site sensitive and negotiated to restrict UNSCOM's access. The Iraqis said that only I, my deputy and my interpreter could enter the Operations Room and balked at opening a safe full of Air Force documents, among them one titled "I-I War Special Munitions." I knew that "special" meant chemical weapons. My translator scanned the seven-page report and our later assessment of that file was that it documented that Iraq falsified its declaration to UNSCOM by exaggerating the expenditure of weapons during the Iran–Iraq War. I asked to copy the document, and the Iraqis considered whether I could copy a redacted version of the report while I took notes on its contents. The chief minder took the document from my hands. I demanded it back and stated the Iraqis were in violation of Security Council resolutions 687 and 715. The chief minder replied that possession of an Iraqi military document was illegal, so I could go to jail. Suddenly, the Special Security Organization soldiers surrounded us with Kalashnikovs. After several hours, UNSCOM headquarters worked out a deal to put UNSCOM tamperproof seals on the document and leave it in Iraq's custody so the Iraqis could give it to the head of UNSCOM a few weeks later. At the end of 2002, Iraq turned the still-sealed document over to the United Nations Monitoring, Verification, and Inspection Commission, UNSCOM's successor organization.

Inspection tools

Another mission was when UNSCOM excavated Al Azzizyah in 1997 to try to confirm Iraq's declaration about the destruction of their biological bombs. We dug up remnants and even found three intact bombs because the explosives the Iraqis used to blow them up misfired. That day, I photographed and took samples from the R-400 bomb nose cones, body parts and pieces. As we moved about the site, our team's explosive ordinance disposal specialist told me to follow his footsteps because the munitions and weapons could blow up. The Iraqis trailed a few meters behind us, smoking and walking wherever, apparently not very concerned about the possibility that a false step or a lit cigarette tossed in the wrong place could cause a deadly explosion.

For other types of weapons satellite data can be a very useful tool for inspectors but it has little utility for biological inspections. Aerial images can identify special air handling systems on buildings, but legitimate facilities use biosafety containment so inspections are still needed to clarify a site's activities. Also, as UNSCOM discovered, Iraq made biological warfare agents without modern biosafety precautions. As the Chief of monitoring and verification, I found on-site cameras and sensors were useful but not definitive for tracking activity at biological facilities. Cameras and sensors were useful for triggering an on-site inspection if we saw something unusual on the real-time images.

Interviewing the Iraqis was sometimes helpful, especially if we had a confirmed, independent data point and could interview the Iraqis sequentially or in a group where we could ask a question and listen as the Iraqis sorted out any discrepancies among themselves. In interviews the Iraqis often just regurgitated what a superior told them to say or made something up on the spot to cover up the truth. With their lives literally on the line if they divulged anything to UNSCOM, this behavior is understandable.

Documents provide an important evidentiary trail, and in the late 1990s UNSCOM conducted document searches to find the paper trail the inspectors thought remained despite the orders from their superiors to destroy everything. The Iraqis kept several copies of every bill, every record had a different colored copy that went to the different ministries. In addition, scientists are meticulous about documenting their work. All sorts of documents can provide useful information. For example, in 1997 we found a pamphlet about post-graduate program at the Al Hazen Institute, the Institute that UNSCOM believed performed Iraq's early biological weapons research and development work. This pamphlet's authors were leads to identify possible weapons scientists. During the UNSCOM-years technical advances like Polymerase Chain Reaction made sampling a much more useful inspection tool. To illustrate, the samples I took from the intact bombs at Al Azziziyah disproved Iraq's declaration. The Iraqis claimed that bombs with black stripes contained anthrax and Botulinum toxin, which they deactivated with formaldehyde and potassium permanganate while those without markings were filled with aflatoxin and inactivated with bleach. However, the bomb without a black stripe, sampled positive for potassium permanganate and the DNA of impure *Clostridium botulinum* and toxin.

Reflections

I paid great attention to detail. At Al Taji I spotted thin pencil markings on the tiles that helped confirm that a single cell protein plant with a methanol pipe connection had previously been installed there. The methanol would not be appropriate for a process making biowarfare agent. These markings, in other words, pointed at Al Taji's original civilian purpose in the Iraqi bioweapons program.

Nothing is black and white; inspectors encounter a lot of grey zones and have to cope with them. I kept an open mindset and tried to think laterally, that the Iraqis could do something differently than I or the team would expect.

As an inspector, my most important findings were the biological growth media related evidence *in situ* and on the chemical side, the Air Force document that exposed that Iraq inaccurately declared its chemical arsenal. In addition, the monitoring system was a deterrent for Iraq to resume the production of biological weapons and also turned up leads to investigate the extent of Iraq's past bioweapons program.

Chapter 6

The South African Biological Warfare Program

Alastair Hay

Introduction

If you were told that others wished to destroy your way of life what would you do? You might just shrug your shoulders and evince disbelief. But if it was claimed that everything you had and valued could be lost, and that your family could be at risk, would you sit idly by? Doubtful! And if it were put to you by those in government that as a scientist with the necessary skills to help your country in its hour of need you could help avert this threat, would you resist this appeal for assistance? Unless you had a heart of steel there would certainly be some wavering of your position. Think about it. How would you explain to your family that its safety was not sufficient to induce you to help? Surely the government had a better appreciation of threats to the country than you as an individual. If you were also told that your enemies to the north were using chemical weapons and that you were required to help develop a biological weapons (bioweapons) program to counter this, where is the flaw in the appeal?

The logic is clear. Paint a picture in the minds of those to whom you appeal for help that their assistance will be crucial in the war being waged for white South Africa's survival and some, at least, will be happy to take on the job. The fact that chemical weapons and biological weapons are two distinct entities and governed by international treaties will be of little consequence if you are not aware of these. More basic factors, many emotional, will dictate how people respond. These, and many other issues besides, influenced the scientists who became active members of the illegal bioweapons program in South Africa which ran from the early 1980s until it was formally ended in 1995 (Hay 2001). Known as "Project Coast" the program was the brainchild of a respected heart specialist Dr Wouter Basson who conceived it as a way of countering the threats posed by possible use of chemical weapons by newly independent, majority rule countries on South Africa's borders.[1]

South Africa's interest in bioweapons

If the threat was from chemical weapons why was a biological weapons program required? This is far from clear. There are no documents written at the time to explain the motivation behind the program. Much of what we know about Project Coast came retrospectively from testimony from participating scientists and military personnel before South Africa's Truth and Reconciliation Commission (TRC) (see Chapter 6, Point of View). Supplementary details were obtained in interviews with key decision makers. What the disclosures indicated was that Project Coast was a small-scale biological weapons program with a larger chemical weapons component designed to develop and produce crowd-control agents both for the South African police and for possible use in a chemical retaliatory capacity should the South African military forces be attacked with chemical weapons.[2] A significant part of the chemical weapons program was to be defensive and this was to develop protective clothing and detection equipment against chemical weapons for South African troops fighting in Angola (Gould and Hay 2006).[3] According to the former Surgeon General DP Knoebel, who was a member of both the Coordinating Management and separate Security committees which had oversight of the program:

> At no time was it ever considered to develop a biological warfare offensive capability, at no time. I just emphasise that. And therefore

all the organisms and toxins that were studied were never considered either for weaponisation or for delivery systems and there was no intent ever to use them.[4]

A secretive affair

Nothing about Project Coast was to be made public; it was to be a secretive affair, so secret in fact that at the outset those employed in the biological weapons section were to have no knowledge of the work on chemical weapons.[5] Authorization to proceed with the chemical and biological warfare (CBW) program was given in 1981 by the then Minister of Defense General Magnus Malan (Gould and Folb 2000) and responsibility for the technological control of the program was devolved to the Surgeon General; Knoebel became Surgeon General in 1988.[6]

Available evidence does not indicate any involvement in biological warfare (BW) work by South Africa before Project Coast (Gould and Hay 2006) nor was there any immediate or envisaged threat from BW according to threat assessments conducted in the early 1970s.[7] With no imminent threat from biological weapons, Project Coast had no real requirement for any work in this area, but evidence indicates there was a part of the BW program which was clearly offensive in nature with work on bacteria and toxins heading the list, and both subsequently used in assassination attempts with food, drinks and cigarettes spiked with the biological material. There is no evidence of work on viruses.[8]

Roodeplaat Research Laboratories

The BW work was to be conducted at a specific facility known as the Roodeplaat Research Laboratories (RRL), a complex on a 70-hectare site to the northeast of South Africa's capital, Pretoria. The laboratories were designed to enable work with highly pathogenic organisms and a high grade BSL4 containment facility for work with highly pathogenic, easily transmissible organisms was considered. This was to enable sensitive military work, according to its director,[9] as the only other BSL4 site in the country was at the National Institute for Virology, in the town of Rietfontein, and this facility was subject to international supervision. To provide a degree of cover RRL was sited close to other agricultural research facilities to avoid standing out, but just far enough away to obviate any accident or leakage affecting them.[10] RRL was also designed for work with primates and the temperate climate of the location enabled cheaper housing for these animals. In the event, RRL had a very short life as a BW facility. Final work on the complex was only completed in 1988; 6 years later RRL was privatized (Gould and Hay 2006).

Delta G Scientific

The production side of the chemical program was carried out in a sister company called Delta G Scientific. Like RRL, Delta G was designed to provide a respectable front and to hide the military connection. Both companies were fronts in other words.[11] Some of the former Soviet Union's offensive biological weapons program was also conducted at a front company: The Institute for Especially Pure Biopreparations (Biopreparat) near St. Petersburg. Ostensibly involved in vaccine work Biopreparat had many scientists engaged in other, highly secret, work including manipulating bacteria to develop strains resistant to antibiotics (Hay 2002) (see Chapter 4). In South Africa's case, with the military involvement disguised, import of any items that may have raised suspicion, particularly dual-use equipment, was much easier. The two companies assisted one another with RRL carrying out occasional chemical syntheses and Delta G scientists working on biological agents for particular projects (Gould and Hay 2006). The available evidence does not suggest a great deal of cooperation between the two companies — which were separated by some 40 miles — so the arrangement was hardly one of cohabitation. According to the Surgeon General, the only person who had a full knowledge of the activities of the two organizations was the project officer in charge of the CBW program, Dr Wouter Basson.[12]

A philosophy (or lack thereof) for bioweapons

Details about the history of RRL, its demise, the sale of the facility as well as the political environment in which Project Coast operated are set out in Gould and Hay (2006). An architect's drawing of the complex and plans for extensions — never completed because the program ended — are available. This chapter is more about the work that was done at RRL and what was achieved, or, more to the point, how little was achieved as far as bioweapons were concerned. It is also necessary to explore the role of the individuals who were employed on Project Coast, and their motivation, as they were working on projects that were illegal under international law.

In assessing what was done at RRL it is vital to retain a measure of skepticism as the lack of contemporaneous documents forces us to rely on later briefing papers for senior government officials prepared by those who ran the program and the testimony of the scientists involved, together with occasional interviews with these individuals. The picture painted by the briefings is incomplete and there is also likely to have been special pleading on the part of some to both obscure their role and minimize it. But some of the revelations indicate work that was unequivocally awful, yet the scientists had the courage to discuss it knowing that many others would find it distasteful. This "baring of the soul" on the part of some lends a measure of authenticity to a number of accounts.

One of the documents describing the work of the CBW program was prepared by Dr Basson as a briefing paper for the President, F W De Klerk, and his Defense Minister Eugene Louw. Perhaps because the briefing paper might later become public, there was little of substance in its two paragraphs on biological weapons and what was written was both vague and obscure. Claiming an inability to describe the then (circa 1990) biological threat to the world because techniques to produce new bacteria were so rapid, it claimed that the South African program was "focussed on staying up to date with the changing threat."[13] To enable this "we are constantly producing new organisms in order to develop a preventative capacity as well as treatment."[14]

As for the aim of Project Coast, Basson was equally unclear in his briefing. The work done, he wrote, was that of "covert research and development of CBW and the establishment of production technology in the sensitive and critical areas of chemical and biological warfare to provide South African security forces with a CBW capacity following the CBW philosophy and strategy."[15] This is such obscure phraseology and one would hope that the president asked for some clarification and perhaps an explanation of what the "CBW philosophy and strategy" was. Basson did not disclose it in print. On the more specific issue of bioweapons, Basson claimed that Project Coast had an objective which was to "establish a research, production and development capacity with regard to biological warfare."[16] This phrasing clearly hints at an offensive program with its reference to "production," but is still vague enough to deny such was in operation if there was a leak and the work became public knowledge.

Limited insight into Basson's motives for adopting obscure phrasing may be found in a document written for the Reduced Defence Command Council later the same year. Having outlined a philosophy on chemical weapons he noted that what he had spelled out did not "cover any aspects of Biological warfare" and that because of "the more controlled nature of Biological Warfare there are many more international control measures. The production of Biological weapons is not allowed anywhere in the world."[17] Here Basson is clearly referring to both the 1925 Geneva Protocol and the 1972 Biological and Toxin Weapons Convention (see Chapter 12). But he does not refer to either international treaty directly. Besides statements of fact about international control measures and the illegality of producing biological weapons, the phrasing is again vague and uninformative. We know from testimony of participants in Project Coast that biological agents were used in assassination attempts, so is Basson being deliberately elliptical in his writing and avoiding writing this? Was he asked to phrase his document vaguely because this suited the military and the less people knew the better? Perhaps. It is even possible that the assassination materials were not considered to be biological weapons. The text may also be explained by Basson not knowing about the attempted assassinations, as he later claimed in court.[18]

Clandestine operations

The first director of RRL was the veterinarian Dr Daan Goosen. Goosen was based at the University of Pretoria. Previously he had been Special Advisor to the Surgeon General for veterinary matters in 1977 whilst doing his military service and later advised on protocols for treatment of animals such as horses and sniffer dogs used by the military. Goosen was recruited by Basson to run RRL sometime in late 1982 or early 1983. At the time one of Goosen's research projects was to develop a medical kit for soldiers to use in the event of snakebites. In the course of a broader discussion on biological weapons with Basson, Goosen discussed his work on venom. Although Goosen is a little vague about the exact date, he claimed Basson asked him for some poison to eliminate an enemy of the state.

A more specific request was then made by Basson for snake venom. Goosen knew the venom to be lethal in small doses. He claimed in testimony before the TRC that he gave Basson venom from the black mamba snake.[19] The transfer was apparently done at 6:00 am to avoid other witnesses. Either Goosen was nervous, or just clumsy, but he dropped the vial containing the venom on the floor where it smashed and the contents spilled. Goosen claimed he had to gather the venom up in a syringe and repackage it for Basson to take away.[20] So, even before RRL was established, a procedure had been instituted to use toxins for assassination.

Goosen claimed that he had many discussions with Basson about the type of company that was to be formed and that some of these discussions also occurred with the then Surgeon General (Nieuwoudt). According to Goosen, his friend General Knoebel (and later Surgeon General) may also have been there, although this has not been established with certainty. General Knoebel certainly acknowledged that he first became aware of Project Coast in 1983 in a briefing he received, but whether it was this same meeting Goosen refers to is unclear.[21]

As for RRL, Goosen claimed that Basson wanted the company to be clandestine, to have no overt links with the military as this would make it difficult to persuade reputable scientists to join, but also because of bureaucratic red tape and delay in getting things approved if the military was involved directly.[22] Another consideration, apparently, for Goosen was that he was in the process of setting up his own company and had to make a decision to abandon this if he was to help establish RRL. Goosen was very remorseful about his decision to change direction. He felt that he had sacrificed his career and placed far too much reliance on what Basson had told him.[23]

In contrast to what Surgeon General Knoebel claimed in the TRC hearings about the aim of the bioweapons program at RRL, Goosen stated that: "There was no doubt in my mind, and there was no doubt in anybody's mind, that it was offensive, intended to be used offensively." The company, he said, started off as one thing and then it expanded. Initially it was to establish an evaluating facility where animals would be used to determine the effectiveness (or lethality) of substances. Referring to the fact that there was already a facility producing chemical weapons (Delta G), Goosen claimed that there was no facility to produce biological weapons. The plans for RRL changed so that RRL had the "ability for the country to test, in the first place; and secondly, develop biological and even chemical weapons."[24]

Toxins for sale

So what was developed? Goosen notes that RRL supplied many crude products that could have been used to kill people. The products Goosen refers to were noted in what the TRC referred to as the "Verkope lys" or sales list,[25] as well as a list of South African Defence Force (SADF)-sponsored ("hard") projects conducted at RRL. The sales list was authored by Dr André Immelman, a toxicologist and head researcher on SADF projects at RRL. In an affidavit to the TRC, Immelman confirmed that he wrote the list as Dr Basson had asked him to provide toxins to a group of individuals.[26] The list covered an 8-month period from March to October 1989 and indicated that some 67 items had been sold on 48 occasions.[27]

Questioned about this list at the TRC hearings Professor Schalk van Rensburg, Director of Laboratory services at RRL, denied ever having seen the list until just prior to his testimony. He claimed to have heard of the lists and overheard a later director of RRL, Wynand

Swanepoel, continually asking Immelman to keep the list of projects up-to-date. Projects also included material containing toxins. Page one of the sales list referred to numerous items including:

- Five beer bottles containing what appears to be Botulinal toxin (a highly potent nerve inhibitor);
- Five beer bottles with thallium (a potent systemic poison);
- Sugar infected with the bacterium Salmonella (a frequent cause of food poisoning);
- Whisky laced with the toxic weed killer Paraquat;
- A baboon fetus (a baboon foetus was later found in the grounds of TRC Chairman Archbishop Desmond Tutu's residence);
- Cigarettes infected with the bacterium *Bacillus Anthracis* (which causes anthrax, a potentially fatal infection);
- Five coffee chocolates laced with *B. Anthracis*;
- Five coffee chocolates laced with Botulinal toxin;
- Peppermints containing the toxic insecticide Aldicarb (similar in properties to the organophosphate insecticides but shorter acting);
- Peppermint chocolates adulterated with Brodifacum (a rat poison which operates by stopping blood clotting, resulting in hemorrhaging);
- Peppermint chocolates laced with Cantharidin (a drug used to remove warts and tattoos, which will stimulate sexual arousal, but which in high doses causes intestinal hemorrhaging and kidney damage);
- Peppermint chocolates with cyanide;
- Whisky with Colchicin (a drug used to treat gout with a range of side effects including peripheral nerve damage, abdominal pain and kidney damage amongst others).

Asked if the list suggested materials for research or more likely a list of murder weapons Van Rensburg said it was undoubtedly the latter,[27] a view with which General Knoebel concurred,[28] as did the Commission.[29] The products listed above were given (sold) to unknown operatives of the Civil Cooperation Bureau (CCB).[30] The CCB was apparently a covert military hit squad, which targeted enemies of the South African state (Gould 2005). It is also important to note that work to determine the lethal dosages of some of the chemicals added to peppermint chocolates (listed above) involved appalling experiments in a range of animal species including dogs and primates with little regard being paid to the welfare of the animals.[31]

Culturing bacteria

Veterinarian and microbiologist Dr Mike Odendaal, employed at RRL for eight and half years, worked on some of the agents referred to above. Odendaal knew that RRL was a front company and in testimony to the TRC said that he worked on three types of projects at RRL. These included what were known as "hard" projects in which the Defence Force was interested, "soft" projects of a commercial nature, and "in-house" schemes. One of his briefs, Odendaal explained, was to develop technology that could be used to develop a limited defensive capability.

Odendaal had responsibility for microbiology. He acknowledged working on many different microorganisms and toxins, including Salmonella, *B. Anthracis* and Botulinum toxin. Odendaal received orders for military projects directly from Immelman and reported back to him directly.[32] Some of these orders required Odendaal to culture a wide range of bacteria, which he freeze-dried and placed in vials before handing them to Immelman. He said he did not know what happened to them after this. Odendaal explained that Immelman had a small bar-room fridge in his office in which he kept all these freeze-dried cultures. This appears to have been the sole storage facility and Odendaal claimed that RRL was not "geared to produce large quantities [of bacteria] and we were not geared to hold large quantities of these organisms."[33]

Maintaining that RRL did not embark on large-scale production of these organisms, Odendall also claimed that they did not produce these organisms continuously as this required a good deal of time and, given their interests, the scientists and technicians were involved in many other projects. The freeze-drying work was only a very small portion of their activities.[34] What Odendaal did not tell the TRC was that in 1987 senior management at RRL had commissioned plans for a major upgrading of the facilities to enable dealing with a wide range of microorganisms and toxins. The plans convinced Odendaal that large-scale production was envisaged (Gould and Hay 2006). The upgrade did not happen.

At the TRC hearings Odendaal did acknowledge that he investigated the solubility of Botulinum toxin in a range of fluids including water, milk, whisky and beer, any liquid in fact that might be used to poison someone. And the reason he did this he said was that he was told that "it could land in one of our own people's drinks" — hence the need to research its solubility.[35] He also admitted adding anthrax spores to five cigarettes and acknowledged that it was hardly likely to be for a mass attack and more likely to be used against particular individuals.[36]

One of Odendaal's larger bacterial culture tasks was to produce 220 milliliters of concentrated cholera organisms', which he claimed he thought initially might be used for testing purposes, but:

> There were hints that this could be used in the war situation in Angola, and it never crossed my mind for one moment that it could be used internally in our own country, because to use organisms or to spread organisms in your own country is a very risky thing, and it's not the — it doesn't go along with the convention of biological warfare that you produce these things to use on your own territory.[37]

That cholera might be used to cause an epidemic amongst opposition forces in Angola was a position put to him, he claimed, by Immelman. Odendaal claimed that Immelman had said that Angolan forces were using similar tactics so what was wrong if cholera was employed against them.[38] But Odendaal did acknowledge that it would be callous to use cholera against whole villages, where women and children would be resident.

Other microorganisms of interest to RRL were ones which might be used to degrade organophosphate compounds,[39] and small quantities of some very potent organophosphate nerve agents, including

Tabun and VX,[40] were synthesized at RRL presumably for this work (Gould and Hay 2006).

One reason the TRC was interested in Odendaal's work was that it had obtained a list of research projects carried out at RRL. In a document referred to as TRC 30, a total of 163 hard projects were listed covering 1985, 1986 and 1990 onwards. Projects for the 3 years, 1987 to 1989, were missing. Of the 163 known projects 66 percent concerned potentially lethal toxins. Most of the projects were toxicity studies in animals, others included preparation of toxins, a few on treatment and neutralizing agents, a few on psychotropic agents, two or three on explosives, some 12 percent of projects being involved with highly pathogenic microorganisms and some 18 percent on fertility and fertility control projects.[41]

Research published openly

What Odendaal was also keen to explain to the TRC was that he was involved in research that he subsequently published openly. Many scientists at RRL published openly. Indeed this was one of the carrots used to recruit scientists. It served several purposes; scientists were able to work on their own projects and so remained visible to their peers and this, in turn, provided cover for secret activity. Odendaal's published work concerned anthrax infection, a major problem in the Kruger National Park where anthrax was endemic. Odendaal had 45 different strains of anthrax in his RRL collection. Some of the strains had been tested for their pathogenicity. They were also interested to see if any were resistant to treatment with penicillin, the first line of defence for any anthrax infection; it does not appear that any were found.[42] Odendaal claimed that as internal talks between the South African government and the African National Congress (ANC) made progress, work on hard projects and cultures declined. Asked to put a date on this, he said 1990. He categorically denied that cultures were produced as late as 1993. The evidence suggests that increasingly from 1990 onwards, RRL was involved in more civilian projects as the company was prepared for privatization under a new director Wynard Swanepoel.[43]

Controlling fertility

One project which was not a civilian one, but started life "in house" before becoming a so-called "hard" project was aimed at producing a female vaccine to limit fertility.[44] The project was considered too sensitive at the time to seek a grant from the likes of the Medical Research Council. There were many publications about fertility vaccines in the open literature at the time and the approach adopted, according to Van Rensburg, technical advisor to the project (and led by Doctor Riana Borman), was to target a protein, or a hormone-like compound, only produced by the embryo and usually in the placenta. These organs, he noted, produced unique proteins. If antibodies were developed against these and injected into a woman it would prevent any developing embryo being implanted causing it to be expelled in the early days of a pregnancy. Van Rensburg had no qualms about developing such a vaccine; it was a legitimate scientific enquiry and the likes of Dr Borman would only be involved if she felt it was ethically sound. Vaccines like this, Van Rensburg said, might be up to 90 percent effective in women for 5 years or so before re-vaccination was required. The aim was to limit the birth rate. But Van Rensburg claimed that they had only reached the stage of safety testing of the vaccine in baboons, and it appeared safe in these animals. The product had not been tested in humans.[45]

Vaccination could be done covertly by misleading women into believing that they were being protected against a disease like yellow fever.[46] And Van Rensburg had been told there was a need for using such a vaccine in refugee camps and for female soldiers fighting for the African military leader Jonas Savimbi, who South Africa supported. Borman denied knowledge of any of the covert uses or knowing that the project had military uses (Gould 2005). Much more controversially, Goosen had stated in his testimony that Basson had spoken to him repeatedly about the need to control the birth rate of the black population in South Africa and this was what the aims of the fertility project were. Even more controversially, Goosen said the project was discussed in the presence of the Surgeon General.[47] In his testimony, Van Rensburg claimed that his director

Swanepoel had repeatedly pressed him to release the product, and even requested some, but he refused to provide it.[48] Swanepoel emphatically denied this.[49]

Project Coast and chemical agents

It is beyond the scope of this chapter to discuss in detail the work at RRL's sister organization Delta G, but some facts are relevant to what became of Project Coast. Dr Basson appears to have been able to have the company produce chemicals for him at will, some of which, like the bacteria produced at RRL, for very dubious purposes. Delta G produced a range of riot control agents including the more potent chemical with the acronym CR; it also investigated incapacitating agents. Of particular interest were the sedative methaqualone and 3, 4-methylenedioxy-methamphetamine (MDMA) otherwise known as Ecstasy, a drug recognized for its ability to increase energy in users, but also feelings of euphoria and empathy. Methaqualone was initially extracted from drugs seized by the police, but a later order was placed for a 500-kilogram delivery from Croatia.[50] Dr Basson was involved in arranging this multimillion rand contract, and he traveled to Europe to facilitate it. Substantial funds involved in this transaction have still not been traced.[51] Some 912 kilograms of 99.5 percent pure crystalline MDMA was prepared by the chemist and research director of Delta G, Dr Johan Koekemoer, following an order from the Surgeon General.[52] The Ecstasy was later divided up into small capsules (possibly numbering in the millions) and collected by Basson.[53]

Arrest, trial, acquittal and misconduct of Wouter Basson

In 1997, Basson was arrested on charges of fraud and when arrested found to be in possession of a large quantity of Ecstasy. He was also found to be in possession of 177 files relating to projects done under Project Coast (Gould and Hay 2006). These files should have been destroyed earlier. Basson had visited numerous countries and his activities were of concern to the U.K. and U.S. governments, who sent their ambassadors in 1994 to meet with the South African

President FW De Klerk. Further meetings occurred at which senior personnel from the U.K. CBW programs were present.[54] Knoebel claimed these individuals judged the South African program to be very sophisticated, and they wanted it stopped.

There had also been agreement on the Chemical Weapons Convention (CWC) in 1993 and South Africa was committed to complying with its terms. This meant destroying any chemicals not permitted under the CWC schedules.[55] Basson was ordered to arrange their disposal and document this. He was also required, as the only person fully knowledgeable about the CBW program, to put all the technical information onto CD rom discs (there were 13 apparently) and to destroy all the files. The discs were subsequently placed in a safe that only very senior personnel had access to. However, as Basson was the only individual who could confirm that everything was placed on disc, and he had lied about destroying the technical reports, Knoebel acknowledged that he could not be certain that everything had been recorded and that the information was safely under lock and key.[56]

This unsatisfactory state of affairs was very embarrassing for South Africa as the TRC noted.[57] It also spoke volumes about how Project Coast was managed. Surgeon General Knoebel was nominally in charge of the CBW program, but completely reliant on Basson for reports on what was being done. Knoebel claimed that Basson was also taking orders from other senior military commanders and that he was concerned about a lack of control.[58] Somewhat in awe of Basson, Knoebel admitted to the TRC that he did not have the technical background to question Basson on what he was directing. It appears no one else in the various oversight committees of Project Coast had this ability either; Dr Basson had a free rein. In general, Dr Knoebel felt that Project Coast was fulfilling its defensive mandate, but he acknowledged that some of the work on toxins was clearly outside this mandate and that he should have been informed about this by Basson, but this did not happen.[59]

The arrest of Basson and his subsequent charge on 67 counts of murder, fraud and illegal possession of banned substances (drugs) clearly shocked Knoebel.[60] Basson's legal counsel successfully argued before the TRC that Basson should not be questioned as this might jeopardize his subsequent trial on the 67 counts. In the event, the outcome of that court case was a "Not Guilty" verdict. The judge in the case (begun in October 1999 and ended in April 2002), Justice Willie Hartzenberg, who earlier had refused to be replaced because of allegations of bias, said in his judgment that Basson was a secret agent; that the state had not proved its case about lack of financial controls in Project Coast, indeed that it had scuppered its case at times; concluded that all front companies established by Basson had served the interests of the SADR; and acknowledged that toxins had been produced which had been used to kill people, but accepted that Basson had no knowledge of this activity. Basson's version of events was accepted throughout. The trial had heard from some 200 witnesses, with 24 of the 30 state witnesses given exemption from prosecution for testifying. Basson's not guilty verdict on the 47 charges heard in court (others were dismissed by the judge) was greeted by applause amongst supporters, including General Knoebel.[61] Counsel gave notice that the state would appeal. No appeal has occurred.

Basson is currently fighting efforts to have him removed from the national roll of doctors. Found guilty of four charges of misconduct in 2012 by the Health Professions Council of South Africa (HPCSA) but not yet sentenced, Basson alleges that two of those judging him are biased. Basson claims that he was found guilty simply because he worked as a doctor for the SADF.[62]

Dirty work and responsibility of scientists

It is clear from the evidence that Project Coast was involved in producing toxins to assassinate enemies of the South African state. Other projects, such as that to develop a vaccine to control population growth, were clearly under development but did not reach fruition. Had they been completed it remains speculation how they would have been used. It is apparent that this work on so-called bioweapons was small scale. Plans to upgrade the facility at RRL for larger scale production of biological agents were abandoned, and it is not clear why they were stopped. The negotiations between the government and ANC may have played a role in this decision. But had the upgrade gone ahead as planned, it is apparent that RRL either had the scientists with the necessary skills to develop biological weapons or could probably have recruited them. Given General Knoebel's claim that the bioweapons program was purely defensive[63] and that there was never any intention to develop a biological weapons offensive capability, the plans for the upgrade remain unexplained and somewhat at odds with Knoebel's assertion.

There are other untidy elements around the closure of Project Coast. That many of those recruited believed that the country was under serious threat from chemical weapons is abundantly clear. It is also clear that numerous scientists felt it their duty to help their country. It was brave of them to openly discuss work at RRL that was extremely unpleasant, knowing how it would be perceived by the public. Some, like Goosen, were certainly in serious financial straits through their involvement at RRL, but it is odd that having cooperated with the TRC and claiming to have worked for South African national intelligence that he should later become involved in a plan to sell the RRL biological agent culture collection together with another genetically manipulated organism to the U.S. government, a plan which failed miserably (Gould and Hay 2006).

Although some scientists who had maintained an academic output, like Odendaal, were able to transfer to other institutions, there was no overall plan on how to deal with the scientists and assist them to relocate or even retrain — a serious omission on the part of the government. Given that a similar problem occurred in Russia following the demise of the Soviet Union's biological weapon's program, advice could have been given to the South African government about national security concerns and keeping its scientists on side. But the seriously distasteful elements of Project Coast probably had an influence on government perceptions on what help it should, or indeed could, offer the scientists. In the event it appears that all the scientists who were involved at RRL did eventually find other employment.[64]

There is also the role of Wouter Basson to consider. Clearly persuasive because of his ability to recruit talented people to his cause, he has remained a sort of teflon-coated (non-stick) individual on whom no formal charges have been pinned, save for several verdicts of misconduct through his role as a doctor.[65] Basson clearly had an agenda and he has been harried about it in court cases for the best part of 20 years, a punishment in itself, many might argue.

Basson also had a very wide range of organizations and projects to oversee. It was not proved in court that Basson was outside the mandate of Project Coast and we only have the testimony of various parties to the TRC, including General Knoebel,[66] that he was. It was not proved in court that he used Project Coast to make toxins to dispatch enemies of the state, or that he recruited others to do this dirty work for him. For dirty it was, and all those associated with this work will be forever tainted.

Although some were convinced on recruitment that they were helping the state there are limits, or ought to be, to define a boundary beyond which work is unacceptable. What effect does secrecy have on someone's principles, particularly if you are an accomplice to murder (assassination, as a term, allows some distancing for those with a conscience)? How do you live with this knowledge? Is the threat to your way of life (as you are led to believe) sufficient justification to put your ethical values on hold? Surely not. There must be a corrosive effect which may well lead to even more distasteful projects appearing acceptable. And, as a scientist, if you know that your work on a vaccine is going to be used deliberately to reduce the fertility in the majority of the population, how do you continue? The South African scientists might argue that not being medical doctors they were neither bound by the Hippocratic Oath (circa 390 BC) nor by the Declaration of Helsinki (World Medical Association 2008) regarding research on human subjects. More's the pity. One of the essential Helsinki principles first adopted in 1964 is that it is the duty of physicians who participate in medical research to protect the life, health, dignity, integrity, right to self-determination, privacy and confidentiality of research subjects. None of these guidelines were remotely considered by those planning to use the vaccine covertly. Their plans to direct research to obtain the vaccine were a real corruption of science and beget no justification.

It is also a matter of deep regret that South Africa has never officially declared the offensive elements of its work on bioweapons though the Biological Weapons Convention (BWC) Confidence Building Measures (see Chapter 12). The fact that it has not done so does not seem to have troubled other nations' party to the treaty. Should it have concerned them? Does this mean that lacing cigarettes with anthrax is not considered a bioweapons program, just a potentially criminal activity if discovered? Or is it because the quantity of anthrax involved is too small to be of concern? Using anthrax to lace cigarettes can hardly be considered to be for defensive or peaceful purposes, nor prophylaxis, which is how the BWC defines legitimacy and the retention of microorganisms. And what of the other activities? Are they just officially forgotten? Is the stain on the country just that, but brought about by a different government? If so, all the more reason to acknowledge that it occurred and ensure it never happens again.

References

Gould C (2005) *South Africa's Chemical and Biological Warfare Program 1981–1995.* Doctorate thesis, Rhodes University.

Gould C and Folb PI (2000) 'The South African chemical and biological warfare program: An overview,' *Nonproliferation Review* Vol. 7(3): 10–23.

Gould C and Hay A (2006) 'The South African biological weapons program' in M Wheelis, L Rozsa and M Dando (Eds.) *Deadly Cultures: Biological Weapons since 1945.* Cambridge, MA: Harvard University Press.

Hay A (2001) 'To know that which is forbidden' foreword in Resolution TTCFC (ed). *Chemical and Biological Warfare. Non-Proliferation and the Ethics of Science.* Capy Town: University of Cape Town.

Hay A (2002) 'Invisible death,' in T Radford (Ed.) *Frontiers 01: Science and Technology, 2001–02.* London: Atlantic Books.

Notes

[1] Gould C (2000) Interview with General Constand Viljoen (former chief of the SADF), Cape Town, May 18, 2000.

[2] Knoebel DP (1998a) Testimony before the Truth and Reconciliation Committee of South Africa, June 12, 1998. See http://www.justice.gov.za/trc/special/cbw/cbw13.htm (accessed July 1, 2015).

[3] Gould (2000), as per note 1.
[4] Knoebel (1998a), as per note 2.
[5] Knoebel (1998a), as per note 2.
[6] Knoebel DP (1998b) Testimony before the Truth and Reconciliation Committee of South Africa, July 8, 1998. See http://www.justice.gov.za/trc/special/cbw/cbw17.htm (accessed June 26, 2015).
[7] De Villiers JP, McGlouglin GE, Joynt VP and Van der Westhuizen CC (1971) Chemical and Biological Warfare in a South African Context in the Seventies. Mechem Archives, February 12, 1971.
[8] Odendaal M (1998) Testimony before the Truth and Reconciliation Committee of South Africa, June 9, 1998. See http://www.justice.gov.za/trc/special/cbw/cbw5.htm (accessed June 29, 2015).
[9] Basson W (1991) Authorisation for the Sale of Assets: Project Coast. HSF/UG/302/6/C123. SADF Top Secret Document, August 19, 1991.
[10] Basson (1991), as per note 9.
[11] Goosen AJ (1998) Testimony before the Truth and Reconciliation Committee of South Africa, June 11, 1998. See http://www.justice.gov.za/trc/special/cbw/cbw9.htm (accessed June 26, 2015). Knoebel (1998a), as per note 2; TRC (1998) Truth and Reconciliation Commission Vol. 2, Chapter 6, Special Investigation: Chemical and Biological Warfare, p. 511, October 29, 1998.
[12] Knoebel (1998a), as per note 2.
[13] Basson W (1990) Briefing of the State President. South African Defence Force Document. South African History Archives, March 26, 1990.
[14] Basson (1990), as per note 13.
[15] Basson (1990), as per note 13.
[16] Basson (1990), as per note 13.
[17] Basson (1990), as per note 13.
[18] Burger M (2002) Record of the trial 'The State v Wouter Basson' South African High Court, Transvaal Division. A daily trial record (1999–2002) prepared for the Centre for Conflict Resolution's CBW research project. See http://www.issafrica.org/uploads/Wouter_Basson_Trail_Summary.pdf (accessed June 27, 2015).
[19] Goosen (1998), as per note 11.
[20] Goosen (1998), as per note 11.
[21] Knoebel (1998a), as per note 2.
[22] Goosen (1998), as per note 11.
[23] Goosen (1998), as per note 11.
[24] Goosen (1998), as per note 11.

25 TRC (1998), as per note 11.

26 Immelman (1998) Testimony of Dr Andre Immelman in the trial 'The State v Wouter Basson', May 19, 2000.

27 Van Rensburg S (1998) Testimony before the Truth and Reconciliation Committee of South Africa, June 9, 1998. See http://www.justice.gov.za/trc/special/cbw/cbw4.htm (accessed June 28, 2015).

28 Van Rensburg S, as per note 27.

29 Knoebel DP (1998c) Testimony before the Truth and Reconciliation Committee of South Africa, July 8, 1998. See http://www.justice.gov.za/trc/special%5Ccbw/cbw14.htm (accessed June 29, 2015).

30 Odendaal (1998), as per note 8; TRC (1998), as per note 11.

31 CBW 126. Available data about Brodifacum. Internal RRL document disclosed in the trial 'The State v Wouter Basson'; CBW 127. Cholicalciferol (sic). Internal RRL document disclosed in the trial 'The State v Wouter Basson'; CBW 137 (1986) Determination of the toxicity of Brodifacum and Sulphaquinoxalin as single doses and in combination. Roodeplaat Research Laboratories (PTY) Ltd. Project No: 86/H/10/50. June 28, 1986. Project report (NR 3). Project leader JH Davies. A Immelman; CBW 140. Ionophore antibiotics. Sensitive. Shareholders meeting August/85. Internal RRL document disclosed in the trial 'The State v Wouter Basson'

32 Odendaal (1998), as per note 8.

33 Odendaal (1998), as per note 8.

34 Odendaal (1998), as per note 8.

35 Odendaal (1998), as per note 8.

36 Odendaal (1998), as per note 8.

37 Odendaal (1998), as per note 8.

38 Odendaal (1998), as per note 8.

39 Gould C (1999) Minutes of meeting with four former RRL scientists (and checked by participants), December 1, 1999.

40 Immelman (1998), as per note 26.

41 Van Rensburg (1998), as per note 28.

42 Odendaal (1998), as per note 8.

43 Swanepoel, WP (1998) Testimony before the Truth and Reconciliation Committee of South Africa, June 9, 1998. See http://www.justice.gov.za/trc/special/cbw/cbw7.htm (accessed June 27, 2015).

44 Goosen (1998), as per note 11; Swanepoel (1998) as per note 44; Van Rensburg (1998), as per note 28.

45 Van Rensburg (1998), as per note 28.

46 Van Rensburg (1998), as per note 28.

[47] Goosen (1998), as per note 11.

[48] Van Rensburg (1998), as per note 28.

[49] Swanepoel (1998) as per note 44.

[50] Knoebel (1998c), as per note 29.

[51] TRC (1998), as per note 11.

[52] Koekemoer J (1998) Testimony before the Truth and Reconciliation Committee of South Africa, June 9, 1998. See http://www.justice.gov.za/trc/special/cbw/cbw3.htm (accessed June 29, 2015).

[53] TRC (1998), as per note 11.

[54] Knoebel (1998c), as per note 29.

[55] Knoebel (1998c), as per note 29.

[56] Knoebel (1998c), as per note 29; TRC (1998), as per note 11.

[57] TRC 1998, as per note 11.

[58] Knoebel (1998c), as per note 29.

[59] Knoebel (1998c), as per note 29; TRC (1998), as per note 11.

[60] Knoebel (1998c), as per note 29.

[61] Burger (2002), as per note 18.

[62] Health Professions Council (2015) http://www.enca.com/south-africa/wouter-basson-takes-health-council-court-claiming-bias (accessed July 1, 2015).

[63] Knoebel (1998c), as per note 2.

[64] Gould, personal communication.

[65] Health Professions Council (2015), as per note 63.

[66] Knoebel (1998c), as per note 2.

Point of View

Open Secrets: "Truth Telling" and Transitional Justice in Revealing Biowarfare Programs

Chandré Gould

In 1998, the South African TRC held a public hearing into "Project Coast": the secret apartheid-era chemical and biological warfare program. At the hearing scientists and military personnel testified about their role in the program. Until then Project Coast had been hidden from public sight.

As one of the TRC investigators responsible for bringing the program to light, in this short commentary I shall attempt to answer the question: What does the experience of the TRC in investigating and revealing details of the apartheid-era (CBW) program tell us about the suitability of transitional justice institutions to enable revelation about otherwise hidden or secret weapons programs?

To get at this question, a number of ancillary questions need to asked and answered: What was the purpose of the truth commission? What kinds of truth were sought? Were the mechanisms, institutional arrangements and enabling legislation of the TRC well suited to the investigation and revelation of weapons programs? Whose interests are, and are not, served by the revelation of secret weapons programs? One way to answer these questions is by describing the purpose of the TRC and how it came to deal with Project Coast, the military code-name assigned to the CBW program.[1]

"Truth": A bridge to the future

The South African TRC, like many others that have since been established, was intended to enable the country to "move forward" (Ojielo 2010; Brakoukis 2011). It was, if you like, a bridge from the past characterized by racial segregation and associated human rights violations to a future where all South Africans would be able to live together peacefully. In the words of the Minister of Justice at the time, Dullah Omar, "...a commission is a necessary exercise to enable South Africans to come to terms with their past on a morally accepted basis and to advance the cause of reconciliation."[2]

Implicit in this formulation of the purpose is the notion that the TRC was a way to enable forgetting, such that the past did not overshadow the present and future. In order to achieve this, "truth" telling about the past was seen to be necessary. But, it was a very particular truth that was sought — a truth about gross human rights violations experienced, and narrated by those who fell victim to them, and those who were responsible for their perpetration.[3] This was both to surface and expose the experiences of individuals, families and collectives, whose victimization and associated suffering had been silenced, or rendered invisible; and to recreate a national narrative that would be acceptable in the context of the new political dispensation (Nelson Mandela Foundation 2013). Further, the TRC was expected to promote national unity, and reconciliation.[4]

It was not only the type of truth sought that informed the TRC's work, but also what was defined as worth telling. The TRC sought to reveal the nature and extent of gross human rights violations, defined very narrowly as "killing, abduction, torture and severe ill-treatment of any person" (Brakoukis 2011). Thus, by its very definition, the TRC's purpose was not to reveal secret weapons programs, unless those programs and the individuals involved in them were (i) responsible for gross human rights violations; and (ii) that information emerged from victims' statements or applications for amnesty.

Truth telling was facilitated by statements made by victims of human rights violations, including from families whose relatives had disappeared and were feared to be dead; and through a parallel process of seeking "truth" about the perpetration of gross human rights violations from those responsible, in exchange for amnesty from prosecution.

Over 2 years, 21,000 statements were taken from victims, and 7,116 applications for amnesty were received. These statements formed the basis for public hearings, "aimed at establishing a social or 'dialogue' truth." There were five kinds of hearings held by the Commission: victim hearings (where victims could share their stories and experiences), event hearings (focused on a particular incident such as the Bisho massacre), special hearings (e.g., children and youth, women and conscripts) and institutional (e.g., health system, prisons, private sector, and the chemical and biological weapons program) (Brakoukis 2011).

For perpetrators of human rights violations, the "truth" was a currency, and telling it a way for them to avoid prosecution for their deeds, through being granted amnesty (Dignan 2014).

But, the process of truth telling offered something more to perpetrators. Since the TRC was very significantly influenced and informed, in nature and structure, by its head, Archbishop Desmond Tutu, and thus by a Christian interpretation of forgiveness and reconciliation; the process of truth telling, particularly public expositions of their deeds, by perpetrators was a form of penance, a way to obtain absolution and thus to be able to present oneself as "reformed", "redeemed", and be welcomed into the "new" South Africa. It was both the prospect of such absolution and an opportunity for revenge for perceived betrayal that led two of the scientists who were part of the chemical and biological weapons program to apply for amnesty, and willingly participate in the public hearing about the program (Burger and Gould 2002).

Franz argues that implicit in the notion that the Commission could uncover the truth of what had happened in the past was the belief that there was "an existing body of knowledge about past violations which is waiting to be discovered by researchers. In this sense, the commission is conceived as the objective seeker of a truth, which is fully-formed and just waiting to be discovered." (Franz 1997) But, nothing could have been further from the truth.

While Franz's interpretation of the absence of such a body of knowledge leads her to consider the Commission's agency in producing the truth, and to assert that the "hearings of the commission are not a process of discovering truth, but of creating it" (Franz 1997), there is a far more practical implication for the recognition that there was no existing body of knowledge that could easily be uncovered and revealed. That is, while possibly motivated by the desire to be "forgiven" — but more likely to avoid prosecution — applicants would apply for amnesty for acts they had reason to believe were already in the public domain; or that would be revealed through victims' statements, or that they had good reason to believe would find their way into the public domain through some other means. There was little or no motivation for amnesty to be sought in cases where the perpetrators were fairly certain their deeds would remain hidden, such as information about the details of military involvement in human rights violations. Indeed, the military closed ranks, effectively boycotting the TRC process, with only a handful of amnesty applications being received from soldiers (Stott 2002).

The investigative units of the TRC were small teams located in each of the provincial offices. They had at their disposal limited tools to unearth information that was not already in the public domain. With over 20,000 statements from victims, and over 7,000 amnesty applications, each of which had to be verified and supporting documentation obtained to enable the Commissioners to make a finding, there was not much capacity to be spared for the kind of expensive and difficult investigation that a secret warfare program, like that into Project Coast.

The TRC did have the power to subpoena individuals to appear before investigative hearings; and powers of search and seizure. But, the latter power was hardly used. Dorothy Shea quotes Commissioner, and head of the Investigative Unit, Advocate Dumisa Ntsebeza as saying that he regrets that these powers were used so sparingly, but explains that the TRC — existing as it was in a very delicate political moment — was cautious not to "upset the apple cart" and undermine the new, and perhaps fragile, government (Shea 2000).

Investigating Project Coast

Timing played a crucial role in the TRC's investigation into Project Coast. Even before the establishment of the Commission, military intelligence had begun to look into the activities of the head of the program, Dr Wouter Basson.[5] By 1996, when the TRC's work got underway, Basson was under investigation by three different government agencies: the Office for Serious Economic Offences (OSEO) was investigating allegations of fraud; the Special Investigation Unit (SIU) of the Traansvaal Attorney General was looking into links between Project Coast and the Civil Co-operation Bureau (a secret military hit squad) and the National Intelligence Service (NIS) was also examining Project Coast and Basson's links to political violence. But, it was detectives from the police's Narcotics Bureau that arrested Basson in 1997, and a day later a major breakthrough was made when the NIS unearthed numerous documents about Project Coast at a home of one of Basson's associates. These documents would be crucial to all of these agencies investigations.

The three agencies — OSEO, NIS and the SIU — and the head of the TRC's research unit were called in when the documents were numbered for archiving, and an agreement was struck that all would have access to the documents for purposes of investigation. But, at this stage the TRC had no compelling reason to initiate an investigation into

Project Coast, and had more than enough on its plate already. Had it not been for two amnesty applications from scientists involved in the program, the TRC may well not have investigated the chemical and biological weapons program at all.

The amnesty applications by Jan Lourens and Schalk van Rensburg, compelled the TRC to investigate, and it soon became necessary for the TRC to access the documents.[6] But, despite the agreements that had been reached, the TRC quickly ran into trouble. The Deputy President, Thabo Mbeki, approached the TRC soon after the investigation began. He requested the Commission to stop investigating, for two main reasons: exposing the identity of the scientists could open them to recruitment by states seeking their chemical and biological weapons expertise, and the TRC's investigation might compromise the investigations of the SIU and OSEO.

When the TRC decided to continue with its investigation despite these concerns, additional arguments were presented for why it should not. Commissioners and investigators were called to President Mandela's office where a second request was made to end the Commission's investigation. Presidential advisor, Dr Jakes Gerwel, also addressed the Commission's staff, saying that the TRC's investigation could have a detrimental effect on the new government's attempts to establish healthy relationships with other states, if revelations were to be made about the role of foreign governments in the program.

Present, but not officially acknowledged in all these interactions, was the concern that something "unknown" to the new government, or uncontrollable, would be revealed by the TRC. By this time, the only information the new government had about the program was based on briefings by the Surgeon General, Dr Niel Knobel; Dr Wouter Basson and Dr Ben Steyn, who had taken over as Project Manager of Project Coast in 1992. The extent to which that information was complete could only be guessed at. Arguably, the ANC state needed to protect a secret that it did not know. In short, what the state itself was "allowed" to know was limited to what was officially told by people who had been instrumental in running the program. And, what the scientists would say was wholly unknown.

These obstacles to the TRC's investigation slowed an already arduous and difficult investigation. By the time the TRC was granted limited, and constrained access to the documents, it was running out of time.

At this stage the TRC's investigation into the CBW program, could justifiably have been limited to obtaining sufficient details to enable the amnesty committee to come to a finding in relation to the two amnesty applications. Some Commissioners were, at first, reluctant to allow a public hearing into Project Coast — not only because of the political risk the Commission would be taking, but also because by the time the investigation had collected enough evidence about the program, toward the end of the first quarter of 1998, there were only a few months left within which the TRC was legally mandated to hold hearings. Furthermore, it was not possible to prove that the program had resulted in any direct gross human rights violations. It was the statements by Van Rensburg and others that they had been instructed to find an anti-fertility vaccine that could be administered to black women, without their knowledge, that convinced the TRC to proceed.

Throwing it open

Since this was the last hearing of the Commission, and the last day of the hearing was the last day on which the TRC was legally mandated to hold public hearings (July 31, 1998); the hearing was vulnerable to legal challenges and delays. These came from many quarters. While Basson was subpoenaed to appear before the Commission, he asserted his right to remain silent, and took the TRC to the High Court in a bid to avoid having to testify. The head of the Nonproliferation of Weapons of Mass Destruction Council appeared before the Commission on the first day of the hearing, making an urgent appeal for the Commission not to hold the hearings in public to prevent the risk of proliferation or of violating the Chemical Weapons Convention or the Biological Weapons Convention.

Before the hearing even began, the TRC had agreed to ensure that documents naming foreign countries would not be used, made public or mentioned in the TRC hearings; and that documents detailing scientific formula or processes would not be placed in the public domain. In this way, the "truth" the TRC could reveal about the program was negotiated and mediated. Furthermore, while some of those subpoenaed to appear before the Commission's hearings did so willingly, those who did not, obsfucated, delayed and ultimately gave very little detail about the program and their role in it.

In the end the "truth" of the CBW program as constructed through the TRC hearings, and reported in the media was shaped and constrained by the Commissions' mandate: to investigate and report on "gross human rights abuses"; by what had been agreed could and could not be revealed during the hearing; and by the willingness, or reluctance of witnesses to testify.

The TRC as a model to uncover truth about past programs

Taking all of this into consideration, one has to conclude that the TRC does not offer a strong "model" for revealing secret weapons programs. However, the TRC did make a significant contribution to the revelation of the program, by placing information about the program, however limited, in the public domain. By defying the pressure placed on the TRC and the requests made to hold the hearing *in camera*, the TRC dispelled fears that testimony by the scientists involved in the program would embarrass the state, lead to a violation of non-proliferation agreements, or open the scientists to recruitment by states wishing to establish their own weapons programs. More importantly, the TRC placed in the public domain many of the formerly top secret military documents, scientific reports and documents that would enable independent researchers, analysts and academics to further study the program.

Since the TRC hearing, more detail about Project Coast has made its way into the public domain. At the time of writing this commentary a public, 3-year long criminal trial of Wouter Basson had been concluded with him being acquitted or found not guilty on all of the charges of fraud and human rights violations against him. The Health Professionals Council of South Africa had held a disciplinary hearing, and found that Basson was guilty of unethical conduct; and South Africans were awaiting the Council's decision about whether he should be allowed to continue practicing medicine. Whatever the outcome of this process, it remains imperative to ensure that scientists and medical doctors of the present and future understand that their involvement in secret weapons programs of this nature is unjustifiable.

References

Burger M and Gould C (2002) Secrets and Lies: Wouter Basson and South Africa's Chemical and Biological Warfare Program. Cape Town: Zebra Press.

Brakoukis L and Viulla Vicencio C (2011) *Truth Commissions: A Comparative Study.* Conflict Resolution Program, Georgetown University, Washington DC. and the Institute for Justice and Reconciliation, Cape Town.

Dignan E (2014) *Reconciliaion Lessons: Verne Harris on South Africa.* Belfaet: Northern Ireland Foundation.

Franz C (1997) *South Africa's Truth and Reconciliation Commission: An Enquiry into the Nature of the 'Truth' Produced at the Hearings of the Committee of Human Rights Violations.* Honours Dissertation, University of Cape Town.

Nelson Mandela Foundation, G. G. L. A. (2013) *The Mandela Dialogues: Dialoguing Memory Work. Report on the Dialogue in South Africa.* Johannesburg: Nelson Mandela Foundation.

Ojielo O (2010) *Critical Lessons in Post-Conflict Security in Africa: The Case of Liberia's Truth and Reconciliation Commission.* Wynberg, South Africa: Institute for Justice and Reconciliation.

Shea D (2000) *The South African Truth and Reconciliation Commission: The Politics of Reconciliation.* Washington DC.

Stott N (2002) *From the SADF to the SANDF: Safeguarding South Africa for a Better life for all?* Violence in Transition Series. Johannesburg:

Centre for the Study of Violence and Reconciliation.

Notes

[1] For detailed discussions of Project Coast see: Gould C (2005) *South Africa's Chemical and Biological warfare program 1981–1995.* Doctorate thesis in fulfillment of a doctorate of History, Rhodes University, and Purkitt, H and Burgess S (2001) *The Rollback of South Africa's Chemical and Biological Warfare Program.* Alabama, United States: United States Airforce Counter Proliferation Centre Air College.

[2] Quoted on the official Truth and Reconciliation Commission website, http://www.justice.gov.za/trc/, (accessed April 20, 2015).

[3] Promotion of National Unity and Reconciliation Act, 34 of 1995.

[4] For a discussion about the way in which the TRC used and interpreted the terms "reconciliation" and, the associated notion of "forgiveness" see Jacques D (2001) 'On forgiveness' in *On Cosmopolitanism and Forgiveness.* New York: Routledge.

[5] For more detail about each of these investigations see Burger, M and Gould, C (2002) *Secrets and Lies: Wouter Basson and South Africa's Chemical and Biological Warfare Program.* Cape Town: Zebra Press.

[6] Ultimately their applications for amnesty were rejected on the basis that they had not broken any laws.

Section II: Bioweapons in Today's Context

Chapter 7

RISE, the Rajneeshees, Aum Shinrikyo and Bruce Ivins

W. Seth Carus

Introduction

Despite the widespread attention given to the risks from bioterrorism, few terrorists have contemplated using biological agents, and fewer still have made any serious effort to develop a capability to employ biological agents. Still fewer ever tried to use them (Carus 2001; Tucker and Sands 1999). This chapter describes four instances in which an individual or small group acquired biological agents, using or intending to employ them.

The four cases differ in many respects. In the first incident, a group of teenagers with fantasies of apocalyptic regeneration for humankind created a group called "R.I.S.E.;" they obtained several biological agents and learned how to grow them but failed to mount planned attacks before being arrested. In the second, more serious case, a cult known as the Rajneeshees actually spread a biological agent, albeit one that typically sickens and rarely kills, infecting more than 750 people. The third instance, perpetrated by the Japanese cult Aum Shinrikyo, involved the failed aerosol dissemination of what the group incorrectly thought were lethal biological agents. The most lethal biological attacks were the 2001 anthrax letters, which killed five and sickened another 17 people, although it is unclear whether it should be considered bioterrorism or a biocrime.

R.I.S.E. (1972)

Chicago, Illinois, had a long history of political violence, including the infamous 1884 Haymarket Riot, but it was the riots during the 1968 Democratic Convention and the subsequent prosecution of the Chicago Seven that defined the environment for R.I.S.E. and its ill-conceived efforts at bioterrorism. Relatively little has been written about R.I.S.E., so this review draws heavily on original documents not cited here but described elsewhere.[1]

R.I.S.E.'s organizers had an apocalyptic vision for creating a new world by killing off the world's population and restarting a new, more ecologically sound society. This objective is evident from the group's name, which was an abbreviation for Reconstruction, Society and Elimination (there is no documentation for the meaning of the 'I').

R.I.S.E. was the brainchild of two teenagers, both would-be community college students. The leader, Allen C. Schwandner, was 19 years old at the time of his arrest. Known by his friends as "Lonnie," Schwandner had experienced a troubled childhood. He did not get along with his adoptive parents and spent time in a psychiatric hospital. In late 1971 and early 1972, he was arrested at least three times for theft, possession of stolen property, burglary and sexual delinquency. According to people who knew him, Schwandner did not like people who he considered as "straights" and had adopted a counter-culture persona in dress and action, including some drug use. Schwandner enrolled in Mayfair College, a 2-year college that eventually became a component of City Colleges of Chicago. He only attended a few classes (Carus 2000a).

The group's biological expertise was provided by 18 year old Steven Pera. Pera was extremely intelligent, even if he did not have an I.Q. of 193, as claimed by people who knew him. He came from a solidly middle-class family (his father was a school principal). Pera apparently had a strong interest in biology, enrolling in a biology course at Mayfair College during the school's 1971 spring term.

Although he dropped out of the course, he was selected for a work-study internship sponsored by a Chicago-based organization, the International Foundation of Microbiology, which was created to promote an interest in microbiology by high school students. He did not get along with others, and was kicked out of the program. Pera volunteered at a clinical laboratory at Presbyterian-St. Luke's Hospital, claiming that he wanted "to gain additional knowledge of biology."[2]

R.I.S.E. apparently was "organized" in November 1971, based on a six-page manifesto written by Schwandner. It argued that humans were destroying the environment, and that it would be better if the slate were wiped clean so that mankind could start afresh. To accomplish this, he proposed eliminating the entire human population, except for a small cadre of like-minded people who would repopulate the planet and create a society based on better principles. The plan was for eight couples to serve as the nucleus of the new society.

Schwandner's first recruit was Pera, who he met in November 1971, and between the two of them they concocted a grandiose plan for mass genocide. They decided that the simultaneous spread of several infectious diseases was the way to accomplish their objective, believing that the appearance of multiple diseases would confuse responders and that immunizations would protect their followers.

Pera began assembling a haphazard collection of readings, including material on biological warfare (such as *Tomorrow's War*, a book on chemical and biological warfare written by a former head of the U.S. Army Chemical Corps), scientific articles and treatises. He also began to collect biological agents. Subsequent investigation confirmed that he possessed isolates of *Corynebacterium diphtheria*, *Niesseria menigitidis*, *Salmonella typhi*, *Shigella sonnei* and possibly *Clostridium botulinum*. Some of these were obtained by simply asking for them. The University of Illinois Hospital provided him with *N. menigitidis* and *S. typhi* in this way, even replenishing the supply on request. It is not known where the other cultures came from. According to people who talked with Schwandner and Pera, they also expressed interest in, or made efforts to acquire, *Bacillus anthracis*, *Vibrio cholera* and *Yersinia pestis*.

Obtaining pathogens, however, was only the first step. Despite Pera's interest in biology, he had little experience or expertise in culturing microorganisms. Microbiologists working at the Illinois Department of Health found his cultures difficult to assess because they were so thoroughly contaminated with extraneous organisms. Nor did he have automatic access to appropriate laboratory space. Ultimately, he divided his work between the clinical microbiology laboratory of Presbyterian-St. Luke's Hospital, Mayfair College, and Schwandner's apartment. This created a problem when Pera was discovered trying to obtain a controlled substance at the hospital and destroyed all his cultures.

Schwandner and Pera discussed spreading diseases in three different ways: contamination of food, through the air and contamination of water. They identified likely targets in the region around Chicago where they could spread biological agents, although it does not seem the target list has survived. Attacks on food apparently focused on retail settings, as they were planning to put pathogens on foods in grocery stores. Why they expected such an approach to cause globally significant consequences is unclear. Their thinking about aerosol sprays was somewhat more sophisticated, apparently reflecting the ideas appearing in writings associated with the U.S. offensive biological weapons program. They understood that many pathogens could be disseminated into the air, and cause disease, even discussing how to ensure that Russia and China were affected by the outbreaks, seeking to ensure that their future was not dominated by survivors in the Communist bloc. It is clear that they had no idea of how to aerosolize a pathogen, and lacked the expertise to do so.

Ultimately, Schwandner and Pera focused on waterborne disease, specifically targeting Chicago area water treatment systems. They visited at least one facility, and collected publicly available information about the operation of the city's water system. They apparently were planning to introduce at least one pathogen into the water system. Although more achievable than an aerosol attack, it is doubtful that such an attack would have had any success. Pera produced only small quantities of biological agent, so what he did have was likely to be heavily diluted if introduced into a water system the size of Chicago's.

Moreover, it is unclear if the pathogens would have survived the chlorinated environment.

By mid-January, the plot had collapsed. Their new recruits were frightened by the group's plans, and at least four of them went to the Chicago Police Department (CPD). They told the CPD about injections that they had received, ostensibly intended to protect them against typhoid, and recounted what they knew about the plans that Schwandner and Pera had concocted. Law enforcement authorities took the allegations seriously, mounted a heavy guard over the city's two main water treatment facilities, and initiated a hunt for Pera and Schwandner. The CPD arrested them at Schwandner's apartment two days later. The Illinois State's Attorney, Edward V. Hanrahan, claimed (incorrectly) that R.I.S.E. was a white supremacist group, apparently not understanding that the underlying ecological concerns that ostensibly motivated Schwandner and Pera.[3]

Subsequent analyses, including tests undertaken by the Centers for Disease Control and Prevention, apparently confirmed that the two had viable cultures of several pathogens, including (using the terminology of the period) *Salmonella typhi*, *Shigella sonnei*, *Clostridium* isolates (but no evidence of toxin) and *Corynebacterium diphtheriae*. There was no evidence of *B. anthracis*.

The pair was released on bail, and immediately fled the United States, ending up in Cuba. Apparently, they hired a plane in Jamaica and forced the pilot to fly them to Cuba in May 1972. Schwandner's stay was ill fated. He was arrested for "counterrevolutionary activities," sentenced to 6 years in prison, and died while in custody.

Pera apparently grew tired of Cuba, developed health problems, and voluntarily came back to the United States in late 1974. He negotiated a plea agreement and was sentenced to 5 years of probation, but in the end the probation was terminated in early 1977. Pera subsequently came to law enforcement attention in 1983, when he was investigated for possible involvement in the Tylenol poisonings.[4]

The R.I.S.E. incident is revealing in several respects. First, it demonstrates the ease with which someone, even a novice, could gain access to dangerous pathogens and suitable laboratory facilities. It also demonstrated the extent to which the microbiology community was willing to assist people with an interest in the field. Second, it demonstrates the vast gulf between the skills of someone able to conduct rudimentary microbiology and those needed to undertake even a small-scale biological attack. Quite simply, Pera would have needed much more experience and knowledge before even their most rudimentary plans could have been brought to fruition. Third, it is clear that anti-government political attitudes did not necessarily translate into a willingness to participate in bioterrorism. Revealingly, fear of disease and a moral repugnance associated with their deliberate spread combined to lead many of those told about the plot to inform the CPD. Finally, neither Schwandner nor Pera had the character to operate secretly, which ultimately destroyed the plot.

Rajneeshees (1984)

On September 16, 1985, the Bhagwan Shree Rajneesh, leader of a religious cult that had settled in rural Oregon, accused some of his followers of a host of crimes, including — among other felonies — biological warfare.[5] This revelation, no surprise to law enforcement officials following the cult's activities, enabled them to launch a massive investigation into the largest bioterrorism attack in U.S. history.[6]

Bhagwan was a remarkable figure. He constantly challenged conventional morality, and encouraged his followers to do the same. That made the group anathema to conservative Hindus, which led him to explore alternative sites for his *ashram*, the Hindi term for religious community. In 1980, Ma Anand Sheela, one of his senior advisors, convinced Bhagwan to relocate to the United States, settling on a ranch in a remote location of Wasco County, Oregon. Over the next several years, the Rajneeshees built a new town, called Rajneeshpuram, on the site (Urban 2005).

The Rajneeshees already were notorious in Oregon. They had feuded with the State of Oregon over violation of land-use laws intended to protect rural land from over development, employed deliberately confrontational tactics against perceived critics, and maintained a collection of 93 Rolls Royce automobiles for Bhagwan's use.[7] Bhagwan was a brilliant, well-read, mesmerizing speaker who had founded the group in India during the 1970s. He increasingly came to attract westerners from the United States and Europe who were seduced by his vision of spirituality and sensuality, including many well-educated professionals (Gordon 1987; Strelley and San Souci 1987). Indeed, his adherents included Harvard-trained lawyers and physicians (Webber 1990).

Sheela was the key figure in the new community. She was the only person who had routine access to Bhagwan, she controlled the group's finances and its many organizations, and she effectively ran Rajneeshpuram — despite the existence of a formal government structure. She seemed to revel in conflict, and made little effort to ameliorate growing tensions with the people in nearby communities or with local, state, of Federal government officials.

The other key figure in the Rajneeshee biological plot was Ma Anand Puja, a nurse with close ties to Sheela. Puja was one of the *ashram's* "big moms." She was in charge of Rajneeshpuram's health care operations, including both its clinic and pharmacy. Puja also had responsibilities for the operation of the Rajneesh Foundation International, which was the corporate organization for Bhagwan's church. Puja also was not well liked, and at least some people came to refer to her as "Dr Mengele," a reference to the notorious Nazi physician who conducted medical experiments on concentration camp inmates. At least some people suspected that she had been involved in other poisonings, including of other cult members.

By 1984, the Rajneeshees had a fully functioning, legally recognized community. Although it had the official structure required by state laws, including an elected mayor, the real power vested in Bhagwan and the people around him. Bhagwan increasingly isolated himself from the rest of the community, leaving the daily management of the cult in the hands of Sheela and her immediate subordinates. Sheela ostensibly consulted regularly with Bhagwan, but privately so no one else knew what was discussed. Although Sheela was the key decider, the leadership group, consisting of about a dozen or so people, operated in a relatively collegial manner. They regularly held brainstorming sessions to work through issues confronting the community and the *ashram*.

As Rajneeshpuram grew, it attracted the negative attention of U.S. government officials, as well as the Oregon government. By 1984, the U.S. Attorney's office in Portland was investigating immigration fraud, among other possible crimes. At the same time, Oregon was trying to enforce land-use regulations designed to protect rural areas from the kind of development that resulted in the construction of a whole new town in an undeveloped area. Relations with the locals were also inflamed, both because of hostility towards the strange outsiders and their loose morals and because of the Rajneeshee's disregard for laws they found inconvenient.

By early 1984, the Rajneeshee's leadership felt that the contentious relationship with local government officials in Wasco County was obstructing their efforts to expand their community. During one of their brainstorming sessions in early 1984, they decided that their community of 4,000 people, many of whom were foreign nationals not eligible to vote, needed to use the upcoming November election to take over the government in a jurisdiction with about 15,000 registered voters. After rejecting as impracticable various schemes for their adherents to cast fraudulent ballots, they adopted a two-part strategy. First, they would exploit Oregon's liberal voter registration laws to swell their ranks by bringing in homeless people and getting them enrolled as voters. Second, they would make the other voters sick and unable to vote on Election Day.

Executing the biological plot also required some consideration. Sheela and Puja researched various methods for making people sick, including reference to the notorious books *How to Kill: Volumes 1 to 4* and more legitimate publications, such as the *Handbook of Poisons*. According to Sheela, she also consulted with Bhagwan, who told her that while they should find non-lethal ways of making people sick, it would be acceptable if a few people died. It appears that they decided against using *S. typhi*, because an outbreak of typhoid fever in Oregon inevitably would attract unwanted attention. Interestingly, an Indian Health Service clinic, trying to be helpful, had given the Rajhneeshees an expired collection of culture isolates, which included *S. typhi*.

Puja also considered hepatitis and other organisms. Ultimately, Sheela and Puja settled on *S. enterica* serotype *typhimurium*.

This organism had several virtues. First, it was a common cause of foodborne disease outbreaks. Second, it was a relatively mild pathogen, likely to make people sick for a few days but unlikely to cause death. Finally, it was easy to acquire. *Salmonella typhimurium* was used routinely to test the ability of clinical laboratories to culture pathogens. As a result, it was possible to order it from a medical supply company.

Their well-equipped clinic was provided with a microbiology laboratory. However, a separate laboratory was built in an isolated part of the Rajneeshpuram to conduct what some other members of the cult called their "germ warfare" activities. It was well equipped, and had both an incubator, not unexpected in a clinical laboratory, and a freeze dryer, not typically found in such facilities. The lab also had facilities for handling animals, as Puja apparently tested her biological agents on rodents collected from the area.

Puja was not a microbiologist, and did not know how to culture the chosen *Salmonella* strain. However, a member of the cult who was a trained laboratory technician had the requisite skill. Despite some reluctance, he apparently produced it in quantity and also taught Puja how to do so. As a result, the group had more than enough of the *Salmonella typhimurium* to conduct their operations in August and September 1984.

The first targets were two of Wasco County's three judges (the title for elected commissioners), during August 29 visit to the *ashram*. Viewed as hostile towards the cult, they were given water laced with *Salmonella*. Both became severely ill, and one had to be hospitalized. They also contaminated vegetables at a grocery store and door handles and other surfaces in the county courthouse. There is no evidence that these efforts caused disease, although a small outbreak might not have been detected.

Sheela decided to target the community's water system in July or August. A member of the group acquired maps of the system. It appears that the group made at least one trip to a large water storage tank located on a hill above the town. Exactly what they did is unclear. They may have poured a quantity of *Salmonella* into the system, or it could have been raw sewage mixed with dead rats. Puja also thought about using beavers, because they were often infected with *Giardia lamblia*, a protozoan that causes a diarrheal disease. Law enforcement officials were unsure whether to take statements seriously that the Rajneeshees had "pureed" beavers before putting them into the water system. In any case, there is no evidence that the contamination caused any disease.

The more serious efforts were aimed at the many restaurants in The Dalles area, which served locals as well as long-distance travelers using the interstate highway that went through the town. The attacks took place in two waves. The first wave, which targeted only two restaurants, occurred from September 11 through 18. The second wave lasted from September 19 to 25, and targeted at least 10 restaurants. The techniques used were rudimentary. Puja gave one of the Rajneeshees a test tube containing a brownish liquid that he poured into the salad dressing at a salad bar. Others contaminated coffee creamers, which was unlikely to result in many illnesses (Miller *et al.* 2001).

At least 751 people became ill due to the contaminations, according to an intensive investigation mounted by local, state and Federal officials. The first cases began to appear on September 17. By the 21st, public health officials had identified 25 cases. Preliminary testing identified *Salmonella typhimurium*, which was confirmed by the Oregon State Public Health Laboratory on September 21. At that point, the number of new cases was declining, and public health officials thought the outbreak was waning. However, on September 24, new cases began appearing, and by September 27 more than 200 cases were reported. This made the outbreak Oregon's largest Salmonellosis outbreak. Ultimately, 751 victims were identified, including 45 who had to be hospitalized. Public health officials suspected that the actual numbers were higher, because many of the victims were long-distance travelers who were never identified.[8]

The outbreak was intensively investigated by a group of public health officials from local, state, and federal agencies, including the Centers for Disease Control and Prevention (CDC) and Food and Drug Administration (FDA). Investigators were mystified by the outbreak, because they could not identify a common source. The restaurants got their food from many different sources, and they could never attach the outbreak to any particular supplier or food. Although a few public health officials suspected that the outbreak was intentional, that was not the predominant view. Indeed, the official position adopted by Oregon officials in late 1984 was that the size of the outbreak resulted from unsafe food handling practices by restaurant workers.[9]

By mid-1985, Federal Bureau of Investigation (FBI) officials believed that the outbreak was due to the Rajneeshees, but felt that they had no way to prove it. This changed when the cult's internal rifts led Bhagwan to accuse Sheela and her cohorts of the biological attack. This led to a massive law enforcement investigation, which resulted in prosecutions for many of the leading Rajneeshees, including the extradition of Sheela and Puja. Those two were the only people actually charged with the biological attack. Oregon prosecuted them for their attacks on the two county judges. They pled guilty, and were given multiple 20-year sentences. In addition, the U.S. Attorney's office prosecuted them for the restaurant contaminations, relying on new product tampering laws enacted in the wake of the recent Tylenol poisonings. They also pled guilty to the Federal charges, and were sentenced to 5 years in prison. They were released by Federal authorities after having served only 2½ years. Although they should have been transferred to state custody, due to a communications mix up, Federal penal authorities allowed them to leave the country. They fled to Switzerland, where Sheela could not be extradited.

The Rajneeshees left Oregon in 1985, abandoning their infrastructure to return to India. Back in India, Bhagwan gave the group a new name, Osho, and reinvented it. It now operates a resort in Pune, India (Goldman 2005; Urban 2005).

The Rajneeshee attack was highly idiosyncratic in many ways. Indeed, some people would not (and have not) consider it an act of terrorism. It is not included in FBI terrorism statistics, even though some FBI officials have identified it as the first successful bioterrorism attack in the United States. Because the attack was intended to mimic a natural event, the group never claimed credit. On the other hand, if terrorism is intended to influence government policy, attempting to affect the outcome of an election would seem to be the definitive example.

The Rajneeshee example also calls into question the usual perception that bioterrorism will be viewed as an escalation from other forms of political violence. In this case, the bioterrorism attack occurred before the group decided to assassinate the U.S. Attorney in Portland, Oregon, who was leading the investigation into the group's immigration fraud.

Only a small group of trusted people knew about the biological attack, largely limited to senior people around Sheela and a few other highly trusted underlings. Clearly, the group thought that most Rajneeshees would have had nothing to do with the plot. Ultimately, this led to problems, because the same people executing the plot became distracted by the difficulties in integrating the many homeless people brought to Rajneeshpuram.

Aum Shinrikyo (1990–1995)

Aum Shinrikyo, a religious cult that started out as a yoga school, strove but failed to execute biological attacks intended to cause catastrophic casualties. Its founder, Shoko Asahara, fascinated by the spiritual side of yoga, structured his movement as a religious organization to exploit protections given by Japan's constitution. He also had a political agenda, which led to a disastrous 1990 foray into electoral politics. This failure motivated Aum to pursue its unconventional warfare activities (Smithson 2000: 74–76). Asahara had a fascination with exotic weapons, reflected in the cult's studies of a device to generate earthquakes invented by Nikola Tesla (Kaplan 2000: 212).[10]

The cult attracted many people with technical degrees, although it is unclear that any had the needed level of biological expertise. Several people played key roles in the group's efforts to develop biological weapons, but by far the most important were Seiichi Endo and Tomomasa Nakagawa. Endo had an undergraduate degree from the Obihiro University of Agricultural and Veterinary Medicine and began graduate studies at Kyoto University in virology. He quit his doctoral program and joined the cult in 1987. His research was focused on virology; he was the lead author on at least one scientific article.[11] Endo quickly entered the cult's inner circle, based on his ability to raise money and his willingness to undergo rites that Asahara demanded of his closest followers. He was given control of Aum's Ministry of Health and Welfare. Nakagawa, a graduate of the Kyoto Prefectural University of Medicine, joined the cult in 1988 and became Asahara's personnel physician the following year. As such, he was part of the cult's inner circle and had the technical knowledge to support Endo's work.

Asahara apparently learned about Botulinum toxin during the planning that led to the November 1989 murder of a Japanese journalist critical of the cult's activities. In February 1990, he ordered members of the cult to obtain *Clostridium botulinum*, the organism that produces the Botulinum toxin. Rather than obtaining cultures from an existing collection, the cult chose to isolate the organism from soil samples. Ultimately, it appears that the cult acquired at least five different strains, although it is not known if any of them were capable of producing toxins.

To produce the Botulinum toxin, the cult built three homemade fermenters, rather than purchasing commercial systems. Between March and July 1990, around 50 batches were made. Because of the size of the fermenters, they might have produced as much as 450 tons of dilute "Botulinum toxin" solution (the quotation marks are used to distinguish the dubious material from the real thing). While Aum's leaders thought that they had grown *C. botulinum*, some of those involved in the effort were doubtful and there is no evidence that they did so. Indeed, given the design of the fermenter, it is unlikely that it was suitable for growing anaerobic organisms and at least some batches included aerobic organisms. After the failed 1990 "Botulinum toxin" attacks, Aum suspended its biological weapons program.

In 1992, Aum resumed its biological efforts. It once again tried to produce Botulinum toxin, but now also wanted to use *B. anthracis*. It developed a new *C. botulinum* fermenter and produced additional quantities of "Botulinum toxin" solution. Allegedly, they had 50 of the new fermenters, capable of generating some 10 tons for each production run. In all, they may have made scores of tons of the dilute "Botulinum toxin" solution. Finally, in 1995 they generated a small quantity of the so-called "Botulinum toxin" in a laboratory.

Aum employed its "Botulinum toxin" on at least four occasions. Between March and July 1990, they used three truck disseminators to mount between 20 and 40 separate attacks. They targeted several sites in Tokyo, including the Diet building, Narita airport, the Imperial Palace and the offices of another religious group, as well as two U.S. Navy bases.[12] A second attack occurred in November 1993, when an estimated 20 liters of "Botulinum toxin" was released from a car-mounted agricultural sprayer in an attack on Daisaku Ikeda, leader of a rival religious organization. On November 4, 1994, they attempted to poison a prominent lawyer who opposed the cult, Taro Takimoto, using their supposed "Botulinum toxin" mixed with fruit juice. Finally, on March 15, 1995, Aum employed three briefcases fitted with ultrasonic humidifiers in a subway station, supposedly using "Recombinant Botulinus toxin," although it is doubtful that the device contained any toxic substances.

Endo focused his primary attention on *B. anthracis.* He developed new fermenters to produce the pathogen and built a rooftop sprayer to disseminate the agent when Asahara discovered that it would take 2 months to take delivery of a commercial system. In any case, the sprayer worked poorly, and one former cult member said that it would "spout like a whale" when in operation (Danzig *et al.* 2012). Even if they had acquired a lethal strain of *B. anthracis*, it is unlikely that the attack would have caused significant damage. Their agent slurry had a low concentration of *B. anthracis* spores, was highly viscous, disseminated poorly and was heavily contaminated with other microorganisms. Reports that Aum released the organism during the daytime suggest that the group had little understanding of agent dissemination.[13]

Aum did not have a systematic approach to acquiring biological agents. Although biological agents were readily available from culture collections, and could be found in many Japanese research laboratories, the group did not pursue such an obvious path. While it is not necessarily difficult to isolate *C. botulinum* from soil samples, the process is highly problematic given the significant variations in toxin production from one strain to another.[14] Some sources claim that Aum tried to obtain the Ebola virus; there is no evidence to suggest that any real effort was made to do so during a 1992 visit to Zaire (Danzig *et al.* 2012: 58; Leitenberg 1999: 153). There were no Ebola outbreaks in Zaire that year, and had not been since 1977.[15]

Aum's *B. anthracis* strain probably was stolen from a university laboratory. Surprisingly, microbiological analyses showed that Aum employed what appeared to be the 34F2 variant, a non-lethal strain used in Japan as a veterinary vaccine.[16] The failure of Aum to acquire a lethal strain of *B. anthracis* is often considered a reflection of Aum's technical ineptitude. While that is an accurate characterization of Aum's lack of biological competence, the actual story appears to be more complex. Danzig and his colleagues report, based on interviews with convicted Aum members, that the group knew that it had a vaccine strain. According to this account, Endo convinced Asahara that he could modify the organisms by reinserting the toxin-producing plasmids missing from the vaccine strain. Plasmids are small DNA segments separate from an organisms chromosomal DNA. The genetic code for *B. anthracis* toxins is found in such plasmids.

Aum's inability to modify *B. anthracis* is not surprising. The required techniques were cutting-edge science in the early 1990s, and only highly skilled researchers had the ability to employ them (Danzig *et al.* 2012). Thus, it would have been surprising if Endo had been successful. Sonia Ben Ouagrham-Gormley (2012) argues that this experience is revealing about Aum's organizational and leadership dysfunction, reflecting the group's fascination with advanced science and technology beyond the skills of its people to employ, its self-reliance fetish that led to preference for home grown solutions — even for highly complex hardware — over commercially available alternatives, and the role of inter-group politics in allowing well-placed people to pursue poorly conceived projects with no peer review and little supervision.

Invariably, the group abandoned scientifically-based practices when they failed to give the desired results. Initially, Aum acquired several thousand mice to test the potency of its "*C. botulinum.*"

In most cases, the mice survived exposure to the solution, suggesting that it had limited or no toxicity. However, some of the mice died, allowing Endo to claim that it in fact was toxic. In any case, Asahara eventually decided that it was morally impermissible to use mice as experimental animals, so the group stopped testing its biological or chemical agents before employing them.

No member of Aum was prosecuted specifically for the biological warfare activities (Sugishima 2003a, 2003b: 104). Japanese authorities chose to focus their prosecution on Aum's sarin attacks, so they never seriously investigated its biological warfare related activities. As a result, much remains unknown about what they tried to do and why.

Aum's experience supports the views of those who worry about the prospects for mass casualty bioterrorism, while its ineffectiveness supports the views of those who are dismissive of the threat (Smithson 2000). Leitenberg (1999) has argued that it shows the barriers to execution are significantly greater than often asserted. Despite its considerable resources and access to people with biological skills, Aum was unable to create a biological weapons capability. Some analysts point to the importance of tacit knowledge (Ouagrham-Gormley 2012; Ouagrham-Gormley and Vogel 2010). Tacit knowledge is the information critical to perform particular tasks that are not written down, either because they are assumed or because it is impractical to document every essential detail.

A slightly different, but complementary perspective, was offered by Richard Danzig and his colleagues. They argue that Aum's biological expertise has been overstated, and some of its failures can be attributed to highly ambitious technical goals that far exceeded the group's technical competence. More interestingly, Danzig also argues that many of the deficiencies were not unique to Aum, but reflected the dysfunction of any secretive research and development teams. This argument was extended by Ouagrham-Gormley (2012), who suggested that intangibles — "organization, program management, structural organization, and social environment" — are decisively important for both state and non-state bioweapons programs, basing her conclusions in part on Aum's experiences. This argument suggests that the impediments to terrorist creation of biological weapons capabilities are substantial. In contrast, Parachini (2005) pointed to examples of organizational learning within Aum, but also noted the failure of the group to provide its members with appropriate technical training once it decided to develop sophisticated weapons.

Amerithrax (2001)

On October 2, 2001, a Florida hospital admitted a seriously ill patient, Bob Stevens, a photograph editor for American Media, Incorporated. His doctor diagnosed inhalation anthrax, a highly unusual condition. As a result, Stevens was the first identified victim of the anthrax letter attack, what epidemiologists call the index case, although subsequent investigation determined that there were seven previous cases (all but one cutaneous). Subsequent investigation determined that between September 22 and November 14 a total of 22 people were infected, five of whom died, half with inhalational and half with cutaneous anthrax.[17]

The anthrax letter attack, called "Amerithrax" by the FBI, was the most deadly use of biological agents in modern U.S. history. On October 4, laboratory testing confirmed that Stevens had anthrax, but it took additional time to identify other cases and to determine that the cases were associated with letters containing *B. anthracis.* The letters were mailed in two groups, all from Trenton, New Jersey. The first batch, postmarked on September 18, probably consisted of five letters sent to media outlets, although only two were located: the New York City news offices of the three major network television networks (ABC, CBS and NBC), the editor of the *New York Post*, and the Florida offices of *The Sun*, a tabloid newspaper published by American Media. In all, 11 people were affected.[18]

Identifying these cases required an intensive effort by public health officials, monitoring hospital admissions in a large geographic area.[19] These efforts led to the identification of two inhalational anthrax cases, Stevens and another American Media employee, Ernesto Blanco, who handled the mail. Stevens was the only fatality. The victims mostly worked at the targeted media companies, except for two postal workers, and all appear to have come into contact with the suspect letters.[20]

Subsequent analysis of the powder in the two recovered letters suggests that it was contaminated with *B. subtilis*, an organism often used to simulate anthrax, and had a consistency like "Purina Dog Chow."[21] This may account for the relatively small number of people with inhalation anthrax. Testing in the AMI building revealed that the *B. anthracis* spores were concentrated on the first floor of the building. Perhaps significantly, there was little evidence to suggest much airborne spread. Only two people tested positive for *B. anthracis* exposure among the many AMI and postal service workers given nasal swabs in the weeks after Stevens' death: Blanco and another AMI employee who was asymptomatic.[22]

The two envelopes in the second mailing, post-marked October 9, were sent to the offices of Senators Thomas Daschle and Patrick Leahy. The Daschle letter was opened on October 15 by a staffer, who noticed a puff of dust and notified security. Ventilation systems were shut down within 45 minutes, which apparently limited contamination to only two floors of the building. Nasal swabs identified 28 people who had positive exposure to *B. anthracis*; around 625 people who had been in the affected area were given prophylactic antibiotic treatment. None of the exposed individuals developed antibodies to *B. anthracis* (Hsu *et al.* 2002).[23]

The most serious problems were faced by postal workers. Initially, it was believed that the spores in the letters would remain in the envelopes until opened, a perception reinforced by the careful taping of seams by the perpetrator. This turned out to be totally incorrect. The forces at work in mail handling facilities ensured that a considerable number of spores seeped out of the envelopes, contaminating adjacent letters and building air. Several postal workers got cutaneous anthrax from the first letters. More seriously, the second letters resulted in six cases of inhalation anthrax amongst postal workers, including two who died.[24]

Despite the intensive effort, public health investigators were unable to determine the routes of exposure for three people.[25] A 61-year-old hospital supply worker became symptomatic with inhalation anthrax on October 25 and died on the 30th. How she became ill was never determined.[26] Also puzzling was the death of a 94-year-old Connecticut resident, Otile Lundgren, although she probably was exposed to some cross-contaminated mail in Connecticut.[27]

The anthrax attack generated a substantial investigative response by the FBI. Microbial forensics were crucial to this effort, although it was only a small part of the overall investigation, which ultimately cost $100 million. The investigation exploited emerging scientific advances, including whole genome sequencing of *B. anthracis* DNA from a clinical specimen, techniques to determine when the organisms were grown, and geolocation studies based on the water in the organisms.[28]

The initial testing of isolates from Stevens demonstrated the presence of Ames strain. This was a rare type, first identified in 1981, and found only in a few biodefense laboratories (Guillemin 2011). As a result, the FBI quickly narrowed its focus to those laboratories, mostly located in the United States, which had access to the Ames strain. The FBI initially focused its attention on Steven Hatfill, a virologist who had worked at U.S. Army Medical Research Institute of Infections Diseases USAMRIID as a visiting researcher. Hatfill had a flamboyant past, including serving in the Rhodesian military at a time when the white regime was employing biological and chemical agents (allegedly including *B. anthracis*) in its campaign to suppress black nationalist movements (Martinez 2002). The FBI and some outside researchers assembled what seemed to them to be a plausible case against Hatfill.[29]

A laboratory researcher supporting the investigation was surprised to discover that colonies formed by *B. anthracis* often formed different shapes. Using new genomic techniques, scientists determined that there was a genetic basis for this variation. By testing a large number of different isolates from every laboratory known to possess Ames strain cultures, the FBI came to focus on a very specific lot, RMR-1029, which the FBI concluded was the source of the Amerithrax *B. anthracis*. A comprehensive assessment of everyone known to have had access to RMR-1029 isolates found that Hatfill never had access to them, forcing them to look at other suspects.[30] The FBI publicly conceded that Hatfill was not implicated and paid him $5.82 million in reparations to settle a lawsuit.[31]

Ultimately, the FBI concluded that the one person who had access, motive and ability to produce and send the anthrax letters was Bruce Ivins, a widely recognized anthrax expert (United States Department of Justice 2010).[32] The Bureau built what they considered to be a strong case against Ivins, although in truth it relied heavily on circumstantial evidence.

Ivins' motivation for mounting the attack was unclear. On the one hand, the Department suggested that the anthrax vaccine program at USAMRIID was failing, and that the attacks were intended to reinforce the need for it. On the other hand, considerable attention was given to Ivins' psychological state of mind, suggesting that they thought he was mentally ill. The Justice Department was preparing an indictment when Ivins committed suicide from an overdose of an over-the-counter drug.[33]

A review of Ivins' psychiatric history by an expert panel made clear the extent of Ivins' psychological dysfunction. The experts, and some of the psychologists who had treated Ivins, found the psychological evidence sufficiently compelling to believe that he was the likely perpetrator, as claimed by the investigators.[34] However, at least one of the experts subsequently wondered whether Ivins' alleged actions are best considered an act of terrorism, a form of extortion, or the result of a debilitating psychological pathology.[35]

There remains considerable skepticism regarding the quality and interpretation of the FBI's microbial forensics.[36] The U.S. General Accountability Office, an organization tasked with auditing the activities of Federal government agencies, expressed concerns about the techniques employed to compare RMR-1029 to other Ames strain samples.[37] This builds on the broader critique made by a National Academies of Science panel commissioned by the FBI to review the case's microbial forensics, which raised a questions about the definitiveness of the FBI's scientific results.[38]

These external assessments seem to challenge a central claim made by the investigators when proclaiming Ivins' guilt. While the microbial forensics showed that Ivins had access to a *B. anthracis* culture consistent with the organisms used in the attacks, it did not definitively demonstrate that those organisms had to have originated in RMR-1029. In other words, the supposedly definitive evidence that ruled out other suspects was not as ironclad as claimed.

It must be stressed that the weakness of the microbial forensics does not necessarily prove that Ivins was innocent. Other investigators, focusing on different evidence, found the case against Ivins to be compelling. Because Ivins committed suicide before he was arrested and tried, and because the case against him was circumstantial, it is possible that the evidence may not have been sufficiently compelling to result in a conviction, even if he were the guilty party. Nonetheless, attribution of the 2001 anthrax letter attack remains highly controversial.

Observations

These four incidents elaborated here offer insights into the prospects for bioterrorism, although caution is warranted. There have been relatively few instances of bioterrorism, and future cases may differ significantly from past ones. Nevertheless, there are suggestive features that can enrich assessments of the current and future threat.

First, bioterrorism can take many forms. It might be motivated by a desire to cause mass casualties, as was true for R.I.S.E. and Aum Shinrikyo. But, it is equally true that the perpetrators may not be focused on killing people at all. The Rajneeshees wanted to disrupt an election, so hoped that their attack would appear to be a natural outbreak. Similarly, if Bruce Ivins was the Amerithrax perpetrator, his motivations clearly did not fit the typical terrorism model. Thus, bioterrorism incidents may be motivated by idiosyncratic considerations.

Second, the skills required to undertake even rudimentary bioterrorism attacks are greater than often assumed. Certain technical and scientific skills are required to culture and disseminate microorganisms, even in crude ways. More sophisticated attacks, involving larger quantities of agent and more complex dissemination methods, as attempted by Aum Shinrikyo, may be beyond the capabilities of even well-organized and funded terrorist groups. While the problems may not be technically insurmountable, terrorist groups rarely engage in the required types of complex research and development, and some of the needed expertise may require access to difficult to obtain tacit knowledge.

Third, organizational factors may be critical. While simpler forms of bioterrorism are within the reach of lone actors, a group effort would be necessary to mount larger, more sophisticated attacks. As Aum Shinrikyo's experience suggests, this may create serious impediments to the solution of the many technical challenges facing a would-be bioterrorist. The complexities of undertaking such activities in a covert manner should not be underestimated.

Finally, the scarcity of bioterrorism incidents is telling. The Rajneeshees demonstrated that it should be possible to undertake crude bioterrorism attacks with little difficulty, and the Amerithrax case showed how disruptive they could become. Nonetheless, few terrorists have shown a serious interest in developing the capabilities to develop biological weapons.

References

Carus WS (2000a) 'R.I.S.E. (1972)' in JB Tucker (Ed.) *Toxic Terror: Assessing Terrorist Use of Chemical and Biological Weapons.* Cambridge, Massachusetts: MIT Press.

Carus WS (2000b) 'The Rajneeshees (1984)' in JB Tucker (Ed.) *Toxic Terror: Assessing Terrorist Use of Chemical and Biological Weapons.* Cambridge, Massachusetts: MIT Press.

Carus WS (2001) *Bioterrorism and Biocrimes: The Illicit Use of Biological Agents Since 1900.* February 2001 Revision. Washington, DC: Center for Counterproliferation Research, National Defense University.

Danzig R, Sageman M, Leighton T *et al.* (2012) *Aum Shinrikyo: Insights into How Terrorists Develop Biological and Chemical Weapons*, 2nd Ed. Washington, DC: Center for a New American Security.

Goldman MS (2005) 'When leaders dissolve: Considering controversy and stagnation in the Osho Rajneesh movement' in JR Lewis and

JA Petersen (Eds.) *Controversial New Religions.* New York: Oxford University Press.

Gordon JS (1987) *The Golden Guru: The Strange Journey of Bhagwan Shree Rajneesh.* Lexington, Massachusetts; New York, NY: S. Greene Press.

Guillemin J (2011) *American Anthrax: Fear, Crime and the Investigation of the Nation's Deadliest Bioterror Attack,* 1st Ed. New York: Times Books.

Hsu VP, Lukacs SL, Handzel T *et al.* (2002) 'The Public Health Response and Epidemiologic Investigation Related to the Opening of a Bacillus Anthracis-Containing Envelope, Capitol Hill, Washington, D.C.' *Emerging Infectious Diseases* Vol. 8(10): 1039–1043.

Kaplan DE (2000) 'Aum Shinrikyo (1995)' in JB Tucker (Ed.) *Toxic Terror: Assessing Terrorist Use of Chemical and Biological Weapons.* Cambridge, Massachusetts: MIT Press.

Leitenberg M (1999) 'Aum Shinrikyo's Efforts to Produce Biological Weapons: A Case Study in the Serial Propagation of Misinformation,' *Terrorism & Political Violence* Vol. 11(4): 149–158.

Martinez I (2002) 'The History of the Use of Bacteriological and Chemical Agents During Zimbabwe's Liberation War of 1965–80 by Rhodesian Forces,' *Third World Quarterly* Vol. 23(6): 1159–1179.

Miller J, Engelberg S and Broad WJ (2001) *Germs: Biological Weapons and America's Secret War.* New York: Simon & Schuster.

Ouagrham-Gormley SB (2012) 'Barriers to Bioweapons: Intangible Obstacles to Proliferation,' *International Security* Vol. 36(4): 80–114.

Ouagrham-Gormley SB and Vogel KM (2010) 'The Social Context Shaping Bioweapons (Non)Proliferation,' *Biosecurity and Bioterrorism: Biodefense Strategy, Practice, and Science* Vol. 8(1): 9–24.

Parachini JV (2005) 'Aum Shinrikyo' in B Jackson (Ed.) *Aptitude for Destruction.* Santa Monica, California: RAND.

Smithson AE (2000) 'Rethinking the lessons of Tokyo,' in AE Smithson and L-A Levy (Eds.) *Ataxia: The Chemical and Biological Terrorism Threat and the U.S. Response.* Washington, DC: Henry L. Stimson Center See http://www.loc.gov/catdir/toc/fy0711/2002727310.html.

Strelley K and San Souci RD (1987) *The Ultimate Game: The Rise and Fall of Bhagwan Shree Rajneesh.* San Francisco: Harper & Row.

Sugishima M (2003a) 'Aum Shinrikyo and the Japanese law on bioterrorism,' *Prehospital and Disaster Medicine* Vol. 18(3): 179–183.

Sugishima M (2003b) 'Biocrimes in Japan' in M Sugishima (Ed.) *A comprehensive Study on Bioterrorism (English part).* Mizuho City, Japan: Legal Research Institute, Asahi University.

The case against Ivins is described in detail in U.S. Department of Justice (2010). U.S. Department of Justice (2010) *Amerithrax Investigative Summary: Released Pursuant to the Freedom of Information Act.* Washington, DC. See http://www.justice.gov/archive/amerithrax/docs/amx-investigative-summary.pdf.

Tucker JB and Sands A (1999) 'An unlikely threat,' *Bulletin of the Atomic Scientists* Vol. 55(4): 46–52.

Urban HB (2005) 'Osho, from sex guru to guru of the rich: The spiritual logic of late capitalism' in TA Forsthoefel and CA Humes (Eds.) *Gurus in America.* Albany, NY: State University of New York Press.

Webber B (1990) *Rajneeshpuram: Who Were Its People? An Oregon Documentary.* Medford, Oregon: Webb Research Group.

Notes

[1] This account of R.I.S.E.'s activities draws heavily on primary sources, including police reports, grand jury and courtroom testimony, and other material in the possession of the Cook County State's Attorney's Office. These documents are described in detail in Carus (2000a).

[2] Koziol R, "Tighten Water Plant Guard After Poison Scare Arrests", *Chicago Tribune*, January 19, 1972.

[3] Koziol 1972, as per note 2.

[4] Arrest Report and other Documents, Chicago Police Department (1983).

[5] Ulrich R, "Sheela, others quit commune", *Oregonian*, September 17, 1985.

[6] This account draws primarily from two sources: Carus (2000b) and Török TJ, Tauxe RV, Wise RP *et al.* (1997) 'A large community outbreak of salmonellosis caused by intentional contamination of restaurant salad bars', *JAMA: The Journal of the American Medical Association* Vol. 278(5): 389–395. Original documents used by Carus (2000b) included law enforcement reports, transcripts of interrogations, and courtroom testimony. Some of the most important of these are available at Rajneesh document archive (n.d.) *Oregon Live*, http://www.oregonlive.com/rajneesh/index.ssf/documents.html (accessed July 2, 2015).

[7] Senior J and Laatz J, "Texas dealer buys Rolls-Royces," *Oregonian*, Portland, Oregon, November 27, 1985.

[8] Török *et al.* 1997, as per note 6.

[9] Török *et al.* 1997, as per note 6.

[10] While much has been written about Aum Shinrikyo, the best single account of its biological and chemical warfare programs is Danzig *et al.* (2012). In addition to drawing on earlier studies, it benefits from interviews with former members involved in the group's illicit activities and other material not previously available. Other studies that contributed significantly to this account include (Leitenberg 1999; Smithson 2000; WuDunn S, Miller J and Broad WJ, "How Japan Germ Terror Alerted World," *New York Times*, May 26, 1998.)

[11] Endo S, Shinagawa M, Sato G *et al.* (1986) "MDBK nuclear factor-binding site of various serotypes of adenovirus DNA," *Microbiology and Immunology* Vol. 30(10): 1011–1022.

[12] WuDunn *et al.* 1998, as per note 10.

[13] Takahashi H, Keim P, Kaufmann AF *et al.* (2004) 'Bacillus Anthracis Incident, Kameido, Tokyo, 1993,' *Emerging Infectious Diseases* Vol. 10(1): 117–120.

[14] Montecucco C and Rasotto MB (2015) 'On Botulinum Neurotoxin Variability,' *mBio* Vol. 6(1); See. http://www.ncbi.nlm.nih.gov/pmc/articles/PMC4313909/ (accessed April 24, 2015).

[15] CDC (2015) *Outbreaks Chronology: Ebola Virus Disease*, http://www.cdc.gov/vhf/ebola/outbreaks/history/chronology.html (accessed April 24, 2015).

[16] Keim P, Smith KL, Keys C *et al.* (2001) 'Molecular Investigation of the Aum Shinrikyo Anthrax Release in Kameido, Japan,' *Journal of Clinical Microbiology* Vol. 39(12): 4566–4567.

[17] It is likely that more has been written about this case than all other incidents of biological terrorism or crime combined, including numerous book-length treatments: Coen B and Nadler ED (2009) *Dead Silence: Fear and Terror on the Anthrax Trail.* Berkeley, California: Counterpoint; Cole LA (2009) *The Anthrax Letters: A Leading Expert on Bioterrorism Explains the Science Behind the Anthrax Attacks.* New York: Skyhorse Publishing; Graysmith R (2003) *Amerithrax: The Hunt for the Anthrax Killer.* New York: Berkley Books; Guillemin 2011; Thompson MW (2003) *The Killer Strain: Anthrax and a Government Exposed.* New York: HarperCollins; Willman D (2011) *The Mirage Man: Bruce Ivins, the Anthrax Attacks, and America's Rush to War.* New York, NY: Bantam Books. The account here draws mainly from Guillemin's book, supplemented by the many numerous scientific and medical articles written about the case. Two important epidemiological overviews are: Jernigan *et al.* (2002) and Sanderson *et al.* (2004). The AMI cases were described in Bush *et al.* (2001) and Traeger *et al.* (2002).

[18] Jernigan DB, Raghunathan PL, Bell BP *et al.* (2002) 'Investigation of Bioterrorism-Related Anthrax, United States, 2001: Epidemiologic Findings,' *Emerging Infectious Diseases* Vol. 8(10): 1019–1028.

[19] Tan CG, Sandhu HS, Crawford DC *et al.* (2002) 'Surveillance for Anthrax Cases Associated with Contaminated Letters, New Jersey, Delaware, and Pennsylvania, 2001,' *Emerging Infectious Diseases* Vol. 8(10): 1073–1077.

[20] Bush LM, Abrams BH, Beall A *et al.* (2001) 'Index Case of Fatal Inhalational Anthrax Due to Bioterrorism in the United States,' *New England Journal of Medicine* Vol. 345(22): 1607–1610; Jernigan *et al.* 2002, as per note 18; Traeger MS, Wiersma ST, Rosenstein NE *et al.* (2002) 'First Case of Bioterrorism-Related Inhalational Anthrax in the United States, Palm Beach County, Florida, 2001,' *Emerging Infectious Diseases* Vol. 8(10): 1029–1034.

[21] Gordon G (2011) 'Was FBI too Quick to Judge Anthrax Suspect the Killer?' *McClatchy DC.* See http://www.mcclatchydc.com/2011/04/20/112520/was-fbi-too-quick-to-judge-anthrax.html (accessed May 7, 2015); The White House Regular Briefing (2001) *Federal News Service, Lexis/Nexis*, October 25.

[22] Traeger *et al.* 2002, as per note 20.

[23] Dewan PK, Fry AM, Laserson K, *et al.* (2002) 'Inhalational Anthrax Outbreak Among Postal Workers, Washington, D.C., 2001,' *Emerging Infectious Diseases* Vol. 8(10): 1066–1072; Dull PM, Wilson KE, Kournikakis B *et al.* (2002) 'Bacillus Anthracis Aerosolization Associated with a Contaminated Mail Sorting Machine,' *Emerging Infectious Diseases* Vol. 8(10): 1044–1047; Jernigan *et al.* 2002, as per note 18; Sanderson WT, Stoddard RR, Echt AS *et al.* (2004) 'Bacillus Anthracis Contamination and Inhalational Anthrax in a Mail Processing and Distribution Center,' *Journal of Applied Microbiology* Vol. 96(5): 1048–1056.

[24] Jernigan *et al.*, 2002, as per note 18, p. 1024.

[25] Holtz TH, Ackelsberg J, Kool JL *et al.* (2003) 'Isolated Case of Bioterrorism-Related Inhalational Anthrax, New York City, 2001,' *Emerging Infectious Diseases* Vol. 9(6): 689–696; Mina B, Dym JP, Kuepper F *et al.* (2002) 'Fatal Inhalational Anthrax with Unknown Source of Exposure in a 61-year-old Woman in New York City,' *JAMA* Vol. 287(7): 858–862.

[26] Barakat LA, Quentzel HL, Jernigan JA *et al.* (2002) 'Fatal Inhalational Anthrax in a 94-year-old Connecticut Woman,' *JAMA* Vol. 287(7): 863–868; Griffith KS, Mead P, Armstrong GL *et al.* (2003) 'Bioterrorism-Related Inhalational Anthrax in an Elderly Woman, Connecticut, 2001,' *Emerging Infectious Diseases* Vol. 9(6): 681–688.

[27] Kreuzer-Martin HW and Jarman KH (2007) 'Stable Isotope Ratios and Forensic Analysis of Microorganisms,' *Applied and Environmental Microbiology* Vol. 73(12): 3896–3908.

[28] Foster D (2003) 'The Message in the Anthrax,' *Vanity Fair.*

[29] Freed D (2010) 'The Wrong Man,' *The Atlantic Monthly.*

[30] U.S. Department of Justice, 2010, as per note 30.

[31] U.S. Department of Justice, 2010, as per note 30.

[32] Expert Behavioral Analysis Panel (2011) *The Amerithrax Case: Report of the Expert Behavioral Analysis Panel.* Vienna, Virginia: Research Strategies Network.

[33] Schouten R (2010) 'Terrorism and the Behavioral Sciences,' *Harvard Review of Psychiatry* Vol. 18(6): 369–378.

[34] Bhattacharjee Y and Enserink M (2008) 'FBI discusses microbial forensics — but key questions remain unanswered,' *Science* Vol. 321(5892): 1026–1027.

[35] General Accountability Office (2014) *Anthrax: Agency Approaches to Validation and Statistical Analyses Could be Improved.* Washington, DC: U.S. General Accountability Office. See http://www.gao.gov/products/GAO-15-80 (accessed 6 May 2015).

[36] Committee on Review of the Scientific Approaches Used during the FBI's Investigation of the 2001 Bacillus Anthracis Mailings (2011) *Review of the Scientific Approaches Used During the FBI's Investigation of the 2001 Anthrax Letters.* Washington, DC: National Academies Press. See http://www.nap.edu/catalog/13098/review-of-the-scientific-approaches-used-during-the-fbis-investigation-of-the-2001-anthrax-letters (accessed February 19, 2015).

Point of View

Inside the Mind of a Bioterrorist

Toby Ewin

The anthrax letters sent in autumn 2001 arguably represent the highest-impact small-scale terrorist attack ever mounted, and the perpetrator's identity is even now controversial. This essay considers what "Amerithrax," as it became know, and other significant cases tell us about terrorist innovation: What makes terrorists choose, or avoid, the use of chemical, biological, radiological and nuclear (CBRN) materials as weapons.

Four fundamental aspects of CBRN terrorism underlie this analysis. First, compared to most other forms of terrorism, there are relatively few important data points (cases of significant terrorist interest in one or more CBRN ideas); so recognizing and appropriately interpreting them is important. Several of these data points are contested, or uncertain, complicating interpretation.

Second, CBRN terrorism often manifests itself in amateurish and small-scale ways. Many aspirations are never fulfilled, and some would-be perpetrators are "lone wolf" individuals, or groups that are not fundamentally terrorist, e.g., most Aum or Rajneeshee members were not involved in terrorism (see this chapter). Yet despite the paucity of *successful* CBRN terrorist attacks, the threat should not be dismissed. There has been, and apparently continues to be, serious terrorist interest.

Third, we are not dealing with a static object to be "uncovered" like an archaeological find, but an evolving threat.

Fourth, societies' or individual targets' vulnerability alone is of limited value in measuring a threat or determining a proportionate response: There are uncountable potential vulnerability scenarios. We must weigh terrorists' intent and capability, too.

Aspects of the Amerithrax case

After a painstaking and lengthy investigation, the FBI identified the Amerithrax spores as having derived from a specific batch of the Ames strain — "RMR-1029" — that had been created and maintained by Dr Bruce Ivins, a microbiologist at the U.S. Army Medical Research Institute of Infectious Diseases (USAMRIID) at Fort Detrick, Maryland.

The investigation then focused on those who had access to RMR-1029, and the FBI came to believe that Ivins had sent the letters for a number of reasons: He had uncharacteristically worked late and alone in the lab where RMR-1029 was stored, just before the letters must have been sent; he admitted being sole custodian of RMR-1029; he had significant psychological problems including bipolar depression and possible split personality; he had a motive — he apparently feared his anthrax work would be discontinued; he had a history of sending mail from distant post offices under pseudonyms; he sometimes provided inaccurate information during the investigation; he could not account for 200 grams of anthrax for which he was responsible; the FBI judged that he was among the few anthrax researchers with sufficient knowledge and ability to create the "highly purified" spores used; and other people with access to RMR-1029 were ruled out (Majidi 2013; Guillemin 2011).

> There is no absolute evidence that directly connects [him] to the mailings. His DNA was not on any evidence collected, no witness observed him producing the anthrax … used in the attack … nevertheless, all other evidence and investigative results point to him as the perpetrator.
>
> (Majidi 2013: 101)

Ivins committed suicide in July 2008; he was never brought to trial and the case against him was never tested in court.

Despite his psychological problems and history of

instability, Ivins had only been barred from "high-containment" research in 2007. In July 2009, Chief Judge Royce Lambert of the U.S. District Court for the District of Colombia authorized a report from an Expert Behavioral Analysis Panel.[1] The Panel's review of sealed psychiatric records supported the Department of Justice's view that Ivins was behind the anthrax letters. In their own words, he was "psychologically disposed to undertake the mailings; his behavioral history demonstrated his potential for carrying them out; and he had the motivation and the means." Some of his colleagues argued that USAMRIID lacked the sophisticated equipment capable of producing the spores within the short time in which the evidence suggests they were produced; but Ivins himself never argued this, "in fact, he named many of his colleagues … as possible anthrax mailers."

Ivins had a long history of "psychological disturbance and diagnosable mental illness at the time he began working for USAMRIID in 1980 that would have disqualified him from a SECRET level security clearance had they been known." He would not then have had access to anthrax. Relevant information was readily available in medical records, had it only been sought. But those investigating Ivins' background "did not pursue inconsistencies in [his] reporting … [and] did not request and review available medical records … [nor] follow up incomplete responses by treating clinicians … [nor] clarify information through direct interview." Meanwhile, many of the mental health professionals who treated Ivins before 2001 did not know he had a security clearance. Failures in supervision, documentation and communication allowed him to avoid scrutiny before and after 2001. His long service, "combined with respect for him as a scientist, appears to have led to a degree of complacency about him."

Most colleagues and acquaintances saw Ivins as eccentric but benign. The Panel thought him devious and manipulative. He admitted some mental health issues to health professionals and his employer, but omitted or distorted others. He had e.g., stalked at least two women, and apparently sabotaged a colleague's research. Key themes in his motivation were judged to include revenge (retribution against perceived enemies, including senators who had incurred his wrath), a desperate need for personal validation, career preservation and professional redemption (showing that anthrax was a threat and that his vaccine was needed to protect the public). His motivation "guided him not only in making the attacks but in choosing his targets and shaping his methods." His reported behaviors suggested, to the Panel, a range of psychological disorders, including "… identity disturbance … recurrent suicidal behaviour … inappropriate, intense anger or difficulty controlling anger; and [words redacted]. He also meets the criteria for diagnosis of Paranoid Personality Disorder…." But even all these diagnoses did not give a full picture of Ivins' personality.

Given his suicide, no hypothesis about Ivins' motivation is provable. Majidi credibly argues that the perpetrator did not initially mean to kill, but to alarm and to make the U.S. government more aware of the risks of anthrax (Majidi 2013); thus the motivation may have included patriotism and a sense of group loyalty towards scientists doing anthrax research (Guillemin 2011). On the other hand, the first victim's death was reported before the final two letters were sent. (The case also generated some red herrings that proved hard to correct; for instance that the anthrax had been "weapons-grade" (Majidi 2013; Guillemin 2011), or that it had been produced using additives (Cole 2009).)

There is no certainty as to why the letters stopped. Had all the available anthrax been used, and no more could be obtained or used without an unacceptable risk of detection or capture? Was the perpetrator mortified by the fact that people were killed who generally had no link with where the letters had been sent? Or was he content that the desired effect had been, or would shortly be, achieved?

As occasional anthrax infections need not be malicious, it was not immediately apparent that the first Amerithrax casualty was a victim of terrorism (Guillemin 2011; Cole 2009).[2] The first people to deal with the challenge were healthcare professionals, not law enforcement. It was the same with the Rajneesh' *Salmonella*, and may well be the case for a future incident. One of the challenges is then that sometimes, quite reasonably, the different concerns and priorities of healthcare and law enforcement may conflict.

A wide range of U.S. departments and agencies were involved in the Amerithrax case including the Departments of Justice, Health and Human Services, Defense, Energy, State, the Centers for Disease Control and the CIA. This is a likely feature of any major CBRN terrorism case. For instance, the U.K.'s national CBRN strategy identified a comparable variety of government bodies as involved in identifying or countering the threat: the Cabinet Office, intelligence and security agencies, Home Office, Ministry of Defense (and through it the armed forces and defense scientists), Foreign and Commonwealth Office, Ministry of Justice, devolved administrations, Departments for Business Innovation and Skills, Communities and Local Government, Transport, Energy and Climate Change, Health, Environment Food and Rural Affairs; plus the Environment Agency, Food Standards Agency and Government Decontamination Service — not to mention law enforcement, and organizations and individuals outside government.[3]

Amerithrax showed that one person, *if* suitably skilled and with access to appropriate laboratory resources and materials, could have a significant bioterrorist impact, even with only a small quantity of material. But the lack of subsequent emulation also suggests that the particular combination of skill, access to materials and laboratory equipment, and desire to cause either mass casualties or great fear, is rare (Tucker 2000). While the case revealed how hard it might be to identify an individual perpetrator, it was not so hard to identify the *type* of person: A capable scientist with access to materials and laboratory equipment. While some doubted whether Ivins acted alone, and some of Ivins' colleagues apparently believed that someone else must have been responsible, the perpetrator would in any case have needed to access the material in RMR-1029; and the FBI believe only Ivins had both means and opportunity.

Terrorist innovation — and predicting it

... while the individual man is an insoluble puzzle, in the aggregate he becomes a mathematical certainty. *You can, for example, never foretell what any one man will do*, but you can say with precision what an average number will be up to ... So says the statistician.

Sherlock Holmes,
in Doyle's (1890)
The Sign of the Four
(emphasis added)

CBRN terrorism, like weapon of mass destruction (WMD) in general, involves a "dread factor" of invisible and unpleasant lethality. It has been the subject of much fictional coverage for decades and, occasionally alarmist, non-fiction literature more recently. Those who want can construct innumerable apparently-plausible scenarios, with individuals or small groups supposedly threatening massive impacts. There is accessible information about terrorist interest in CBRN, about cases of criminal activity (such as product tampering), and about accidents (e.g., fires at chemical plants). Some states which had WMD programs, and/or which poisoned individual dissidents and émigrés, have collapsed, so their expertise and materials might have come onto the market. Why has all this not had more impact on terrorists? Do some terrorists simply not notice, or do they "screen out," such data? The nature of terrorist innovation has been studied much less than other terrorism topics, though there is now some excellent work available (Ranstorp and Normark 2015; Ackerman 2014; Dolnik 2007).

Whatever the radicalism of their politics or theology, terrorists are often seen as conservative and reactive in their weapons technology; and when they do innovate, it is often incremental rather than mould-breaking. But some groups have also readily adopted new technologies outside the realm of weapons, e.g., various Islamist groups' effective use of the

Internet for communications and propaganda. Over a decade ago, a study of 28 case histories by the Monterey Institute suggested that the leadership's interest and mindset were among the most important factors in a group choosing to pursue CBRN (Parachini 2003). And at the time of their most significant known CBRN activity, groups such as Aum Shinrikyo, al-Qaeda, and the Tamil Tigers all operated in relatively "permissive" environments, where they could explore CBRN with a low risk of discovery and interruption by the state in which they were based (Parachini 2003).

Except for Aum and the Rajneeshees, we lack a clear case of (by terrorist standards) mass-casualty CBRN terrorism. The other cases we have — smaller incidents or plans — necessarily get used as what Gary Ackerman calls "proxy data." This sort of data must be used with caution: Even detailed case studies are hampered by "the opacity of the terrorist decision-making process ... subsequent interviews with protagonists can be marred by doubts about the subjects' veracity" (Ackerman 2009: 18). The most serious CBRN cases are obviously a sort of "outlier" because of their rarity, and the likely requirement for a perpetrator to have an unusual amount of expertise, time, money and a safe space for research and development. But arguably all CBRN cases are outliers, as they clearly involve atypical judgements and actions. We must therefore be circumspect in extrapolating from them.

The available information suggests that most terrorists have not been interested in CBRN (see this chapter). This should be no surprise: CBRN is much harder than firearms and explosives, and not every terrorist can even make even those work. For all its wealth and resources, and success in making sarin, Aum's biological work was so flawed that it worked with a vaccine rather than a lethal anthrax strain. Rolf Larssen observed that al-Qaeda "probably learned in trying to weaponize anthrax, [that] biological pathogens may seem simple enough to produce, but such weapons are not easy to bottle up and control" (Mowatt-Larssen 2010: 7). Those wishing to avoid collateral casualties are unlikely to want a relatively indiscriminate weapon. Those whose existing weapons deliver sufficient impact to achieve their desired political and other effects, do not need to explore CBRN.[4] And many CBRN weapons only moderately increase destructive power compared with a kinetic attack.[5]

CBRN, like any novel weapon, requires users to divert scarce human and financial resources to develop or otherwise acquire it. It could also prompt practical or moral qualms, such as: Whether it is compatible with the terrorists' skills; will it work; might it harm the terrorists themselves; will it increase the risk of being caught; is it compatible with a group's, or its members' and supporters', values? The "dread factor" of CBRN might be an attraction, but how much is this worth to a group such as Islamic State — "a slave-holding gangster regime that practises mass rape as an instrument of policy as well as pleasure and which is held back from genocide only by its lack of power?"[6]

There are a number of cases where a terrorist used a toxic material, but only once. For instance, in 1990 the Tamil Tigers mounted a chlorine gas attack on a Sri Lankan army base, though it was not entirely successful and some chlorine blew back over the Tigers themselves (Hoffman 2000). The Tigers' leader, Vellupillai Prabhakaran, apparently liked films and books about military, terrorist and criminal exploits, from which he took ideas for innovative attacks. But after this single incident there were no more confirmed chemical attacks. In another example, the Kurdistan Workers' Party (PKK) poisoned the drinking water supply of a Turkish air force compound in 1992 with lethal quantities of cyanide, but the contamination was detected before anyone was poisoned, and there is no record of the group seeking to mount such an attack again (Gurr and Cole 2002).

Much has been written about al-Qaeda, its descendants and potential use of CBRN (see for instance Mowatt-Larssen 2010; Stenersen 2008). A useful way to categorize terrorist CBRN is to divide them into large- and small-scale, rather than into scientific categories. On CBRN innovation, significant data points include:

- Correspondence attributed to Bin Laden's then deputy, Aiman al-Zawahiri, found in Afghanistan after the U.S. invasion — "Despite their extreme danger, we only became aware of them [from the context, chemical and biological weapons] when the enemy drew our attention to them by repeatedly expressing concerns that they can be produced simply with easily available materials" (Cullison 2004). This risk has been highlighted by Leitenberg (2007) among others: What if well-publicized concern increases the very threat it was intended to deter?
- Al Qaida's pre-9/11 contact with several officials who had worked in Pakistan's nuclear program; its recruitment of a Pakistani government microbiologist to work on anthrax, and its related attempt to set up a laboratory in Afghanistan (Mowatt-Larrsen 2010). The microbiologist visited the U.K. on al-Qaeda's behalf, seeking material and equipment, though his attempts were frustrated. This type of research was kept secret even within al-Qaeda.
- al-Qaeda apparently considered U.S. nuclear sites as potential targets for the 9/11 attacks, but decided such targets would be too hard, or, according to some senior members, because "things might get out of control," presumably meaning that it might provoke more retaliation than al-Qaeda wanted to handle (Stenersen 2008: 34; see also Fouda and Fielding 2003: 114).
- By one account, the late 1990s saw a reported difference of opinion among al-Qaeda leaders on the need to pursue WMD. Some were concerned about U.S. retaliation; others argued WMD were necessary. Some felt primitive WMD would create fear and earn credibility and prestige (Stenersen 2008).
- Correspondence found at Bin Laden's final hiding place in Abbottabad included a letter apparently written by someone of Egyptian origin to an

Islamic legal scholar, seeking guidance on the use of chlorine gas in Iraq — though the concern was not about theological or ethical justification, but about whether collateral casualties might damage public support.[7]

- Instructions about how to make and use a poison gas dispersal device, the Mobtakar, included warning about locations where (the designer thought) it would or would not be wise to try to deploy it. Suggested targets included brothels, bars, restaurants, theaters, banks, shopping malls, cinemas, synagogues, gyms, dancing halls, casinos, trains, churches, schools, government offices and hospitals; but use in airports was discouraged lest checkpoints or dogs detect it (Salama 2006).

It seems increasingly clear that al-Qaeda's own CBRN research and development in Afghanistan was at least temporarily disrupted by military action after 9/11, and the related capture of key personnel. But in autumn 2006, the then leader of al-Qaeda in Iraq issued a call for scientists from various fields, including unconventional weapons, to join him, as U.S. bases in Iraq were ideal for "biological and so-called dirty bombs" (Stenersen 2008: 42). And, addressing the Australia Group in June 2015, Australia's foreign minister said "the use of chlorine by [Islamic State], and its recruitment of highly technically trained professionals, including from the West, have revealed far more serious efforts in chemical weapons development."[8] The idea of recruiting scientists evidently did not end with al-Qaeda and Aum.

It remains hard to predict whether and how a given terrorist or group might explore a CBRN topic. That is because, in the early stages of an individual's or group's development as a terrorist entity, it is unlikely that law enforcement or intelligence agencies, or academic researchers, will have sufficient data about them to be able to make an informed judgement whether they will develop in a particular way. By the time enough information is available, the question may have begun to answer itself.

Weather forecasting is a useful analogy for our understanding of CBRN innovation, or indeed for the process of "radicalization" into terrorism. The advent of computing and consequent ability to process more data meant weather prediction improved. But even improved models and computing do not permit us to predict in detail, with accuracy, a significant distance in advance. We can look *in hindsight*, working out how a past situation developed. We can predict "actuarially," so we know roughly when and in what areas dangerous phenomena occur. Likewise in terrorism, we can examine a past incident and sometimes discover enough to make relatively informed judgements about why people turned to "the Dark Side", or why they chose what weapons they did. We may get better at the actuarial, the "how often" and "how serious," helping policymakers — politicians and senior officials — get a feel for the general trends of an issue's "climate." But it does not identify exactly *which* person will turn into a terrorist, or whether a particular group will pursue a CBRN idea, the sort of detailed prediction that would help law enforcement agencies. There are simply too many variables, and the relationship between these multiple variables is *itself* a variable.

References

Ackerman G (2014) *More Bang for the Buck: Examining the Determinants of Terrorist Adoption of New Weapons Technologies.* Doctoral thesis, King's College London.

Ackerman G (2009) 'Defining knowledge gaps within CBRN terrorism research' in M Ranstorp, and M Normark (Eds.) *Unconventional Weapons and International Terrorism: Challenges and New Approaches.* London: Routledge.

Cole LA (2009) *The Anthrax Letters: A Bioterrorism Expert Investigates the Attacks that Shocked America.* New York: Skyhorse Publishing.

Cullison A (2004) 'Inside al-Qaeda's hard drive,' *The Atlantic*, September.

Dolnik A (2007) *Understanding Terrorist Innovation: Technology, Tactics and Global Trends.* London: Routledge.

Fouda Y and Fielding N (2003) *Masterminds of Terror.* Edinburgh: Mainstream Publishing.

Guillemin J (2011) *American Anthrax: Fear, Crime and the Investigation of the Nation's Deadliest*

Bioterror Attack. New York: Times Books.

Gurr N and Cole B (2002) *The New Face of Terrorism: Threats from Weapons of Mass Destruction*. London: I B Tauris.

Hoffman B (2000) 'New and continuing forms of terrorism and the debate over future terrorist use of CBRN weapons,' *Centre de recherche des Menaces Criminelles Contemporaines*, http://60gp.ovh.net/~drmcc/IMG/pdf/41b392ea6326b.pdf (accessed September 2, 2015).

Leitenberg M (2007) 'Evolution of the current threat,' in A Wenger and R Wollenmann (Eds.) *Bioterrorism: Understanding a Complex Threat*. London: Lynne Reinner Publishers.

Majidi V (2013) *A Spore on the Grassy Knoll: An Insider's Account of the 2001 Anthrax Mailings*. CreateSpace Independent Publishing Platform.

Mowatt-Larssen R (2010) *Al Qaeda Weapons of Mass Destruction Threat: Hype or Reality?* Belfer Center for Science and International Affairs paper, http://belfercenter.ksg.harvard.edu/publication/19852/al_qaeda_weapons_of_mass_destruction_threat.html (accessed September 2, 2015).

Parachini J (2003) 'Putting WMD terrorism into perspective,' *Washington Quarterly* Vol. 26: 4.

Ranstorp M and Normark M (Eds.) (2015) *Understanding Terrorism Innovation and Learning: Al Qaeda and Beyond*. London: Routledge.

Salama S (2006) 'Special Report: Manual for producing chemical weapon to be used in New York subway plot available on al-Qaeda websites since late 2005,' Monterey Institute, Center for Nonproliferation Studies, http://cns.miis.edu/other/salama_060720.htm (accessed September 2, 2015).

Stenersen A (2008) *Al-Qaida's Quest for Weapons of Mass Destruction: The History Behind the Hype*. Saarbrücken: VDM.

Tucker JB (Ed.) (2000) *Toxic Terror: Assessing Terrorist Use of Chemical and Biological Weapons*. Cambridge Massachusetts: MIT Press.

Notes

1 Expert Behavioral Analysis Panel (2011) *The Amerithrax Case: Report of the Expert Behavioral Analysis Panel*. Vienna, Virginia: Research Strategies Network.

2 U.S. Department of Justice (2010) *Amerithrax Investigative Summary: Released Pursuant to the Freedom of Information Act*. Washington, DC. See http://www.justice.gov/archive/amerithrax/docs/amx-investigative-summary.pdf (accessed September 2, 2015).

[3] *The United Kingdom's Strategy for Countering Chemical, Biological, Radiological and Nuclear (CBRN) Terrorism*, 2010.

[4] A FARC commander is quoted saying "What is the point of using acid? We use the bombs to destroy the buildings, as we do not have artillery or tanks. Acid is of no use against concrete or bricks" (Parachini 2003: 45).

[5] For instance, releasing chlorine gas by destroying a train carrying it has potential to kill thousands, but a dirty bomb's physical impact might be less than from conventional high explosive (Fishman B and Forest J (2009) 'WMD and the four dimensions of Al Qaida,' in M Ranstorp and M Normark (Eds.) *Unconventional Weapons and International Terrorism: Challenges and New Approaches*. London: Routledge.

[6] *The Guardian* 16 June 2015, http://www.theguardian.com/commentisfree/2015/jun/16/guardian-view-on-fighting-terror-we-must-win-war-for-young-imaginations (accessed September 2, 2015).

[7] Don Rassler *et al.* (2012) *Letters from Abbottabad: Bin Ladin sidelined?* Item SOCOM-2012-0000011 dated March 28, 2007. Combating Terrorism Center, http://www.ctc.usma.edu/posts/letters-from-abbottabad-bin-ladin-sidelined (accessed September 2, 2015).

[8] 'Islamic State likely has "expertise to build chemical weapons," says Julie Bishop' *The Guardian*, June 6, 2015. http://www.theguardian.com/australia-news/2015/jun/06/islamic-state-has-expertise-to-build-chemical-weapons-says-julie-bishop (accessed September 2, 2015).

Chapter 8

Aftershocks of the 2001 Anthrax Attacks

Kathleen M. Vogel

Introduction

Exactly one week after the September 11, 2001 attacks, five envelopes containing anthrax bacteria were sent via mail to ABC News, CBS News, NBC News and the New York Post in New York City, and the American Media International (AMI) in Boca Raton, Florida (Guillemin 2011) (see Chapter 7). On October 4, Robert Stevens, a photo editor at AMI was hospitalized and subsequently died of inhalational anthrax after being exposed to one of these letters. This initial anthrax death sent shock waves across the United States, as intelligence analysts, policy officials, and the public worried that al-Qaeda was launching a new and more deadly set of terrorist attacks.[1] On October 9, two more anthrax letters were mailed to the Washington, DC offices of Senators Tom Daschle and Patrick Leahy. It was subsequently learned that the mail sorting and delivery process had created aerosolized anthrax from these letters, resulting in the infection of several U.S. postal workers, and had caused cross-contamination with other letters that subsequently infected additional mail recipients. By November 2001, 22 people in New York, New Jersey, Connecticut, Florida and the District of Columbia had contracted anthrax, with half manifesting cutaneous anthrax and the other half inhalational anthrax (the more deadly form) from these attacks. These events triggered public fears about receiving and opening mail, and led to a U.S. buying spree of bleach, duct tape, plastic sheeting and Cipro in public attempts to secure against future bioterrorist attacks.[2]

In terms of impact of the attacks, 5 of the 11 victims who contracted inhalational anthrax died. Beyond those who were known to have been infected, more than 10,000 individuals who might have come into contact with the letters were put on antibiotics as a precautionary measure.[3] In addition, because the contaminated letters passed through several government buildings, a massive decontamination effort ensued, taking several years and costing $320 million dollars (Schmitt and Zacchia 2012). After a long and difficult investigation, the U.S. Department of Justice declared in 2008 that it had identified the perpetrator of the 2001 anthrax attacks as Bruce E. Ivins, a government biodefense scientist who had worked for decades at the U.S. Army Medical Research Institute of Infectious Diseases (USAMRIID), one of America's top biodefense research laboratories (U.S. Government Accountability Office 2014; U.S. National Research Council 2011) (see Chapter 7).[4]

The "Amerithrax" attacks, as the anthrax mailings were later code-named by the U.S. Federal Bureau of Investigation, revealed serious shortcomings in U.S. biosecurity and also raised fears about the growing potential for bioterrorism on American soil. Soon after the attacks, a variety of experts stated that a technological threshold had been crossed, indicating that terrorists would seek to develop and use biological weapons in order to further their mass casualty aims (Tucker 2002).[5] In response to these concerns a series of new U.S. government policies, programs and evaluations were put in place in the early- to mid-2000s to beef up U.S. preparedness and response to bioterrorism. These initiatives built on the significant biodefense efforts of the Clinton Administration (Wright 2007; Guillemin 2005; Miller *et al.* 2002).

Although important initiatives were put in place to secure pathogens, improve medical countermeasures and enhance disease surveillance efforts, there has been little improvement since 2001 in how the

U.S. government assesses current and future bioweapons threats. Furthermore, there has been a systematic failure by the U.S. government (as well as non-government analysts) to learn empirically from the Amerithrax attacks, real-world bioweapons programs, and other subsequent bioweapons-related incidents, such as the 2001 capture of an al-Qaeda laboratory in Afghanistan, or concerns about new potential threats (e.g., lone wolf scientists, DIY biologists, teenagers with PCR kits). Instead, U.S. intelligence officials and policymakers have become fixated on threats from the life sciences, largely abstracted from real world actors or contexts. As a result, the conventional, unchallenged wisdom that has emerged after the anthrax attacks is that terrorists are intent to use technology, like bioweapons, to cause mass casualties and are enabled to do so by the ease of access to bioweapons-related materials and technology that result from our increasingly globalized and commoditized world.[6] Few, either inside or outside the government, have moved beyond the conventional wisdom to interrogate these claims (Leitenberg 2005; Wright 2007; Smith III 2014; Ben Ouagrham-Gormley 2014; Jefferson *et al.* 2014; Rappert 2014; Lentzos 2014).

Furthermore, no attention at the government level seems to be given to trying to sort out the complex interaction involving people and science and technology in bioweapons assessments, to look at how bioweapons developments are shaped by real world actors and various contextual factors. Instead, bioweapons assessments and policy making since September 11 seem to be driven largely by speculative forecasting, without grounding in serious empirical inquiry that considers the range of social, contextual and technical factors shaping near and long-term bioweapons threats (Leitenberg 2005). New models and practices in bioweapons assessments are needed in order to rectify these shortcomings and better inform policy. Such a change will require new government and institutional approaches and resources that need to dramatically depart from what has been the focus over the past 15 years.

This chapter begins by discussing key U.S. government legislation and programs that were passed in the aftermath of the September 11 and Amerithrax attacks to deal with what was seen as a growing bioterrorist threat. In doing so, the chapter focuses largely on the efforts put in place by the Bush Administration, as these were enacted as a direct response to the 2001 anthrax attacks. Later, it is discussed how these compare and contrast with the Obama Administration's focus on biosecurity, and how these have intersected with new and worrisome developments in the life sciences. The chapter concludes with a discussion on the serious analytic shortcomings that remain in U.S. bioweapons analysis and preparedness efforts, and what is needed to move forward in the future.

A. Policy and intelligence responses after the Amerithrax attacks

In the immediate weeks and months of the anthrax attacks, the Bush Administration implemented a series of new regulations and programs to safeguard dangerous pathogens and toxins in U.S. laboratories, as well as provide enhanced screening of individuals working with those materials. In subsequent years, additional programs and strategies were developed to further strengthen U.S. preparedness against a bioweapons attack. This section focuses only on a set of pivotal regulations, activities and programs; other accompanying efforts passed by the Bush Administration have been described by Poulin (2009).

PATRIOT Act (2001)

In October 2001, President Bush signed the "Uniting and Strengthening America by Providing Appropriate Tools Required to Intercept and Obstruct Terrorism" Act, otherwise known as the USA PATRIOT Act.[7] The purpose of the PATRIOT Act was to create new U.S. governmental authorities designed to deter and punish terrorist acts in the United States and abroad, and to enhance law enforcement and surveillance tools against terrorism. In Section 817 of the Act, new penalties were outlined for possessing biological agents in types and quantities that are not for peaceful purposes. The section also introduced the new rule of certain "restricted persons" being barred access from dangerous biological materials. A "restricted person" is defined as someone who:

> (A) is under indictment for a crime punishable by imprisonment for a term exceeding one year; (B) has been convicted in any court of a crime punishable by imprisonment for a term exceeding one year; (C) is a fugitive from justice; (D) is an unlawful user of any controlled substance (as defined in section 102 of the Controlled Substances Act (21 U.S.C. 802); (E) is an alien illegally or unlawfully in the United States; (F) has been adjudicated as a mental defective or has been committed to any mental institution; (G) is an alien (other than an alien lawfully admitted for permanent residence) who is a national of Cuba, Iran, Iraq, Libya, North Korea, Sudan or Syria, or any other country to which the Secretary of State, pursuant to applicable law, has made a determination (that remains in effect) that such country has repeatedly provided support for acts of international terrorism; (H) has been discharged from the Armed Services of the United States under dishonorable conditions.[8]

These provisions were made to significantly enhance control of dangerous biological pathogens and toxins from regulations already in place by the 1996 Antiterrorism and Effective Death Penalty Act, which had only prohibited the transfer of some dangerous biological materials to laboratories that were not registered with the U.S. Centers for Disease Control (CDC). In addition, Section 1013 of the PATRIOT Act, allows for increased funding for bioterrorism preparedness and response.[9] This led to a significant increase in civilian biodefense funding, from around $400 million per year before the anthrax attacks to $3.6 billion in FY2002, $4.9 billion in FY2003, and has led to an average of $5–7 billion per year in subsequent years (Schuler 2004; Boddie *et al.* 2014).

U.S. Public Health Security and Bioterrorism Preparedness and Response Act (2002)

U.S. Public Law 107–188, the Public Health Security and Bioterrorism Preparedness and Response Act of 2002, directed the Secretary of

U.S. Department of Health and Human Services to create a strategy for responding to acts of bioterrorism, including the development of medical countermeasures against biological agents and toxins and the maintenance of a national stockpile of drugs, vaccines and other supplies in the event of a bioterrorist attack.[10] Furthermore, the act called for enhanced control (new procedures for registration, inventory, transfer and security) of certain biological agents and toxins related to human and animal health, which has become known as the Select Agent Program (bioweapons-related pathogens are now referred to as Select Agents). These rules included a new security risk assessment of individuals, involving FBI background checks, who have access to Select Agents. These new provisions in the Act were created to strengthen those introduced into the PATRIOT Act. Both the PATRIOT Act and this law were designed to control direct access to, and increase accountability of, bioweapons-related pathogens. Although the 2002 law did have a minor provision for threat assessments (Section 126), it was primarily focused on evaluating new technologies that could be used in bioterrorist attacks and not on a more holistic assessment of how technologies would interact with different state and non-state actors.

Fink Committee (2003)

In light of the growing concern about bioterrorism and the potential for misuse of biotechnology by hostile individuals and states, the U.S. National Academies of Science set up the Committee on Research Standards and Practices to Prevent the Destructive Application of Biotechnology (see Chapter 9, Point of View). The committee was chaired by MIT biologist Gerald Fink and was composed of academics, primarily scientists, and focused its attention on two issues: "(1) the risk that dangerous [biological] agents that are the subject of research will be stolen or diverted for malevolent purposes; and (2) the risk that the research results, knowledge, or techniques could facilitate the creation of 'novel' pathogens with unique properties or create entirely new classes of threat agents" (U.S. National Research Council 2004). The Committee was charged to find ways to decrease bioweapons threats without hindering the progress of biotechnology.

What is interesting to note here is that the Fink Committee was responding not only to the Amerithrax concerns, but also to a set of published scientific experiments in the early 2000s, involving the creation of genetically engineered mousepox and smallpox variants and the artificial synthesis of poliovirus.[11] These experiments raised policy and public concerns that the scientific papers could be downloaded from the Internet by terrorists and used to launch a bioweapons attack. Around this time, the discourse of bioweapons threats began to conflate concerns over cutting-edge scientific experiments with the Amerithrax case, and other types of potential bioterrorist events, with little differentiation of the types of factors that might shape each of these distinct threats.

The Fink Committee issued its influential "Fink Report" — *Biotechnology Research in an Age of Terrorism* — in early 2004. This was the first National Academies report to examine the role of the life sciences in national security, and its focus was on the dual-use dilemma, e.g., how the life sciences could have peaceful and beneficial, but also malicious applications. The Committee identified seven classes of experiments that would raise misuse concerns, and that should necessitate further review before they are conducted or published. These include those that (1) would demonstrate how to render a vaccine ineffective; (2) would confer resistance to therapeutically useful antibiotics or anti-viral agents; (3) would enhance the virulence of a pathogen or render a non-pathogen virulent; (4) would increase the transmissibility of a pathogen; (5) would alter the host range of a pathogen; (6) would enable the evasion of diagnostic/detection modalities; and (7) would enable the weaponization of a biological agent or toxin.[12] The Report also recommended the creation of a new National Science Advisory Board for Biosecurity (NSABB) to provide guidance for the review and oversight of such experiments and other dual-use research concerns. The focus in this report remained on scientific experiments, with little detailed examination or discussion of how the ability to master and conduct experimental work depends upon particular kinds of know-how that is shaped by a variety of social and contextual factors. With this report, the government focus on bioweapons threats begins to increasingly focus on the scientific dimensions of the threat, and less on the human dimension.

NSABB (2004)

In response to the Fink Committee, the NSABB was chartered in 2004 by the Executive Office of the President to provide advice to the U.S. government regarding the review and oversight of dual-use research.[13] This mandate was larger than that concerned with scientists working on anthrax bacteria or other Select Agents, but aimed to encompass a broad array of existing and emerging science and technologies that could be misused. Some of the Fink Committee members were chosen to serve as voting members on the NSABB. In addition to the voting members, the Board also included *ex officio* representatives from each of the interested federal agencies.

When the NSABB became fully operational in June 2005, five working groups were created to (1) outline the criteria for dual-use research; (2) assemble a code of conduct for scientists; (3) develop strategies and guidelines for the communication of dual-use research; (4) advise on the usage and regulation of synthetic genomes and (5) foster international cooperation regarding the oversight of dual-use research.

In the first years of its existence, the NSABB was focused on defining and providing oversight recommendations for dual-use research, as well as making recommendations regarding the emerging field of synthetic genomics. At the time, and into the present, the NSABB has been primarily concerned with providing guidance on scientific and technological developments in the life sciences, and how these might lead to biological weapons or bioterrorism threats. In their oversight and evaluation recommendations, the focus of the NSABB has been almost exclusively on the materials and methods sections in scientific papers and also the availability and use of new technologies to produce advanced bioweapons threats.

HSPD-10 (2004)

The 2004 Homeland Security Presidential Directive (HSPD)-10 was designed to provide a roadmap across the U.S. government for U.S. biodefense capabilities, "… to prevent, protect against, and mitigate bioweapons attacks on the United States and our global interests."[14] It established four pillars for U.S. biodefense: (1) *Threat awareness*, focused on timely, accurate and relevant intelligence, threat assessment and the anticipation of future threats; (2) *Prevention and protection*, focused on limiting access to agents, technologies and knowledge to certain groups and countries as well as protecting critical infrastructure from the effects of biological attacks; (3) *Surveillance and detection* to provide early warning or recognition of biological attacks to permit a timely response and mitigation of consequences as well as attribution and (4) *Response and recovery* which included pre-attack planning and preparedness, capabilities to treat casualties, risk communications, physical control measures, medical countermeasures and decontamination capabilities.

In terms of threat awareness, this Directive emphasized the importance of science-based threat assessments on bioweapons issues. Also, HSPD-10 had an explicit emphasis on assessing futuristic, technologically oriented bioweapons threats. In addition, under HSPD-10, the Department of Homeland Security was responsible for conducting national risk assessments of new biological threats every 2 years, involving traditional biological agent threats (e.g., anthrax, smallpox), as well as new forms of modified agents or emerging agents (e.g., newly emerging diseases). Here again, however, the focus on threat assessments has remained on narrow scientific and technological issues, with little attention to the more complex ways in which people contribute and modulate a potential bioweapons threat.

BSEG (2006)

In November 2006, the National Counterproliferation Center (NCPC) within the Office of the Director of National Intelligence

(ODNI) established the Biological Sciences Experts Group (BSEG) to improve the Intelligence Community's access to biological expertise.[15] The BSEG grew out of high-profile public recommendations from the 2005 Final Report of the Commission on the Intelligence Capabilities of the United States Regarding Weapons of Mass Destruction, the National Academy of Sciences and the U.S. House of Representatives Subcommittee on Prevention of Nuclear and Biological Attack of the Committee on Homeland Security.[16]

The BSEG consisted of a cadre of external life science and bioweapons experts from universities, companies and non-governmental organizations, who served as independent consultants to the NCPC. The BSEG charter states that members may be assigned the following types of projects: (1) Supporting intelligence customers in the design of scientific/technical experimental protocols, intelligence analyses or collection methodologies against biological threat agents, biological warfare agents and/or state and non-state actors that do or may pose threats to the United States; (2) Advising on strategies to improve the execution or interpretation of results of experimental protocols, analysis and collection; (3) Undertaking technical assessments and performance reviews of the Intelligence Community's scientific/technical programs, analytical products and collection methodologies.[17] The establishment of the BSEG made new, in-depth scientific expertise available to the U.S. intelligence community to help assess the security implications of new biological developments. This narrow technical focus of BSEG, however, has not provided important social science expertise to the intelligence community in order to produce more holistic bioweapons assessments (Vogel 2013c).

WMD Commission Report (2008)

The Commission on the Prevention of Weapons of Mass Destruction Proliferation and Terrorism (commonly known as the Graham/Talent WMD Commission) was set up by Congress in 2008 "to assess, within 180 days, any and all of the nation's activities, initiatives, and programs to prevent weapons of mass destruction proliferation and terrorism."[18] The Commission was a legacy of the 9/11

Commission, which recommended the creation of a new commission to study the possibility of future terrorist threats. The Commission issued a report in December 2008 stating that:

> Unless the world community acts decisively and with great urgency, it is more likely than not that a weapon of mass destruction will be used in a terrorist attack somewhere in the world by the end of 2013. The Commission further believes that terrorists are more likely to be able to obtain and use a biological weapon than a nuclear weapon.[19]

The Commission argued that the acquisition, weaponization and use of biological weapons for harm would be much easier than for nuclear capabilities. In its recommendations, the report suggested additional measures to secure dangerous pathogens, improve bioforensic capabilities, and tighten government oversight of high containment laboratories. In addition, the Commission argued for the creation of a new scientific advisory board for intelligence in order to better anticipate emerging threats from advances in the life sciences. This report, as the various U.S. government initiatives that preceded it, remained focused on science and technology issues surrounding bioweapons threats.

Cooperative Threat Reduction (2006)

The Nunn–Lugar Cooperative Reduction Program was launched in 1991 to mitigate the weapon of mass destruction (WMD) proliferation threats from the breakup of the Former Soviet Union. While the original policy focus was on the Soviet nuclear establishment, additional Nunn–Lugar efforts in 1998 began to engage the former Soviet bioweapons program that consisted of over 40 facilities. Starting in 2006, the Cooperative Threat Reduction (CTR) program began to expand its programmatic activities to countries outside of the former Soviet Union, with new Congressional appropriations (Woolf 2010). As one strategy paper for this new initiative noted: "The threat of bioterrorism is increasing due to gradual lowering of the technical and financial barriers to purchase the materials, technologies, and expertise to develop biological weapons that are linked to the worldwide growth in biotechnology ... particularly in states with rapidly expanding bioscience sectors that never had biological weapons programs."[20] New threat reduction efforts were launched in Asia, the Middle East and Latin America. As reflected in the quote above, this program was based on a simplistic understanding of scientific and technological developments and technology transfer, without a more robust understanding of how particular kinds of know-how are developed to enable successful acquisition and use of science and technology.

B. Developments since the George W. Bush administration

In 2009, the Obama administration announced the *National Strategy for Countering Biological Threats*, which was the new administrations' first major policy initiative on biosecurity.[21] Although the Bush Administration efforts were focused on biodefense, Obama's new strategy was focused on prevention (Koblentz 2012). Also, the new strategy placed an emphasis on linking both naturally occurring disease outbreaks and bioweapons/bioterrorist events in its prevention strategy to create a more seamless and integrated link across all types of biological threats. The strategy also worked to create more linkages between health and security, e.g., by enhancing disease surveillance, bioforensics, cooperation between public health, life science and security communities. Furthermore, Obama's strategy also emphasized the need for international cooperation and partnerships to deal with the global nature of the threat, and called for expansion of bioengagement activities into Africa and South Asia.

A focus on threats emanating from advances in the life sciences has also persisted in this strategy: "(1) the risk is evolving in unpredictable ways; (2) advances in the enabling technologies will continue to be globally available and (3) the ability to exploit such advances will become increasingly accessible to those with ill intent as the barriers of technical expertise and monetary costs decline."[22] Also, in July 2010, the President issued an executive order to optimize laboratory biosecurity that was focused on the Administration's general interest in securing dangerous materials by "building higher fences around smaller yards."[23] The executive order created a tiered system that calibrates the level of security to the degree of risk posed by the pathogen. Personnel reliability measures have also been included in laboratory biosecurity regulations, but only for researchers working on the most dangerous pathogens. This new change has attempted to further address the problems of human error and misconduct in facilities that work with dangerous pathogens. As one can see, the persistent focus on dangerous materials and information, and the theme of ease of science and technology development, acquisition and use, underpins the Obama Administration's perspective on the threat and its focal point for new government policies and programs.

In late summer 2011, the NSABB was called in to deal with a controversial set of biological experiments that raised scientific concern. In 2011, two leading influenza scientists, Ron Fouchier and Yoshihiro Kawaoka, attempted to publish details of how their research teams had mutated the H5N1 bird flu virus to make it transmissible via aerosol (Gronvall 2013b) (see Chapter 9). The U.S. government became concerned that terrorists might be able to use this scientific information if these papers were published. The scientists initially faced objections to publish the papers from the NSABB, who argued that the methods sections of the papers could enable replication of the experiments by terrorists.[24] The NSABB eventually reconsidered its original recommendation and the researchers published their work in full.[25] After the resolution of this controversy, the U.S. government subsequently issued new regulations stipulating that federally funded life science research is subject to increased oversight and security review, and the U.S. government can issue restrictions for publications of data if security concerns exist.[26]

In August 2014, the U.S. Office of Science and Technology Policy issued a memorandum titled "Enhancing Biosafety and Biosecurity in the United States."[27] This memo urged all federal departments and agencies to use Select Agents to perform a Safety-Stand Down to include an immediate sweep of their facilities to identify Select Agents and ensure proper registration, safe stewardship and secure storage or disposal of such agents. The memo also urged non-government facilities to do the same. During this period, facility leaders were urged to devote significant, dedicated time to review laboratory biosafety and biosecurity best practices and protocols, as well as to develop and implement plans for sustained inventory monitoring. This new set of recommendations was issued in light of a series of incidents at the Centers for Diseace Control and Prevention (CDC) and National Institutes of Health (NIH) in summer of 2014 in which CDC and NIH laboratories mistakenly handled and shipped Select Agents.[28] The insider threat has remained a concern of many policy discussions and reports — typically this is envisioned as a malicious employee wishing to take Select Agents for harm, rather than the more mundane ways in which human workers can produce errors (Gronvall 2013a, 2013b: 189).

As one can see from the earlier descriptions, the Obama Administration has largely continued the Bush Administration's focus on material, information, and science and technology in its biosecurity agenda — with increasing concerns about the ease of diffusion and globalization of the life sciences for harm. This consistency across administrations is not surprising: many of the specific initiatives featured in the Obama strategy were initially developed during the Bush presidency, with some of the Bush government officials staying through into the Obama Administration.

C. Progress and shortcomings

At the time of the anthrax attacks, the CDC could not definitely state who had access to *B. anthracis* as there was no reliable accounting system. With the new biosecurity legislations that have been passed, there are now more strict measures (written protocols, security technologies, clearance procedures) for the accounting and safeguarding of Select Agents and those with access to them. In addition, a host of U.S. government programs and funding streams have been established since 2001 to increase U.S. bioterrorism preparedness. Yet, even with all these measures, more accurate bioweapons threat assessments are lacking. There remains too much focus on the materials, equipment, and published information about biological materials and technologies, with much less attention on how to make sense of these tangible items as they might be used by specific state and non-state actors, who have access to varying resources, capabilities and contexts in which to work with Select Agents.

In terms of specific analytic shortcomings, there has been a failure to conduct in-depth empirical studies of past bioweapons-related actors and learn from these real-world examples to inform threat assessments. During the 21st century there have been a number of state and terrorist examples of bioweapons threats (e.g., Soviet Union, Iraq, al-Qaeda), as well as concerns about potential threats from new actors (DIY biologists, lone wolf scientists, teenagers) that could have been subject to more rigorous case study analysis and comparison.

For example, the Amerithrax case provides an interesting case to study from a non-state actor perspective. Although there was a lot of attention focused on Bruce Ivins and his peculiar behavioral patterns and fetishes, there was little discussion or analysis about how to assess his capabilities to conduct the attack (see Chapter 7, Point of View). There could have been more examination of his particular educational background/training, know-how and expertise, as well as greater scrutiny of the kinds of materials, infrastructure, publications, pedagogical associations, collaborations and resources that he had at hand as a result of working for many years in a sophisticated defense department research laboratory. Studying these factors in more detail and how they connect to a specific actor would allow one to better understand the scope of requirements needed to produce the anthrax for the attacks — and to what extent these requirements could be overcome/substituted by others wishing to cause harm. Similarly, in 2002, U.S. military forces captured a crude laboratory that members of al-Qaeda had tried to assemble to develop a bioweapons capability (Petro and Relman 2003; Commission on the Intelligence 2005: 267–278; Leitenberg 2005: 21–42). This was not a laboratory that was capable of functioning at the time of capture, but it did include some basic infrastructure, a few pieces of equipment, and sets of scientific and policy papers regarding anthrax and bioterrorism. Also, one PhD-level microbiologist from Pakistan and another Malaysian biological technician were connected to this work. These real-world actors could have also been examined with known information about materials, equipment and know-how contextualizing their work, and perhaps comparing that with other non-state actors, such as Ivins, or other historical examples of actors conducting bioterrorism. This would then allow analysts to start constructing a map of the various factors relevant to bioweapons work and identifying important indicators and patterns.

Furthermore, there were a number of state-level bioweapons programs that could have been investigated in the early 2000s to further inform assessment. The Soviet's bioweapons program is one that could have been beneficial to study (see Chapter 4). Although the Soviets had the largest, most advanced, covert bioweapons program in history, its output was a mixed picture. At one bioweapons mobilization facility in Kazakhstan, the Soviets needed 5 years to develop an enhanced Soviet anthrax weapon based on an existing scientific protocol (Vogel 2006). This is because there was specific technical know-how, employee training, and management practices needed, as well as the need to reconfigure the facility and conduct painstaking work to translate the older protocols to work in a new facility. Although the Soviets were ultimately able to construct a military-grade weapon, it required specific socio-technical inputs over a sustained time period to make it happen. This case suggests the importance of taking into account the range of factors needed to develop a sophisticated bioweapons capability in a facility not optimized for bioweapons work.

But beyond looking at a single facility, studying the Soviet program also reveals that managerial, organizational, economic and political factors posed problems for bioweapons work within and across facilities. For example, in comparing two Soviet bioweapons research facilities, Obolensk and Vektor, very different managerial styles are apparent, which ultimately stymied work at one facility (Obolensk) while promoting innovations at the other (Vektor) (Ben Ouagrham-Gormley and Vogel 2010). This illustrates that management matters in the conduct of bioweapons work. By looking at the broader political context, it is also apparent that the Soviet program suffered from constant political interventions and micromanagement which created multiple disruptions in bioweapons work (Ben Ouagrham-Gormley 2014: 91–121). For instance, Soviet scientists and technical staff were sometimes promoted because of their loyalty to the Communist party and not because of their technical skills. Extreme political pressure for progress led other Soviet scientists to lie about their results, also hindering progress. The Soviet bioweapons program suffered from extreme secrecy and compartmentalization resulting in a lack of collaboration within and across facilities, which led to barriers in knowledge transfer and integration across the entire R&D, production and weaponization chain. In a final example, the peculiarities of the Soviet supply system created problems for scientists with access to needed materials and supplies, even when the financial resources were available for these supplies. So although the Soviets had extensive technical expertize, almost unlimited funding, and a high political priority for its bioweapons work, scientists across the program encountered substantial problems leading to many delays and a lack of progress in certain areas. This underscores the importance of understanding the broad range of internal and external factors working within the particular context of a particular actor that can stymie weapons development.

Another timely case that could have been studied in more detail in the early to mid-2000s was Iraq's bioweapons program (see Chapter 5). After the 1991 Gulf War, UN weapons inspectors determined that Iraq had hidden a bioweapons program that had produced thousands of liters of anthrax bacteria and Botulinum toxin loaded onto missiles and bombs. In the years between 1991 and 2003, there were continued suspicions that Iraq had maintained a covert bioweapons program that had grown more advanced and sophisticated with the march of time; U.S. intelligence analysts even suspected that the Iraqis had developed mobile bioweapons labs that could move covertly across the Iraqi desert.[29] After the war, we learned that Saddam Hussein had in fact not kept an offensive bioweapons program since 1996, due to the challenges of UN weapons inspections, sanctions, U.S. and coalition partners' bombing campaigns, and massive corruption in the Hussein government.[30]

It was also uncovered that the Iraqis faced numerous technical problems across the course of its 20-year bioweapons program (Ben Ouagrham-Gormley 2014: 122–143). Work was cyclical and disconnected, and scientists worked in a compartmentalized effort with little collaboration across scientific teams. Similar to the Soviet program, there was significant political intervention which promoted a culture of false reporting of scientific results to please the leadership. The failure to examine these kinds of issues in U.S. intelligence analysis on Iraq's weapons of mass destruction programs was noted by Richard Kerr, former deputy director of the CIA who was called in to conduct an independent assessment of the intelligence failures leading up to the 2003 war. Kerr found:

> The national intelligence produced on the [Iraqis] technical and cultural/political areas ... remained largely distinct and separate. Little or no attempt was made to examine or explain the impact of each area on the other. Thus, perspective and a comprehensive sense of understanding of the Iraqi target per se was lacking ... The bifurcation of analysis between the technical and the cultural/political in the analytic product and the resulting implications for policy indicates systemic problems in collection and analysis.
>
> (Kerr *et al.* 2005: 48)

The Iraq example illustrates the detrimental impacts from bad assessments on U.S. policymaking and the public.

Finally, one could look at the range of controversial scientific experiments that were published in the early to mid-2000s that raised bioterrorism concerns, from genetically engineering mousepox, to reconstruction of the 1918 influenza virus, to the artificial synthesis of poliovirus and other synthetic genomes, to the genetic engineering of the H5N1 virus (see Chapter 9). In all of the assessments of these experiments and their potential for harm, the government and non-government focus has remained on the materials and methods sections of these papers, and to what extent the published information could be used by terrorists. No government analysis has sought to look at what individuals and/or teams were required to do the work, with particular kinds of expertise and know-how and management/laboratory disciplines/team arrangements, nor how these human factors then combine with access to particular kinds of materials, equipment, infrastructure and financing to be able to do the work. Each of these experiments could have provided an opportune moment to conduct a more sophisticated socio-technical analysis in which a broader range of social and technical factors is examined as part of the threat assessment. Instead, what has resulted is an abstracted, generalized notion of threat from these experiments, with little evaluation of human factors that can shape the threat.

These problems in assessment are problematic not only for intelligence and policymakers, but also for how they are used for bioweapons response planning. In talking with a local medical official responsible for emergency response in case of a serious disease outbreak (malicious or natural outbreak), I was told that investment in bioterrorism preparedness has made resources and training available for particular kinds of outbreaks: those focused on anthrax and plague bacteria, which has then led to the provision of particular kinds of bioterrorism-related response equipment, training and protocols, which are not well equipped or prepared to deal with a more complex, natural infectious disease outbreak such as the one involved in the 2014–2015 Ebola outbreak (see Chapter 10).[31]

Furthermore, the continued mishandling of Select Agents, even with the introduction of more stringent protocols and technologies, signifies inherent challenges with the human/social dimension of biosecurity. In June 2015, news reports surfaced that 68 laboratories, in 19 states and 4 countries, had inadvertently received shipments of live anthrax bacteria from U.S. Department of Defense laboratories.[32] At the time of this writing, the Defense department has launched an internal probe to determine how this breach in security could have happened in light of the rigorous measures put in place after September 11. Although it will likely take time to know the full scope of the problem, it is likely that the breach will be connected to lapses in personnel reliability (Weiss *et al.* 2015). This is a sober reminder that we need to take into account human factors, along with protocols and technologies, across all aspects of biosecurity preparedness programs.

Conclusion

Science and technological development (including bioweapons development) is messy, contingent, local and thoroughly social — as a close examination of the 2001 anthrax attacks reveals. The attacks should have prompted the U.S. government to improve its bioweapons assessments and look at specific actors and capabilities, and how these are modulated by an array of messy, contingent, local and social contextual factors. There remains a need to study specific socio-technical factors and conditions of how a particular state or non-state actor might develop a bioweapons capability that include studies of know-how, knowledge networks, management/organizational components and dynamics and the larger socio-political-economic context in which bioweapons work is conducted.

We also need to devote more time and resources to learn empirically from cases of success and failure; to date, there have been few assessments that have interrogated historical and contemporary cases and have gone beyond espousing the conventional wisdom. To do more holistic bioweapons assessments, however, requires higher-level policy support, resources and new forms of analysis. This kind of work would also require the creation of new experimental interdisciplinary knowledge teams to conduct the assessments in order to draw on multiple sets of expertise (Vogel 2013a, 2013b; Johnston 2003).

This kind of analysis would allow for a more useful measure of the ease (or difficulty, or chokepoints) involved in establishing a bioweapons capability by state or non-state actors, and allow for the creation of a refined spectrum of indicators to better inform intelligence and policy about current and future threats. Fifteen years after the anthrax attacks, it is high time the U.S. and international public and policy communities have access to better knowledge about bioweapons threats to more effectively and efficiently guide security planning and taxpayer resources.

References

Ben Ouagrham-Gormley S (2014) *Barriers to Bioweapons: The Challenges of Expertise and Organization for Weapons Development.* Ithaca: Cornell University Press.

Ben Ouagrham-Gormley S and Vogel KM (2010) 'The Social Context Shaping Bioweapons (Non)Proliferation,' *Biosecurity and Bioterrorism: Biodefense Strategy, Practice, and Science* Vol. 8(1): 9–24.

Boddie C, Sell TK and Watson M (2014) 'Federal Funding for Health Security in FY2015,' *Biosecurity and Bioterrorism: Biodefense Strategy, Practice, and Science* Vol. 12(4): 163–177.

Commission on the Intelligence Capabilities of the United States Regarding Weapons of Mass Destruction. *Report to the President of the United States.* March 31, 2005.

Gronvall GK (2013a) 'Biosecurity policy, bioterrorism, and the future,' in R Burnette (Ed.) *Biosecurity: Understanding, Assessing, and Preventing the Threat.* Hoboken: John Wiley and Sons, Inc., pp. 187–196.

Gronvall GK (2013b) *H5N1: A Case Study for Dual-Use Research.* Report, New York: Council on Foreign Relations.

Guillemin J (2005) *Biological Weapons: From the Invention of State Sponsored Programs to Contemporary Bioterrorism.* New York: Columbia University Press.

Guillemin J (2011) *American Anthrax.* New York: McMillan/Henry Holt.

Jefferson C, Lentzos F and Marris C (2014) 'Synthetic Biology and Biosecurity: Challenging the Myths,' *Frontiers in Public Health* Vol. 2: 115.

Johnston R (2003) 'Integrating Methodologists into Teams of Substantive Experts: Reducing Analytic Error,' *Studies in Intelligence* Vol. 47(1): 57–65.

Kerr R, Wolfe T, Donegan R and Pappas A (2005) 'Collection and Analysis on Iraq: Issues for the US Intelligence Community,' *Studies in Intelligence* Vol. 49(3): 47–54.

Koblentz GD (2012) 'From Biodefence to Biosecurity: The Obama Administration's Strategy for Countering Biological Threats,' *International Affairs* Vol. 88(1): 131–148.

Leitenberg M (2005) *Assessing the Biological Weapons and Bioterrorism Threat.* Report, U.S. Army War College Strategic Studies Institute, 1 December. See http://www.strategicstudiesinstitute.army.mil/pubs/display.cfm?PubID=639 (accessed June 29, 2015).

Lentzos F (2014) 'The Risk of Bioweapons Use: Considering the Evidence Base,' *BioSocieties* Vol. 9(1): 84–93.

Miller J, Broad WJ and Engelberg S (2002) *Germs: Biological Weapons and America's Secret War.* New York: Simon and Schuster.

Petro JB and Relman DA (2003) 'Understanding Threats to Scientific Openness,' *Science* Vol. 302(5652): 1898.

Poulin D (2009) *A U.S. Biodefense Strategy Primer.* Report May 15 http://www.nti.org/media/pdfs/05_us_doe.pdf?_=1316627912 (accessed June 29, 2015).

Rappert B (2014) 'Why has There not Been More Research of Concern?' *Frontiers in Public Health* Vol. 2: 74.

Schmitt K and Zacchia NA (2012) 'Total Decontamination Cost of the Anthrax Letter Attacks,' *Biosecurity and Bioterrorism: Biodefense Strategy, Practice, and Science* Vol. 10(1): 98–107.

Schuler A (2004) 'Billions for Biodefense: Federal Agency Biodefense Funding, FY2001–FY2005,' *Biosecurity and Bioterrorism: Biodefense Strategy, Practice, and Science* Vol. 2(2): 86–96.

Smith FL III (2014) *American Biodefense.* Ithaca: Cornell University Press.

Tucker JB (2002) 'What the Anthrax Attacks Should Teach Us,' http://www.hoover.org/research/what-anthrax-attacks-should-teach-us (accessed June 29, 2015).

U.S. Government Accountability Office (2014) *Anthrax: Agency Approaches to Validation and Statistical Analyses Could be Improved, GAO-15-80,* December 19, 2014.

U.S. National Research Council (2004) *Review of the Scientific Approaches Used During the FBI's Investigation of the 2001 Anthrax Letters.* Washington, DC: The National Academies Press.

Vogel KM (2006) 'Bioweapons proliferation: Where Science Studies and Public Policy Collide,' *Social Studies of Science* Vol. 36(5): 659–690.

Vogel KM (2013a) 'Intelligence Assessment: Putting Emerging Biotechnology Threats in Context,' *Bulletin of the Atomic Scientists* Vol. 69(1): 43–52.

Vogel KM (2013b) *Phantom Menace or Looming Danger?: A New Framework for Assessing Bioweapons Threats.* Baltimore: The Johns Hopkins University Press.

Vogel KM (2013c) 'Necessary Interventions: Expertise and Experiments in Bioweapons Intelligence Assessments,' *Science, Technology and Innovation Studies* Vol. 9(2): 61–88.

Weiss S, Yitzhaki S and Shapira SC (2015) 'Lessons to be Learned from Recent Biosafety Incidents in the United States,' *The Israel Medical Association Journal* Vol. 17(5): 269–273.

Woolf AF (2010) *Nonproliferation and Threat Reduction Assistance: US Programs in the Former Soviet Union, CRS Report to Congress,* February 4, 2010.

Wright S (2007) 'Terrorists and Biological Weapons: Forging the Linkage in the Clinton Administration,' *Politics and the Life Sciences* Vol. 25(1–2): 57–115.

Notes

1 Wade N (2001) 'A Nation Challenged: The Disease; Natural Cause Appears Unlikely in 2 Anthrax Cases,' *The New York Times,* October 9, 2001. See http://www.nytimes.com/2001/10/09/us/nation-challenged-disease-natural-cause-appears-unlikely-2-anthrax-cases.html (accessed June 29, 2015).

2 CBS News (2001) 'U.S. Anxious After Anthrax Attacks,' December 20, 2001. See www.cbsnews.com/news/us-anxious-after-anthrax-attack/(accessed June 29, 2015); Petersen L and Pear R (2001) 'A Nation Challenged: Cipro; Anthrax Fears Send Demand For a Drug Far Beyond Output,' *The New York Times,* October 16, 2001. See http://www.nytimes.com/2001/10/16/business/a-nation-challenged-cipro-anthrax-fears-send-demand-for-a-drug-far-beyond-output.html (accessed June 29, 2015); Meserve J (2003) 'Duct Tape Sales Rise Amid Terror Fears,' *CNN,* February 11, 2003. See http://www.cnn.com/2003/US/02/11/emergency.supplies/index.html?_s=PM:US (accessed June 29, 2015); Clemetson L (2003) 'Reshaping Message on Terror, Ridge Urges Calm with Caution,' *The New York Times,* February 20, 2003. See http://www.nytimes.com/2003/02/20/us/threats-responses-domestic-security-reshaping-message-terror-ridge-urges-calm.html (accessed June 29, 2015).

3 Stolberg SG (2002) 'A Nation Challenged: Anthrax Protection; Antibiotics Found to Have Helped Limited Anthrax Infections,' *The New York Times,* March 8, 2002. See http://www.nytimes.com/2002/03/08/us/nation-challenged-anthrax-protection-antibiotics-found-have-helped-limit-anthrax.html (accessed June 29, 2015).

4 There is still controversy remaining about whether Ivins conducted the attacks, as well as whether he might have acted alone, see: Shane S (2015) 'Former FBI Agent Sues; Claiming Retaliation Over Misgivings in Anthrax

Case,' *The New York Times*, April 8, 2015. See http://www.nytimes.com/2015/04/09/us/ex-fbi-agent-claims-retaliation-for-dissent-in-anthrax-inquiry.html?ref=topicsand_r=0andgwh=9984683C3672CF1418C227CD452CBDC3andgwt=pay (accessed June 29, 2015).

5 Lemonic MD (2001) 'Bioterrorism: The Next Threat?' *Time*, September 24, 2001. See http://content.time.com/time/nation/article/0,8599,176066,00.html (accessed June 29, 2015).

6 For an exemplar of this mindset see Clapper, JR (2014) *Statement for the Record Worldwide Threat Assessment of the US Intelligence Community Senate Select Committee on Intelligence*, January 29, 2014, p. 5. See http://www.dni.gov/files/documents/Intelligence%20Reports/2014%20WWTA%20%20SFR_SSCI_29_Jan.pdf (accessed August 18, 2015); U.S. Central Intelligence Agency (2003) *The Darker Bioweapons Future*, http://fas.org/irp/cia/product/bw1103.pdf (accessed June 29, 2015).

7 U.S. Public Law 107-56 (2001) Uniting and Strengthening America by Providing Appropriate Tools Required to Intercept and Obstruct Terrorism (USA PATRIOT ACT) Act of 2001, October 26, 2001. See http://www.gpo.gov/fdsys/pkg/PLAW-107publ56/pdf/PLAW-107publ56.pdf (accessed June 26, 2015).

8 U.S. Public Law, 2001, as per note 8.

9 U.S. Public Law, 2001, as per note 8.

10 U.S. Public Law 107-188 (2002) Public Health Security and Bioterrorism Preparedness Response Act of 2002, June 12, 2002. http://www.gpo.gov/fdsys/pkg/PLAW-107publ188/pdf/PLAW-107publ188.pdf (accessed June 29, 2015).

11 Jackson RJ, Ramsay AJ, Christensen CD, Beaton S, Hall DF and Ramshaw IA (2001) 'Expression of Mouse Interleukin-4 by a Recombinant Ectromelia Virus Suppresses Cytolytic Lymphocyte Responses and Overcomes Genetic Resistance to Mousepox,' *Journal of Virology* Vol. 75(3): 1205–1210; Cello J, Paul AV and Wimmer E (2002) 'Chemical Synthesis of Poliovirus cDNA: Generation of Infectious Virus in the Absence of Natural Template,' *Science* Vol. 297(5583): 1016–1018; Rosengard AM, Liu Y, Nie Z and Jimenez R (2002) 'Variola Virus Immune Evasion Design: Expression of a Highly Efficient Inhibitor of Human Complement,' *Proceedings of the National Academies of Science USA* Vol. 99(13): 8808–8813.

12 U.S. National Research Council (2004) *Biotechnology Research in an Age of Terrorism*. Washington, DC: National Academies Press, p. 5.

13 National Institutes of Health (2004) 'HHS Announcement — March 2004 RE: Establishing the NSABB,' March 4, 2004. http://osp.od.nih.

gov/announcement/thu-2004-03-04-0000/hhs-announcement-march-2004-re-establishing-nsabb (accessed March 10, 2016).

14 The White House (2004) *Homeland Security Presidential Directive 10*, See http://fas.org/irp/offdocs/nspd/hspd-10.html (accessed June 29, 2015).

15 Office of the Director of National Intelligence (undated) 'Biological Sciences Expert Group Concept Paper,' http://fas.org/irp/eprint/bseg-concept.pdf (accessed June 29, 2015).

16 Commission on the Intelligence Capabilities of the United States Regarding Weapons of Mass Destruction (2005) Report to the President of the United States, March 31, 2005, http://fas.org/irp/offdocs/wmd_chapter3.pdf (accessed June 29, 2015); U.S. National Research Council (2006) *Globalization, Biosecurity, and the Future of the Life Sciences.* Washington, DC: The National Academies Press; U.S. House Committee on Homeland Security, Subcommittee on the Prevention of Nuclear and Biological Attack (2005/2006) *Bioscience and the Intelligence Community. Part I and II Hearing before the Subcommittee on [the] Prevention of Nuclear and Biological Attack of the Committee on Homeland Security.* Report November 3 and May 4. See http://babel.hathitrust.org/cgi/pt?id=pst.000061502635;view=1up;seq=1 (accessed June 29, 2015).

17 Office of the Director of National Intelligence, as per note 16.

18 Commission on the Prevention of Weapons of Mass Destruction Proliferation and Terrorism (2008) *World At Risk.* New York: Vintage Books.

19 Commission for the Prevention 2008, as per note 19, p. xv.

20 U.S. Department of State's National Security Council paper, personal communication, May 2006.

21 The White House (2009) *National Strategy for Countering Biological Threats.* Report, November. Washington DC: National Security Council.

22 The White House 2009, as per note 22 p. 2.

23 The White House (2010) 'Executive Order 13546: Optimizing the security of biological Select Agents and Toxins in the United States,' July 2, 2010; the Administration's export control reform plans remarks by General Jones, National Security Advisor, June 30, 2010, p. 5, See http://www.aia-aerospace.org/assets/speech_jones_06302010.pdf

24 National Institutes of Health (2011) 'Press statement on the NSABB review of H5N1 research,' December 20, 2011. See http://www.nih.gov/news/health/dec2011/od-20.html (accessed March 10, 2016). Berns KI *et al.* (2012) 'Policy: Adaptations of Avian Flu Virus are a Cause for Concern,' *Nature* Vol. 482(7384): 153–154.

[25] National Science Advisory Board for Biosecurity (2012) *Findings and Recommendations: March 29–30, 2012*. Report, March. See http://osp.od.nih.gov/sites/default/files/resources/03302012_NSABB_Recommendations_1.pdf (accessed June 29, 2015).

[26] U.S. Government (2012) *United States Government Policy for Oversight of Life Sciences Dual Use Research of Concern*, March 29, 2012. See http://www.phe.gov/s3/dualuse/Documents/us-policy-durc-032812.pdf (accessed June 29, 2015).

[27] The White House (2014) 'Enhancing Biosafety and Biosecurity in the United States,' August 18, 2014. See https://www.whitehouse.gov/sites/default/files/microsites/ostp/enhancing_biosafety_and_biosecurity_19aug2014_final.pdf (accessed June 29, 2015).

[28] U.S. Centers for Disease Control (2014) 'CDC lab determines possible anthrax exposures: Staff provided antibiotics/monitoring,' June 19, 2014. See http://www.cdc.gov/media/releases/2014/s0619-anthrax.html (accessed June 29, 2015); McNeil DG Jr (2014) 'CDC Closes Anthrax and Flu Labs After Accidents,' *The New York Times*, July 11, 2014. See http://www.nytimes.com/2014/07/12/science/cdc-closes-anthrax-and-flu-labs-after-accidents.html (accessed June 29, 2015); Sun LH and Brady D (2014) 'Second Probe Finds More Safety Lapses at CDC Anthrax Lab,' *The Washington Post*, July 14, 2014. See http://www.washingtonpost.com/national/health-science/second-probe-finds-more-safety-lapses-at-cdc-anthrax-labs/2014/07/14/b792d4fe-0b91-11e4-8c9a-923ecc0c7d23_story.html (accessed June 29, 2015); Grady D and McNeil DG Jr (2014) 'Ebola Sample is Mishandled at CDC Lab in Latest Error,' *The New York Times*, December 24, 2014. See http://www.nytimes.com/2014/12/25/health/cdc-ebola-error-in-lab-may-have-exposed-technician-to-hvirus.html?_r=0 (accessed June 29, 2015).

[29] U.S. Central Intelligence Agency (2002) 'Key Judgments: Iraq's continuing programs for Weapons of Mass Destruction,' *National Intelligence Estimate*, October 2002. See http://nsarchive.gwu.edu/NSAEBB/NSAEBB129/nie_judgments.pdf; U.S. Central Intelligence Agency and U.S. Defense Intelligence Agency (2003) 'Iraqi mobile biological warfare agent production plants,' May 28, 2003. See https://www.cia.gov/library/reports/general-reports-1/iraqi_mobile_plants/ (accessed June 29, 2015).

[30] Duelfer C (2004) *Comprehensive Report of the Special Advisor to the DCI on Iraq's WMD*,' September 30, 2004. See https://www.cia.gov/library/reports/general-reports-1/iraq_wmd_2004 (accessed June 29, 2015).

[31] Personal communication with local official, Raleigh, NC, May 2015.

[32] Lamothe D (2015) 'How Anthrax Became an Unexpected Challenge for the Pentagon,' *The Washington Post*, June 1, 2015. See http://www.washingtonpost.com/news/checkpoint/wp/2015/06/01/how-anthrax-became-an-unexpected-challenge-for-the-pentagon/ (accessed March 10, 2016) Baldor LC (2015) 'Pentagon says More Labs Got Shipments of Live Anthrax Samples as Investigation Continues,' *US News and World Report*, June 9, 2015. See http://www.usnews.com/news/politics/articles/2015/06/09/pentagon-more-labs-got-shipments-of-live-anthrax-samples (accessed June 29, 2015).

Point of View
The Threat of Misuse

Gigi Kwik Gronvall

A great deal of the scientific knowledge, materials and techniques required for legitimate, beneficent biological research could also be used to make a biological weapon. For instance, laboratory research conducted to uncover critical information about how a pathogen manipulates the human immune system to cause disease could be exploited to make a disease harder to treat. Yet, the aspiration to protect the life sciences from deliberate misuse is clear. As stated in the seminal National Academies of Science report, *Biotechnology in an Age of Terrorism*, scientists have an "affirmative moral duty to avoid contributing to the advancement of biowarfare or bioterrorism."[1] It is how you implement this in practice that is the real challenge. The NSABB has considered this problem, and has codified 'Dual Use Research of Concern' (known as DURC) as "life sciences research that, based on current understanding, can be reasonably anticipated to provide knowledge, information, products, or technologies that could be directly misapplied to pose a significant threat with broad potential consequences to public health and safety, agricultural crops and other plants, animals, the environment, materiel, or national security."[2] DURC research review is now required for U.S. federally funded research with regulated pathogens; scientists are required to develop a risk mitigation plan and assess risks and benefits of the research.

Assessing the risks of DURC is complicated by determining who might misuse the research. There are multiple actors to be considered, with different levels of skill. On one end of the spectrum there may be biological science amateurs who are looking for step-by-step guidance from the internet, and who are unlikely to be able to incorporate new insights into how to make an already serious disease worse. Even though the methods sections of scientific papers exist to enable replication of the work, these sections are not nearly as descriptive as a recipe in a cookbook; a great deal of knowledge is assumed, not explained. On the other end of the spectrum, there may be state-sponsored scientists with the time and resources to perform R&D, and who are looking at the scientific literature for weaponizable insights; given the incremental nature of science, it is not clear how one particular paper could affect their pursuits or significantly lower their barriers to biological weapons development. Without a defined malevolent actor in mind who might misuse the information to create a biological weapon — who has the necessary skills to manipulate biological systems as well as the resources — it is a challenging process to balance the risks of publication and subsequent potential misuse along with the potential for more positive outcomes.

There is an abundance of dual-use research that could give insights into the development of many different types of biological weapons; well-resourced groups have an almost limitless array of technical options they could pursue for harm. There are many well-known demonstrations of legitimate scientific work that could be misused in order to make pathogens more effective as biological weapons, including making antibiotic resistant bacteria,[3] engineering viruses that can escape their vaccines,[4] engineering anthrax bacteria so that the vaccine is ineffective,[5] and making viruses more transmissible.[6] In addition, there have been advances in neuroscience and its effects on behavior that could be misused.[7] So too could the emerging field of paleovirology, where scientists have been able to resurrect extinct retroviruses that are millions of years old and then demonstrate their ability to infect human cells *in vitro*.[8]

Scientific information is not static, but expands constantly, exposing new areas of dual-use concern. It is difficult to project changes in technologies that may cause some threats to become more urgent. The historical example of the sequencing of the smallpox virus demonstrates this point. Once smallpox was extinct in the natural world, a strict, international regulatory regime coordinated by the World Health Organization was developed to control each and every experiment on the virus, and to make sure that the intact virus was present in only two facilities in the world. Sequencing of the virus was performed when it became technically feasible to gain understanding of how this virus was able to defeat the human immune system so thoroughly, and to investigate whether other pox viruses in the world were likely to mutate into a smallpox-like virus. For example, a cousin to smallpox, monkeypox, can infect humans and even spread from person to person, though it does not spread like smallpox. When the sequencing work was published, in 1994, technologies for "reading" DNA (DNA sequencing) were much more advanced than those for "writing" DNA (gene synthesis).[9] It was not remotely possible to synthesize a genome the size of smallpox, which is over 186,000 base pairs of DNA (a string of 30 base pairs would have been a challenge at the time). However, the ability to write DNA caught up rapidly with advances in technology. When smallpox was originally sequenced, nobody anticipated that, as a 2010 World Health Organization report put it, "advances in genome sequencing and genome synthesis would render substantial portions of [smallpox virus] accessible to anyone with an internet connection and access to a DNA synthesizer."[10]

Determining who might misuse research is further complicated by the sparse empirical data available to assess the likelihood that bioweapons will threaten national security. Thankfully, there have been only a handful of historical examples of bioterrorism or biowarfare, although multiple nations and terrorist organizations have developed the capability to varying degrees. Intelligence about bioweapons programs and intent to use them has been difficult to acquire; miscalculations include type 1 errors (Iraq was thought to have a BW program during the lead up to the Second Gulf War, at which time it did not) and type 2 errors (the former Soviet Union was not thought to have a BW program but, in fact, employed tens of thousands of weapons scientists). Given the paucity of other data, judgments about the bioweapons threat rest largely on expert opinions. Understanding how experts in national security, biosecurity and biosafety perceive the bioweapons threat is therefore important for assessing the threat, and for assessing the potential for misuse of legitimate research.

To assess collective judgments about the bioweapons threat, colleagues and I carried out a Delphi method study that surveyed 59 U.S. experts in biosecurity, from the U.S. government, academia, nongovernmental sector, and industry organizations.[11] We asked participants to estimate the percentage likelihood of a large-scale biological weapons attack occurring within the next ten years in any country. We defined a large-scale attack conservatively, as resulting in more than 100 ill people. There was a wide diversity of opinions. Participants' answers ranged from one to 100 percent likelihood, with a mean of 57 percent. In general, those trained as biological scientists perceived a lower likelihood of bioweapons use than other participants, although that was certainly not true in every case.

Participants were also asked about the likelihood of different types of state and non-state actors to be the perpetrator of a biological weapons attack within the next 10 years. Although participants held a wide range of opinions, overt state bioweapons use was considered to be less likely than covert use by a state or use by a non-state group. An overt attack by a state actor was rated significantly less likely than even the next lowest rated actor: criminal groups. Religious extremists were judged to be the most likely group to perpetrate an attack — significantly more likely than a covert attack by a state actor or any other attack by a state, but not significantly more likely than a right-wing violent non-state actor, or a disgruntled or mentally ill individual.

We also asked about types of biological agents likely to be used as weapons within the next 10 years. Participants felt that the likelihood of use was highest for biological toxins; this was followed by spore-forming bacteria, non–spore-forming bacteria, and viruses. Participants generally did not think that fungi and prions were likely to be weaponized and felt that the likelihood of a synthetic pathogen being used as a weapon in the next 10 years was fairly low.

Our study also obtained participants' judgments about acceptable limits for U.S. biodefense, particularly "threat characterization" laboratory studies (usually classified) that are performed to gain knowledge about potential bioweapons for purposes of defense (i.e., is there a "red line" that should not be crossed?). Most said yes (51), but there was a wide variety of opinions of what types of research would cross that line. A total of 27 participants mentioned gain-of-function experiments as a situation where a red line could be drawn.

The diversity of views, even in this experienced group of participants, demonstrates that it will be more challenging to assess the risks that research would be misused and to develop a regulatory system for legitimate dual-use research. Whenever the next DURC publication is propelled into the news, inspiring discussion and debate, it is likely that the conversation about what should be done about such research will begin anew, and be tied to the specifics of the problematic case. Proponents and opponents of the research will place different weight on the variables of the case — the specifics of the research in question, the researchers involved, the urgency of the threat that the research is trying to address, and assessment of the danger that the information could be applied toward a biological weapon, and by which actors. These qualities are difficult to predict, particularly in global, diversified fields like biological research and biotechnology.

Notes

1 U.S. National Research Council (2004) *Biotechnology Research in an Age of Terrorism.* Washington, DC: National Academies Press, 5–6.

2 *United States Government Policy for Oversight of Life Sciences Dual Use Research of Concern.* March 29, 2012.

3 Athamna A, Athamna M, Abu-Rashed N *et al.* (2004) 'Selection of Bacillus Anthracis Isolates Resistant to Antibiotics,' *Journal of Antimicrobial Chemotherapy* Vol. 54(2): 424–428; Brook I, Elliott TB, Pryor HI *et al.* (2001) '*In vitro* Resistance of Bacillus Anthracis Sterne to Doxycycline, Macrolides and Quinolones,' *International Journal of Antimicrobial Agents* Vol. 18(6): 559–562.

4 Jackson RJ, Ramsay AJ, Christensen CD *et al.* (2001) 'Expression of Mouse Interleukin-4 by a Recombinant Ectromelia Virus Suppresses Cytolytic Lymphocyte Responses and Overcomes Genetic Resistance to Mousepox,' *Journal of Virology* Vol. 75(3): 1205–1210.

5 Pomerantsev AP, Staritsin NA, Mockov Yu V and Marinin LI (1997) 'Expression of Cereolysine AB Genes in Bacillus Anthracis Vaccine Strain Ensures Protection Against Experimental Hemolytic Anthrax Infection,' *Vaccine* Vol. 15(17–18): 1846–1850.

6 Russell CA, Fonville JM, Brown AE, *et al.* (2012) 'The Potential for Respiratory Droplet-Transmissible A/H5N1 Influenza Virus to Evolve in a Mammalian Host,' *Science* Vol. 336(6088): 1541–1547; Imai M, Watanabe T, Hatta M, *et al.* (2012) 'Experimental Adaptation of an Influenza H5 HA Confers Respiratory Droplet Transmission to a Reassortant H5 HA/H1N1 Virus in Ferrets,' *Nature* Vol. 486(7403): 420–428.

7 Dando M (2011) 'Advances in Neuroscience and the Biological and Toxin Weapons Convention,' *Biotechnology Research International* 2011: 973851. See http://www.ncbi.nlm.nih.gov/pubmed/21350673 (accessed September 18, 2015); Requarth T (2015) 'This is Your Brain. This is Your Brain as a Weapon,' *Foreign Policy.* See http://foreignpolicy.com/2015/09/14/this-is-your-brain-this-is-your-brain-as-a-weapon-darpa-dual-use-neuroscience/ (accessed September 18, 2015).

8 Soll SJ, Neil SJ and Bieniasz PD (2010) 'Identification of a Receptor for an Extinct Virus,' *Proceedings of the National Academies of Sciences USA* Vol. 107(45): 19496–19501.

9 Massung RF, Liu LI, Qi J *et al.* (1994) 'Analysis of the Complete Genome of Smallpox Variola Major Virus Strain Bangladesh-1975,' *Virology* Vol. 201(2): 215–240.

10 World Health Organization (2010) *Scientific Review of Variola Virus Research 1999–2010*, p. 45. See http://apps.who.int/iris/bitstream/10665/70508/1/WHO_HSE_GAR_BDP_2010.3_eng.pdf (accessed September 18, 2015).

11 Boddie C, Watson M, Ackerman G and Gronvall GK (2015) 'Assessing the Bioweapons Threat,' *Science* Vol. 349(6250): 792–793.

Chapter 9

Searching for Cures or Creating Pandemics in the Lab?

Nancy D. Connell & Brian Rappert

Ye can call it influenza if ye like, said Mrs. Machin.
There was no influenza in my young days. We called a cold a cold.
Enoch Arnold Bennet, 1867–1931

The influenza transmissibility experiments

In the autumn of 2011, a prominent influenza researcher, Ron Fouchier, gave the keynote address at the Fourth European Scientific Working Group on Influenza (ESWI) Influenza Conference in Malta. One of the more pressing questions in global influenza research is the nature of influenza transmissibility, and what genes control host specificity. Fouchier revealed that his group at Erasmus Medical Center in Rotterdam had succeeded in creating a novel strain of influenza that had altered transmissibility properties. Yoshihiro Kawaoka and his colleagues, working at University of Wisconsin and Tokyo, were performing similar studies. The path of eventual disclosure and publication of these two lines of inquiry in May/June of 2012 was accompanied by a fierce controversy on the justification of the research, the intersection of biosafety and biosecurity, and the role of the media in interpreting contemporary science.

To study the genetic determinants of transmissibility, these researchers started with a specific virus — avian influenza Type A — known to infect aquatic birds as well as domestic poultry. There are two classes of avian influenza viruses, low pathogenic avian influenza (LPAI) A viruses, and highly pathogenic avian influenza (HPAI) A viruses. HPAI causes severe disease in birds and is often fatal. These viruses have also been known occasionally to infect humans (over 840 cases since 2003), with an approximately 50 percent mortality rate for reported cases.[1] In most instances, these human infections are associated with intimate contact with an infected bird — for example, a young girl holding a chicken on her lap, or a butcher working in a live poultry market where infected chickens are processed.

The experiments of Kawaoka and Fouchier addressed the following question: Could the influenza genome be altered in the laboratory to result in a changed virus that would now be transmitted by aerosol? While there are differences between the approaches used by the two scientists,[2] they both started with an HPAI strain and used the ferret as a model for human influenza.[3] The results of the two studies were similar: a small number of mutations can give rise to a viral strain of HPAI with the ability to pass among ferrets via the respiratory route. This virus, normally spread among birds and poultry, had been engineered to spread among members of a different species. The organism had thus acquired a new property and the experiments would later be assigned the descriptive term "gain of function (GOF)." Research that fell in this category would be subject to considerable scrutiny. Before examining the history leading up to GOF and state of policy at the time of writing in 2015, we address the basic question: What does this term actually mean?

"Gain of Function" — historical use and current appropriation

The mutagenesis and subsequent reverse engineering used by Fouchier and Kawaoka to alter the viral genome are classic approaches to the genetic analysis of gene function in negative strand RNA viruses.[4] Traditionally, GOF is a term used to describe a kind of mutation, of which there are many different kinds: deletion, over/under or loss of expression, regulatory, loss of function, dominant, dominant negative, recessive, etc. The original assignment of the term "gain of function" was to a certain class of genetic mutation — an experimental device — characterized by the acquisition of a property, any property. The earliest citing of the term as a genetic tool in PubMed is 1968[5]; GOF mutations have routinely been used for decades as a powerful method to dissect the role of a gene and its product.

Casadevall and Imperiale have analyzed the term "gain of function" and point out that it is now synonymous with "something dangerous, risky, and possibly nefarious," and only as "something that can be used to confer dangerous properties to a microbe."[6] They describe the methods used to create vaccines using human pathogens: The polio virus was serially passed in monkey cells, leading to an attenuated live strain that has contributed to the 99 percent reduction in polio cases worldwide (Sabin 1965).[7] Indeed, the same technique was used to generate the tuberculosis[8] and rabies[9] vaccines, among others. GOF in the context of the controversy over influenza transmissibility studies is an entirely inappropriate use of the term. Replacement terms have been proposed[10] but "GoF" has been firmly ensconced in the lay and scientific literature.

The important thing is not to stop questioning…
Never lose a holy curiosity.
Albert Einstein (1879–1955)

On the need for curiosity

Influenza viruses circle the globe every year, returning in a new version and eluding the previous year's vaccine(s). The numbers associated with influenza disease are staggering. Almost 100,000 papers have been published on influenza. In 1918, as many as 20 million (some estimates put the number closer to 50 million) died of influenza. The WHO's Global Influenza Surveillance and Response System has been in place for over half a century to "monitor[s] the evolution of influenza viruses and provide[s] recommendations in areas including laboratory diagnostics, vaccines, antiviral susceptibility and risk assessment...and to also serve[s] as a global alert mechanism for the emergence of influenza viruses with pandemic potential."[11] The basic research that is part of the global attempt to control pandemic influenza is essential both for the development of vaccines (methods for flu vaccine production have not changed since 1938[12]) and the increased precision of surveillance. The controversy sparked by Kawaoka and Fouchier's work rages on, and other viral agents enter the fray (for example, the corona viruses MERS and SARS). In the remainder of this chapter we will discuss the elements of biosafety, biosecurity, regulatory agencies and the media that have contributed to this perfect storm. Particular reference is given to the U.S., where discussions have been full-blown and significant policies have been introduced.

Where is the concern? The pre-history to "GOF"

To appreciate the debate that ensued over the H5N1 experiments as well as "Gain of Function" research more generally, it is important to note that, in recent decades across much of the globe, civilian life science research has been comparatively free in relation to other areas of science from associations with matters of malign use, the military and national security. With some exceptions, for many it was not until 9/11 and the mailing of anthrax letters in the U.S. that questions were prominently voiced whether the data, conclusions and techniques generated through fundamental civilian research might enable the production of biological weapons. Since then a number of efforts have been made to identify how individuals, substate groups or states might use advances in the life sciences to make bacteria resistant to existing antibiotics, to increase the virulence or lethality of viruses, to lengthen the environmental stability of agents, to lower the body's ability to defend itself against disease, to make non-pathogenic organisms pathogenic, etc.

As well, since 2001 considerable efforts have been made to identify and assess what are known as the "biosecurity" implications of research. In response, additional controls have been introduced on how biological agents identified as dangerous can be stored and transferred, along with who can legitimately access them. Proposals have been offered for how fundamental research could be scrutinized and restrictions imposed because of concerns about the potential malign use of data and findings. The set of H5N1 experiments were one in a series of experiments scrutinized this way.

Going back in time, perhaps the most well-known statement on the question of whether some forms of research should be done, under what conditions, and whether it should be communicated was the 2003 report by the Natural Research Council of the U.S. National Academies titled *Biotechnology Research in an Age of Terrorism: Confronting the Dual Use Dilemma.*[13] As part of this discussion, the committee set out the problem in this way:

> ...almost all biotechnology in the service of human health can be subverted for misuse by hostile individuals or nations. The major vehicles of bioterrorism, at least in the near term, are likely to be based on materials and techniques that are available throughout the world and are easily acquired. Most importantly, a critical element of our defense against bioterrorism is the accelerated development of biotechnology to advance our ability to detect and cure disease. Since the development of biotechnology is facilitated by the sharing of ideas and materials, open communication offers the best security against bioterrorism. The tension between the spread of technologies that protect us and the spread of technologies that threaten us is the crux of the dilemma.

In brief, the fear was with how modern research could *further* rather than just *prevent* the spread of disease.

The biosecurity policy and public discussion about what research should be done and how it should be communicated would become bound up with a handful of identified experiments. Perhaps the best-known instance is that of the Australian mousepox experiment.[14] Australian scientists wished to find a way of dealing with the large numbers of rodents that plague the agricultural industry in that country. Their plan was to develop an anti-fertility treatment for mice by genetically modifying the mousepox virus. To do so they inserted the gene encoding an egg protein into the mousepox genome, believing this would cause treated mice to have an anti-body response to their own eggs, and thus reject them, resulting in sterility. When the results were not as satisfactory as they hoped, they did a further modification of inserting the interleukin-4 (IL-4) gene into the mousepox, since IL-4 had been shown to elevate anti-body responses in other situations. This time the results were dramatic. The researchers found that they had produced a recombinant virus that was lethal to all normal mice, including some that had been bred to be genetically resistant to mousepox, and even some of those vaccinated against mousepox. In other words, they had created an extremely lethal form of the mousepox virus. The researchers identified a further implication of their findings — that if such a simple modification to other pox viruses were to have the same effect (an open question at the time), the prospects for the creation of a highly lethal vaccine resistant form of smallpox might also be within reach.[15]

Another of the handful of examples of what would become widely labeled as "dual-use research" was the reconstruction of the 1918 Spanish flu by researchers in the U.S. in 2005. In this case, the scientists sought to understand what it was about the 1918 Spanish flu that made it so deadly. The researchers were aware from the outset that by reconstructing the virus they were doing work, the results of which, could potentially be used to create more virulent, dangerous forms of the flu virus. They also knew that accidental release from the laboratory would be potentially disastrous. Yet, they went ahead on the basis that identifying the factor that causes virulence could also result in better, more effective vaccines and treatments.[16] A similar set of issues was previously raised in 2002 by a group of researchers of the successful artificial chemical synthesis of poliovirus that brought to the fore a way to create other viruses from scratch (Cello *et al.* 2002).[17]

The question of what should be done in response to such dual-use research was the topic of significant discussion in the 2000s by government agencies, professional societies, science publishers and funders, as well as others. While recognizing the potential malign applications of such experiments, the researchers involved and many others have defended their undertaking and publication because of their value in providing warnings as well as in elaborating basic biological mechanisms. These kinds of studies can inform surveillance and forensics methodologies as well as contribute to vaccines and therapeutics.

For such reasons, it was not the case that debates in the 2000s were split between intelligence and law enforcement agencies pressing for biosecurity controls on what gets done, how, and its communication on the one hand, and scientists resisting such efforts on the other. Indeed, government agencies have repeatedly expressed an unwillingness to impose regulations, and elite representatives of the international scientific community have been the most active to initiate discussions about what needs to be done, albeit often openly with a view to devising forms of voluntary self-regulation. For instance, in 2003 a group of prominent scientific journal editors agreed to factor into their publication decision-making procedures, the possible security harms and benefits of submissions[18] and some science funding bodies[19] introduced questions about misuse into their grant application procedures; the National Institutes of Health has followed suit.

As another strand of activity, following a recommendation in *Biotechnology Research in an Age of Terrorism*, the National Science Advisory Board for Biosecurity was formally set up in 2005 in the U.S.[20] As part of its mandate, it was tasked with devising guidelines for the pre-project approval review of the security costs and benefits of research proposals by local institutional biosafety review boards. As part of doing so, in 2007, it offered the term "dual-use research of concern" (DURC) as a category for research needing review. This was defined as "research that, based on current understanding, can be reasonably anticipated to provide knowledge, products, or technologies that could be directly misapplied to pose a threat to public health and safety, agricultural crops and other plants, animals, the environment, or material."[21]

What is notable about such review procedures is that up until the 2011 H5N1 controversy, only a very small percentage of grant applications, publications and institutional reviews have identified instances of research as 'of concern' (Rappert 2014). For instance, of 74,000 submissions to the Nature Publishing Group between 2005 and

2008, only 28 were identified as having a dual-use potential.[22] Perhaps more notably, it appears that no grant applications, publications and institutional reviews had dissemination restrictions imposed until H5N1 or been forgone outright because of the outcomes of formal DURC review assessments. Reasons identified for the limited identifications and the absence of restrictions have included: The difficulty of assessing the future risks and benefits of individual pieces of research; the limited awareness by most civilian research practitioners about dual use issues despite the need for this as part of review procedures; the limited knowledge held by civilian researchers about the motivations and capabilities of would be malign users; the manner in which the identification of a dual use potential has been identified as positive because of the need to assess threats and countermeasures; and the assumptions often made about the likelihood of benefits stemming from research (Rappert 2014).

DURC: What should be done?

One of the mandates for the National Science Advisory Board of Biosecurity's (NSABB) first years was to devise policy for dual-use oversight. Its *Proposed Framework for the Oversight of Dual-Use Life Sciences* was unveiled in 2007[23] and then languished, facing an uncertain future while U.S. administrations changed.

When the H5N1 influenza virus experiments became high profile in 2011, the NSABB took center stage. The two research groups lead by Ron Fouchier at Erasmus Medical Center and Yoshihiro Kawaoka at the University of Wisconsin, Madison, submitted manuscripts to *Science* and *Nature*, indicating how genetically mutated forms of the H5N1 influenza virus could become transmissible by aerosol among ferrets.[24] Until that time, H5N1 was known to be transmitted to mammals from birds only through direct physical contact. The NSABB reviewed the publications and concluded that to reduce their malign potential, certain details must be redacted. During the wide-ranging and, at times, heated debate that followed, a yearlong moratorium was initiated by a group of 40 flu researchers and lifted in January 2013 (Fouchier *et al.* 2013).[25]

Meanwhile, a series of meetings ensued. The New York Academy of Sciences hosted a lively panel on February 2, 2012; WHO held a confidential international meeting in the same month that concluded that full versions of the articles should be published once issues associated with public messaging had been addressed. The NSABB met again in March 2012, and relented, with a split vote, to support the publication of the two studies. The reversal of the decision was justified by requiring that the publications cite new information that would reduce the possibility of malign use of the material and by the introduction of additional strategies to protect public health. The NSABB stated: "The Board's discussions were informed by the analytical frameworks that it previously developed for considering the risks and benefits associated with the communication of DURC." That framework was the original 2007 *Proposed Framework for the Oversight of Dual-Use Life Sciences Research.*[26] Yet this framework did not specify how potential future benefits and harms could be assessed and weighed in practice. Instead, it laid out organizational processes for handling DURC instances.

However, a rift within NSABB about what should be done regarding H5N1 was reflected in a letter leaked by one of its members who wrote:

> I believe there was a bias toward finding a solution that was a lot less about a robust science- and policy-based risk–benefit analysis and more about how to get us out of this difficult situation. I also believe that this same approach in the future will mean all of us, including life science researchers, journal editors and government policymakers, will just continue to "kick the can down the road" without coming to grips with the very difficult task of managing DURC and the dissemination of potentially harmful information to those who might intentionally or unintentionally use that information in a way that risks public safety.[27]

Some believe that weighing risk and benefits for DURC is not possible[28] while others stress the need for "careful consideration of the scope and magnitude of the potential risks and benefits associated with the research proposal, evaluation of whether the risks outweigh the benefits, and strategies for mitigating potential risks" — as stated in the early 2013, National Institute of Health (NIH) guides for U.S. Department of Health and Human Services' framework for funding decisions on individual proposals involving highly pathogenic avian influenza H5N1 viruses.[29] International attention to devising processes for identifying and evaluating research along these lines continue. The need for DURC-type oversight frameworks has been made elsewhere, including by some governments in the context of the Biological Weapons Convention.

Spurred on by the raging controversy, the U.S. Department of Health and Human Services issued a revised policy for DURC life science research in 2012.[30] These events reignited debates about the security implications of the life sciences — typically framed in terms of whether the freedom of science should be jeopardized in the name of security. During the months of debate, the scientific community split into two basic camps: those who supported work on potentially dangerous pathogens and felt it should move forward, and those who thought these kinds of experiments should not be performed. In fact, two organizations were founded along these lines: Scientists for Science[31] supported work with dangerous pathogens and argues it can be performed safely; the Cambridge Working Group,[32] on the other hand, maintain that a small but measurable rate of accidental release of infectious agents from research laboratories has been documented, and that experiments with potential pandemic organisms "should be curtailed until there has been a quantitative, objective and credible assessment of the risks, potential benefits, and opportunities for risk mitigation, as well as comparison against safer experimental approaches."[33] More generally, those in favor of the work stress the value of experiments in our understanding and ability to control pandemic flu, and those who oppose the work emphasize the inherent dangers. The two camps remain polarized.

Laboratory breaches shift the DURC and GOF landscape

2014 saw a number of high-profile laboratory-related breaches that would have significant implications for debates about DURC and

GOF research. In June of that year, the CDC announced that many of its scientists might have been exposed to *Bacillus anthracis*, the result of insufficient deactivation of the anthrax spores. This event was followed in rapid succession by a series of revelations: Influenza virus sent from a Centers for Disease Control and Prevention (CDC) laboratory was contaminated with a strain of highly pathogenic bird flu. Vials of smallpox virus — under lock and key in ostensibly only two places on the planet since the 1970s[34] — were discovered in a storage room at the NIH; a few weeks later, more vials of potential biological agents were found in the same room. As of this writing, the most recent and large-scale safety and security breach comprises the mailing of incompletely inactivated anthrax spores to 595 shipments, 192 institutions, 500 states, 1 district, 3 territories and 7 foreign countries; these materials were released by the U.S. Department of Defense's premier biological warfare laboratory, the Dugway Proving Ground in Utah, over a period of 10 years.[35]

These lapses in federal oversight alarmed both the scientific community and the public, and, coupled with the controversy of the H5N1 transmission studies, appear to have stimulated a forceful response from the Obama Administration in relation to gain-of-function (GOF) research — one that hitherto had been absent. In October of 2014, the White House Office of Science and Technology Policy and the Department of Health and Human Services moved to stop all U.S. government-funded so-called "GOF" studies in three viruses. The ruling applies to new studies "that may be reasonably anticipated to confer attributes to influenza, MERS, or SARS viruses such that the virus would have enhanced pathogenicity and/or transmissibility in mammals via the respiratory route."[36] For the small subset of ongoing work that is determined to meet the GOF funding pause criteria, the contract-funded work has been paused and the grant-funded work is subject to a voluntary pause. There is some confusion over the specific application of this third pause in pandemic pathogen research. A small number of laboratories (around 18) have been directly affected by these changes: "for the small subset of ongoing work that is determined to meet the gain-of-function funding pause criteria, the contract-funded work has been paused and the grant-funded work is subject to a voluntary pause."[37]

The 2014 ruling led to the following timeline. First, the NSABB was to draft a series of recommendations for a study of the issues surrounding GOF research that would be reviewed by the broader scientific community. This task has been completed ("Framework for conducting risk and benefit assessments of GOF research".[38] The National Research Council (NRC) of the U.S. National Academies was to convene a conference to bring the scientific community together to discuss assessment of GOF research. This conference took place on December 15–16 at the National Academies.[39] Together, these activities are to inform the design and execution of a risks and benefits assessment of GOF research, which will be performed during 2015. The NRC will host another conference to discuss the results of the study, and the study and recommendations for a "policy governing funding and conduct of GOF research" will be presented to the U.S. government (USG).

In the weeks and months between the voluntary moratorium and the Obama administration's mandatory moratorium, the GOF work continued abate. June 2014 saw the publication by groups in Maryland and Italy of a study of the potential pandemic avian influenza H7N1 described.[40] Using serial passages, novel strains of the virus were generated, with ability to be transmitted to cohoused ferrets and no loss of virulence; four amino acid changes were involved. Simon Wain-Hobson, of the Cambridge Working Group, commented in October 2014:

> The ostrich H7N1GOF paper is far from the last. Some insiders have spoken of a tidal wave of viral GOF studies working their way toward publication. Some researchers are even engineering human influenza viruses such that they can escape extant vaccine coverage. I urge funders, universities, and learned societies to foster discussion on this topic from a diverse spectrum of thinkers. And fast, for we are already up against an airborne route-transmissible H7N1 virus that is "more virulent in humans than the 1918 influenza virus A H1N1 pandemic strain."[41] As there appear to be no checks in place, is it wise to continue such work until such a discussion has taken place? I think not. In the meantime, we can all do something simple and take a mental Hippocratic oath.[42]

In the meantime with the roll-out of these activities, researchers Imperiale and Casadevall, writing in *mBIO*, claimed to "have numerous concerns about this third stoppage, including the timing of the announcement relative to the ongoing debate, the vagueness in the wording of the statement, and the potential effects on the fields of influenza virus and coronavirus research."[43] They conclude:

> As we have written previously, understanding the pathogenicity of these viruses is necessary if we want to develop new therapies and vaccines and ensure useful surveillance.[44] Clearly, the research must be performed under biocontainment conditions that minimize the risk of accidental release. The discussion that the White House is asking for must occur because the *status quo* is not acceptable. We call on the government to provide clarity regarding what truly should be paused and for how long. We call on the NSABB and the National Academies to move rapidly on this issue, to consider whether the current biosafety practices put in place after the earlier moratoriums are sufficient, and if found to be so, to state so without a need for new layers of mandates for what is already a highly supervised field. To repeat ourselves, we must get this right.[45]

Critics of the research met the news of the mandatory moratorium positively. "Opponents of this type of research, called gain of function — for example, attempts to create a more contagious version of the lethal H5N1 avian influenza to learn which mutations made it that way — were elated."[46] Marc Lipsitch and colleagues in the Cambridge Working Group argue that "a moratorium is the right approach until a rigorous, objective, and credible risk assessment process can be established."[47] At the time of writing, scientific communities around the world await the results of this year-long exercise in real-time policy evolution.

What is the question, what is the concern?

The survey presented in this chapter of the shifting scrutiny given to civilian life science research in relation to its malign use potential, military relevance and national security implications illustrates a few important themes associated with the interaction of research, policy and biological weapons.

Events as agenda setting: The history of attention to DURC and GOF has very much been driven in response to a limited number of events that captured significant eminence. Initially, much of the attention to dual use research owed its impetus to the events in 2001: The publication of the IL-4 mousepox experiments, 9/11, and the anthrax attacks in the U.S. In the years that followed, a handful of experiments would define (and delimit) how dual-use research was conceived. The attention to this topic was dramatically elevated starting in 2011 with the announcements associated with H5N1. Save for this work, regard for DURC might well have faded into a position of insignificance in the U.S. and beyond.

Events as agenda shifting: Yet while the H5N1 case brought renewed attention to the question of what purposes might be served by civilian research (therefore whether it should be done and how it should be communicated), it did not have significant implications for other DURC. Forceful preventative measures in relation to GOF in the U.S. followed only in response to a number of high-profile laboratory-related breaches in 2014 — breaches associated with improper storage and shipment.

With these events the issues at hand also shifted in important ways. The original focus of the H5N1 controversy was the problem of communication. Should these data be released, and would their dissemination be an overall security risk? In fact, it is the *safety* of the H5N1 transmissibility that has come to dominate discussions and has reinvigorated attention to designing and implementing review procedures. The evolution of the controversy from biosecurity to more traditional matters of biosafety is largely a question of the scientists involved backing off on their original claims for how dangerous the work was, as well as the attention to the safety implications of the breaches in U.S. laboratories.

In relation to shifting agendas, Peter Sandman has meticulously tracked the shift in focus from biosecurity to biosafety in a fascinating analysis of the risk communications provided by the scientists themselves; his interpretation of the procession of events is as follows.[48] Beginning with the initial meeting in Malta, Sandman notes that the experiments were described by Fouchier thus: "The virus is airborne and as efficiently transmitted as the seasonal virus...This is very bad news, indeed."[49] Indeed, in two other accounts — Harmon in *Scientific American*[50] and MacKenzie in the *New Scientist* [51] — Fouchier was quoted as characterizing the decisive manipulation in this manner: "Someone finally convinced me to do something really, really stupid". In her report, Mackenzie continued:

> Then the researchers gave the virus from the sick ferrets to more ferrets — a standard technique for making pathogens adapt to an animal. They repeated this 10 times, using stringent containment. The tenth round of ferrets shed an H5N1 strain that spread to ferrets in separate cages — and killed them.[52]

This version of the experiment was the most prominent one until February 29, 2012, (and perhaps a short time earlier, at the closed WHO meeting), when Fouchier offered a significantly different account during the question and answer period at an ASM panel: "These [lab-mutated] viruses do not kill ferrets if they are sneezed upon....If anything, our data suggest that this virus spreads poorly."[53] No longer portrayed as a "really, really stupid experiment", the H5N1 work became something akin to a snivel.

The limits of analysis

Much of the debate about what needs to be done in response to DURC and GOF research has been couched in terms of the importance of weighing the risks and benefits of research through formal assessments. Perhaps the most comprehensive discussion to date of potential risk and benefits of the GOF work in the context of this specific controversy can be found in the NRC report detailing a meeting held at the National Academies December 15–16, 2014. The workshop tackled the discipline of risk assessment itself, potential benefits and risks of the GOF work, and the policy implications by in-depth presentations followed by lively Q&As. "If there is any area of commonality," said Fineberg, "it is around the acceptance of the legitimacy of the concerns that have been raised on all sides of this issue."[54] No consensus was requested or attempted. Despite nearly 15 years of attention to the overall topic and the centrality of risk assessment, the elaboration of how the potential for future malign use ought to affect civilian research today has been limited. Whether an effective risk analysis can be done and whether it should be done remain unsettled and unsettling concerns.

References

Cello J, Paul AV and Wimmer E (2002) 'Chemical Synthesis of Poliovirus cDNA: Generation of Infectious Virus in the Absence of Natural Template,' *Science* Vol. 297: 1016–1018.

Fouchier RA, Garcia-Sastre A and Kawaoka Y (2013) 'H5N1 virus: Transmission Studies Resume for Avian Flu,' *Nature* Vol. 493: 609.

Rappert B (2014) 'Why has Not There been More Research of Concern?,' *Frontiers in Public Health* Vol. 2: 74.

Sabin AB (1965) 'Oral Poliovirus Vaccine. History of its Development and Prospects for Eradication of Poliomyelitis,' *JAMA* 194: 872–876.

Notes

1 WHO (2015) *Cumulative Number of Confirmed Human Cases for Avian Influenza A(H5N1) reported to WHO, 2003–2015.* See http://www.who.int/influenza/human_animal_interface/EN_GIP_20150501CumulativeNumberH5N1cases.pdf?ua=1 (accessed September 17, 2015).

2 Enserink L (2012) 'Free to Speak, Kawaoka Reveals Flu Details While Fouchier Stays Mum,' *ScienceInsider.*

3 Enkirch T and von Messling V (2015) 'Ferret Models of Viral Pathogenesis,' *Virology* Vol. 479–480: 259–270.

4 Hatta M, Neumann G and Kawaoka Y (2001) 'Reverse Genetics Approach Towards Understanding Pathogenesis of H5N1 Hong Kong Influenza A Virus Infection,' *Philosophical Transactions of the Royal Society London B: Biological Sciences* Vol. 356: 1841–1843; Ozawa M and Kawaoka Y (2011) 'Taming Influenza Viruses,' *Virus Research* Vol. 162: 8–11.

[5] Dalgarno L and Sinsheimer RL (1968) 'Process of Infection with Bacteriophage PhiX174. XXIV. New Type of Temperature-Sensitive Mutant,' *Journal of Virology* Vol. 2: 822–829.

[6] Casadevall A and Imperiale MJ (2014) 'Risks and Benefits of Gain-of-Function Experiments with Pathogens of Pandemic Potential, Such as Influenza Virus: A Call for a Science-Based Discussion,' *mBio* 5: e01730–01714.

[7] Sabin AB (1965) 'Oral Poliovirus Vaccine. History of its Development and Prospects for Eradication of Poliomyelitis,' *JAMA* 194: 872–876.

[8] Calmette AG, (1909) 'Sur Quelques Propriétés du Bacille Tuberculeux d'Origine, Cultivé sur la Bile de Boeuf Glycérinée,' *Comptes Rendus de l'Academie des Sciences* Vol. 149: 716–718.

[9] Smith KA (2012) 'Louis pasteur, the father of immunology?' *Frontiers in Immunology* Vol.3: 68.

[10] Duprex WP and Casadevall A (2014) 'Falling Down the rabbit hole: aTRIP toward lexiconic precision in the "gain-of-function" debate,' *mBio* 5(6):e02421–14.

[11] WHO (2015) *Global Influenza Surveillance and Response System (GISRS)*, http://www.who.int/influenza/gisrs_laboratory/en/ (accessed September 17, 2015).

[12] Gerdil C (2003) 'The Annual Production Cycle for Influenza Vaccine,' *Vaccine* Vol. 21: 1776–1779.

[13] National Research Council (2004) *Biotechnology Research in an Age of Terrorism*. Washington, DC: National Academies Press.

[14] Jackson RJ, Ramsay AJ, Christensen CD *et al.* (2001) 'Expression of Mouse Interleukin-4 by a Recombinant Ectromelia Virus Suppresses Cytolytic Lymphocyte Responses and Overcomes Genetic Resistance to Mousepox,' *Journal of Virology* Vol. 75: 1205–1210.

[15] Finkel E (2001) 'Australia. Engineered Mouse Virus Spurs Bioweapon Fears,' *Science* Vol. 291: 585.

[16] Tumpey TM, Basler CF, Aguilar PV *et al.* (2005) 'Characterization of the Reconstructed 1918 Spanish Influenza Pandemic Virus,' *Science* Vol. 310: 77–80.

[17] Cello J, Paul AV and Wimmer E (2002) 'Chemical Synthesis of Poliovirus cDNA: Generation of Infectious Virus in the Absence of Natural Template,' *Science* Vol. 297: 1016–1018.

[18] Atlas R, Campbell P, Cozzarelli NR *et al.* (2003) 'Statement on the Consideration of Biodefence and Biosecurity,' *Nature* Vol. 421: 771; Atlas R, Campbell P, Cozzarelli NR *et al.* (2003) 'Statement on Scientific Publication and Security,' *Science* Vol. 299: 1149; Atlas R, Campbell P, Cozzarelli

NR *et al.* (2003) 'Uncensored Exchange of Scientific Results,' *Proceedings of the National Academies of Sciences USA* Vol. 100: 1464.

19 Such as the U.K. Biological Sciences Research Council, the U.K. Medical Research Council, and Welcome Trust.

20 National Research Council 2004, as per note 13.

21 NSABB NIoH (2007) *Proposed Framework for the Oversight of Dual Use Life Sciences Research: Strategies for Minimizing the Potential Misuse of Research Information*, http://osp.od.nih.gov/sites/default/files/resources/NSABB_Framework_for_Risk_and_Benefit_Assessments_of_GOF_Research-APPROVED.pdf (accessed September 17, 2015).

22 Society R (2012) 'Science as an open enterprise,' in R Society (Ed). London.

23 NSABB NIoH 2007, as per note 21.

24 Imai M, Watanabe T, Hatta M *et al.* (2012) 'Experimental Adaptation of an Influenza H5 HA Confers Respiratory Droplet Transmission to a Reassortant H5 HA/H1N1 Virus in Ferrets,' *Nature* Vol. 486: 420–428; Herfst S, Schrauwen EJ, Linster M *et al.* (2012) 'Airborne Transmission of Influenza A/H5N1 Virus Between Ferrets,' *Science* Vol. 336: 1534–1541.

25 Fouchier RA, Garcia-Sastre A and Kawaoka Y (2013) 'H5N1 virus: Transmission Studies Resume for Avian Flu,' *Nature* Vol. 493: 609.

26 NSABB NIoH 2007, as per note 21.

27 Osterholm MT (2012).

28 Committee on Science Technology, Law, Policy (2013) *Perspectives on Research with H5N1 Avian Influenza: Scientific Inquiry, Communication, Controversy: Summary of a Workshop.* Washington, DC: National Academies Press.

29 Health NIo. (2013) *A Framework for Guiding U.S. Department of Health and Human Services Funding Decisions about Research Proposals with the Potential for Generating Highly Pathogenic Avian Influenza H5N1 Viruses that are Transmissible among Mammals by Respiratory Droplets.* Bethesda, MD: NIH.

30 USG Policy for Institutional Oversight of Life Sciences Dual Use Research of Concern, 2012. See http://osp.od.nih.gov/sites/default/files/announcements/United_States_Government_Policy_for_Oversight_of_DURC_FINAL_version_032812.pdf (accessed September 17, 2015).

31 http://www.scientistsforscience.org/ (accessed September 17, 2015).

32 http://www.cambridgeworkinggroup.org/ (accessed September 17, 2015).

33 As per note 32.

[34] Connor S (2002) 'How Terrorism Prevented Smallpox Being Wiped off the Face of the Planet For Ever,' *The Independent*.

[35] Department of Defense. (2015) *Department of Defense Laboratory Review*, http://archive.defense.gov/home/features/2015/0615_lab-stats/(accessed September 17, 2015).

[36] White House (2014) *U.S. Government Gain-of-Function Deliberative Process and Research Funding Pause on Selected Gain-of-Function Research Involving Influenza, MERS, and SARS Viruses.*

[37] Imperiale MJ and Casadevall A (2014) 'Vagueness and Costs of the Pause on Gain-of-Function (GOF) Experiments on Pathogens with Pandemic Potential, Including Influenza Virus,' *MBio* 5.

[38] NSABB NIoH (2015) *Framework for Conducting Risk and Benefit Assessments of Gain-of-Function Research*, http://osp.od.nih.gov/sites/default/files/resources/NSABB_Framework_for_Risk_and_Benefit_Assessments_of_GOF_Research-APPROVED.pdf_(accessed September 17, 2015).

[39] Workshop summary: http://www.nap.edu/catalog/21666/potential-risks-and-benefits-of-gain-of-function-research-summary (accessed September 17, 2015).

[40] Sutton TC, Finch C, Shao H *et al.* (2014) 'Airborne Transmission of Highly Pathogenic H7N1 Influenza Virus in Ferrets,' *Journal of Virology* Vol. 88: 6623–6635.

[41] Dermody TS, Sandri-Goldin RM and Shenk T (2014) 'Sequence Changes Associated with Respiratory Transmission of H7N1 Influenza Virus in Mammals,' *Journal of Virology* Vol. 88: 6533–6534.

[42] Wain-Hobson S (2014) 'An Avian H7N1 Gain-of-Function Experiment of Great Concern,' *mBio* 5: e01882–01814.

[43] Imperiale and Casadevall 2014, as per note 37.

[44] Casadevall A, Howard D and Imperiale MJ (2014) An Epistemological Perspective on the Value of Gain-of-Function Experiments Involving Pathogens with Pandemic Potential. *MBio* 5: e01875–01814.

[45] Imperiale and Casadevall 2014, as per note 37.

[46] McNeil DG (2014) 'White House to Cut Funding for Risky Biological Study,' *The New York Times*.

[47] Lipsitch M and Inglesby TV (2014) 'Moratorium on Research Intended to Create Novel Potential Pandemic Pathogens,' *MBio* 5; Lipsitch M and Inglesby TV (2015) 'Erratum for lipsitch and inglesby, moratorium on research intended to create novel potential pandemic pathogens,' *MBio* 6.

[48] Sandman P (2012) *Risk Communication Aspects of the Debate Over H5N1 Transmission Studies*, http://www.psandman.com/gst2012.htm - H5N1; Sandman P (2012) 'Talking about H5N1 Research,' *Genetic and Engineering News* 32.

[49] Influenza ESWGo (2011) Fourth ESWI Influenza Conference.

[50] Harmon K (2011) 'What Will the Next Influenza Pandemic Look Like,' *Scientific American*.

[51] MacKenzie D (2011) 'Five Easy Mutations to Make Bird Flu a Lethal Pandemic,' *New Scientist*.

[52] MacKenzie 2011, as per note 50.

[53] Microbiology ASf (2012) Discussion of NSABB's publication recommendations for the NIH-funded research on the transmissibility of H5N1, February 29, 2012.

[54] Sciences BoL (2015) Potential Risks and Benefits of Gain-of-Function Research: Summary of a Workshop. *The National Academies Collection: Reports funded by National Institutes of Health*. Washington, DC: National Academies Press.Point of View.

Point of View

Dangerous Life Sciences Research

David R. Franz

The concepts "dual-use research," "dual-use research of concern," "gain-of-function" and even "responsible life sciences research" have found an unsettled place in the vocabulary of life scientists, particularly those working with infectious microbes, just since the turn of the 21st century. Was it the biotech and information revolutions or some other more subtle change in societal norms that sparked these challenges, this thinking and the debates? I served on both the U.S. National Academy of Sciences committee that developed the early thinking on these issues and on the resulting U.S. NSABB. In this contribution, I present my perspective on how our thinking about dangerous life sciences research has developed over the last 15 years.

Biotech in an age of terrorism

In 1996, Larry Wayne Harris, using forged letterhead stationary requested an isolate of *Yersinia pestis,* causative agent of plague, from the American Type Culture Collection,[1] a non-profit source for reference microbiological specimens. There were no laws in the U.S. making Harris's actions illegal, but the FBI became suspicious of potential malevolent intent because of other erratic behavior. He was eventually arrested, released on probation and required to serve 200 hours of community service (Tucker

2000). Within the next year, the USG enacted a new law to control *the exchange* between laboratories of a short list of bacteria, viruses and toxins. It was called the Select Agent Rule of 1997.[2]

Just a few years later, in 2001, Australian researchers published the most widely-known example of what we now consider "dual-use research" in biology.[3] The scientists used standard molecular biological techniques to insert the gene coding for interleukin-4 into ecteromelia (mousepox) virus in an attempt to develop a means of causing infertility in mice, a significant pest species in Australia. To their surprise they found that the altered virus killed naturally resistant mice and even mice immunized against native mousepox virus. Their publication of the work triggered a sometimes-heated debate, critics arguing the authors had given would-be terrorists a roadmap to developing a biological weapon. Unlike the Harris case, these were legitimate scientists in a credible laboratory simply trying to address a real and practical ecological problem.

In September of 2001, Middle Eastern terrorists flew passenger jets into the World Trade Center in New York City and only weeks later, after exposure to anthrax spore laced letters, five Americans died of inhalational anthrax; others were sickened and hundreds were given post-exposure antibiotic prophylaxis (Guillemin 2011). Legislatively, the U.S. political leadership reacted to the anthrax letters by introducing the USA PATRIOT Act and the Bioterrorism Acts, which significantly expanded the regulation of select agents (see Chapter 8). It also reacted by increasing the biodefense budget from $137 million (S&T and mostly in DoD) in 1997 to more than USD $6 billion for all departments in 2002 (Franco and Sell 2010). The Department of Health and Human Services, recipient of the largest funding increase during this period, began construction of 10 BSL-3 laboratories and two BLS-4 laboratories, mostly on academic campuses spaced regionally around the country. Other universities and government contractors opened new labs to work with Select

Agent threat pathogens or expanded work in existing labs. The number of scientists in the U.S. with access to these pathogens increased many-fold in the first few years of the 21st century.

Soon the academic community, represented by the U.S. National Academy of Sciences, began to consider the implications of the greatly increased research and development activity related to Select Agents. In 2003, a committee, chaired by Prof Gerald Fink of MIT, began to consider the implications of *Biotechnology in an Age of Terrorism* and coined the challenge for the infectious disease community as the "Dual-Use Dilemma" (National Research Council 2004).[4] The "Fink report," as it has come to be known, is still mentioned and referenced regularly more than 10 years later.

The Fink report

The committee was not charged to consider how to "stop terrorist use of biological agents." Rather, it was asked to consider firstly the risk that pathogens might be stolen or diverted for malevolent purposes and secondly the risk that research results, knowledge or techniques could facilitate creation of novel pathogens, which might be misused. In brief, it was asked to review current rules and regulations governing research, assess their adequacy and recommend any changes that "could improve U.S. capacity to prevent the destructive application of biotechnology research while still enabling legitimate research to be conducted." The report made seven substantive recommendations:

1. That the USG assure biological scientists receive education on the dual-use dilemma and their responsibilities to mitigate the risks.
2. That the National Institutes of Health augment the extant system for reviewing experiments involving DNA research to also review plans for experiments that might potentially be considered 'experiments of concern'. The committee provided seven categorical examples of 'experiments of concern'.
3. That the community of scientists and journal editors

take the responsibility for reviewing manuscripts before publication for their potential 'national security risks.'
4. That the government create a 'National Science Advisory Board for Biosecurity,' preferably within Department of Health and Human Services to provide advice and guidance to the USG.
5. That the USG rely on the implementation of current legislation and regulation with periodic review for adequacy (rather than adding additional regulations at that time).
6. That the national security and law enforcement communities develop new channels of communication with the life sciences community.
7. That there be developed an 'international forum on biosecurity' to promote harmonized national, regional and international measures on the matter.

Having served initially on the Fink Committee and subsequently on the NSABB[5] from 2005 to 2014, it is my opinion that the Fink committee's guidance was sound with one simple, but strategic exception. The fact that the report described the scope of the problem as "dual-use research" and the NSABB would later call it "dual-use research of concern" (DURC)[6] put all eyes on the technology, the knowledge and research outcomes. Were we to do it again, I would argue for a central and greater emphasis on "responsible life science research." While molecular and genetic tools to manipulate the "bugs" have clearly advanced during this period, tools don't make decisions about right or wrong or about safe or unsafe. It is the rational or irrational decisions and the careful or careless ones made by humans, not the availability of technologies, knowledge or even the pathogens, which lie at the heart of the problem. It is here that the "DURC" issue and the "insider threat" issues come neatly together around a common behavioral pathology and must be dealt with using some of the same leadership and cultural tools (Franz 2013).

The Fink report was widely accepted by the science, policy and security communities at the time and the example "experiments of concern" quickly became known as the "seven deadly sins." A board of 25, made up of senior scientists and security personnel as voting members and *ex officio* members from 15 departments and agencies of government, began meeting regularly in 2005. By 2007, the board had published a series of guidance documents including the comprehensive *Proposed Framework for the Oversight of Dual Use Life Sciences Research: Strategies for Minimizing the Potential Misuse of Research Information*[7] and held four international roundtables in Washington DC and a series of regional interactive video teleconferences with international colleagues around the world.[8] The international meetings and teleconferences were an effort to share our perceptions, views and challenges with friends around the globe and gain their insights and experiences regarding what had come to be known as DURC. The 2007 end-to-end plan to manage DURC, which called for thinking about risks from the beginning — at the stage of research hypothesis development — was the keystone of the board's recommended guidance documents. This document, like the others, was approved at the NIH and forwarded to the relevant White House staff via the Secretary of the DHHS.

A real-world test for NSABB's proposed system

The U.S. NIH funded one group at the University of Wisconsin and another at Erasmus Medical Center in Rotterdam to conduct what would later come to be called "gain-of-function" research on the H5N1 highly pathogenic avian influenza virus.[9] The ultimate purpose of the work was to advance our understanding regarding what is possible — and what nature might do — regarding human-to-human transmissibility of this virus. As background, there had occurred a global pandemic of H1N1 influenza beginning in 2009. The virus spread rapidly from person to person but was fortunately not highly lethal in humans, estimated to have killed around 12,000 while infecting up to 89 million.[10] Then in late 2003, the H5N1 virus spread rapidly, again globally, among domestic and wild birds yet only around 700 human cases were reported worldwide.[11] The mortality rate in humans was suspected to be as high as 60 percent; however that rate was not clear due to the difficulty in estimating the number of subclinical and total cases. Most of the relatively few humans diagnosed with clinical disease were infected from close contact with sick birds. Therefore, H5N1 was not easily transmitted from human to human. The scientific teams were funded to modify the virus to make it transmissible between mammals. Ferrets were used as animal models.

In Malta, in September of 2011, Ron Fouchier, one of the two scientists funded to carry out the genetic modification work, said: “This virus [H5N1] is airborne and as efficiently transmitted as the seasonal virus.”[12] In November of 2011, he described his virus in *Science* as “Probably one of the most dangerous viruses you can make.”[13] He then submitted a manuscript to that journal while Yoshihiro Kawaoka, who headed the other team from the University of Wisconsin, submitted a similar manuscript describing their work to the journal *Nature*. The journal editors asked the NSABB to review the two papers. In December 2011, the NSABB recommended that details of the specific mutations be redacted, asked that flu experts from the international community be appraised of the results, questioned the safety (not security) of the laboratories’ practices and called for a 2-month moratorium on this type of work.[14] In response, the USG requested an invitation-only international meeting at the World Health Organization (WHO) headquarters in Geneva; the meeting was held in February of 2012.[15] Both Fouchier and Kawaoka were present and provided the WHO committee additional information about their findings. Others in attendance included flu experts from at least 10 nations; they echoed the NSABB’s safety concerns, asked for a security review, but concluded that the findings would both contribute to our understanding of pathogenesis and facilitate surveillance for natural emergence of a transmissible virus. They concluded that the subject viruses should stay in the labs of origin but the moratorium should continue. Finally, the WHO committee stated that redacting and limiting distribution of the manuscripts was not feasible.

In March of 2012, the NSABB was asked to review the latest versions of the manuscripts. Board members were informed that redaction would not occur and limiting distribution of information to legitimate international flu experts was not possible. After hearing from both authors again and receiving briefings by senior USG personal the board voted unanimously to approve one of the manuscripts and by simple majority the other.[16]

In December 2012, the USG published *A Framework for Guiding U.S. Department of Health and Human Services Funding Decisions About Highly Pathogenic Avian Influenza H5N1 Gain of Function Research.*[17] In 2014, scientists at the University of Maryland produced an aerosol transmissible of H7N9 influenza virus in ferrets simply by multiple passage in that species[18] and the Rotterdam team published previously withheld sequences of their initial controversial virus.[19] Later in the year 2014, after several highly publicized safety lapses at the U.S. Centers for Disease Control in Atlanta,[20] the White House halted research into what were called "super strains" of infectious disease agents.[21]

Too dangerous?

A common response of government to complex and poorly understood risk is to attempt to "regulate" the enterprise most closely associated with it. The implications of failure to find the balance in the safety-security-regulation equation can impact the progress in the life sciences, which can in-turn impact domestic and global health. Finding that balance in laboratory and pathogen *safety* is relatively straight forward and the methods proven. For more than 50 years, government, academic and industrial laboratories in many countries working with dangerous pathogens have protected their employees and communities from harm and made continuous advancements in infectious disease research.

Finding that balance for (bio) *security*, only really an issue in the last 15 years, has been much more difficult.

The potential of a bioterrorist to cause harm is enormous, but the low frequency of such events makes measuring success at preventing them essentially impossible. The experience base and denominator for laboratory biosafety incidents is measurable; the denominator for biosecurity events occurring in our legitimate laboratories is not. Thus, the tendency to add another layer of regulation to the practice of science, particularly by those who don't understand the science or those whose political ambitions make them excessively risk averse.

Practitioners who understand the *safety* risk have long supported the necessary regulation to reduce it and protect themselves and their communities. However the same groups have pushed back at what they believe to be excessive regulation of the broader community to protect from terrorist or insider *security* risk. Regulation for both laboratory safety and laboratory security is necessary, but it must be done wisely and with attention to the real risk of public harm. Unnecessary regulation can harm the enterprise. We must find the right balance.

Is there research that should not be done? Yes. Certainly, we can all think of combinations of microbe, research team, setting and protocol that should not be approved because the potential for harm just outweighs the public good that might come from the work. This is not the first risk-benefit dilemma in science and it will not be the last. Very recently a technology called CRISPR/Cas9 that allows modification of germ lines — even human germ lines — raises more really thorny questions, this time outside the field of infectious disease. Use for "good" to eradicate familial disease with technologies such as CRISPR will now be weighed against the potential for costly mistake or even malevolent use...but can a balance be found in this case that will allow that?

The more mature controversy regarding GOF experiments with H5N1 influenza virus has demonstrated that there can be serious disagreement among rational, intelligent and highly experienced scientists. One pattern that can be observed, anecdotally, is that individual experts are less concerned about high-risk work with "their virus" than are otherwise equally qualified individuals whose expertise lies with another family of pathogens. It is difficult to parse what part of this is "we're afraid of what we don't understand" and what part if any might be related to "turf and funding" issues.

If we ask individual experts to bin experiments as "safe", "unsafe" or in some "grey area" in between, we might expect that the greater the individual's expertise the fewer the experiments categorized as dangerous and the narrower the grey space. Laboratory risk, community risk and population risk must be considered and the implications of known or potential "pathogenicity", "infectivity" and particularly "transmissibility" thoughtfully reviewed for each case. We have a history of working safely and comfortably with highly pathogenic and highly infective organisms in our high-containment laboratories. Even setting aside the potential for intentional misuse, high transmissibility seriously ups the anti. And understanding what a densely populated world of coexisting ducks, pigs and humans will do to further evolve the products that come out of our labs may be the greatest unknown in the case of influenza strains. The answers to that question lie most likely in more laboratory research. Thus the dilemma.

We scientists must do more than complain. We must demonstrate individual responsibility and develop cultures of corporate responsibility in our laboratories. We must include the public in this discourse and be ever mindful of the value and frailty of public trust in science. We must educate, mentor and make opportunities for those who will follow us, but not only technologically; morally, ethically and with honesty and integrity we must challenge ourselves and those around us. Joining with our best subject matter experts from around the globe to ask hard questions and hammer out answers on the anvil of corporate experience will probably always be the best way to bring balance to the necessary but sometimes over-zealous community of regulators who also believe what they are doing is in the best interest of global safety and security.

The science community a generation before us appears to have done a better job at the now famous 1975 Asilomar, California meeting on recombinant DNA research than we did with the H5N1 gain-of-function discovery response.[22] It would be worth our time to carefully understand *why* we didn't do as well this time and ready our approach to yet unknown but certain potentially dangerous life sciences research now.

References

Franco C and Sell TK (2010) 'Federal Agency Biodefense funding, FY2010-FY2011,' *Biosecurity & Bioterrorism: Biodefense Strategy, Practice & Science* Vol. 8: 129–130.

Franz DR (2013) 'The Dual-Use Dilemma: Crying Out for Leadership,' *St Louis University Journal of Health, Law & Policy* Vol. 7(1): 5–57.

Guillemin J (2011) *American Anthrax: Fear, Crime and the Investigation of the Nation's Deadliest Bioterror Attack.* New York: Times Books.

National Research Council (2004) *Biotechnology Research in an Age of Terrorism*, http://www.nap.edu/catalog/10827/biotechnology-research-in-an-age-of-terrorism (accessed April 19, 2015).

Tucker JB (2000) *Toxic Terror: Assessing Terrorist Use of Chemical and Biological Weapons.* Cambridge, Massachusetts: MIT Press.

Notes

1 ATCC (2015) http://www.atcc.org/ (accessed April 19, 2015).

2 Code of Federal Regulations http://www.gpo.gov/fdsys/pkg/CFR-2009-title42-vol1/pdf/CFR-2009-title42-vol1-sec73-17.pdf (accessed April 19, 2015).

3 Jackson RJ, Ramsay AJ, Christensen CD *et al.* (2001) 'Expression of Mouse Interleukin-4 by a Recombinant Ectromelia Virus Suppresses Cytolytic Lymphocyte Responses and Overcomes Genetic Resistance to Mousepox,' *Virology* Vol. 75: 1205–1206.

4 National Research Council (2004) *Biotechnology Research in an Age of Terrorism*, http://www.nap.edu/catalog/10827/biotechnology-research-in-an-age-of-terrorism (accessed April 19, 2015).

5 NSABB(2005)http://osp.od.nih.gov/office-biotechnology-activities/biosecurity/nsabb (accessed April 19, 2015).

6 NSABB FAQ http://osp.od.nih.gov/office-biotechnology-activities/biosecurity/nsabb/faq(accessed April 19, 2015).

7 NSABB (2007) http://osp.od.nih.gov/sites/default/files/resources/Framework%20for%20transmittal%20duplex%209-10-07.pdf (accessed April 19, 2015).

8 NSABB (2015) International Activities, http://osp.od.nih.gov/office-biotechnology-activities/biosecurity/nsabb/nsabb-meetings-and-conferences/international-engagement (accessed April 19, 2015).

9 Walsh B (2012) 'H5N1 Paper Published: Deadly, Transmissible Bird Flu Could be Closer than Thought' in *The Healthland Blog*. See http://healthland.time.com/2012/05/03/h5n1-paper-published-deadly-transmissible-bird-flu-could-be-closer-than-thought/ (accessed April 19, 2015).

10 CDC (2009) 'CDC Estimates of 2009 H1N1 Influenza Cases, Hospitalizations and Deaths in the United States.' See http://www.cdc.gov/h1n1flu/estimates_2009_h1n1.htm (accessed April 19, 2015).

11 CDC (2003) 'Highly Pathogenic Asian-Origin Avian Influenza A (H5N1) in People.' See http://www.cdc.gov/flu/avianflu/h5n1-people.htm (accessed April 19, 2015).

12 ESWI (2011) News from Malta. *Influenza Times*, http://labs.fhcrc.org/cbf/Papers/H5N1_docs/FEIC_news_from_Malta.pdf (accessed April 19, 2015).

13 Enserink M (2011) 'Controversial Studies Give a Deadly Flu Virus Wings,' *Science* Vol. 334: 1192.

14 NIH (2011) 'Press Statement on the NSABB Review of H5N1 Research' (December 20, 2011), http://www.nih.gov/news/health/dec2011/od-20.htm (Accessed April 19, 2015).

15 WHO (2012) 'News Release: Public Health, Influenza Experts Agree H5N1 Research Critical, But Extend Delay,' February 17, 2012, http://www.who.int/mediacentre/news/releases/2012/h5n1_research_20120217/en/ (accessed April 19, 2015).

16 NIH (2011) 'Press statement on the NSABB Review of H5N1 Research,' December 20, 2011, http://www.nih.gov/news/health/dec2011/od-20.htm (accessed April 19, 2015).

17 USG (2012) 'Path Forward: Framework for Guiding United States Department of Health and Human Services Funding Decisions About Highly Pathogenic Avian Influenza H5N1 Gain-of-Function Research,' http://osp.od.nih.gov/sites/default/files/Proposed_Framework_for_Guiding_HHS_Funding_Decisions_about_

HPAI_H5N1_GOF-12-11-12.pdf (accessed April 19, 2015).

[18] Sutton TC, Finch C, Shao H *et al.* (2014) 'Airborne Transmission of Highly Pathogenic H7N9 Influenza Virus in Ferrets,' *Journal of Virology* Vol. 88(12): 6623–6635.

[19] Linster M, van Boheemen S, de Graaf M *et al.* (2014) 'Identification, Characterization, and Natural Selection of Mutations Driving Airborne Transmission of A/H5N1 Virus,' *Cell* Vol. 157(2): 329–339.

[20] Sun L (2014) 'CDC chief admits pattern of safety lapses after mishandling anthrax, other pathogens,' http://www.washingtonpost.com/national/health-science/cdc-chief-admits-pattern-of-safety-lapses-after-mishandling-anthrax-other-pathogens/2014/07/16/af778ce2-0cfe-11e4-8c9a-923ecc0c7d23_story.html (accessed April 19, 2015).

[21] Lapatto E (2014) 'White House Halts Research into Super Strains of Infectious Diseases,' http://www.theverge.com/2014/10/20/7020249/white-house-halts-research-into-super-strains-of-infectious-diseases (accessed April 19, 2015).

[22] Berg P (2004) 'Asilomar and Recombinant DNA,' http://www.nobelprize.org/nobel_prizes/chemistry/laureates/1980/berg-article.html (accessed April 19, 2015).

Chapter 10

Ebola: From Public Health Crisis to National Security Threat

Nicholas G. Evans

Introduction

After more than 28,000 infections, 11,300 deaths, and 10 countries,[1] we are witnessing the protracted end of an 18 month-long outbreak of Ebola virus disease (EVD) due to Ebola virus (EBOV) infection that dwarfs all other outbreaks combined. The three countries worst affected — Guinea, Liberia and Sierra Leone — have been devastated, losing $1.6 billion, or 12 percent of their combined GDP over the course of the outbreak.[2] The healthcare infrastructure of these countries has collapsed, leaving hundreds of thousands of people without access to basic medicines or clinical care. It is estimated that 20 percent of the healthcare workforce in Liberia has died — ominous news for those left to respond to future public health threats. And approximately 40 percent of the survivors of EVD have presented with what is now known as "post-Ebola syndrome," whose symptoms and clinical signs include chronic pain and blindness. You would be forgiven for thinking a war ripped through these countries; the analogy reflects the reality of EVD's transition from a public health crisis to a national security threat.

The gradual framing of the EVD outbreak in the language of security can be marked with milestones. On August 8, 2014, the

World Health Organization (WHO) declared the Ebola outbreak a Public Health Emergency of International Concern (PHEIC):

> ...an extraordinary event, which is determined, as provided in [the International Health Regulations (IHR), 2005]:
>
> (i) to constitute a public health risk to other States through the international spread of disease and
> (ii) to potentially require a coordinated international response.[3]

Much like a declaration of war, the framework of the PHEIC couches infectious disease in the language of risk. A PHEIC, properly defined, constitutes a threat to *states* rather than individuals, and calls for a coordinated, international response.

Yet, more than a mere public health risk, EBOV was considered a *security* risk. WHO Director-General Margaret Chan described the outbreak as a "social crisis, a humanitarian crisis, an economic crisis, and a threat to national security well beyond the outbreak zones."[4] Chan's audience was the United Nations (UN) Security Council, the 15-member arm of the UN charged with making decisions regarding collective and international security. This was the Security Council's first briefing on a health matter in the history of the UN. Their response was just as momentous: Resolution 2177, in which they declared the EVD outbreak a threat to international peace and security.[5] The ensuing attempt to raise funds to combat the outbreak involved the coordination of considerable resources by nation states in an attempt to break the chains of transmission that fueled the outbreak.

This chapter examines the response to the Western African EVD outbreak, particularly in terms of its perceived status as a security threat. First, the response effort is described in brief. Second, the way that EBOV was "securitized," or framed as a security issue, is detailed. Third, the EVD outbreak is used as a case study on the perils of securitization. I conclude with an argument for how we "take securitization seriously;" that is, how we approach characterizing the security implications of infectious disease in principled terms, and what this means for decision-making in future outbreaks.

Combatting Ebola

The response effort within Western Africa reflected the urgency of the Security Council's report. In Liberia, the United States Army was deployed to provide logistical and infrastructure support to aid workers, later called "Ebola fighters" by *TIME*[6] and "Ebola Warriors" by the United Nations.[7] The iconic site of the battle against EVD became the "Ebola Treatment Center," the partitioned medical structure in which patients came in, were sorted by their disease status and progression of symptoms, and supported by healthcare workers. The logistics of the outbreak response were described by the United Nations in explicitly militaristic terms:

> The Ebola war is being fought on many fronts. On the frontlines, social mobilizers strive to educate local communities, contact tracers go door-to-door searching for new cases, and doctors and nurses work to save lives in Ebola Treatment Units. In Monrovia, Conakry, and Freetown — the three capitals of the countries still affected by Ebola — men and women are also hard *at* work in the Situation Rooms, culling through data, charting contacts of Ebola patients, and planning for the end of the epidemic. The Situation Rooms are the nerve centres of the Ebola Response.[8]

Abroad, governments instituted liberty-violating measures with the justification of protecting citizens from the disease. In the United Kingdom, returning healthcare workers were subject to restrictions on their movement, including on their ability to use public transport.[9] In Australia, the Department of Immigration and Citizenship ceased issuing visas to travelers from Western Africa, including humanitarian visas, under the guise of protecting Australian citizens from the outbreak.[10] In the United States, hysteria over Ebola — used as a proper noun, as if describing the Islamic State/ISIS or al-Qaeda — led some to describe "being besieged" by a disease, and the need to "[screen] for Ebola the same way [we] screen for terrorists."[11] This included the enforcement, by Governor Chris Christie of New Jersey, and Governor Andrew Cuomo of New York, of the mandatory quarantine of healthcare workers returning from Western Africa — using "whatever steps

[were] necessary" to protect the (United States) public against an external threat (Swaine and Glenza 2014).[12] The director of the California department of public health, in describing the state's blanket quarantine policy, couched his comments in terms of "containing the potential spread of the disease," by way of preventing it from being introduced into the population in the first place.[13]

Securitizing Ebola virus

The 2013-present EVD outbreak was framed, and ultimately declared, as a threat to national and global security. EVD became a *securitized* disease. That is, EVD outbreaks, potential or actual, are public health issues framed in terms of their effects on — their threat to — human security.[14] Securitization is, moreover, the process of generating ideas about what is, and is not, a threat to security (Balzacq 2010).

Securitization occurs in a variety of ways — and to a variety of degrees — in civil life and medicine in particular. People wage war against cancer, AIDS, terror and drugs. Yet not all kinds of securitization are the same. In the context of the HIV/AIDS epidemic and the ensuing "war on AIDS," for example, militant rhetoric took a back seat to *criminalization*. The disclosure of (or failure to disclose) one's infection status; and the transmission of, testing for, and the isolation of individuals infected with HIV/AIDS are framed in terms of criminal justice.[15]

The EVD outbreak, unlike HIV/AIDS, is chiefly described in terms of an externally imposed threat to national security. This framing parallels that of armed conflict: "Ebola" is *militarized*. Militarizing as a way of securitizing health arose, in part, in the context of defining infectious disease public health threats in terms of "emerging infectious diseases." This system replaced a more juridical system of "disease lists" that required mandatory reporting between countries, shifting the quanta by which infectious disease outbreaks are defined from individual cases, to outbreaks as events in themselves. The criterion for concern was also shifted to an emergent threat to sovereignty or the political life of a nation or group of nations, rather than to their citizens (Weir 2012).

There are good reasons to frame EVD in terms of armed conflict. Virulent infectious disease outbreaks can and do mirror other more conventional threats to national or community security in terms of their impact on communities. Infectious disease destroys economies through the deaths of citizens, lower volume of street traffic, the loss of export and import abilities and social distancing. The spread of infectious disease harms social relations, turning casual contact into a potentially lethal activity, or — in the case of EVD — the burying of bodies into a proscribed practice (Hewlett and Hewlett 2007). In terms of sheer numbers of deaths, an infectious disease outbreak can easily exceed mortality in war. The 1918–1919 H1N1 "Spanish flu" influenza outbreak is estimated to have killed 50–100 million people, more than both World Wars combined (Taubenberger and Morens 2006). There is a real sense in which disease is a security threat, insofar as we conceive of security threats in terms of the scale and scope of the damage they inflict on communities.[16]

This securitization of infectious disease has extended, following the anthrax attacks in the United States in 2001, to conceptions of EBOV as a *weapon*. The Center for Disease Control and Prevention (CDC) classifies EBOV as a "Category A" bioterrorism agent:

> Category A [agents] have greatest potential for adverse public health impact with mass casualties, and most require broad-based public health preparedness efforts (e.g., improved surveillance and laboratory diagnosis and stockpiling of specific medications). Category A agents also have a moderate to high potential for large-scale dissemination or a heightened general public awareness that could cause mass public fear and civil disruption.[17]

EBOV was most likely chosen precisely for its capacity to cause widespread disease and death in the Soviet bioweapons program (see Chapter 4). The Scientific-Production Association (SPA) "Vektor" conducted extensive research on the EBOV, though the Soviets probably never successfully weaponized EBOV. They did, however, succeed in preparing a dry fermentation (i.e., powdered viral particles) of the Marburg virus — another filovirus and distant relative of EBOV — for weaponization and use, though we still do not know whether any explosion tests were ever successful (Leitenberg *et al.* 2012: 218–219).

The use of EBOV as a weapon by a state is possible, albeit unlikely, but it is far less clear how a terrorist would be able to mobilize such resources. EBOV is highly infectious, but its mode of transmission — primarily bodily close contacts, or exposure of mucosal membranes or open wounds to bodily fluids — makes it difficult to implement as a bioweapon, particularly on a small scale. Moreover, unlike more transmissible candidates,[18] the reproductive capacities of EBOV are usually limited to close contacts, and only when an infected individual is presenting with clinical signs.[19] This means that, unlike other potential bioweapons, individuals that have EVD are typically identifiable before they have a chance to transmit the virus to secondary contacts, and the disease moves slowly enough through the population that a developed healthcare system would have no trouble getting ahead of the virus. This is not in principle a reason against the use of EBOV as a bioweapon by terrorists, but it provides significant limitations on its use.

Given the considerable lethality of EVD and the magnitude of the current outbreak, it is not difficult to understand the tendency to frame this EVD outbreak as a national security issue. There is a clear analogy between the effects of an EVD outbreak — particularly this EVD outbreak — on a community, and those of war. Moreover, there is evidence that EBOV has been manufactured with the aim of using it as a weapon of war. Combined with the intense focus over the 21st century on the potential for diseases to be used by aspiring bioterrorists[20] (see Chapter 8), the securitization of EBOV is understandable. How far this analogy extends, and what the consequences of such an analogy entail, is contentious.

The perils of the security analogy

Like most framing devices, securitizing EVD (or any other infectious disease outbreak) has both benefits and costs. Securitization is a common narrative that binds a variety of emergency situations, and provides a basis for understanding complex situations. It is no coincidence that ordinary language has "fire*fighters*;" we "combat" disease; and we use phrases like "brothers in arms" in a wide range of context beyond the armed forces. Security threats allow us to understand the idea of *emergency* and *threat* in a common language, and this has pragmatic value insofar as it provides a common index for a variety of problems.

Securitization of an issue defines priorities for governance and community action, in virtue of the urgent nature and threat posed by infectious disease outbreaks. In keeping with concepts of armed conflict, these threats are conceived of as a threat to nations, if not the world. After the Security Council declared the 2013–present EVD outbreak as an international security concern, EBOV rose to become a national priority for a range of countries. The United States, for example, experienced a rare moment of bipartisanship, appropriating $5.4 billion to respond to the outbreak.[21] President Barack Obama also appointed an executive officer to coordinate the response effort, the so-called "Ebola Czar" Ron Klain.

The language of armed conflict also removes individual *responsibility* from much of the ethical discourse around infectious disease outbreaks. Where criminalization as a securitization modality assigns responsibility for both possessing a disease and for actions taken while infected, the framing device of armed conflict does not necessitate ascribing responsibility to individuals afflicted with a disease. The aim of public health measures framed in the language of armed conflict does not seek to deter or punish infected individuals in an attempt to change their behavior as a recipe to ending the outbreak. Rather, liberty-violating public health measures, such as mandatory screening or quarantine, are justified only when the harms inflicted are so serious that they outweigh other competing considerations, such as the right to freedom of movement.

Securitization, however, has serious drawbacks. First, securitization places an existential finger on the scales of health priorities. Securitization defines certain emergent issues as priorities, but often at the expense of other, potentially more harmful health issues. Measles, for example, killed 145,700 people in 2012,[22] yet it is typically not considered to be a security issue in the same way as EVD, despite the significantly larger annual burden it places on healthcare around the world. Securitized diseases are often prioritized in terms of scientific and health research for their potential to cause harm, while those diseases that *actually* kill are left understudied.

Moreover, coherently framing a particular disease in terms of either criminal justice or armed conflict is difficult in practice. Thomas Eric Duncan, a Liberian national admitted to Texas Presbyterian Hospital in Dallas in October 2014 with EVD after initially being turned away, was the victim of intense criminalization, in contrast with the dominant militaristic narratives of the remainder of the response. The immediate, visceral reaction to Duncan's presentation with EVD was to charge him with lying on his exit interview from Liberia and entrance exam to the United States. The reaction was severe to the point that Ellen Johnson Sirleaf, President of Liberia, criticized Duncan's alleged acts as "unpardonable," and the Texas District Attorney raised the possibility of charging Duncan with criminal intent (Baden and Moss 2014).[23]

In other cases, heroic healthcare workers returning from Western Africa became suspected belligerents. Kaci Hickox, for example, faced a wave of criticism after refusing to enter into home quarantine upon her return to her home in Maine. Craig Spencer, a New York physician who presented with symptoms days after returning from Western Africa, was heavily criticized for not entering into a precautionary 21-day self-quarantine upon returning to the United States. In Hickox's case, she never presented with clinical signs; in Spencer's, there was no secondary transmission — he presented to an emergency department as the first signs of his condition manifested. Casting healthcare workers as villains is reminiscent of the war crime of perfidy: when an enemy masquerades as a protected class of non-combatant, namely a civilian or an aid worker. Hickox and Spencer, returning as heroes, were framed as potential foes disguised as friends.

Conceptual mistakes about the language of security are of serious concern, because the normative basis of different kinds of security — independent of whether or not they can be justified for infectious diseases — are fundamentally different. Typically, criminal justice is predicated on respecting the rights of citizens, and is subject to a series of important due process laws that limit the degree to which police officers can collect evidence and bring charges to bear. The normative basis of criminal justice, however, is one in which individuals are subject to punishment based on their responsibility for a particular crime. In armed conflict, however, this responsibility is absent. Individual warfighters are typically not held personally responsible for the acts of their state, except in rare cases where they commit war crimes. The response that war entails, however, is far more extreme, and has fewer limits than the criminal justice system.

Using both frames simultaneously conflates the basis on which we can make and justify particular decisions in the context of our infectious disease response. This is a perilous prospect at the best of times, but more fraught in the context of extreme measures that can occur in responding to disease epidemics such as the case of the 2013–present EVD epidemic. The language of security can be invoked to justify repugnant deeds, and thus is constantly prone to abuse.

This conceptual slipperiness can also be informed by, or lead to, the smuggling of other beliefs into our language and decisions. In the case of Duncan, a serious issue raised was the latent racism in his treatment by media and Dallas Presbyterian Hospital. Duncan was initially dismissed from the hospital, despite presenting with a high fever; when he was eventually treated, he was subject to intense scrutiny and violation of privacy far in excess of any other individuals suffering from EVD in the U.S. His family was monitored by the press; his address and the location of his house, and where his children went to school, were given by local media outlets. These kinds of violations are more indicative of a court case than a hospital visit, and no other patient in the U.S. suffered to nearly the same degree.

Other instances also highlight the introduction of racism into the reaction to EVD. Children in Texas were banned from attending school on the purported risk of being infected with EBOV, despite their nationality being Rwandan, not Liberian (Rwanda is close to Liberia in much the same way as London is close to Mumbai). Duncan himself waited almost a week to receive access to experimental treatments for EVD, whereas other (white) patients received them almost immediately — sometimes even more than one.[24] Further afield, while foreign healthcare workers infected with Ebola were repatriated for care, domestic healthcare workers who were arguably more essential to the relief effort were left to fend for themselves. In the most public case, Dr Sheik Umar Khan, Liberia's infectious disease specialist, was denied access to experimental therapeutics to treat EVD.[25]

These issues converge on a central issue regarding the status of public health crises as national security threats: *medical exceptionalism.* The securitization of disease has the effect of promoting the concept that particular diseases are somehow more important, or at least sufficiently different from all others to warrant special attention. These diseases tend to receive preferential attention for their ability to affect certain (usually white, affluent) communities, draw funds disproportionate to the burden of disease they represent, and lead to the neglect of other pressing health issues. Moreover, this treatment tends to favor certain methods of resolving medical issues, such as the stockpiling of pharmaceuticals over reinforcing public health infrastructure.

In the 2013–present EVD outbreak, medical exceptionalism was most evident in terms of the sheer number of therapeutics and vaccines that emerged over the course of the outbreak; far more than would be expected for a less securitized virus. Many of these candidate therapies were already in development prior to the outbreak, as a result of the United States Biomedical Advanced Research and Development Authority (BARDA) funding research into potential bioterror agents. This, however, only drives home the exceptional status given to EBOV. Exceptionalism also occurred as individual countries split their time worrying equally about the response effort in Western Africa (and its 28,000 cases), and containing and responding to the disease in developed countries (and their six cases).[26] This kind of exceptionalism reflects the mistaken priorities that can occur through, and because of, the securitization of public health emergencies.

Taking health securitization seriously

A reaction to the serious pitfalls of securitization might lead us to conclude that divorcing public health completely from the language of security in infectious disease is the best decision. I want to suggest, as a final thought, that the 2013–present EVD outbreak itself should lead us to the opposite conclusion. The first reason for this is that I doubt we are *capable* of such an effort. Consider firefighting: fires clearly aren't something we fight in the same way as "fighting crime," much less armed conflict. Nonetheless, we have common but nuanced language to describe all three. It is a natural extension to regard disease, and infectious disease in particular, in partly securitized terms. I'm not confident we could avoid the comparison even if we tried.

The second reason is that there are certain parallels between infectious disease outbreaks and armed conflict. Let us return to the opening paragraph of this chapter. The survivors of this catastrophe have been marked by the event. Huge resources have been poured into turning back the tide of the outbreak. As Ebola Treatment Centers are torn down — often burned to the ground — in an effort to decontaminate areas, there will be zones in cities and communities that will be marked by the outbreak for some time. Few have even begun to consider the toll the outbreak has taken on the survivors, healthcare workers, and population of Western Africa in terms of mental health. The resulting health burden on these countries as other, seasonal diseases enter the fray has yet to be foreseen. What does this sound like, if not a war?

The alternative to resisting securitization is taking securitization seriously. Given that emerging infectious diseases are linked with the language of armed conflict, we ought to apply our best tools to understand what this analogy means for the ethics of infectious disease response, and where the analogy breaks down. There is a broad and detailed literature on the normative foundations of security — in both military and criminal justice spheres — that can inform our thinking on what kinds of public health events constitute security threats, and what responses are justified in response to those threats.

Three important *desiderata* for such a project are clear. The first is to develop an account of what counts as a militarized public health emergency. The language of the PHEIC serves an important role here, but it need not be our only tool. Importantly, armed conflict arises and is justified in terms of a threat to the sovereignty of a community. For our purposes, this threat to sovereignty can be cashed out in terms of the impact that an infectious disease outbreak, left unchecked or without an aggressive response, could compromise the integrity of a community. Importantly, this situates a "war against [infectious] disease" in a particular *theatre*, much like a war. This prescribes important limits to infectious disease response and priority setting: Ebola may be a PHEIC, but it is merely *concerning* to, say, the U.S. or U.K.; it is not *happening* in the U.S. or U.K.

The second is to understand priorities of securing against infectious disease in broad strategic and ethical terms. Avoiding these outbreaks should be a global priority. Like avoiding war, this requires diplomacy and a commitment to common norms for collective health security. A broad commitment to building global health infrastructure — the basic defenses against disease — should be a part of both the strategic and normative basis for defending against infectious disease. Public health is still our best weapon against disease, and we should structure our priorities towards it.

Finally, the language of war over the last millennia has refined a set of basic principles that limit the justification for war to those that are in the service of a just cause, are proportionate to a threat, and as a last resort (Allhoff *et al.* 2013). We ought to look to the principles of military ethics to inspire a justificatory basis for engaging in a collective defense against a public health crisis, what can be permissibly accomplished within these emergent situations, and what our obligations are in the aftermath. The principles developed in response to war can guide our future thinking about how we deal with an emerging disease outbreak that threatens national, international or global security.

Conclusion

Not all public health crises are national security threats. But sometimes, the magnitude and intensity of a public health crisis can present as real a threat to the sovereignty and integrity of communities as armed conflict. This is to be expected: for all that humans are skilled at killing each other, diseases are still the uncontested first and best killer of humans.

Understanding public health crises as national security threats, as in the case of the EVD outbreak, is not a straightforward task. Our language provides a proxy for understanding infectious disease as security threats, but much like security threats themselves, more work must be done to make sense of what a disease threat entails, and what is justified as a result. Analogy is easy, but the step to *analysis* is much more difficult. We need, collectively, to do more to secure that second move.

References

Allhoff F, Evans NG and Henschke A (2013) *Routledge Handbook of Ethics and War*. New York: Routledge.

Baden J and Moss C (2014) 'Thomas Eric Duncan and Craig Spencer: Race, Nationality, and Rhetoric of Ebola patients,' *Slate*. See http://www.slate.com/articles/health_and_science/medical_examiner/2014/10/thomas_eric_duncan_and_craig_spencer_race_nationality_and_rhetoric_of_ebola.single.html (accessed April 6, 2015).

Balzacq T (Ed.) (2010) *Securitization Theory: How Security Problems Emerge and Dissolve*. New York: Routledge.

Hewlett B and Hewlett B (2007) *Ebola, Culture and Politics: The Anthropology of an Emerging Disease*. Cengage Learning.

Leitenberg M, Zilinskas RA and Kuhn JH (2012) *The Soviet Biological Weapons Program: A History*. Cambridge, Massachusetts: Harvard University Press.

Swaine J and Glenza J (2014) 'New York and New Jersey Issue Tough New Ebola Quarantine Measure,' *The Guardian*. See http://www.theguardian.com/us-news/2014/oct/24/ebola-quarantine-new-york-new-jersey-west-africa (accessed April 6, 2015).

Taubenberger JK and Morens DM (2006) '1918 Influenza: The Mother of all Pandemics,' *Revista Biomédica* Vol. 17: 69–79.

Weir L (2012) 'A Genealogy of Global Health Security,' *International Political Sociology* Vol. 6(3): 322–325.

Notes

[1] World Health Organization (2015) 'Ebola Situation Report 16 September 2015.' See http://apps.who.int/iris/bitstream/10665/184623/1/ebolasitrep_16Sept2015_eng.pdf (accessed September 17, 2015).

[2] Smith G, Cruz M, Himelein K *et al.* (2015) *The Economic Impact of Ebola on Sub-Saharan Africa: Updated Estimates for 2015.* 1st Ed. See *documents.worldbank.org.*

[3] World Health Organization statement on the 1st meeting of the IHR Emergency Committee on the 2014 Ebola outbreak in West Africa. See *http://www.who.int/mediacentre/news/statements/2014/ebola-20140808/en/* (accessed September 17, 2015); World Health Organization (2005) *International Health Regulations, http://apps.who.int/iris/bitstream/10665/43883/1/9789241580410_eng.pdf.*

[4] World Health Organization (2014) 'WHO Director-General addresses UN Security Council on Ebola.' See http://www.who.int/dg/speeches/2014/security-council-ebola/en/ (accessed May 8, 2015).

[5] United Nations Security Council (2014) *Resolution 2177.* See www.un.org.

[6] McGregor J (2014) 'The Ebola fighters are Time Magazine's 'Person of the Year,'' *The Washington Post.* See http://www.washingtonpost.com/blogs/on-leadership/wp/2014/12/10/the-ebola-fighters-are-time-magazines-person-of-the-year/ (accessed May 13, 2015).

[7] United Nations Global Ebola Response (2015) 'Sierra Leone: The Ebola Warriors in the Situation Room.' See https://ebolaresponse.un.org/sierra-leone-ebola-warriors-situation-room (accessed May 13, 2015).

[8] United Nations Global Ebola Response 2015, as per note 7.

[9] McVeigh T (2015) 'NHS Ebola Staff 'Insulted' by UK Travel Ban,' *The Guardian.* See http://www.theguardian.com/world/2014/dec/21/nhs-ebola-staff-insulted-by-uk-travel-ban (accessed April 6, 2015).

[10] Hill-Cawthorne G and Kamradt-Scott A (2014) 'Mandatory Ebola quarantine is about politics, not public health,' *The Conversation.* See http://theconversation.com/mandatory-ebola-quarantine-is-about-politics-not-public-health-33531 (accessed April 6, 2015).

[11] Baden J and Moss C (2014) 'Thomas Eric Duncan and Craig Spencer: Race, Nationality, and Rhetoric of Ebola patients,' *Slate.* See http://www.slate.com/articles/health_and_science/medical_examiner/2014/10/thomas_eric_duncan_and_craig_spencer_race_nationality_and_rhetoric_of_ebola.single.html (accessed April 6, 2015).

[12] Swaine J and Glenza J (2014) 'New York and New Jersey Issue Tough New Ebola Quarantine Measure,' *The Guardian.* See http://www.theguardian.com/us-news/2014/oct/24/ebola-quarantine-new-york-new-jersey-west-africa (accessed April 6, 2015).

[13] Serna J (2014) 'California Issues Quarantine Policy for Ebola Exposure,' *Los Angeles Times.* See http://www.latimes.com/local/lanow/la-me-ln-california-orders-ebola-quarantine-protocols-20141029-story.html (accessed April 6, 2015).

[14] In Balzacq's terms, securitization is "the set of interrelated practices, and the processes of their production, diffusion, and reception/translation that brings threats into being" (2010). I simplify this definition for my purposes here; it is clear that securitization in this formal sense is operating in terms of both HIV/AIDS and EBOV/EVD, but does so through different referents.

[15] Burris S and Cameron E (2008) 'The Case Against Criminalization of HIV Transmission,' *JAMA: The Journal of the American Medical Association* Vol. 300(5): 578–581; Gostin LO (1989) 'Public Health Strategies for Confronting AIDS,' *JAMA: The Journal of the American Medical Association* Vol. 261(11): 1621.

[16] Though this ought not to be taken as an exhaustive conception of what constitutes a threat to security. For more on this, see Herington J (2012) 'The concept of security,' in C Enemark and MJ Selgelid (Eds.) *Ethics and Security Aspects of Infectious Disease Control.* Farnham Ashgate, pp. 7–26; Selgelid MJ (2012) 'The value of security: A moderate pluralist perspective,' in C Enemark and MJ Selgelid (Eds.) *Ethics and Security Aspects of Infectious Disease Control: Interdisciplinary Perspectives* Farnham Ashgate Publishing, p. 258.

[17] Rotz LD, Khan AS, Lillibridge SR *et al.* (2002) 'Public Health Assessment of Potential Biological Terrorism Agents,' *Emerging Infectious Diseases* Vol. 8(2): 226.

[18] I set aside the counterexample of anthrax, which although unable to transmit between humans, is relatively easy to convert into a slurry or powder for the purpose of dissemination. What it lacks in reproductive capacity, anthrax makes up for in ease of production and use.

[19] Centers for Disease Control and Prevention (CDC) (2014) *Guidance on Personal Protective Equipment to be Used by Healthcare Workers During Management of Patients with Ebola Virus Disease in U.S. Hospitals, Including Procedures for Putting On (Donning) and Removing (Doffing).* See http://www.cdc.gov/vhf/ebola/healthcare-us/ppe/guidance.html (accessed April 11, 2015).

[20] Directorate of Intelligence (2003) *The Darker Bioweapons Future.* Langley: Central Intelligence Agency.

[21] Plitsch JL and Evans T (2015) 'President signs act authorizing $5.4 billion in emergency funding to combat Ebola,' *National Law Review*. See http://www.natlawreview.com/article/president-signs-act-authorizing-54-billion-emergency-funding-to-combat-ebola (accessed May 13, 2015).

[22] Perry RT, Gacic-Dobo M, Dabbagh A *et al.* (2014) 'Progress Toward Regional Measles Elimination — Worldwide, 2000–2013,' *Morbidity & Mortality Weekly* Vol. 63(45): 1034–1038.

[23] Baden and Moss 2014, as per note 11.

[24] Karimi F and Shoichet CE (2014) 'Thomas Eric Duncan: 7 ways his Ebola case differs from others in U.S.' *CNN*. See http://www.cnn.com/2014/10/09/health/ebola-duncan-death-cause/ (accessed May 13, 2015).

[25] Pollack A (2014) 'Opting against Ebola drug for ill African doctor,' *New York Times*. See http://www.nytimes.com/2014/08/13/world/africa/ebola.html?_r=0 (accessed May 13, 2015).

[26] World Health Organization 2015, as per note 1.

Point of View

Building a Sustainable Biodefense Industry

Jacob Thorup Cohn

The financial model of the biodefense industry is complicated, rightfully questioned[1] and discussed in detail below. This contribution is based on my working experience at Bavarian Nordic since 2008. Bavarian Nordic (BN) is a biopharmaceutical company focused on development and manufacturing of cancer immunotherapies and vaccines for infectious diseases. Since 1999, Bavarian Nordic partnered with the U.S. Government (USG) to build a sustainable response to various biological threats. So far, this partnership has delivered:

- A Flexible, multi-purpose vaccine manufacturing facility[2];
- A stockpiled non-replicating smallpox vaccine that has been licensed in more than 30 countries[3];
- An Ebola vaccine development project (initiated in 2010) enabling BN to partner with Johnson & Johnson and produce 500,000 vaccines in 6 months to battle Ebola[4];
- A versatile technology platform for new vaccine candidates that led to a commercial agreement with Bristol Myers Squibb[5] in cancer (Prostvac).[6]

The Private–Public Partnership between the USG and Bavarian Nordic has proven that a mutual long-term commitment can yield positive results benefitting both taxpayers and investors.

The birth of an industry

Most people in the western hemisphere remember where they were on 9/11, but what most do not know is that there is a direct link between the ashes from the towers and the vaccines we are throwing into the battle against Ebola.

In the aftermath of 9/11 and Amerithrax (see Chapter 7), the USG reflected on threats posed to the nation.[7] One immediate conclusion was that "we must do more to protect our civilian population from biological weapons."[8] The threat from a biological attack was known to the USG long before 9/11; already in 1998 President Clinton asserted: "We will pursue R&D to create the next generation of vaccines. ...It is critical to our national security."[9] In June 2001, the Dark Winter exercise demonstrated potential impact to public health infrastructure when facing a lethal biological agent.[10]

In July 2004, President George W. Bush signed "Project BioShield" finally moving words, reports and recommendations from paper into action.[11] The biodefense industry was born.

The purpose of the pharmaceutical industry in defense

Traditional biopharmaceutical R&D and production is designed to address unmet medical needs for which there is acknowledged demand driven by a market request. For biopharmaceutical firms in biodefense it is different. We are named defense industry for the simple, but not well understood, reason that we are developing defense systems to protect humanity from a different kind of threat — a threat of biological warfare — a war for which the defense is not a gun, tank, navy vessel or a fighter plane, but a Medical Counter Measure (MCM).

A MCM — a vaccine, drug or diagnostic — should be considered a bulletproof armament ready to be deployed in battle. There is no shortage of words to describe the impact of a lethal biological agent in action. The WHO described it as "A threat to international peace and security."[12] The Obama administration's national strategy on countering biological threats characterizes the threat as "placing at risk the lives of hundreds of thousands of people" with a "direct impact on our way of life and the public's trust in the government."[13] These descriptions are why biological threats are potential issues of national security and not "just" health issues.

The economic impact and the fear associated with a pandemic outbreak were poorly understood until SARS, H1N1, H5N1, MERS and recently Ebola created global spread or global attention (Keech and Beardsworth 2008; Lee and McKibbin 2004).[14] Through these five experiences, the purpose of BioShield and its creation of the biodefense industry have moved from being a good idea to a needed health security asset.

The market place

The most significant challenge for biodefense industry players is that the concept of "health security" is not owned by any one policy area or administrative agency. Decisions on MCM investments in biodefense do not, therefore, have an established decision process or a dedicated responsibility within government. As a result, decision-making procedures are either invented ad hoc or are disorganized, sometimes even non-existent, and this prevents long-term investments and achievements.

In order to create policies that meet the gravity of the threat and its impact on society, it is imperative for decision makers to understand the conditions and the main stakeholders in the market place. There are three significant pillars in the biodefense marketplace:

Policy: Increasing global interconnectivity is transforming emerging infectious diseases, whether naturally or deliberately introduced, from biodefense into global health security. Global health security includes elements from both health and defense; but policies and decision processes are not yet in place to combine the two areas and direct actions. The decision process involves cross-departmental discussions and a large number of stakeholders with conflicting interests, but rarely a final decision maker. This makes the process slow, lengthy and subject to evolving threat assessment and shifting political priorities. For the industry this creates uncertainty, which complicates strategic decision-making; for governments it prevents the ability to react quickly or to prevent crisis.

Product: MCM development, in particular vaccines, is costly, risky, scientifically challenging, legally complicated and time consuming (Matheny *et al.* 2007; Duong 2011).[15] Successful development of a vaccine roughly equals three political terms (and elections), and this length of time generates exceptional uncertainty for an industry making investments entirely dependent on government policy. Vaccine development and production requires highly skilled staff who are not easily replaced. Stability and long-term vision are therefore important aspects of a successful product.

Profitability: No industry will develop if there are no profit prospects, and no investors will commit funds unless they see a growth potential. The profit prospect of an outbreak that might never happen, or if it happens, could be subject to either re-negotiation[16] or dictation of price[17] is not attractive when comparing the risk/profit ratio with the traditional pharmaceutical industry. R&D risk and sales possibilities must, therefore, be addressed more transparently, and this requires government acceptance of their responsibility to: support R&D activities; support and maintain manufacturing capacity through long-term (12yrs+) commitments in planning and procurement (manufacturing facilities are crucial assets in case of an outbreak); put in place agreements for managing product liabilities and long-term pricing.

The stakeholder map has three main groups:

The political establishment: Since biodefense falls between health and defense, final decisions often involve the President (or Prime Minister). Placing decisions in the highest office underlines the importance of biodefense, but it slows the administrative process and demonstrates the need for sustainable policy in the field.

Additionally, changes in government may lead to changes in policy, but to build a sustainable biodefense industry we need long and bipartisan commitments that benefit the nation, not the next election.

The commercial players: The traditional pharmaceutical industry is not engaged in the biodefense sector. However, as evident from Ebola, when a "biodefense disease" becomes a public health issue, we see immediate involvement. Johnson & Johnson, Merck and GlaxoSmithKline are driving the industry response in the battle against Ebola through both investments and acquisitions. However, unless there are existing technologies and research to invest in, their engagement comes too late. The biopharmaceutical industry is engaged in R&D against biothreats, and it is driven through USG investment in small- and medium-sized companies. However, these companies are generally struggling with profitability or with the ability to manufacture basic quantities (scale up), as in the case with MAPP for the Ebola response.[18] Investors are needed to support government investment and to sustain the industry base. The biodefense industry is viewed with caution due to the small number of success stories and the limited transparency on government long-term ambitions and priorities. A quick look at the Bavarian Nordic stock from 2012 to 2015 indicates that investors have plenty to gain from the industry, yet without consistent government policy industry will not have investor support and government will lose a funding partner in sustaining an industry base.

The NGOs and IGOs: Disease knows no borders, and intergovernmental organizations (IGOs) and non-governmental organizations (NGOs) are significant players in pushing government responsibility and development of policy — as was the case, for example, with the standards of the International Health Regulations or addressing the types of diseases and threats that cause particular concern for the global community. IGOs and NGOs can also provide helpful frameworks for procurement to benefit developing countries.

Current reality demonstrated through the EU Ebola response

In a press release during the recent Ebola outbreak, the European Union (EU) noted that it "has been engaged in efforts to contain the spread since its first appearance."[19] 'First appearance' is a question of definition: in 1976 Ebola was discovered; in 2002 USG initiates Ebola R&D with U.S. industry; in 2006 Ebola is declared a high priority threat; in 2010 EU-based Bavarian Nordic initiates Ebola R&D with USG; in 2014 the rising death toll hits the media and the EU responds "immediately."

One of the EU's responses to the Ebola outbreak has been to offer attractive loans to companies willing to invest, but the EU provides no policy or commitment to procure MCMs, making a calculation of the investment risk impossible. By providing loans with no guarantee of purchase, the EU essentially leaves the entire financial risk of R&D to commercial companies — a financial model unsuitable for biodefense sector development and which highlights that the EU has not yet understood the gravity of the situation. Loans can be useful if combined with long-term ambitions, but these must be ambitions directed by policies, not sudden media focus.

The current reality of the biodefense market outside North America is that biothreats are recognized but not prioritized. There are no policies or assigned responsibilities in place to deal with emerging infectious diseases that can threaten national security. In the absence of clear responsibility, the issue circles between various layers in national bureaucracies. This failure to engage has three significant consequences for national preparedness plans: the plans have not been exercised; there is no clear communication strategy; there is no policy for MCMs.

Towards sustainability

Creating MCMs do not only prevent diseases from being dangerous, but the development process creates a strengthened technology platform which can be utilized in the civilian sector or lead to the development of other medical products. When nurtured appropriately, the biodefense industry can become a vital part of national security as well as an asset to global health in the battle against emerging infectious diseases — both the known and the unknown. The next emerging disease might not be limited in scope as Ebola was, but may, for instance, combine the fatality of Ebola with the spread of H1N1. To counter this threat we need an industry base ready to be deployed, not invented for the occasion.

Investing in preparedness is like having an insurance policy. There are three outcomes of the investment. When not needed, it seems wasted. When it *is* needed, we wish we had invested more. When it is needed but not there at all, we wonder how we were so ignorant. As noted during the Global Health Security Agenda meeting in Washington during the height of the Ebola epidemic in 2014, "the consequences of inaction are simply too great."[20] This implies that ignorance and unwillingness to assume responsibility cannot be accepted.

Today we know what it takes to create a sustainable industry. It takes political understanding of the benefits of Private–Public Partnerships; acceptance that profit is necessary for a sustainable industry; the allocation of one responsible agency within government to enable long-term policies and create collaboration internationally; robust funding of MCM development; and clear procurement guidelines to sustain manufacturing facilities.

The drivers for a sustainable industry are not complicated to provide, the tools for being prepared *are* possible to create. The real question is whether there is *political will* to create models like BioShield, and to continue nurturing them when they are created.

At the Global Health Security Agenda meeting, the EU Commissioner for Health asserted: "This is a global crisis which concerns all of us. It is a tragic reminder that we must never let down our guard. We pay the price of complacency with human suffering and loss of life."[21] After Ebola, we can no longer accept human suffering of this magnitude due to complacency, but if we fail to prepare for the next emerging infectious disease, it is a political choice, not complacency.

References

Duong D (2011) *Developing Biodefense Countermeasures: Lessons from the Orphan Drug Act and Project Bioshield Anthrax Contracts.*

Doctorate thesis, George Mason University.

Keech M and Beardsworth P (2008) 'The impact of influenza on working days lost: A review of the literature,' *Pharmaeconomics* Vol. 26: 911–924.

Lee JW and McKibbin WJ (2004) 'Estimating the global economic cost of SARS,' in S Knobler *et al.* (Eds.) *Learning from SARAS: Preparing for the Next Disease Outbreak.* Washington, DC: National Academies Press.

Matheny J, Mair M, Mulcahy A and Smith BT (2007) 'Incentives for biodefence countermeasure development,' *Biosecurity & Bioterrorism* Vol. 5(3): 228–238.

Notes

1 Salinsky E and Werble C (2006) 'The Vaccine Industry: Does it Need a Shot in the Arm?' National Health Policy Forum background paper. See http://www.nhpf.org/library/background-papers/BP_VaccineIndustry_01-25-06.pdf; Lentzos F (2007) 'The American Biodefense Industry: From Emergency to Non Emergence,' *Politics and the Life Sciences* Vol. 26(1): 15–23; Kadlec R (2013) 'Renewing the Project Bioshield Act: What has it Brought and Wrought?' Policy Brief. See https://www.bio.org/sites/default/files/CNAS_RenewingTheProjectBioShieldAct_Kadlec.pdf (accessed September 9, 2015).

2 www.bavarian-nordic.com, http://www.pharmaceutical-technology.com/projects/bavarian_nordic/

3 US stockpile details: http://www.niaid.nih.gov/topics/smallpox/Pages/research.aspx; EU registration file: http://www.ema.europa.eu/ema/index.jsp?curl=pages/medicines/human/medicines/002596/human_med_001666.jsp&mid=WC0b01ac058001d124; Canadian registration; http://www.hc-sc.gc.ca/dhp-mps/prodpharma/applic-demande/regist/reg_innov_dr-eng.php.

4 http://www.bioworld.com/content/johnson-johnson-bavarian-nordic-ink-187m-deal-ebola-virus-vaccine.

5 http://news.bms.com/press-release/rd-news/bristol-myers-squibb-signs-exclusive-agreement-bavarian-nordic-prostvac-prosta.

6 www.bavarian-nordic.com.

7 The 9–11 commission report 2004, http://www.9-11commission.gov/report/911Report.pdf.

8 The 9-11 commission report 2004, as per note 7, p. 102.

9 President Clinton commencement address at the US Naval academy in Annapolis, Maryland May 22, 1998, http://edition.cnn.com/ALLPOLITICS/1998/05/22/clinton.academy/transcript.html.

[10] http://www.upmchealthsecurity.org/our-work/events/2001_dark-winter/index.html.

[11] http://www.gpo.gov/fdsys/pkg/PLAW-108publ276/pdf/PLAW-108publ276.pdf.

[12] http://theglobalobservatory.org/2014/12/security-council-response-ebola-action/; WHO DG Chan addresses the UN security council 2014, http://www.who.int/dg/speeches/2014/security-council-ebola/en/.

[13] NSC, National Strategy for countering biological threats (Nov 2009), www.whitehouse.gov/sites/default/files/National_Strategy_for_Countering_Biothreats.pdf.

[14] The socio economic impacts of Ebola in Sierra Leone by the World Bank. See http://www-wds.worldbank.org/external/default/WDSContentServer/WDSP/IB/2015/06/16/090224b082f3b78a/1_0/Rendered/PDF/The0socio0econ0survey-00round0three0.pdf.

[15] A significant layer of complexity and uncertainty is added where animal models have to be used as a disease substitute or due to the fatality risk associated with human testing for 'biodefense diseases.'

[16] U.S. "negotiation" on purchase of Cipro during Amerithrax, http://www.ncbi.nlm.nih.gov/pmc/articles/PMC1121539/ and http://content.healthaffairs.org/content/24/3/706.full.

[17] The U.S. Government effectively forced Bayer to reduce the price of Cipro during Amerithax, http://patentlyo.com/patent/2008/10/intellectual-pr.html and http://www. cptech.org/ip/health/cl/cipro/americanlawyer012002.html.

[18] http://www.cnbc.com/2014/10/17/, http://www.nytimes.com/2014/10/02/world/us-to-increase-production-of-experimental-drug-but-may-not-meet-demand.html?_r=0.

[19] http://europa.eu/rapid/press-release_SPEECH-14-633_en.htm.

[20] U.S. National Security Advisor Susan E Rice, September 26, 2014: https://www.whitehouse.gov/the-press-office/2014/09/26/opening-remarks-national-security-advisor-susan-e-rice-global-health-sec

[21] EUcomment:http://europa.eu/rapid/press-release_SPEECH-14-633_en.htm.

Chapter 11

Quandaries in Contemporary Biodefense Research

Gregory D. Koblentz

Introduction

Following the terrorist attacks on September 11, 2001 and the anthrax letters mailed that fall, governments around the world strengthened their efforts to prevent, prepare for and respond to an attack with a biological weapon. Since 2001, the United States alone has spent over $78 billion on biodefense programs to improve public health infrastructure, increase the readiness of hospitals to handle mass casualties, enhance biosurveillance systems to detect a disease outbreak, create stockpiles of medical countermeasure such as therapeutic drugs and vaccines, conduct basic research on dangerous pathogens, and develop new medical countermeasures, diagnostic tests, detection systems, and forensic tools (Kirk Sell and Watson 2013). The threat of bioterrorism also led to an increase in the number of biodefense programs around the world. In 2007, 25 countries declared having such programs (Lentzos 2008). Concerns about bioterrorism and emerging infectious disease have also triggered a construction boom in high biocontainment laboratories in the United States and around the world.[1] There are 13 biosafety level (BSL)-4 laboratories in operation or under construction in the United States and at least 24 such laboratories in operation in the rest of the world

(Gronvall and Bouri 2008). In addition, there are more than 1,400 BSL-3 laboratories registered to work with dangerous human, plant or animal pathogens in the United States and an unknown number of such laboratories around the world (Kaiser 2011).[2]

Biodefense research is just one part of a global public health and medical infrastructure, including university labs, hospitals, biotech companies, the pharmaceutical industry, government agencies and public health laboratories, that tackles the threats posed by infectious diseases using diagnosis, treatment, research and drug development. Gaining a better understanding of pathogens and toxins that can have catastrophic effects on human health, strengthening the medical and public health infrastructure to respond to naturally occurring and man-made disease outbreaks, and developing improved medical countermeasures, diagnostic tests, detection systems and forensic tools, are all laudable goals. While some programs and facilities are designed specifically and primarily to address the threat posed by the use of pathogens as weapons by states or terrorists, most of them are embedded in or contribute to the larger struggle against naturally occurring infectious disease outbreaks.

Developing defenses against the threat of bioterrorism, and even naturally occurring disease outbreaks such as pandemic influenza, Severe Acute Respiratory Syndrome (SARS) and Ebola, poses several quandaries for policymakers, scientists and the public (Koblentz 2010). By dramatically increasing the number of facilities and researchers working with dangerous pathogens, the recent biodefense research boom has increased the risk of such materials being stolen, insiders using their knowledge and skills for malevolent purposes or the accidental release of a pathogen. In addition, the knowledge and methods used to understand the pathogenicity, virulence and transmissibility of a pathogen is dual-use: it can be used for peaceful purposes such as developing new medical countermeasures or it can be misused for malicious purposes. The dramatic increase in biodefense funding after 2001 has also been accused of distorting research priorities too heavily toward biodefense pathogens at the expense of diseases that pose severe public health threats every day around the world. Developing defenses against biological weapons also runs the risk of crossing, or appearing to cross, the sometimes blurry line that separates legitimate research from offensive activity that is prohibited under international law. As states establish or expand biological defense research programs and high biocontainment laboratories to combat bioterrorism, other states may perceive these activities as threatening, thereby providing a justification for initiating or continuing an offensive biological warfare (BW) program. Sound biodefense policy needs to take into account these types of trade-offs when deciding how to prevent, prepare for and respond to existing and emerging biological threats. The rest of this article describes the main quandaries facing contemporary biodefense programs: how to develop defenses against biological threats securely, responsibly, safely, legally, transparently and in alignment with public health priorities.

Optimizing laboratory biosecurity

The dramatic increase in the number of laboratories and scientists working on dangerous pathogens and toxins has created more opportunities for these agents to be stolen, and it has increased the number of individuals with expertise that could be misused (Choffnes 2002; Schwellenbach 2005). As of July 10, 2014, there were 11,034 workers cleared to work in 324 facilities registered with the Centers for Disease Control and Prevention (CDC) and U.S. Department of Agriculture to handle dangerous pathogens known as Select Agents.[3] Historically, laboratories and culture collections were the preferred source of pathogens and toxins for terrorists and criminals. In contrast, there is no evidence that any terrorist or criminal group has successfully acquired a pathogenic microorganism from nature (Carus 2001: 8).

In 2002, in the aftermath of the anthrax letter attacks, Congress passed several laws to strengthen the physical security of dangerous pathogens, known collectively as the Select Agent regulations. These regulations were initially designed to prevent undesirable individuals from being hired to work in laboratories and to prevent outsiders from gaining unauthorized access to the pathogens stored there. Relations between scientists and law enforcement agencies got off to a rocky start after the 2001 anthrax letter attacks with the imposition of new laboratory biosecurity regulations and several high-profile cases in which scientists were seen as being treated unfairly.[4]

After the Federal Bureau of Investigation (FBI) alleged that Bruce Ivins, an anthrax researcher at the U.S. Army Medical Research Institute of Infectious Disease, the military's premier biodefense research facility, was responsible for the 2001 anthrax letter attacks, attention shifted to the threat posed by insiders. The difficulties that previous terrorists groups faced in developing biological weapons capable of causing mass casualties led the Commission on the Prevention of Weapons of Mass Destruction Proliferation and Terrorism to warn in 2008 that "the United States should be less concerned that terrorists will become biologists and far more concerned that biologists will become terrorists."[5] In 2012, the Select Agent regulations were "optimized" by creating a tiered system that calibrates the level of security to the degree of risk posed by the pathogen. For the highest risk pathogens, called Tier 1, personnel reliability measures, which include pre-access suitability screening and ongoing monitoring, were added to address the problem of what happens when a "good" researcher goes "bad."[6]

Scientists have criticized laboratory biosecurity measures on several grounds. First, they argue that since virtually all pathogens and toxins (with the exception of the viruses that cause smallpox and rinderpest) exist in nature, terrorists and criminals do not need access to a laboratory to acquire a biological agent (Rambhia *et al.* 2011). In addition, advances in synthetic biology, which it is anticipated will easily enable scientists to create infectious agents from scratch using published genomes of pathogens and DNA synthesizers, could be used to circumvent laboratory biosecurity measures designed to restrict access to dangerous pathogens.[7] Scientists also argue that greater laboratory biosecurity regulations, especially the types of intrusive measures associated with personnel reliability programs, will increase costs and deter researchers from entering or staying in the biodefense research field (Franz *et al.* 2009). As a result, they claim, the number and quality of biodefense researchers will be reduced. According to Jean L. Patterson, Chairwoman of the Department of

Virology and Immunology at the Southwest Foundation for Biomedical Research in San Antonio, Texas, which conducts extensive biodefense research: "We need people doing countermeasures work in this country, and if they find that it's too onerous and the rules aren't clear-cut, people might be reluctant to do it."[8]

Other countries, such as Australia, Canada, Denmark, Germany, Israel and the United Kingdom, have also imposed stricter regulations on the handling of dangerous biological materials (Tucker 2007; Friedman *et al.* 2008; Danish Ministry of Health and Prevention 2009; Rappert 2010). In contrast, relatively little has been done on the international level. In April 2004, the United Nations Security Council passed Resolution 1540 (UNSCR 1540), which requires states to ensure that weapons of mass destruction (WMD)-related materials are properly secured.[9] Although the resolution does not provide guidance on how states can achieve that objective, the World Health Organization (WHO) and the European Committee for Standardization (CEN) have published guidelines for implementing laboratory biosecurity measures.[10] By creating a legally binding obligation on all members of the UN, UNSCR 1540 has also stimulated a strong interest among a number of countries in improving the security of their biological materials and motivated several countries and non-government organizations to offer legal and technical assistance in the area of laboratory security (Perkins 2015).

Conducting research responsibly

The life sciences and biotechnology are characterized by a dual-use dilemma: the facilities, material and knowledge used for peaceful purposes, such as biomedical research and pharmaceutical production, can also be used to produce biological weapons. Advanced dual-use biotechnologies could enable states and terrorists to modify organisms to be more lethal as well as harder to detect, protect against and treat (Petro *et al.* 2003; Chyba and Greninger 2004). Due to the dual-use nature of the life sciences, efforts to develop defenses against naturally occurring or man-made biological threats have the potential to provide new knowledge or tools to malicious actors.

Two high-profile experiments demonstrated the potential for advances in the life sciences to be misused, and focused new attention on the security implications of biotechnology. In 2001, an experiment with mousepox demonstrated a possible method for engineering a highly virulent and vaccine-resistant form of variola, the virus that causes smallpox.[11] In 2002, scientists synthesized a virus — the poliovirus — from scratch for the first time, raising the prospect that more complex viruses, such as variola, could be synthesized in the future (Tucker and Zilinskas 2006). The emergence of the "do-it-yourself biology" movement, where amateur biologists engage in molecular biology and synthetic biology research outside of an institutional laboratory setting, adds another dimension to the safety and security concerns generated by the biotechnology revolution (Bennett *et al.* 2009).

In 2002, the National Academy of Sciences was commissioned to provide recommendations for how to balance the costs and benefits posed by dual-use research. The Fink Report (named after the chairman of the committee) formulated criteria that could be used to identify dual-use research of concern, proposed establishing a mechanism for oversight of such research, and recommended the creation of an advisory group composed of leading experts from the life sciences and national security communities to provide advice on establishing the proposed oversight system (see Chapter 9, Point of View).[12] As a result of this study, the George W. Bush administration created the National Science Advisory Board for Biosecurity (NSABB) to advise the government on dual-use research oversight. In 2007, the NSABB proposed a framework for governing dual-use research similar to the one proposed by the Fink Report, but its recommendations were not acted upon.[13]

The challenge of dual-use research in the life sciences re-emerged on the national and international stage in 2011 as scientists and policymakers debated what to do about article manuscripts that described how to modify the H5N1 avian influenza virus so that it could spread between mammals (see Chapter 9). Since H5N1 emerged in Southeast Asia in 2003, it has sickened over 600 people and caused almost 400 human deaths, as well as the deaths of millions of domestic and wild birds. The virus has not, however, demonstrated the ability to engage in sustained human-to-human transmission. If a new strain of H5N1 emerged with that capability, and it retained a high level of virulence, it could cause a global pandemic. The experiments by Yoshihiro Kawaoka from the University of Wisconsin-Madison and Ron Fouchier from Erasmus Medical Center in the Netherlands not only demonstrated that mammalian transmission of the virus was possible, but also provided information on how to construct such a virus.[14]

The H5N1 controversy highlighted the widely divergent views on the benefits and risks of dual-use research held by different stakeholders, including scientists, publishers, biosecurity experts, the national security community and public health officials. On the one side, proponents of the research focused on the public health benefits of knowing that H5N1 can be transmitted between mammals and which specific mutations can confer this ability on the virus. Opponents of the research highlighted the risks of a laboratory accident and the potential for a nefarious actor such as a terrorist group or rogue scientist to replicate the research and deliberately release the virus (Koblentz 2014).

The confusion and controversy surrounding the H5N1 experiments galvanized the United States to issue new policies for the funding and conduct of dual-use research. In March 2012, a process of regular Federal review of dual-use research of concern conducted by or funded by the U.S. government was established.[15] In a major departure from the Fink Report and NSABB recommendations, the new policy only applies to experiments with certain high-consequence pathogens and toxins (Tier I Select Agents plus H5N1 avian influenza and reconstructed 1918 pandemic influenza virus) which dramatically narrows the scope of life sciences research covered by the policy. In 2013 and 2014, the government issued a new policy requiring institutions receiving Federal funding to conduct oversight of their own life sciences research to identify potential dual-use research of concern and provided guidance for how these institutions could mitigate the risks posed by such research (but see Chapter 8, Point of View).[16] As a result of concerns about biosafety (discussed in the next section), the U.S. government launched a new review process in fall 2014 to develop a new policy for overseeing dual-use research.

Despite the potential risks posed by dual-use research, there are serious questions about the capability and intention of terrorist groups to exploit these breakthroughs. One line of argument is that terrorists are simply not sophisticated enough to conduct biological attacks with "high-tech" means (Suk *et al.* 2011). Vogel (2013) and Ben Ouagrham-Gormley (2014) argue that developing biological weapons, especially using advanced techniques such as synthetic biology, requires high levels of expertise, extensive tacit knowledge, and conducive work environments that terrorists do not typically have access to. In addition, even a group that was able to develop a deadly pathogen would still face significant hurdles in disseminating that agent in a way capable of causing mass casualties. Based on this analysis, the greater risk comes from "rogue" scientists, an issue addressed within the context of laboratory biosecurity. The scientific community continues to raise questions about the costs of increased regulations on ill-defined categories of research such as "gain of function" or limitations on studying viruses that pose significant immediate threats to global health.[17]

Ensuring biosafety

Conducting research on dangerous pathogens in order to develop defenses against them poses an intrinsic risk of accidents that could lead to the infection of a laboratory worker or the escape of a pathogen into the environment. Historically, the greatest risks of laboratory accidents have been posed by state-run BW programs that produced large quantities of dangerous pathogens, conducted particularly hazardous laboratory activities such as aerosolization studies, and engaged in field-testing of biological weapons. The Soviet BW program suffered at least two major accidents. In 1971, a field test of variola virus at its BW test site on Vozrozhdeniye Island in the Aral Sea resulted in a small outbreak of smallpox that required extraordinary public health measures to contain (Tucker and Zilinskas 2002). In April 1979, an accident at a military BW facility in

Sverdlovsk (now Yekaterinburg, Russia) released *Bacillus anthracis* (the bacterium that causes the disease anthrax), which caused an outbreak of inhalation anthrax that killed at least 66 civilians in the city (Guillemin 1999).

To date, laboratory accidents associated with biodefense research have posed the greatest risk to individual researchers.[18] From 2006 through 2013, laboratories in the United States reported about 1,500 incidents involving the exposure, release, theft or loss of a Select Agent, resulting in more than 800 cases of workers receiving medical treatment or evaluation. During this time, 15 laboratory acquired infections (LAIs) associated with Select Agent research and three unintended infections of animals were reported to the CDC.[19] No fatalities resulted from these infections and there were no reported cases of secondary transmission to other humans.[20]

The risk to local communities from laboratory accidents, however, is increasing as a result of the proliferation of high biocontainment laboratories around the world. Although BSL-4 laboratories in the United States have not experienced a LAI or environmental release of a pathogen, several BSL-4 laboratories outside of the United States have experienced lethal LAIs and secondary transmission of a disease from a researcher to individuals outside of the laboratory.[21] In 2007, a breach of containment at the Pirbright BSL-4 laboratory in the United Kingdom caused an outbreak of foot-and-mouth disease at several local farms. Although this outbreak was quickly contained at a cost of approximately £150 million, a naturally occurring epidemic of this highly infectious disease in the U.K. in 2001 cost taxpayers over £3 billion (Pennington 2007).[22]

Biosafety measures in the United States have been criticized on three points. First, the rules governing the design, construction, commissioning and operation of high-containment laboratories are not based on a national standard with clear verification and enforcement mechanisms.[23] Second, oversight of this research is weak and fragmented. For example, a 2008 study found that the institutional biosafety committees, which every biological research facility must have in order to receive federal funding, are weak, non-existent or opaque (Race and Hammond 2008). A 2015 investigation documented continuing problems with these committees exercising effective oversight of the research activities under their jurisdiction.[24] Third, oversight of biosafety is complicated by a lack of transparency that impedes accountability and reduces the public's confidence in biodefense and public health research.

Public concern about the safety of research in high biocontainment labs was initially localized to communities in close proximity to such labs. The most high-profile such confrontation occurred in Boston where Boston University sought to build a BSL-4 laboratory next to a densely populated neighborhood comprised primarily of low-income and minority residents. Although the university completed its $200 million New England Infectious Disease Laboratory (NIEDL) in 2008, it has yet to move into the lab's BSL-4 suite due to continued opposition by local residents and politicians.[25]

Biosafety became a national-level issue during the summer of 2014 when two world-class research institutions, the CDC and the National Institutes of Health (NIH), experienced a number of biosafety failures. In June, the CDC discovered that one of its laboratories had improperly inactivated samples of *B. anthracis*, which resulted in live bacteria being handled without appropriate safety precautions. The CDC's investigation into this incident revealed several other lapses in biosafety including shipping to other laboratories of improperly inactivated samples of *Clostridium botulinum*, virulent strains of *Brucella*, and a supposedly harmless avian influenza strain that had been contaminated with the highly pathogenic H5N1 strain.[26] Fortunately, there were no reported infections associated with these incidents. In July, six vials of variola (the virus that causes smallpox) were unexpectedly discovered in a storage room at NIH. Variola, which has been eradicated from nature, is supposed to be held at only two secure repositories: The CDC in Atlanta and Vektor in Novosibirsk, Russia. The vials were intact and no one was exposed or infected with the virus.[27] National biosafety concerns were reignited in 2015 when it was revealed that for over 8 years Dugway Proving Ground, the military's primary chemical and biological defense testing facility, had been shipping improperly inactivated samples of anthrax to labs across the United States and at least eight other countries.[28] As of August 2015, no infections associated with this failure of biosafety had been reported.

The discovery of variola virus at the NIH highlighted the risk that a laboratory accident could reintroduce a contagious disease that has already been eradicated or otherwise contained. The last known cases of smallpox and SARS were both caused by laboratory exposures, and both viruses were able to spread from infected researchers to a small number of individuals outside of the laboratory.[29] The growth in dual-use research has also raised a number of biosafety concerns. One concern is that genetically engineered pathogens might escape a laboratory. This risk was highlighted by experiments that re-created the influenza virus that caused the 1918–1919 pandemic that killed 50 million people around the world and used genes from this virus to make contemporary influenza viruses more virulent.[30] These concerns were further amplified by the H5N1 experiments in 2011, which were an example of "gain of function" research whose purpose is to generate pathogens with enhanced virulence and/or transmissibility. These "potential pandemic pathogens" pose a significant public health risk if they were to escape a laboratory (as the result of an accident or intentional release) due to the lack of population immunity and effective medical countermeasure against them (Lipsitch and Bloom 2012; Klotz and Sylvester 2014). The burgeoning field of synthetic biology also raises the conundrum of determining the proper biosafety level for experiments with artificially created organisms that have no naturally occurring analogue (Tucker and Zilinskas 2006).

Concerns about the safety of creating and studying "potential pandemic pathogens" were reignited by the 2014 biosafety failures at the CDC and NIH. In response to those incidents, the White House announced a moratorium on so-called "gain of function" experiments that could increase the transmissibility or pathogenicity of viruses that cause influenza, SARS and Middle East Respiratory Syndrome (MERS). The government, in cooperation with the NSABB and the National Academies of Science, is engaged in a year-long review to devise a new policy to balance the benefits and risks of such research.[31]

Demonstrating compliance and transparency

Governments face a quandary in demonstrating that their biodefense programs are in compliance with the 1972 Biological and Toxin Weapons Convention (BWC), which prohibits the development, production, acquisition and transfer of biological weapons (see Chapter 12). The best way for states to demonstrate their compliance with the treaty is to be transparent about their biodefense research activities in order to build confidence and allay suspicions. At the same time, there is a tension between transparency and the need to safeguard sensitive information on vulnerabilities that could be exploited by another nation or by terrorists. Certain states, such as the Soviet Union, Russia, Iraq and South Africa, have exploited the ambiguity inherent in the treaty's definition of permitted activities to hide their offensive programs (Koblentz 2009: 69).

The BWC was a groundbreaking treaty, the first international treaty to outlaw an entire class of weapons. The language in the treaty walks a fine line between the aspirations of the drafters to achieve a clear and unequivocal prohibition against biological weapons, and the reality of the dual-use nature of biological agents and biological research. As a result, while state parties are obligated "never in any circumstances" to develop, produce or possess biological weapons, the borders demarcating prohibited and legitimate activities are either vague or undefined. The Convention does not prohibit research on biological weapons in recognition of the great difficulty in determining whether such activities were being undertaken for permitted or prohibited purposes. Furthermore, the Convention does not define what activities are considered research, and therefore fall outside the scope of the treaty, and what activities constitute development, and therefore subject to the treaty's provisions. In addition, the treaty allows the development, production and stockpiling of biological agents of appropriate "types and quantities" so long as they have "prophylactic, protective or other peaceful purposes." However, the types, quantities and purposes that are permitted are not further defined in the treaty. This ambiguous wording and lack of definitions was required to allow states to continue conducting legitimate medical, scientific, public health, commercial and defensive work with organisms that could also be used as BW agents.

Conducting research to develop defenses against biological weapons has long been recognized as the type of activity that was permitted by the treaty, but could also be used as a cover for an offensive program, or be perceived as doing so. For this reason, parties to the BWC have agreed to provide an annual declaration of national biodefense programs as a confidence-building measure. The lack of transparency by one state regarding its defensive activities provides other states with a convenient excuse for resisting greater transparency in their own ostensibly defensive programs. In the worst case, a secretive biodefense programs could be viewed as threatening by other states, which might lead them to launch their own secret defensive or offensive programs which in turn could trigger a biological weapon arms race. The goal of this BWC confidence-building mechanism is to avoid this type of security dilemma that feeds on secrecy, suspicion and worst-case estimates of other states' intentions and capabilities. The growth of biological defense programs around the world, especially in the United States, requires a greater level of transparency to ensure that these activities are subject to appropriate domestic oversight and are not being used, or perceived as being used, to mask an offensive program (Lentzos 2011).[32]

When the United States abandoned its offensive program in 1969, it committed itself to conducting its defensive program as openly as possible. Nonetheless, an interagency group determined that the performance of detection systems, threat assessments and vulnerability studies may require classification.[33] The lack of a clear boundary between offensive and defensive activities, and the tension between secrecy and transparency, has been a source of continuing controversy for the United States' biodefense program. During the 1980s, the U.S. Army increased its spending on defensive biological research in response to intelligence that the Soviet Union had an active BW program, including the application of genetic engineering. The U.S. military's research on genetically modified organisms and exotic diseases, and the construction of a new aerosol test facility, were subsequently criticized and restricted due to their perceived association with offensive activities (Koblentz 2009). The question of U.S. compliance with the BWC came to the fore in 2001 when it was reported that the Central Intelligence Agency, Defense Intelligence Agency, and Department of Defense were conducting classified biodefense projects that entailed the small-scale production of *B. anthracis* spores in dry powder form, the construction of a pilot plant capable of producing a simulant for *B. anthracis* spores, the design and testing of a bomblet to disseminate biological agents, and the creation of a genetically modified strain of *B. anthracis* that could overcome the protection offered by some vaccines.[34] Some of these projects had not been subject to an official arms control compliance review, and none of them were included in annual confidence-building declarations of biodefense activities to the United Nations (Leitenberg 2005: 54–70, 84). The United States claimed that the purpose of these research projects was defensive and legal under the BWC, but the combination of capabilities under development and the secrecy of the work raised questions at home and abroad about the commitment of the United States to complying with the BWC.[35]

The most problematic types of biodefense research are those related to threat assessment. Threat assessment research includes determining the feasibility of an adversary's offensive BW capabilities, gauging an adversary's ability to exploit vulnerabilities in existing defenses, and discovering potential avenues to develop new defenses against these threats. After September 11, 2001, the United States established a new facility, the National Biodefense Analysis and Countermeasures Center (NBACC) within the Department of Homeland Security (DHS), to conduct research on the physical and biological properties of traditional, genetically modified and emerging BW agents as part of a threat assessment program (Leitenberg *et al.* 2004; Tucker 2004; Petro and Carus 2005). Critics pointed out that the research necessary to characterize biological threats as described by NBACC scientists could cross the line into activities prohibited by the BWC. Without greater transparency into the facility, its activities, and the measures it was taking to ensure that it remained in compliance with the BWC, U.S. biodefense research might be misinterpreted as being for offensive purposes or to provide justification for other states to conduct such work in the context of an offensive program (Leitenberg *et al.* 2004; Ember 2005). In response to these concerns, DHS adopted a formal, structured process to ensure that its research is in compliance with the BWC and provided greater transparency of its compliance assessment process.[36]

There is, of course, a tension between transparency and the need to safeguard sensitive information on vulnerabilities that could be exploited by another nation. States developing defenses against biological weapons may need to keep certain activities, such as intelligence on foreign biological threats, specific vulnerabilities, and the range of medical countermeasures available, secret to ensure the effectiveness of their preparations. Making such information available publicly, or even on a confidential level with other governments, could enable an adversary to identify and exploit weaknesses in defensive preparations and intelligence gathering. Given the diversity of BW agents, an adversary could select an agent for which it knows the target state lacks any or adequate defenses. On the other hand, although an adversary might use such knowledge to develop different agents for which no defenses are available, such agents are unlikely to be as well studied and may not be as suitable for use as mass casualty-producing weapons. Furthermore, full disclosure of all facets of a nation's biodefense program is unlikely to be required to reassure other states that no offensive program is underway. The U.S. military's program to develop biodefense detection and diagnostic systems, and medical countermeasures, is unclassified, and is already subject to extensive reporting requirements from Congress. Indeed, the regulatory process in advanced industrialized nations required to field a medical countermeasure makes it impossible to develop and produce such a countermeasure in secret.

Increasing the confidence of domestic and foreign observers that biodefense research, especially research that is classified and engaged in threat assessment, is in compliance with the BWC could be achieved by vesting this oversight responsibility in an interagency review group capable of balancing the competing needs of secrecy and transparency. This group would be required to submit annual reports to the appropriate Congressional committees to ensure accountability. Given the inherent secretiveness of intelligence agencies and the research capabilities already available within military and civilian institutes, the role of intelligence agencies in biodefense research should be strictly limited. Transparency of biodefense programs would not only promote accountability, reduce suspicion and build confidence in compliance with the BWC, but could also serve a deterrent function by demonstrating the availability of defenses against a range of biological threats.

Balancing public health priorities

The increased attention to preparing for and responding to bioterrorism has led to a closer linkage between public health and national security, which carries both benefits and risks to public health (see Chapter 10). In January 1999, at the unveiling of President Bill Clinton's counterterrorism budget, Secretary of Health and Human Services Donna Shalala stated, "This is the first time in American history in which the public health system has been integrated directly into the national security system."[37] At the time, this statement was a gross exaggeration of the extent of collaboration between the public health and national security communities, but it captured the growing securitization of public health. The public health and national security communities, however, approach risk assessment and risk management from very different perspectives. In public health, risk is assessed on a utilitarian basis, which leads to a focus on threats that are currently causing the most severe health effects to the largest number of people. Due to a lack of resources, public health also favors responses that promise the largest reduction in harm to the greatest number of people at the lowest cost. In contrast, the national security community tends to focus on risks that could potentially inflict catastrophic consequences, even if the probability of that event (such as bioterrorism) is low. Since national security agencies tend to be well-funded, they have the luxury of engaging in worst-case planning and being prepared for a wide range of contingencies.

Given the rarity of bioterrorism and chronic underfunding of public health programs for addressing diseases that impose much higher levels of morbidity and mortality on the population, some members of the public health community have questioned both the ethical and practical implications of biodefense (Sidel *et al.* 2002). One criticism of biodefense programs is that they divert funding away from more urgent public health needs. For example, Klotz (2007) argues that assessing bioterrorism and public health threats separately has led to a disproportionate investment in biodefense at the expense of more serious public health threats such as influenza, HIV, methicillin-resistant *Staphylococcus aureus*, and tuberculosis, which cause far more deaths than bioterrorist threats such as anthrax and smallpox and therefore deserve a larger share of research dollars. In 2005, a group of prominent scientists accused NIH of distorting research priorities too heavily toward biodefense pathogens at the expense of diseases that pose severe public health threats every day around the world.[38] NIH has been able to alleviate this concern by defining biodefense broadly to include research on emerging infectious diseases and supporting laboratories and research applicable to a broad range of pathogens. In addition, programs to develop medical countermeasures against exotic pathogens such as Ebola, which was categorized as a high-priority Category A bioterrorist threat agent in 1999, have proven useful as that disease turned into a global health threat in 2014 (see Chapter 10, Point of View).[39]

Public health officials have also questioned the value of highly specialized programs that are designed only to defend against bioterrorism threats. A prime example is the BioWatch program, overseen by DHS, which is a network of air samplers deployed in over 30 major cities that is designed to provide early detection of an aerosolized biological weapon attack. The program has been criticized for generating too many false alarms, being too expensive, imposing an additional burden on public health labs, and not being integrated into the public health system. In 2014, the Obama Administration cancelled a technological upgrade to the program that was supposed to provide quicker and more reliable results.[40] In 2004, the CDC established the Cities Readiness Initiative (CRI) with the goal of distributing oral antibiotics to an entire city within 48 hours of an anthrax attack. Progress in achieving the CRI's objective has been slow. In 2007, the

Bush Administration found that "few if any cities are presently able to meet the objective of dispensing countermeasures to their entire population within 48 hours after the decision to do so."[41] In 2011, the bipartisan WMD Terrorism Center concluded that "no local jurisdiction has demonstrated the ability to rapidly dispense medical countermeasures on a large scale under realistic conditions."[42] CRI has also been criticized by public health officials for its unrealistic demands on overstretched local health departments.[43]

Proponents of biodefense counter that programs for addressing bioterrorism have utility against a wide range of threats. According to the Center for Health Security, approximately 90 percent of biodefense programs contribute to non-biodefense needs as well (Sell and Watson 2013). While this "synergy thesis" is typically overstated (Fidler and Gostin 2007), there are clear examples where programs established to counter biological terrorism provided valuable capabilities for addressing natural disease outbreaks. For example, the CDC established the Laboratory Response Network (LRN) in 1999 to improve the ability of state and local public health labs to detect biological agents that might be used by terrorists. The network performed admirably during the 2001 anthrax letter attacks.[44] Subsequently, the scope of LRN expanded to include emerging infectious diseases that public health labs would not ordinarily be prepared for such as SARS, MERS and Ebola. Likewise, the Strategic National Stockpile, which was established in 1999 to serve as a repository for critical medical countermeasures needed to respond to a bioterrorist attack, has expanded to include pharmaceutical and medical supplies needed to respond to an influenza pandemic.

From the national security perspective, such investments are seen as a worthwhile form of insurance (see Chapter 12, Interview by Smith & Lentzos). Epstein (2007) has argued that the value of investments in biodefense countermeasures can't be measured solely using an analysis of "cost per avoided fatality" but also has to take into account the political, psychological and social benefits of the government's ability to respond to a bioterrorist attack. In short, "Security entails more than public health" (Epstein 2007: 353). National security experts also point to the deterrent value of biodefense. Bob Graham and Jim Talent, former chairmen of the Commission on the Prevention of Weapons of Mass Destruction Proliferation and Terrorism, have claimed that by strengthening its public health and medical systems, the United States can deter terrorists from launching a biological attack since the odds of successfully causing mass casualties will be so low.[45]

Public health practitioners have also warned that the securitization of public health to address bioterrorism would have a negative impact on the ability of the public health community to fulfill its core mission (Sidel 2003). The downsides of the securitization of public health became evident in 2003, when the public health community was put in charge of implementing a large-scale smallpox immunization program for public health and health-care workers. The program was motivated by national security concerns stemming from the imminent invasion of Iraq, and not by public health assessments of the benefits and risks of the vaccine. As a result, instead of immunizing 500,000 civilians, fewer than 40,000 received the vaccine and the program was ignominiously suspended (Baciu *et al.* 2005). One way to encourage synergistic policies is to replace threat-specific responses with "all-hazard" strategies. The concept of public health emergency preparedness, which encompasses defenses against bioterrorism as well as natural disasters and disease outbreaks, provides a sustainable model for improving the ability of the public health community to respond to extraordinary events, regardless of their cause.[46]

Conclusion

The biodefense research enterprise is subject to a number of dilemmas and trade-offs, some obvious and some not. Since the character of threats from natural and man-made disease outbreaks are constantly evolving and the life sciences is such a dynamic field, biodefense policymakers need to continuously evaluate their programs and policies to ensure that their activities are maximizing the benefits of research while minimizing the risks. Traditionally, however, each of the five areas discussed in this chapter — safety, security, dual-use research, compliance and public health priorities — has been treated in isolation. Jessica Stern has warned that the failure of policymakers to recognize the cross-cutting nature of these issues may result in policymakers being "more prone to choose remedies that substitute new risks for old ones in the same population, transfer risks to new populations, or transform risks by creating new risks in new populations" (Stern 2002/2003: 91). Integrating the benefits and risks of biodefense research across these five areas is a daunting prospect, but increasingly necessary, as such research proliferates and the power of biotechnology grows and diffuses globally. Establishing a flexible, sustainable governance structure for life sciences research, particularly when conducted for biodefense purposes, will be one of the most important policy challenges of the 21st century.

References

Baciu A, Pernack AA, Stratton K and Strom B (Eds.) (2005) *The Smallpox Vaccination Program*. Washington, DC: National Academies Press.

Ben Ouagrham-Gormley S (2014) *Barriers to Bioweapons: The Challenges of Expertise and Organization for Weapons Development*. Ithaca: Cornell University Press.

Bennett G, Gilman N, Stavrianakis A *et al.* (2009) 'From Synthetic Biology to Biohacking: Are we Prepared?' *Nature Biotechnology* Vol. 27(12): 1109–1111.

Carus WS (2001) *Bioterrorism and Biocrimes: The Illicit Use of Biological Agents in the 20th Century*. Washington, DC: National Defense University.

Choffnes E (2002) 'Bioweapons: New Labs, More Terror?' *Bulletin of the Atomic Scientists* Vol. 58(5): 28–32.

Chyba CF and Greninger AL (2004) 'Biotechnology and Bioterrorism: An Unprecedented World,' *Survival* Vol. 46(2): 143–162.

Danish Ministry of Health and Prevention (2009) *Executive Order on Securing Specific Biological Substances, Delivery Systems, and Related Materials*. Document no. 69710, June 30, Copenhagen, Denmark.

Ember LR (2005) 'Testing the Limits,' *Chemical and Engineering News* Vol. 83: 26–32.

Epstein GL (2007) 'Security is More Than Public Health: Commentary on "Casting a Wider Net for Countermeasure R&D Funding Decisions,"' *Biosecurity and Bioterrorism* Vol. 5(4): 353–357.

Fidler DP and Gostin LO (2007) *Biosecurity in the Global Age, Biological Weapons, Public Health, and the Rule of Law*. Stanford: Stanford University Press.

Franz DR, Ehrlich SA, Casadevall A *et al.* (2009) 'The "Nuclearization" of Biology is a Threat to Health and Security,' *Biosecurity and Bioterrorism* Vol. 7(3): 243–244.

Friedman D, Rager-Zisman B, Bibi W *et al.* (2008) 'The Bioterrorism Threat and Dual-use Biotechnological Research: An Israeli Perspective,' *Science and Engineering Ethics* Vol. 16(1): 1–13.

Gronvall GK and Bouri N (2008) 'Biosafety Laboratories,' *Biosecurity and Bioterrorism* Vol. 6(4): 300.

Guillemin J (1999) *Anthrax: The Investigation of a Deadly Outbreak.* Berkeley: University of California Press.

Kaiser J (2011) 'Taking Stock of the Biodefense Boom,' *Science* Vol. 333(6047): 1214.

Klotz LC (2007) 'Casting a Wider Net for Countermeasure R&D Funding Decisions,' *Biosecurity and Bioterrorism* Vol. 5(4): 313–318.

Klotz LC and Sylvester EJ (2014) 'The Consequences of a Lab Escape of a Potential Pandemic Pathogen,' *Frontiers in Public Health* Vol. 2(116): 1–3.

Koblentz GD (2009) *Living Weapons: Biological Warfare and International Security.* Ithaca: Cornell University Press.

Koblentz GD (2010) 'Biosecurity Reconsidered: Calibrating Biological Threats and Responses,' *International Security* Vol. 34(4): 96–132.

Koblentz GD (2014) 'Dual-Use Research as a Wicked Problem,' *Frontiers in Public Health* 2: 1–4.

Leitenberg M (2005) *Assessing the Biological Weapons and Bioterrorist Threat.* Carlisle Barracks, PA: Strategic Studies Institute Press.

Leitenberg M, Leonard J and Spertzel R (2004) 'Biodefense Crossing the Line,' *Politics and the Life Sciences* Vol. 22(2): 1–2.

Lentzos F (2008) 'Preparing the Ground for the CBM Content Debate: A Study on the Information Exchange that Builds Confidence Between States Parties to the Biological and Toxin Weapons Convention (BTWC),' Report, London School of Economics, U.K.

Lentzos F (2011) 'Strengthening the BWC Confidence Building Measures: Towards a Cycle of Engagement,' *Bulletin of the Atomic Scientists* Vol. 67(3): 26–33.

Lipsitch M and Bloom BR (2012) 'Rethinking Biosafety in Research on Potential Pandemic Pathogens,' *mBio* Vol. 3(5): 1–3.

Pennington TH (2007) 'Biosecurity 101: Pirbright's Lessons in Laboratory Security,' *Bio Societies* Vol. 2(4): 449–453.

Perkins D (2015) 'The Past and Future of 1540 and the Biological Weapons Convention,' *1540 Compass* Vol. 8(4): 28–32.

Petro JB and Carus WS (2005) 'Biological Threat Characterization Research: A Critical Component of National Biodefense,' *Biosecurity and Bioterrorism* Vol. 3(4): 295–308.

Petro JB, Plasse TR and Mcnulty JA (2003) 'Biotechnology: Impact on Biological Warfare and Biodefense,' *Biosecurity and Bioterrorism* Vol. 1(3): 161–168.

Race MS and Hammond E (2008) 'An Evaluation of the Role and Effectiveness of Institutional Biosafety Committees in Providing Oversight and Security of Biocontainment Laboratories,' *Biosecurity and Bioterrorism* Vol. 6(1): 19–35.

Rambhia KJ, Ribner AS and Gronvall GK (2011) 'Everywhere You Look: Select Agent Pathogens,' *Biosecurity and Bioterrorism* Vol. 9(1): 69–71.

Rappert B (2010) *Education and Ethics in the Life Sciences: Strengthening the Prohibition of Biological Weapons.* Canberra: Australian National University E Press.

Schwellenbach N (2005) 'Biodefense: A Plague of Researchers,' *Bulletin of the Atomic Scientists* Vol. 61(3): 14–16.

Sell TK and Watson M (2013) 'Federal Agency Biodefense Funding, FY2013–FY2014,' *Biosecurity and Bioterrorism* Vol. 11(3): 1–21.

Sidel VW (2003) 'Bioterrorism in the United States: A Balanced Assessment of Risk and Response,' *Medicine, Conflict, and Survival* Vol. 19(4): 318–325.

Sidel VW, Gould RM and Cohen HW (2002) 'Bioterrorism Preparedness: Cooptation of Public Health?' *Medicine & Global Survival* Vol. 7(2): 82–89.

Stern J (2002/2003) 'Dreaded Risks and the Control of Biological Weapons,' *International Security* Vol. 27(3): 91–92.

Suk JE, Zmorzynska A, Hunger I, Biederbick W *et al.* (2011) 'Dual-Use Research and Technological Diffusion: Reconsidering the Bioterrorism Threat Spectrum,' *PLoS Pathogens* Vol. 7(1): 1–3.

Tucker JB (2004) 'Biological Threat Assessment: Is the Cure Worse than the Disease?' *Arms Control Today*: 13–19.

Tucker JB (2007) 'Strategies to Prevent Bioterrorism: Biosecurity Policies in the United States and Germany,' *Disarmament Diplomacy* Vol. 84(Spring): 36–47.

Tucker JB and Zilinskas RA (2002) *The 1971 Smallpox Epidemic in Aralsk, Kazakhstan and the Soviet Biological Warfare Program.* Monterey, CA: Center for Nonproliferation Studies.

Tucker JB and Zilinskas RA (2006) 'The Promise and Perils of Synthetic Biology,' *New Atlantis* Vol. 12(Spring): 32–34.

Vogel K (2013) *Phantom Menace or Looming Danger? A New Framework for Assessing Bioweapons Threats.* Baltimore, MD: Johns Hopkins University Press.

Notes

1 High biocontainment labs include biosafety level (BSL)-3 and 4 labs. Work in BSL-3 labs involves agents, such as *Francisella tularensis* (tularemia), SARS coronavirus, and West Nile virus that may cause serious and potentially lethal infection although vaccines or effective treatments may be available. Work in BSL-4 labs involves the most dangerous agents for which there are no effective vaccines or treatments available such as Ebola, Marburg and variola virus (smallpox).

2 Kaiser J (2011) 'Taking Stock of the Biodefense Boom,' *Science* Vol. 333(6047): 1214.

3 Subcommittee on Oversight and Investigations (2014) *Memorandum on review of CDC Anthrax Lab Incident.* Report for the House Energy and Commerce Committee. July 14, Washington DC. p. 8.

4 Enserink M and Malakoff D (2003) 'The Trials of Thomas Butler,' *Science* Vol. 302(5653): 2054–2063; Annas G (2006) 'Bioterror and "Bioart" — A Plague o' both your houses,' *New England Journal of Medicine* Vol. 354(25): 2715–2720.

5 Commission on the Prevention of Weapons of Mass Destruction Proliferation and Terrorism (2008) *World at Risk.* New York: Vintage Books.

6 Department of Health and Human Services (2012) Possession, use, and transfer of Select Agents and Toxins. *Federal Register* 77(194): 61804–61115.

7 National Science Advisory Board for Biosecurity (2006) *Addressing Biosecurity Concerns Related to the Synthesis of Select Agents.* Bethesda, MD: National Science Advisory Board for Biosecurity.

8 Dishneau D (2011) 'Federal panel recommends tighter scrutiny of those who handle deadly pathogens,' *Associated Press*, January 11.

9 United Nations Security Council (2004) Resolution 1540, http://www.un.org/en/sc/1540/ (accessed 6 August 2015).

10 World Health Organization (WHO) (2006) *Biorisk Management: Laboratory Biosecurity Guidance.* Report, Geneva: WHO; European Committee for Standardization (CEN). (2011) *Laboratory biorisk management.* CWA 15793. Brussels: CEN.

[11] Jackson RJ, Ramsay AJ, Christensen CD *et al.* (2001) 'Expression of Mouse Interleukin-4 by a Recombinant Ectromelia Virus Suppresses Cytolytic Lymphocyte Responses and Overcomes Genetic Resistance to Mousepox,' *Journal of Virology* Vol. 75(3): 1205–1210.

[12] National Research Council (NRC) (2004) *Biotechnology Research in an Age of Terrorism*. Washington DC: National Academies Press.

[13] National Science Advisory Board for Biosecurity (2007) *Proposed Framework for the Oversight of Dual Use Life Sciences Research*. Washington, DC: National Science Advisory Board for Biosecurity.

[14] National Research Council (NRC) (2013) *Perspectives on Research with H5N1 Avian Influenza: Scientific Inquiry, Communication, and Controversy*. Washington, DC: National Academies Press.

[15] United States Government (2012) *United States Government Policy for Oversight of Life Sciences Dual Use Research of Concern*, http://osp.od.nih.gov/sites/default/files/resources/United_States_Government_Policy_for_Oversight_of_DURC_FINAL_version_032812_1.pdf (accessed August 6, 2015).

[16] United States Government (2013) *United States Government Policy for Institutional Oversight of Life Sciences Dual Use Research of Concern*, http://www.phe.gov/s3/dualuse/documents/us-policy-durc-032812.pdf (accessed August 6, 2015).

[17] National Research Council (NRC) (2015) *Potential Risks and Benefits of Gain-of-Function Research*. Washington, DC: National Academies Press.

[18] Willyard C (2007) 'Lack of Training in Biodefense Research Leading to Dangerous Leaks,' *Nature Medicine* Vol. 13(9): 1004; Kimman TG, Smit E and Klein MR (2008) 'Evidence-Based Biosafety: A Review of the Principles and Effectiveness of Microbiological Containment Measures,' *Clinical Microbiology Reviews* Vol. 21(3): 403–425.

[19] Young A and Penzenstadler N (2015) 'Inside America's secretive biolabs,' *USA Today*, May 28. See http://www.usatoday.com/story/news/2015/05/28/biolabs-pathogens-location-incidents/26587505/ (accessed August 6, 2015).

[20] Henkel RD, Miller T and Weyant RS (2012) 'Monitoring Select Agent Theft, Loss and Release Reports in the United States: 2004–2010,' *Applied Biosafety* Vol. 17(4): 171–180.

[21] Johnson KM (2004) 'Biosafety at BSL-4: More than 20 years experience at three major facilities,' in National Institutes of Health (NIH) *Rocky Mountain Laboratory Integrated Research Facility Final Environmental Impact Statement*. Washington, DC, pp. D5–D11; Heymann DL, Aylward RB

and Wolff C (2004) 'Dangerous Pathogens in the Laboratory,' *Lancet* Vol. 363(9421): 1566–1568.

22 Anderson I (2008) *Foot and Mouth Disease 2007: A Review and Lessons Learned.* London: The Stationery Office.

23 Government Accountability Office (GAO). (2014) *High-Containment Laboratories: Recent Incidents of Biosafety Lapses.* Report for the United States Government. GAO-14-785T, 16 July. Washington DC: GAO.

24 Young and Penzenstadler 2015, as per note 19.

25 Schnirring L (2014) 'Steps move Boston lab closer to BSL-4 work,' *CIDRAP News*, May 15. See http://www.cidrap.umn.edu/news-perspective/2014/05/steps-move-boston-lab-closer-bsl-4-work (accessed August 6, 2015).

26 Centers for Disease Control and Prevention (2014) *Report on the Potential Exposure to Anthrax*, http://www.cdc.gov/about/pdf/lab-safety/Final_Anthrax_Report.pdf (accessed July 8, 2015).

27 Centers for Disease Control (2014) 'Media statement on newly discovered smallpox specimens'. See http://www.cdc.gov/media/releases/2014/s0708-nih.html (accessed July 8, 2015).

28 Young A (2015) 'Army Lab Cited Eight Years Ago for Failing to Properly Kill Anthrax Samples,' *USA Today*, June 12. See http://www.usatoday.com/story/news/2015/06/12/dugway-live-anthrax-shipments/71093540/ (accessed August 6, 2015).

29 Heymann, Aylward and Wolff (2004), as per note 21.

30 Kobasa D, Takada A, Shinya K *et al.* (2004) 'Enhanced Virulence of Influenza A Viruses with the Haemagglutinin of the 1918 Pandemic Virus,' *Nature* Vol. 431(7009): 703–707; Tumpey TM, Basler CF, Aguilor PV *et al.* (2005) 'Characterization of the Reconstructed 1918 Spanish Influenza Pandemic Virus,' *Science* Vol. 310(5745): 77–80.

31 National Research Council 2015, as per note 16.

32 Between 1993 and 2007, the number of countries with declared biodefense programs grew from 11 to 25.

33 Interdepartmental Political Military Working Group (1970) *Annual review of United States chemical warfare and biological research programs as of 1 November 1970.* Washington, DC.

34 Miller J, Engelberg S and Broad WJ (2001) 'U.S. Germ Warfare Research Pushes Treaty Limits,' *New York Times*, September 4: A1; Miller J, Engelberg S and Broad WJ (2001) *Germs: Biological Weapons and America's Secret War.* New York: Simon and Schuster; Shane S (2001) 'Army Confirms Making Anthrax in Recent Years,' *Baltimore Sun*, December 13.

[35] Miller J (2001) 'When is a Bomb Not a Bomb? Germ Experts Confront U.S.,' *New York Times,* September 5: A5; Harris E (2001) 'Research Not to be Hidden,' *New York Times,* September 6; Dando MR and Wheelis M (2003) 'Back to Bioweapons?' *Bulletin of the Atomic Scientists* Vol. 59(1): 41–45.

[36] Center for Arms Control and Non-Proliferation (2008) *Ensuring compliance with the Biological Weapons Convention.* Meeting report, Washington, DC, February; Gerstein DM (2011) *U.S. biodefense & treaty compliance,* http://geneva.usmission.gov/wp-content/uploads/2011/12/Dec.8GersteinPresentation.pdf (accessed June 14, 2015).

[37] Office of Press Secretary (1999) Press briefing by Attorney General Reno, Secretary of HHS Donna Shalala, and Richard Clarke, President's National Coordinator for Security, Infrastructure and Counterterrorism. See http://www.presidency.ucsb.edu/ws/?pid=47819 (accessed June 20, 2015).

[38] Altman S *et al.* (2005) 'An Open Letter to Elias Zerhouni,' *Science* Vol. 307(5714): 1409c–1410c.

[39] Boddie C (2015) 'Federal Funding in Support of Ebola Medical Countermeasures R&D,' *Health Security* Vol. 13(1): 3–8.

[40] Willman D (2014) 'Homeland Security Cancels Plan for New Biowatch Technology,' *Los Angeles Times,* April 25. See http://www.latimes.com/nation/la-na-biowatch-20140426-story.html (accessed August 6, 2015).

[41] Bush GW (2007) *Countermeasure Stockpiling and Distribution.* Homeland Security Presidential Directive (HSPD) 21. October 18. Washington: DC.

[42] WMD Terrorism Research Center (2011) *Bio-Response Card.* Report, Washington DC, October. p. 45.

[43] Khan S and Richter A (2012) 'Dispensing Mass Prophylaxis: The Search for the Perfect Solution,' *Homeland Security Affairs Journal* Vol. 8(3): 1–20.

[44] Snyder JW (2005) 'The Laboratory Response Network: Before, During, and After the 2001 Anthrax Incident,' *Clinical Microbiology Newsletter* Vol. 27(22): 171–175.

[45] Graham B and Talent J (2009) 'Bioterrorism: Redefining Prevention,' *Biosecurity and Bioterrorism* Vol. 7(2): 1–2.

[46] Nelson C *et al.* (2007) 'Conceptualizing and Defining Public Health Emergency Preparedness,' *American Journal of Public Health* Vol. 97(S1): S9–S11.

Section III: Disarmament and Non-Proliferation

Chapter 12

The Traditional Tools of Biological Arms Control and Disarmament

Marie Isabelle Chevrier & Alex Spelling

Introduction

The traditional tools of biological arms control and disarmament have a long and complicated history. This chapter focuses on critical concepts of arms control and places the cornerstone of the biological regime, the 1972 Biological and Toxin Weapons Convention (BWC), in the historical context of its negotiation.

The BWC is an extraordinary treaty. Negotiated in a relatively short period of time it is the first treaty to outlaw an entire class of weapons. The political atmosphere in the late 1960s, early 1970s when the BWC was negotiated was dramatically different from the international political situation today. The U.S. and the USSR were engaged in the ideological, political and military conflict known as the Cold War. Taking place over nearly half a century, the Cold War impacted every aspect of U.S. and USSR foreign and international policy and policy analysis. Nuclear weapons and nuclear deterrence dominated the arms control agenda. Even in multilateral fora, the Cold War severely limited progress in arms control and disarmament. Occasionally, however, the Cold War provided windows of opportunity to advance arms control. BWC negotiators took advantage of one of these windows to successfully draft and approve the final text of the Convention.

During the Cold War there was a stalemate between the USSR and its Warsaw Pact allies on the one hand, and the United States and its NATO allies on the other. Simply speaking and condensing a complex topic, the U.S. argued for the inclusion of on-site inspections to verify compliance with arms control agreements. The USSR responded that it did not need on-site inspections and that the U.S. only wanted on-site inspectors in order to spy on the Soviet Union. Some nuclear agreements — including the Strategic Arms Limitation Talks (SALT) I and II, the Intermediate Range Nuclear Forces agreement, and the Strategic Arms Reduction Talks — were concluded between the U.S. and the USSR despite the absence of intrusive on-site verification provisions. Other agreements — including the Chemical Weapons Convention (CWC) — languished in protracted negotiations because a solution to the on-site inspection impasse could not be found. The U.S. and the USSR both had huge stockpiles of chemical weapons, and sophisticated and widespread chemical weapons production facilities. Moreover, the 1969 Nixon review of chemical and biological warfare policies determined that the U.S. needed to retain its chemical weapons capabilities. Keeping its chemical weapons arsenal was thought to be important in deterring the USSR from using chemical weapons, particularly in an attack on Western Europe. At the same time, the chemical weapons program in the U.S. had greater political and private sector support for continued production of weapons and research of chemical agents than the biological weapons program had.

The BWC was concluded with 85 initial signatories without the intrusive on-site verification provisions that held up the negotiation of the CWC. The only provisions contained within the Convention that are concerned with what could loosely be called verification tools are contained in Articles V and VI. According to Article V, treaty parties agree to consult and cooperate with one another if problems arise in the implementation of the Convention. Article VI allows a state to file a complaint with the United Nations Security Council (UNSC) if it finds that another party is not in compliance with the treaty. How one state could make such a finding without any mechanism for inspections or investigations is unclear. The official consultation and cooperation process has been engaged only once (see below), and no complaint has ever been filed with the UNSC under Article VI. The rareness of the use of the tools in these articles is not a demonstration of satisfaction with treaty compliance. Rather it shows the weakness of the tools and the futility of filing a complaint with the UNSC when any of the permanent members could veto any resolution related to such a complaint, and surely would do so if the complaint concerned its own compliance.

This chapter outlines the principle international tools of biological arms control and disarmament. It contextualizes the aims and provisions of the 1925 Geneva Protocol and the 1972 Biological Weapons Convention, and it details the tools that were negotiated around the drafting of the BWC and those that were subsequently agreed, namely: Articles V and VI of the BWC, the Trilateral Process, the Consultative Committee Process, and the Confidence Building Measures (CBMs). National intelligence is a further tool of traditional arms control and disarmament common to most countries. The chapter describes these tools and discusses how they came about, how they have operated during the implementation of the BWC and what their limitations are in providing information to accurately assess compliance.

The 1925 Geneva Protocol and the historical context of the BWC origins

Attempts to limit the use of poison in war has been attempted as far back as the St. Petersburg Convention in 1868, then more concertedly through the 1899 and 1907 Hague Declarations (see Chapter 2). These attempts, however, were jettisoned in the weapons-technology driven atmosphere of World War I. The extensive use of gas was responsible for approximately 100,000 fatalities, with many more wounded or incapacitated by chlorine, phosgene and mustard agents. Despite the industrial scale of killing wrought by conventional weapons during the conflict, the use of CW developed a special moral opprobrium; indeed their deployment arguably carried a greater psychological threat than military necessity, and the psychological fear of such weapons remains prevalent today.

As part of the WWI peace treaties, ad hoc CW restrictions were meted out to the defeated Central Powers and the 1922 Washington Naval Treaty also contained provisions relating to poison gas. At the League of Nation's Geneva Conference for International Arms Traffic in 1925, a suggestion by the U.S. and France to build upon these earlier treaties was extended at Poland's request to include bacteriological (biological) weapons. This led to the drafting and signing of the "Geneva Protocol for the Prohibition of the Use in War of Asphyxiating, Poisonous or Other Gases, and of Bacteriological Methods of Warfare." The Protocol did not cover development, production or possession of CW however, and several signatories reserved the right to retaliate in kind if chemical or biological weapons were used against them. Hence it assumed the character of a no first-use agreement, entering into force 3 years later and covering international conflict. The treaty is not a perfect instrument. Lacking enforcement machinery, the value of the Protocol lies in its moral and practical commitments towards regulating norms of behavior and rules of engagement (Spelling *et al.* 2015).

Although Italy used chemical weapons in Ethiopia and Japan used biological weapons in China, the Protocol prohibition on the use of chemical and biological weapons (CBW) held up remarkably well during the World War II era. In practice, most policy on CBW battlefield use was governed by operational difficulties and fear of retaliation.

The BWC emerged in the Cold War period commonly referred to as the "era of détente". Whilst détente, the geopolitical "relaxation of tensions", is popularly seen as an element of the 1970s, which certainly fits with the signing of the BWC, one can see an earlier beginning through arms control measures of the early 1960s. Indeed, these efforts arguably went back to November 1959 when the United Nations (UN) General Assembly adopted resolution 1378 on "general and complete disarmament", which included CBW disarmament. Responsibility was passed to the newly created the Ten-Nation Disarmament Committee in Geneva, which became the Eighteen Nation Disarmament Committee (ENDC) in 1961. The ENDC negotiated the introduction of the White House–Kremlin telephonic "hotline" in the aftermath of the Cuban Missile Crisis in November 1962 and this progress was solidified in 1963 with the conclusion of the Nuclear Partial Test Ban Treaty, of which the U.S., U.K. and USSR were depository powers. Similarly, the conclusion of the Nuclear Non-Proliferation Treaty (NPT) in 1968 and the Seabed Treaty in 1971 (with the U.S., U.K. and USSR again depositories) continued to highlight arms control (and the ENDC, later renamed the Conference of the Committee on Disarmament — CCD) as an area which could deliver strategic security and cooperation outside of diplomatic summitry. This activity occurred despite the geopolitical climate of the time. The building of the Berlin Wall and the substantial American military involvement in Vietnam thereafter seemed to confirm the East–West divide of the era.

The Vietnam War and BWC negotiations

The issue of alleged chemical warfare became a prominent public issue during the Vietnam War, with firstly, U.S. use of large quantities of chemicals — herbicides and defoliants — to clear or destroy vegetation in the Vietnamese countryside, and secondly, extensive employment of another chemical, CS (tear) gas against personnel. The use of these agents attracted international criticism, particularly from the Eastern Bloc and non-aligned countries. In 1966, Hungary for example charged that they were prohibited by the Geneva Protocol and international law and attempted to introduce a UN General Assembly resolution to this effect. The controversy over U.S. use of these chemicals began a process of measures to reaffirm the importance of the Geneva Protocol in the UN and a concurrent effort at the ENDC in studying proposals for "general and complete disarmament" of which a CBW prohibition was a priority. Such measures were codified in the July 1969 UN experts report on CBW, which again stressed the importance of adherence to the Geneva Protocol and for new measures on prohibiting production and possession of such weapons.

The origins of what would become the BWC initiative lay in work conducted by the U.K. Foreign and Commonwealth Office's (FCO) Arms Control and Disarmament Research Unit (ACDRU) and the Atomic Energy and Disarmament Department (AEDD) between

1966 and 1968, which included consultations with the U.S. Arms Control and Disarmament Agency (ACDA). Concurrently CBW issues were also being regularly debated in disarmament non-governmental organizations (NGOs) such as Pugwash and the Campaign for Nuclear Disarmament (CND). The contested nature of U.S. use of CS and herbicides in Vietnam on the one hand, and allegations of CW use by forces of the Yemen Arab Republic in the Yemeni civil war, also demonstrated a potential requirement for more clarity in respect of CBW policy, whether through strengthening or amending the Geneva Protocol, or introducing new legislation. The successful conclusion of the NPT negotiations in January 1968 then provided an impetus to move towards other areas of disarmament. British disarmament officials ultimately decided to move forward with the idea of separating CW and BW on the basis that a new agreement prohibiting production of the latter was more immediately achievable and practicable in the current international climate. The process of arriving at this point was complex, involving detailed discussions, suggestions and papers across government departments and the advice of scientific experts, mindful of many different issues. Nevertheless, the U.K. "working paper on microbiological warfare" was duly presented to the ENDC on August 6, 1968. Following discussions in Geneva and continued work in London, this was duly turned into a draft treaty almost 1 year later on July 10, 1969 when the U.K. tabled its "Convention for the Prohibition of Biological Methods of Warfare" (Walker 2012a; Wright 2002).

At the same time, a confluence of domestic and international pressure in the U.S. surrounding CBW led to an intensive multi-agency review of policy under the new Nixon Administration (see Chapter 12, Witness Seminar). The conclusions led in November to an announcement by President Nixon that the U.S. would cease production of BW, destroy its existing stockpiles, resubmit the Geneva Protocol (which it had signed but not ratified) to the Senate for consideration, and, shortly thereafter, to end its toxin weapons program as well (see Chapter 3). At the CCD meanwhile, 2 years of further intensive negotiations and redrafts took place with contributions from many countries. These would form the basis of the amended and renamed "Biological and Toxin Weapons Convention", presented on September 28, 1971 and cosponsored by 12 members, with the U.K., U.S. and USSR acting as depository powers.

A weakened verification regime

The BWC as it was presented in 1971 contained the principle elements of the U.K. draft presented to the ENDC in 1968, with some significant exceptions, including:

- Provisions for access by authorities to "all research which might give rise to allegations" of noncompliance
- Openness of relevant research to international investigation and public scrutiny

(Chevrier 2006: 312–319)

These two elements — tools to investigate suspicions of noncompliance — had been dropped in the final text. Why did the U.S. and its Western allies agree to the BWC without any provisions to document the extent of the USSR's or other states' biological and toxin weapons stockpiles? Why did they forego verification of the destruction of "agents, toxins, weapons, equipment and means of delivery" as required under Article II of the Convention? Why did the U.S. and the U.K. become signatories of the Convention without the ability to monitor or inspect facilities that they suspected might be in violation of the treaty? How have these provisions operated since the treaty was implemented in 1975? How have states parties augmented these provisions?

The answers to these questions lie, in part, in working papers produced by the U.K.'s Ministry of Defense (MOD) assessing CW and BW policy. The paper summarizing the policy assessments emphasized three elements that motivated the U.K. BW policy initiative throughout the 1960s: (1) the U.K. was vulnerable to a BW attack; (2) BW had limited strategic and limited military tactical value for the U.K. and (3) the USSR was not a suitable BW target (Balmer 2001: 177).

When the U.K. tabled its 'Convention for the Prohibition of Biological Methods of Warfare' in 1969, Article III contained provisions for complaints of treaty violations. Allegations of breaches of the Convention were to be taken to the UN Secretary General along with a recommendation for an investigation, the report of which would be submitted to the UNSC. Allegations of treaty breaches that did not involve use were to be taken to the Security Council with the request that the complaint be investigated. Each of the parties was obliged to cooperate with the Secretary General in any investigation (Chevrier 2006: 317). U.S. President Nixon's dramatic decision to entirely abandon biological weapons significantly changed the momentum of the negotiations.

In November 1969, the group of U.S. policymakers assessing chemical and biological warfare policy reported to the U.S. National Security Council. The report did not make recommendations; it only listed the advantages and disadvantages of maintaining a BW program:

> PROS:
>
> - Maintenance of such a capability could contribute to deterring the use of such agents by others.
> - Without any production capability and delivery means for lethal weapons, the United States would not be able to reconstitute such a capability within likely warning times.
> - Retains an option for the United States at very little additional cost as a hedge against possible logical surprise or as a strategic option
>
> CONS:
>
> - Control of the area of effect known BW agents is uncertain
> - A lethal BW capability does not appear necessary to deter strategic use of lethal BW.
> - Limits our flexibility in supporting arms control arrangements."
>
> (Tucker 2002: 125)

According to Tucker, President Nixon was influenced by a report from the President's Scientific Advisory Committee,

> which pointed out that biological weapons were subject to the vagaries of weather and had delayed effects … As a result, biological

> weapons had limited tactical utility on the battlefield and did not constitute a reliable and effective deterrent. Lack of institutional support for biological warfare from within the armed services — with the sole exception of the Army — eased Nixon's decision to abandon what was generally considered to be a marginal capability.
>
> (Tucker 2002: 127)

Nixon decided to renounce the use of biological warfare agents and destroy its stockpile of agents and munitions. The U.S. also agreed to support the U.K. draft convention (Tucker 2002: 128).

When President Nixon unilaterally renounced biological weapons, he said, in effect, that we do not want biological weapons even if other countries have them. In his study of the "motives that can lead countries to bargain about armaments," Schelling describes U.S. policy on biological weapons as a dominant negative preference — "*not* having the weapon is preferred *irrespective of whether the other side has it*" (Schelling 1984: 244; emphasis in original). Schelling says this reference can describe "an infinity of ridiculous weapons that nobody is interested in having even if the other side is foolish enough to procure them" (1984: 253).

In a surprise move in 1971, the Soviet Union introduced its own draft convention on biological warfare, dropping its long held opposition to separate disarmament agreements on CBWs. The Soviet draft differed from the U.K. draft in several crucial respects. Importantly, it required all complaints concerning a breach of obligation to go to the UNSC rather than the Secretary General, and it substituted the U.K. draft's language on investigation of complaints by the Security Council or the Secretary General, depending on the severity of the allegation, with significantly weaker language on consultation and cooperation procedures to resolve problems of implementation. The U.S. ultimately joined the Soviet Union in yet another version of the text that included the weaker provisions for dealing with treaty breaches and which made their way into the final Convention (Chevrier 2006: 316–325). One analyst describes these verification provisions as "symbolic" (Clemison 1985), defined as: "A regime in which the verification capability is known to be inadequate through a combination of lack of technology and/or of low probability of compliance. Nevertheless, the contracting parties consider the nature of the treaty is such as to override the inadequacy of verification" (Rowell 1986: 81; emphasis in original).

The U.K. voiced objections to the Soviet draft convention with weaker verification tools in an internal document. Among the U.K. reservations of the Soviet draft were concerns that the "language of consultation and cooperation procedures to resolve problems of implementation of the Convention was not a realistic deterrent to would-be violators."[1] Nevertheless, after consultation among Western allies, the U.S., the U.K. and others agreed to proceed with negotiations that included the weaker language.

The BWC opened for signature in 1972 and entered into force in 1975. Testifying at U.S. Senate hearings on the ratification of the BWC, Fred Ikle, director of the ACDA, described why the U.S. should ratify a treaty with such weak verification tools:

> First, the military utility of these weapons is dubious at best: The effects are unpredictable and potentially uncontrollable, and there exists no military experience concerning them. Hence prohibitions of this Convention do not deny us a militarily viable option and verifiability is therefore less important.[2]

The Senate accepted these arguments and unanimously ratified the BWC along with the long over-due 1925 Geneva Protocol. In testifying before the House of Representatives, Ikle said:

> It has been our decision that it was in our net interest to have this agreement even though, in a strict sense, it is not fully verifiable. Why? It is not only because biological weapons are so undesirable from a moral point of view but because it is very dubious what role they would play in a military manner and for military purposes. It does seem to be in our net interest to rather dampen the competition in biological weapons.[3]

It appears that the U.S. entered into an agreement to ban the possession of biological and toxin weapons in the hopes that other states would follow its example, because it had already determined that it did not need the weapons militarily.

The Trilateral Process — Sverdlovsk and suspicions of Soviet violations

Analysis of U.S. Central Intelligence Agency spy plane photographs raised suspicions that the Soviet Union was defying its obligations to dismantle its BW program shortly after the USSR signed the treaty in 1972. These photographs and U.S. suspicions continued after the Convention entered into force in 1975. What the spy plane photos delivered to Secretary of Defense Melvin Laird appeared to show was that the Soviets were constructing new structures at their BW installations rather than getting rid of BW agents and munitions. After the CIA leaked photos to the press, there were two types of reaction in the U.S. Government. Convinced that the Soviets were in violation of the Convention, Laird wanted to confront the USSR, perhaps using the processes set forth in Articles V and/or VI. In contrast, the ACDA was not convinced that the photos provided sufficient proof that the Soviet Union was violating the BWC. Without on-site inspections there was no way to know what was going on inside the buildings and whether those unknown activities were a continuation or expansion of a biological weapons program. Moreover, ACDA did not want to jeopardize ongoing negotiations with the USSR on reductions of nuclear weapons (Mangold and Goldberg 2001). ACDA's views carried the day. The U.S. did not call for a consultative meeting, nor did it lodge a complaint with the UNSC even after a Soviet defector, Arkady Shevchenko, provided more damning evidence of the Soviet BW program (Mangold and Goldberg 2001; Shevchenko 1985).

The first conference to review the operations of the BWC was held in March 1980, in the period often referred to as the "second Cold War." At that conference, Sweden proposed amending Articles V and VI to establish a Consultative Committee to investigate issues of non-compliance with the treaty. The Committee would have the ability to conduct fact-finding missions with on-site inspections.

The USSR objected, arguing that a review conference was not the appropriate forum to introduce amendments to the Convention. The Soviets may well have had other reasons to object to the Swedish proposal. In the spring of 1979, there was an outbreak of anthrax in the Soviet city of Ekaterinburg, then known as Sverdlovsk. Because the city was home to a facility the U.S. long suspected was a biological warfare laboratory, intelligence analysts in the West suspected that a leak or explosion at the facility caused the outbreak. The U.S. made its suspicions public at the first BWC review conference and raised allegations that the outbreak was due to a biological weapon accident, charging the Soviets with treaty violation. The Soviets responded to the allegation by acknowledging the existence of the anthrax epidemic and blaming it on the ingestion of tainted meat. Commenting on the effect of the U.S. allegations, Julian Perry Robinson made the following observations:

> The Sverdlovsk allegation very much affected the content of the Final Declaration on the thorny issue of the Consultative Committee. On the one hand it illustrated most graphically the need for some form of international verification procedure. On the other hand it suggested that the USSR would be the subject of the first complaint to be brought before the committee, and few states were happy to contemplate the political furor that would ensue, and the attendant threat to the BWC's continuation … [so it] paradoxically strengthened the position of the USSR.
>
> (Robinson 1980: 393)

Ultimately, the controversy was resolved by abandoning the amendment process, and including language in the final declaration that clarified that the consultation and cooperation provision in Article V of the Convention included the right to call a consultative meeting open to all treaty members at the expert level. The controversy over the cause of the anthrax outbreak lingered until independent scientific investigations conducted after the collapse of the Soviet Union revealed that, indeed, the U.S. suspicions of a leak at a biological weapons facility was the cause of the outbreak (Guillemin 2001; Meselson *et al.* 1994).

Today much is known about the massive offensive BW program that the Soviet Union conducted in complete violation of its commitments under the BWC (see Chapter 4). Scientists who defected from the Soviet Union, notably Ken Alibek, Vladimir Pasechnik, Arkady Shevchenko and others who left after the downfall of the USSR provided detailed information about the program. Following the dissolution of the USSR in December 1991, Russian President Boris Yeltsin somewhat obliquely acknowledged the existence of the illegal Soviet BW program. Yet, the U.K. and U.S. remained unconvinced that Russia had terminated all aspects of the program as Yeltsin had promised to do (Hart 2009; Leitenberg *et al.* 2012: 637–639). These worries led the U.S., U.K. and Russia to hold informal and formal discussions, and to host reciprocal visits to biological institutes. They formalized this process in the "Trilateral Agreement" among the three governments. According to Hart: "The U.S. (and U.K.) did not publicly discuss the Soviet BW program during the trilateral process ... because they believed that quiet diplomacy would be more effective in promoting transparency and appropriate follow-up steps" (Hart 2009: 149). The process was suspended in 1996 when the participants saw no further utility in continuing the process (Walker 2012a, 2012b).

The visits conducted during the trilateral process uncovered some details of the Soviet program that were not known beforehand, but also demonstrated the limits of the process. Discussions and visits without more intrusive tools are unlikely to come to definitive conclusions about treaty compliance or non-compliance where biological agents and weapons are concerned. Leitenberg *et al.* (2012) authoritative history of the Soviet BW program underscores that there are still unanswered questions about the Soviet program; the Russian leadership, in an about face from Yeltsin's admission, now denies that an illicit BW program existed in the USSR; and the legacy of secrecy, military obstruction and dishonesty may have profound implications for biological disarmament and the BWC.

The Consultation Process — Cuban allegations of U.S. use of BW

The second Review Conference of the BWC took place in 1986 and delegations once again recognized the limitations of Article V and VI to address questions of compliance. They changed the language around the consultative meeting and developed procedures for such a meeting. They also initiated an information exchange, discussed in more detail in the following section.

Since 1986, only one state — Cuba — has requested that a consultative meeting be called. Over the years Cuban leaders had made numerous informal allegations that the U.S. had used BW against the island nation (Zilinskas 1999). In April 1997, Cuba requested that a consultative meeting be called to investigate charges that a U.S. government airplane sprayed a substance over Cuba containing an insect, *Thrips Palmi,* which causes a plant disease. Raymond Zilinskas (1999) has written the most comprehensive description of the consultative meeting process and the scientific evidence brought by the Cuban government and rebutted by the U.S. government.

The meeting took place over 3 days in August 1997, each government presented reports as evidence for and against the charges that the U.S. used a biological agent in violation of its BWC obligations. States that attended the meeting could issue findings and submit them to the consultative meeting chair, who along with six vice chairs issued a final report. Twelve governments submitted findings and Zilinskas reports on 10 of them (he does not include a description of Cuba's submission, presumably as unnecessary; and he notes that North Korea's submission was not included in submissions sent to BWC state parties). A total of 8 of the 10 states — Australia, Canada, Denmark, Germany, Hungary, Japan, The Netherlands and New Zealand — found that the evidence did not support Cuba's allegation. Two states — China and Vietnam — said they could not draw conclusions from the evidence presented (Zilinskas 1999: 214–215). In the consultative meeting report issued in December 1997, U.K. Ambassador Soutar concluded that "due inter alia to the technical complexity of the subject and the passage of time, it has not proved possible to reach a definitive conclusion with regard to the concerns raised by the Government of Cuba" despite the evidence and findings from the majority of states who provided submissions (Soutar 1997, quoted in Zilinskas 1999). Zilinskas makes an important point in his discussion: Cuba did not share the insect specimens with the international community and, therefore, "the Cuban government's allegation is unsupported by an international authority" (Zilinskas 1999: 216). Cuban and/or independent scientists could have applied "sophisticated molecular biology techniques ... to compare *Thrips Palmi* samples collected in Cuba with those from other parts of the world. If it had done so a determination could have strengthened Cuba's case, or weakened it" (Zilinskas 1999: 216). Zilinskas examines the scientific evidence for the allegations and concludes that political rather than scientific motives were behind the Cuban allegations and that "governmental decisions, which had nothing to do with science, were made to put blame ... on U.S. imperialists to gain political and diplomatic ends" (Zilinskas 1999: 218).

Consultative processes and committees were somewhat popular during the latter part of the 20th century as part of arms control agreements like the SALT I, Anti-Ballistic Missiles treaty and within institutions such as NATO (Blacker 1984).[4] In the BWC context they have not been very effective; there has only been one consultative meeting called in nearly 30 years. There may, of course, be several reasons for this. All states parties to the BWC are invited to attend any consultative meeting, and states may prefer to discuss compliance concerns in a more private setting. Second, concerns about BWC compliance may not be a priority in states' diplomacy with one another. They would not want allegations of non-compliance with the BWC to damage relationships in areas that they consider to be more important. Third, the technical difficulty of proving BWC non-compliance may make diplomats, who might not understand technically dense arguments, reluctant to press their suspicions. But still, the reluctance of states to use the process even when they have suspicions of non-compliance is damning.[5] A tool that is not used may become rusty to the point that it is unusable. In the BWC context non-use of the consultative meeting in the already murky landscape of BW arms control and disarmament leads to even less than optimum transparency.

Annual information exchange — CBMs

Recognizing the weakness of Articles V and VI, the second BWC review conference instituted the beginnings of an annual information exchange, commonly known as the Confidence Building Measures (CBMs). Beginning in 1987, all member states have been obliged to submit data on facilities and activities relevant to the Convention. The third review conference in 1991 added to the existing CBMs. Further improvements were made to allow states to submit information electronically, and delegations modestly revised the CBMs at the seventh review conference in 2011. BWC states parties must now submit information on the following:

- Research centers and laboratories
- National biological defense research and development programs
- Unusual outbreaks of infectious diseases
- Publication policies
- Relevant legislation, regulations and other measures
- Past activities in offensive and/or defensive biological research and development programs
- Vaccine production facilities

Analysts disagree about the value of the CBMs. There are several concerns (Lentzos 2011). First, a large number of countries ignore their obligation to submit information. For more than 20 years, the annual number of States Parties submitting CBMs has been somewhere between 30 at its lowest (1987) and 72 at its highest (2010).[6] Annual CBM submissions are thus made on average by less than 40 percent of the states parties to the BWC. This relative lack of participation in the CBM process is particularly unfortunate as the mechanism will only command limited transparency until more states honour their commitments and submit declarations. Ignoring the mechanism weakens the concept of CBMs and may ultimately reduce, rather than build, confidence among States.

The relative lack of participation in the CBM mechanism is compounded by inconsistent submissions, where states submit returns in some years but not in others, as well as by incomplete submissions, where only some of the seven forms are submitted (Lentzos 2009). A notably bad year was 1991, for example, in which approximately half of the returns submitted were incomplete. In other years somewhere between 15 percent and 25 percent of submissions are incomplete. Where forms are submitted, they are sometimes only partially filled out, or filled out with information that provides little transparency about national programes and activities related to the BWC. Moreover, no mechanism exists for states to challenge inaccurate or missing information in CBMs.[7] Inconsistent participation and incomplete submissions make it more difficult to establish national patterns of normal activity, and thereby reduce transparency.

Third, there is only a subset of states actually using the CBMs.[8] The annual report of the Implementation Support Unit provides aggregate statistics on the number of States Parties that have accessed the restricted area of the BWC website. This area is currently the only place States Parties can access CBM submissions, and although it also provides some other information, the statistics provide a good proxy for the number of States Parties accessing CBM returns. In 2008, when these statistics were first made available, 44 States Parties had used the restricted area. In 2009, 45 States Parties had used it; in 2010, 37 States Parties had used it. This equates to less than one-third of BWC states in 2008 and 2009, and only about one-fifth of BWC states in 2010. While there may be many reasons for this, ranging from lack of resources and language barriers, through lack of perceived utility, to low threat assessments of national biodefense programmes, the number of States Parties accessing CBM returns is remarkably low.

In the interest of maximizing transparency, and disseminating the relevant information as widely as possible, many states (about a third of those submitting CBMs) are now making their returns publicly available or are working towards doing so. So far, in 2015, 27 out of the 67 states submitting CBMs have made their returns publicly available.[9] This is certainly an improvement, but nowhere near adequate transparency.

Fifteen years ago one of us concluded that "the efforts to institutionalize and augment the CBMs have not to date lived up to expectations ... compared to a strong compliance protocol, these CBMs are a feeble bag of tools" (Chevrier and Hunger 2000: 35). While CBMs continue to have potential "there is little evidence that CBMs, as defined and implemented in the BWC, have increased confidence in countries' treaty compliance or in the effectiveness of the BWC" (Chevrier and Hunger 2000: 40). Events since 2000 have not changed this conclusion.

Intelligence

This chapter has so far discussed the traditional international tools available to enhance the ability to accurately judge others' compliance with the BWC. Yet national tools also play a significant role in assessing the activities of other states in the biological context, most notably a state's intelligence apparatus. Regrettably, intelligence agencies do not have a sterling record of accurate intelligence on state BW programs. Moreover, since so much of national intelligence is secret, it is frequently impossible to know the evidence upon which the intelligence experts are making their judgments.

The Soviet Union got it wrong when it concluded that the U.S. did not end its biological and toxin weapons programs following Nixon's decision to terminate them in 1969 and 1970, respectively. The Soviets were duped by a disinformation campaign that used spies to pass on information to them that the U.S. had a covert BW program. The USSR went on to justify its own covert BW program following the entry into force of the BWC, at least in part, because it believed that the U.S. was doing the same (Garthoff 2000; Leitenberg *et al.* 2012).

The U.S. got it wrong when assessing whether Iraq had a covert, mobile BW program in early 2002. Its national intelligence estimate of Iraq's biological weapons program was utterly exaggerated and completely unfounded. The report cited that "it had a high degree of confidence in this assessment" (National Intelligence Council 2002, quoted in Koblentz 2009: 141). George W. Bush, his administration and members of Congress relied on this specious assessment in deliberately misleading the international community and the U.S. public while seeking support for its ill-fated invasion of Iraq in 2003.

The U.S.' prolonged assessment of the Soviet BW program demonstrates how intelligence assessments can find some information about BW programs even in a country with a government that rules with secrecy and disinformation. Yet even then the intelligence was incomplete. Koblentz finds that between 1971 and 1990.

> U.S. intelligence was able to outline the basic contours of the Soviet offensive program ... Although many of the Soviet Union's BW research and production sites were identified at one time or another by U.S. intelligence agencies, there does not appear to have been a consistent assessment of the role of these facilities over time or an appreciation of the range of other facilities involved in the BW program.
>
> (Koblentz 2009: 157)

Koblentz, as well as Leitenberg and Zilinskas, emphasize the role of human intelligence in biological arms control, as the history of Soviet defectors has amply shown. But they emphasize that human intelligence can be a "two-edged sword" (Koblentz 2009: 194). It can be difficult or impossible to independently establish the accuracy of human informants. Indeed the U.S. estimate of Iraq's covert BW program relied on human intelligence in making its faulty assessment (Vogel 2012). The lesson from these cases is that intelligence alone is very unlikely to provide an accurate picture of illicit BW programs.

Intelligence, of course, is only one component of assessing threats to national and international security and can take many forms, including human intelligence, aerial photography, signal intelligence and open source intelligence (Koblentz 2009: 193–194). Koblentz convincingly argues that "biological weapons are a notoriously difficult target for intelligence agencies" (Koblentz 2009: 142). As a consequence, intelligence errors go in both directions; intelligence can fail to detect clandestine BW programs that exist while mistakenly concluding that there are secret biological weapons programs where there are none.

Verification, confidence and compliance

States that agree to limit, control or eliminate certain types of weapons and their delivery systems ordinarily do so only if they have sufficient *confidence* that other states will abide by the same rules they have agreed to be bound by. If treaty parties are confident that other states are in *compliance* with international agreements on arms control, they may choose to acknowledge that other states are in compliance; that is they make a judgment that constitutes *verification* of compliance. Conversely if states are not confident that others are in compliance, they may publicly acknowledge that they cannot verify others' compliance with agreements. Confidence, compliance and verification have technical as well as common meanings or understandings. In arms control those understandings of what exactly constitutes confidence, compliance and verification can differ across countries and professional cultures.

Some in the arms control community understand the term verification, for example, as the activities that states or international agencies engage in to gather and assess information about compliance.[10] In contrast, others in the arms control community stress that the definition of verification is a state's prerogative and involves a judgment that a state is in compliance. This might boil down to a difference of emphasis rather than a disagreement about the nature of verification, but these differences of opinion, emphasis and priority can nevertheless have consequences in treaty negotiation and implementation (Chevrier 1990).

Verification of compliance is considered essential if a breach of treaty obligations would harm national security. Tools that enable states to be confident about another state's compliance often involve states agreeing to a degree of intrusiveness, or limits to a state's sovereignty. And this can cause the negotiation of these tools to be lengthy and contentious. The more important treaty compliance is to national security the more intrusive the tools of verification must be to provide evidence of compliance. There are different levels of confidence that can lead to a judgment of verification. A state can rarely have absolute or complete confidence in another's compliance. Each party to a treaty must be comfortable that one's own national technical means of gathering information about treaty compliance, along with additional tools negotiated within a treaty, will provide sufficient evidence of compliance that any militarily significant breach of compliance will be detected and responded to, before it constitutes a threat to national or international security.

Conclusion

The traditional tools of BW arms control and disarmament have varied during the negotiation and implementation of the BWC. Left with measures to assess compliance within the BWC that are symbolic, or inadequate at best, states have attempted to make the best of these measures and augment them with national means of assessing treaty compliance. None of these measures, even in combination, have accomplished the increased confidence in compliance that is desirable.

The failed attempt between 1994 and 2001 to add a legally binding compliance protocol to the BWC has left the treaty in a state of limbo. Annual meetings of experts and governmental representatives have kept an international focus on the obligations of the Convention. NGOs have tried to keep states parties' feet to the fire, for example, in assisting parties to implement Article IV of the treaty which requires states to draft implementing legislation that would make the prohibitions contained in the Convention part of their domestic criminal law and other aspects of BWC relevant activities.[11] The Implementation Support Unit and successive Chairs have promoted universalization of the treaty urging states to ratify or accede to the Convention. But still, the BWC remains an arms control treaty whose provisions are notoriously difficult to verify, and one that provides very few traditional tools to carry out the process of verification and to make an informed and accurate verification judgment.

What can be done, if anything to rectify this situation? Many detailed proposals for strengthening the BWC have appeared over the years from Sweden's initial proposal to amend the treaty at the 1980 review conference to more recent proposals. France, Australia, Canada, the Czech Republic, Japan, New Zealand, Switzerland, the United States and the Russian Federation have all submitted proposals to enhance confidence in compliance in recent yearly meetings and at the most recent review conference. Independent analysts and academics have also contributed numerous proposals (Lentzos 2014, 2015; Koblentz and Chevrier 2011; Lennane 2011; Sims 2009).

These proposals have a number of features in common. First, is an acceptance that there are weaknesses in the verification and compliance mechanisms of the BWC and that there are routes to address those weaknesses. Second, they recognize that a return to the mandate for a legally binding protocol to the BWC is unlikely to garner the necessary political support to proceed. Third, creative thinking combined with voluntary action could lead to substantial contributions to increased confidence in compliance with all the articles of the Convention.

For example, France has proposed conducting peer review assessments of national implementation legislation and practices.[12] It carried out a pilot exercise in 2013 to demonstrate the mechanism in practice, and further exercises are in process in Belgium, Luxembourg and the Netherlands. Among the most promising framework for addressing weaknesses is the catchy "3D Bio: Declare, Document and Demonstrate" proposed by Filippa Lentzos (2015). Building on work by Sims (2009) and Lennane (2011), as well as working papers submitted by states, Lentzos hits the nail on the head by finding the elements that are most likely to enhance confidence in compliance in the absence of legally binding obligations. The first element of 3D BIO — declare — simply requires states to reaffirm their commitment to renounce the possession and use of biological weapons already enshrined in ratification or accession to the BWC. The second element — document — tackles the issue of CBMs, but also moves beyond it urging states to document all implementation efforts and engage the scientific community. The third element — demonstrate — would ask states to host on-site visits to high containment and/or biodefense facilities, and demonstrate how those facilities are in compliance with the BWC.

A weakness of all the voluntary proposals, however, is whether any increased confidence in compliance reaches and convinces the most suspicious. Would Cuba, for example, be convinced of U.S. compliance with a report of a visit if the visitors were all friends and allies of the U.S.? Legally binding obligations, as unlikely as they may be, would increase confidence in compliance far more than voluntary measures.

Ultimately, all of these suggestions for action require that states and NGOs make BW arms control a priority. Advances in science could make BW more insidious, more lethal and more horrifying. The international community has known about the weaknesses of the BWC and the potential for a growing BW threat for a long time. The question is whether members of the community are willing and able to gather and sustain momentum to create stronger obstacles to the threat coming to fruition.

Acknowledgments

Research for Alex Spelling's contribution to this chapter was supported by AHRC grant AH/K003496/1 "Understanding Biological Disarmament: The Historical Context for the Biological Weapons Convention."

References

Balmer B (2001) *Britain and Biological Warfare: Expert Advice and Science Policy, 1930–65.* New York: Palgrave.

Blacker CD (1984) *International Arms Control: Issues and Agreements.* 2nd Edition. Stanford: Stanford University Press.

Chevrier MI (1990) 'Verifying the Unverifiable: Lessons from the Biological Weapons Convention,' *Politics and the Life Sciences* Vol. 9(1): 93–105.

Chevrier MI (2006) 'The Politics of Biological Disarmament,' in M Wheelis, L Rozsa and M Dando (Eds.), *Deadly Cultures: Biological Weapons since 1945.* Harvard: Harvard University Press.

Chevrier MI and Hunger I (2000) 'Confidence-building Measures for the BTWC: Performance and Potential,' *The Nonproliferation Review* Vol. 7(3): 24–42.

Cleminson FR (1985) 'Verification of Compliance in the Areas of Biological and Chemical Warfare', In WC Potter (Ed.), *Verification and Arms Control.* Maryland Lexington Books.

Garthoff RL (2000) 'Polyakov's Run,' *Bulletin of the Atomic Scientists* Vol. 56(5): 37–40.

Guillemin J (2001) *Anthrax: The Investigation of a Deadly Outbreak.* Berkeley: University of California Press.

Hart J (2009) 'The Soviet biological weapons program,' in M Wheelis, L Rozsa and M Dando (Eds.), *Deadly Cultures: Biological Weapons since 1945*, Harvard: Harvard University Press.

Koblentz GD and Chevrier MI (2011) 'Modernizing confidence-building measures for the Biological Weapons Convention,' *Biosecurity and Bioterrorism: Biodefense Strategy, Practice, and Science* Vol. 9(3): 232–238.

Koblentz GD (2009) *Living Weapons Biological Warfare and International Security.* Ithaca: Cornell University Press.

Leitenberg M, Zilinskas RA and Kuhn JH (2012) *The Soviet Biological Weapons Program: A History.* Cambridge, Massachusetts: Harvard University Press.

Lennane R (2011) 'Verification for the BTWC: If not the Protocol, Then What?' *Disarmament Forum* No. 1: 39–50.

Lentzos F (2009) 'Reaching a Tipping Point: Strengthening the BWC's Confidence-Building Measures,' *Disarmament Diplomacy* Vol. 89 (winter): 52–57.

Lentzos F (2011) "Strengthening the BWC Confidence-Building Measures: Toward a Cycle of Engagement" *Bulletin of the Atomic Scientists* Vol. 67(3): 26–33.

Lentzos F (2014) *Confidence & Compliance with the Biological Weapons Convention*: Workshop Report. Submitted to the BWC 2014 Meeting of States Parties by the United Kingdom BWC/MSP/2014/INF.3

Lentzos F (2015) *3D Bio: Declare, Document and Demonstrate.* EU Non-Proliferation Consortium Non-Proliferation Papers No. 45.

Mangold T and Goldberg J (2001) *Plague Wars: The Terrifying Reality of Biological Warfare.* New York: St. Martin's Griffin.

Meselson M, Guillemin J, Hugh-Jones M *et al.* (1994) 'The Sverdlovsk Anthrax Outbreak of 1979,' *Science* Vol. 266(5188): 1202–1208.

Robinson JP (1980) 'East–West fencing at Geneva,' *Nature* Vol. 284: 393.
Rowell WF (1986) *Arms Control Verification: A Guide to the Policy Issues for the 1980's*. Cambridge, Massachusetts: Ballinger.
Schelling TC (1984) *Choice and Consequence*. Cambridge Massachusetts: Harvard University Press.
Shevchenko AN (1985) *Breaking with Moscow*. 1st Edition. New York: Knopf.
Sims NA (2009) *The Future of Biological Disarmament: Strengthening the Treaty Ban on Weapons*. 1st Edition. London: Routledge.
Spelling A, Balmer B and McLeish C (2015) 'The Geneva Protocol at 90: An Anchor for Arms Control?' *The Guardian*, June 17, 2015. See http://www.theguardian.com/science/the-h-word/2015/jun/17/the-geneva-protocol-at-90-an-anchor-for-arms-control?CMP=share_btn_tw (accessed August 4, 2015).
Tucker JB (2002) 'A Farewell to Germs: The U.S. Renunciation of Biological and Toxin Warfare, 1969–70,' *International Security* Vol. 27(1): 107–148.
Vogel KM (2012) *Phantom Menace or Looming Danger?* Baltimore, Maryland: Johns Hopkins University Press.
Walker JR (2012a) *Britain and Disarmament: The UK Nuclear, Biological and Chemical Weapons Arms Control and Programmes, 1965–1975*. Farnham: Ashgate.
Walker JR (2012b) 'The Leitenberg–Zilinskas history of the Soviet Biological Weapons Programme' *Harvard Sussex Program Occasional Paper* Issue 02.
Wright S (2002) 'Geopolitical origins,' in S Wright (Ed.) *Biological Warfare and Disarmament: New Problems/New Perspectives*. Maryland: Rowman and Littlefield.
Zilinskas RA (1999) 'Cuban Allegations of Biological Warfare by the United States: Assessing the Evidence,' *Critical Reviews in Microbiology* Vol. 25(3): 173–227.

Notes

[1] Confidential Saving Telegram, FCO to Abidjan, September 29, 1969, DEFE 24/551, PRO.

[2] U.S. Congress. Senate. Committee on Foreign Relations (1974) *Hearings on the Prohibition of Chemical and Biological Weapons*. 93rd Congress, 2nd Session. Washington, DC: U.S. Government Printing Office.

[3] U.S. Congress House. Committee on Armed Services (1974). *Review of Arms Control and Disarmament Activities: Hearings before the Special Subcommittee on Arms Control and Disarmament.* 92nd Congress, 2nd Session. Washington DC: U.S. Government Printing Office.

[4] Group of Experts on a New Strategic Concept for NATO (2010) *NATO 2020: Assured Security; Dynamic Engagement.*

[5] Department of State (2014) 2014 Compliance Report. See http://www.state.gov/t/avc/rls/rpt/2014/index.htm (accessed August 10, 2015).

[6] Germany, Norway and Switzerland (2011) Review and update of the Confidence-Building Measures. Working Paper submitted to the Seventh BWC Review Conference: BWC/CONF.VII/WP.9

[7] See Leitenberg and Zilinskas (2012: 634–638) for a discussion of problems with Russian CBMs.

[8] Germany, Norway and Switzerland 2011, as per note 5.

[9] BWC website www.unog.ch/bwc (accessed August 28, 2015).

[10] And hence the "Annex on Implementation and Verification" in the 1993 CWC, "sets out all of the detailed procedures to be followed by the States Parties and by OPCW [Organization for the Prohibition of Chemical Weapons] inspection teams during verification/inspection activities at chemical weapons facilities or sites and industrial facilities" (OPCW 2015).

[11] For example, VERTIC a not-for profit NGO provides assistance to countries to draft implementing legislation. The BioWeapons Prevention Project published yearly publications from 2010–2014 monitoring open source information on certain states activities relevant to the BWC.

[12] France (2011) 'A Peer Review Mechanism for the Biological Weapons Convention: Enhancing Confidence in National Implementation and International Cooperation,' Working Paper submitted to the BWC Review Conference 2011, BWC/CONF.VII/WP.28

Witness Seminar

Origins of the Biological Weapons Convention

Jeanne Guillemin, Matthew Meselson, Julian Perry Robinson & Nicholas Sims

Editor's note: A witness seminar is a method of gathering oral history from a group of people who were historical "witnesses" to an event or series of events. Witness seminars thereby offer access to communal (though by no means consensual) recollections, tempered by "real-time peer review".[1] This witness seminar, on the history of the BWC took place on October 10, 2014 at the University of Sussex in front of a small specialist audience.

The panelists were: Jeanne Guillemin, a medical anthropologist and author, who for 25 years was a Professor of Sociology at Boston College and for the last 10 years has been a Senior Fellow in the security studies program at Massachusetts Institute of Technology. Matthew Meselson, Professor in the Department of Molecular and Cellular Biology at Harvard University, which he joined in 1960. Julian Perry Robinson, Emeritus Professor at the University of Sussex Science Policy Research Unit, which he joined in the early 1970s. Together, Meselson and Perry Robinson established the Harvard Sussex Program, an ongoing collaborative effort, formally initiated in 1990, but extending back many years before that, to provide research, training, seminars and information on CBWs dis-armament. The final panelist, Nicholas Sims, holds an Emeritus Readership in International Relations from the London School of Economics and Political Science, where he taught from 1968 until his retirement in 2010.

The witness seminar was part of a 3-year research project run by Brian Balmer, Caitríona McLeish and Alex Spelling, funded by the U.K. Arts and Humanities Research Council.[2] The full transcript of the 3-hour event runs to about 21,000 words; what follows is a version, edited by the project team and Filippa Lentzos, of about 9,000 words. After the witness seminar all participants were provided with the opportunity to comment on or amend the text. So, while the majority of the transcript remains a verbatim record, readers should bear in mind that participants have been allowed to tidy up, correct and in a very few instances remove part of their contributions.

Brian Balmer (Department of Science and Technology Studies, University College London, and chair of the witness seminar) There are four broad questions we would like you to consider:

1. Why do you think biological warfare was given time on the international diplomatic calendar given everything else that was going on in the period that could have crowded the issue out?
2. What was the role of public opinion — particularly when a lot of press coverage and media coverage tended to focus on chemical warfare issues?
3. How important and influential do you think NGOs and individuals such as scientists and national politicians were?
4. What was your reaction, and the reaction of those you worked with, when chemical and biological warfare came to be treated as separate issues in Geneva?

Julian Perry Robinson In the late 1960s, I began working for the Stockholm International Peace Research Institute (SIPRI), which had just started up as a non-governmental research organization. In its early work, SIPRI had a biological weapons project that had been running since 1966 under the instigation of particular figures within the Pugwash movement (Pugwash Conferences on Science and World Affairs) and especially, the late Martin Kaplan, a veterinary virologist …

So SIPRI was embarking upon a biological weapons

project and soon taking into its head the idea that maybe the project ought to be broadened into chemical warfare as well, whereupon I, who had published a bit on chemical warfare already, was engaged for 3 months to run a conference on chemical weapons and introduce the subject into the scope of the biological weapons project.

SIPRI was studying the possibility of constraint in the application of biology to military affairs and was looking for ways of coming to grips with this potentially burgeoning area of military technology. Biological warfare was a small, esoteric, little-known subject at that time, less known even than chemical warfare. CBW had scarcely figured in World War II nor since. The number of people expert in the subject was therefore small and becoming smaller, but with the one exception of those involved with CBW on the science and technology front, within the scientific community. These were the people, and others in the intelligence community too, whose job it was, pretty much in secret, to understand the subject — in contrast to the rest of the world, so I thought then, which knew nothing whatever about chemical biological warfare. It was that pervasive ignorance that led SIPRI to expand its small biological weapons project into something which within the next few years had produced six closely documented volumes: "A study of the historical, technical, military, legal and political aspects of CBW, and possible disarmament measures".[3]

SIPRI believed that a lot more ought to be known about CBW within the disarmament community, especially with the ENDC/CCD (Eighteen Nation Disarmament Committee/ Conference of the Committee on Disarmament) in Geneva choosing, under several influences, to have CBW enter its active agenda. SIPRI decided its archetypal reader should be the technical advisor of one of the smaller delegations in Geneva who were becoming involved in these CBW talks, delegations starting essentially from zero in comparison with the delegations of the co-chairmen of the ENDC/ CCD — the USSR and the U.S.A. — who could easily learn much about the subject from within their own resources ...

To do that well we read as widely as we could, and we took advantage of certain trends in the information flows within governments that caused some secret matters suddenly to pop up in the open domain. It was thereby possible to amass a sort of picture of CBW and that's what those six volumes were about.

Another key part of our research was getting to know as many people as possible in different countries whose job it was to follow the subject, to know about it, to set policy for Geneva … so that was our contribution at that time …

Which gets me away from the first question, and into the second question: What is the influence which non-governmental bodies can have on these types of negotiations? Almost negligible is the answer, to my mind, but not totally negligible if there is good information. Finding it then became the main function of the SIPRI work and of all those many other bits of work which the SIPRI folk got involved in over the years down to the days of the Harvard Sussex Program, when Meselson and I were collaborating on trying to produce a systematic record of what was happening in the world of chemical and biological weapons negotiation and publishing a quarterly journal: *The CBW Conventions Bulletin.*

But back to question one: Why do you think biological warfare was given time on the international diplomatic calendar? I don't actually think that's the right question. You know, it is striking the way so many diplomatic words were spoken in Geneva on the subject of BW but really they were not for the international diplomatic agenda. They were consequences of happenstance: of an arms control and disarmament forum having been created in Geneva. In fact this produced some very good products, latterly the NPT, but what was then to be done next? So the case was made for putting CBW onto the Geneva agenda. So that was how it got there, not that very many people noticed.

Nicholas Sims I'd like to answer the first question rather narrowly. The main thing that in the end ensured that BW received negotiation and, to my mind, had a very deleterious effect on it, was the overshadowing influence of the SALT, and particularly the timing.

The SALT talks, as I understood at the time, were about to start when the Soviet Union and its allies invaded Czechoslovakia in August 1968. That postponed the start of the talks for a whole year, which I think is very significant given that the ENDC/CCD, as Julian said, was at the end of a very significant period of nuclear negotiations culminating in NPT, which had been opened for signature in July. It then had to take up something quite different, initially the Seabed Treaty, then CBW. But CBW became important in the ENDC/CCD from July 1968 onwards, partly because of the NPT just having been concluded and because of SALT being a strictly bilateral process.

I do think that needs to be emphasized. SALT was incredibly important in the international diplomatic calendar but it was a negotiation strictly between the U.S. and the Soviet Union. I remember a U.K. minister saying, "Of course we stay out of it, they don't want us breathing down their necks." And I was thinking to myself, though I was too polite to say at the time, "Chance would be a fine thing."

The U.S. and Soviet Union were determined to keep this strictly bilateral, they did not want advice from anybody else and they wanted the timing to be theirs. And I think it's very significant that in early 1971 it became clear that a first SALT agreement could be reached by May 1972, as indeed it was. So from about a year before May 1972, the pressure was on. Nothing must be allowed to get in the way and that was an overarching goal. It was a superordinate goal into which the conclusion of the BWC had to fit and the U.S. attitude was: "It didn't matter what was in the treaty, the important thing was to get it finished and out of the way." And so it was.

Jeanne Guillemin I'd go back to the Archbishop of Canterbury using the phrase "weapons of mass destruction," a very unfortunate phrase, which then very quickly began to include nuclear, chemical and biological, and became a kind of mantra over time to the United Nations and other venues.

The intractability of nuclear weapons, the difficulty of arbitrating anything about them or ever getting rid of them, made biological and chemical weapons look ever more easy. This is tractable, maybe this is something you can do. We can go on from there to the nuclear weapons discussion but one might say from the point of view of the Nixon decision, or from Nixon himself, stopping the U.S. biological weapons program was easy pickings. It was not a big investment, by the way, for the United States, a rather small program relatively, and then Nixon put some restraints on chemicals too.

So this is a happenstance in a way. The thing that people forget, which I think is very important to include, is that if you look at the development of molecular and cellular biology and genetics in the 1950s, you have a very dangerous period in terms of their possible exploitation for biological weapons.

Matthew Meselson There are several paths that led to putting biological warfare abolition on the U.S. and international agenda. I'll confine myself as much as I can to things I saw close up.

In 1963, I was offered the possibility of serving with the United States ACDA for a summer. A friend of mine had a house in Georgetown, which was going to be unoccupied and that added to the attraction. The person I interacted with most strongly was Freeman Dyson; we were office mates. Freeman was working on exotic ABM defense and I was assigned to work on European theater nuclear arms control, which I knew nothing about. I worked on it for maybe a week or two, and very high-level people were sent to brief me: Paul Nitze, then Assistant Secretary of Defense for International Security Affairs, and Llewellyn Thomson who was our ambassador to Moscow. I could see there was nothing I could contribute; but I was expected to write something. Henry Kissinger had already written *The Necessity for Choice*, a thoughtful and influential book on the subject.

So I went to my boss at the time, Franklin Long, Director of the Science and Technology Bureau at ACDA. … and I told Frank, who was a chemist, that I was wasting his time working on European nuclear arms control. Why couldn't I, since I was a biologist and a chemist, do something in that area? And he said, "Fine." I do not remember if I knew about it at the time, but on June 8, 1963, 2 days before I started at ACDA, Long had written a memo to the files saying that initial steps had been taken in responding to a suggestion by Secretary of State Dean Rusk that "would link a ban on the use of biological weapons with a program for peaceful study of biological problems." In his memo, Long cited initial conversations about the idea with Jerome Weisner, President Kennedy's science advisor and with Harold Brown, then Director of Defense Research and Engineering at the Pentagon and with their staffs. Let me quote Long's memo at length because it shows how already in 1963 the groundwork leading to the BWC was being laid (Reads):

In a very preliminary way, the picture seems to be as follows: Biological weapons are not yet being used or planned-for to any extent by either the U.S. or the USSR although both countries have research programs on them. Even though biological weapons seem to hold potential in various possible branches of warfare the total analysis has not yet led to any feeling of urgency in producing, stockpiling or developing specific weapon systems which employ them.

Outside of those directly concerned with BW research and development, there was no great support for a BW capability within the U.S. military. As Long's memo reported (Reads):

The idea of a ban is reasonable in that it would not interfere with major proposed programs, nor would it apparently deprive either this country or the USSR of a significant weapon, i.e., national security would not be seriously affected if a ban were violated. On the other hand there are some difficulties [differentiating BW from CW; proposing a ban without inspections; assessing military potential of BW and of Soviet program].

Franklin Long discussed the idea with ACDA Director William Foster, a well-liked Republican that President

Kennedy had wisely put at the head. Foster wrote to McGeorge Bundy, President Kennedy's National Security Advisor, who suggested in a memo of November 5, 1963, that ACDA initiate a study and develop proposals that could be discussed by the Committee of Principals for ultimate decision by the President. The Committee of Principals then included Foster, Rusk, Bundy, Wiesner and Robert McNamara, the Secretary of Defense and John McCone, the Director of Central Intelligence.

But shortly before that, something had happened that added momentum to the proposed reappraisal of CBW policy. Von Hassel, the German Minister of Defense, asked the U.S. to supply Germany with chemical weapons. That was very serious business. The political problem would be immense. First of all, the release authority for chemicals at that time was the same as the release authority for nuclear weapons. And this was at a time when there was much discussion of a multilateral nuclear force and the idea of "many fingers on the trigger." So this was a really hot potato and only the President could decide that and it meant that people who were studying this proposal, this modest proposal that had started with Rusk, at lower levels, suddenly now principals had to get into the act. In the event, the reappraisal of U.S. policy for CBW was seen as a reason for delaying action on Von Hassel's request.

So a staff study gets done in November 1963. By then I had gone back to Harvard. The staff study was almost entirely on chemicals, basically saying only that there are important CBW arms control dimensions that should be given future attention. By then the U.S. use of herbicides in Vietnam and, subsequently, of CS, greatly complicated official consideration of CBW arms control. Nevertheless, ACDA continued to follow up the 1963 Rusk suggestion, and in a long memo dated November 19, 1968, a few days after Richard Nixon was elected President, produced policy recommendations for a government-wide review of CBW policy and for CBW arms control and eventual "far-reaching agreements aimed at the eventual elimination of CB weapons of mass destruction."

Now as to what I did at ACDA in 1963. I remember reading all the documents that were in the office. There had been a man before me who was studying CBW ... He had accumulated a lot of classified documents, so I read them. And then I went to the CIA to see what they thought the Russians were doing in BW. We had fairly decent photographs of the island in the Aral Sea, but it had just been realized that the prevailing wind blew from what looked, and was, a test grid on the island, toward a village on the shore. And so the conclusion at that time was that this was unlikely to be a BW testing site. But of course it was.

Then I went to Fort Detrick and was given a tour by Dr LeRoy Fothergill, a microbiologist and one of the old time members of the U.S. BW program ... And I asked Dr Fothergill "why do we do this?" And he said that it's cheaper than nuclear weapons, it will save us money. That, I think, is the first time that it dawned on me that there was an irrefutable argument to not push this stuff because we certainly didn't want to make the equivalent of a cheap hydrogen bomb that others might emulate.

I also had a feeling as a biologist, a sort of gut feeling, that biology was going to take off and sooner or later you could do anything — you could modify anything in a human being, and change maybe what it means to be human.

Brian Balmer Do you have any recollections about what role public opinion was playing at those times?

Julian Perry Robinson What you read in the newspapers was the basis of lots of information about all sorts of things including, what little there was, about chemical biological warfare. So the question then is: Is this a reliable source of information? Only extremely rarely. In cases where a figure like Josh Lederberg is writing that's one thing, but if it's an anonymous reporter writing, it's quite another ... So at SIPRI we lost confidence in the press coverage and in the media as our primary source of information.

Brian Balmer But what about in terms of just keeping the issue alive?

Julian Perry Robinson Yes, that is another question altogether. And we eventually came to the view that it wasn't the Egyptian technical advisor in Geneva we were writing for, but actually much more usefully it was for people who were so well connected in the media that they could command columns of print.

So we thought our role should be as propagandists, which is maybe putting it a bit extremely. There were largely unrecognized people who, in England, were raising consciousness of what chemical biological warfare was. The prime example is Elizabeth Compton, now Elizabeth Sigmund … She is somebody who was an exceptionally good interface person; she could talk to people who understood the science and technology of CBW and then with journalists or politicians who might take up the subject, even read some of those six volumes. And yes we felt that was a big value …

Nicholas Sims I'm convinced press and media coverage from the time tended to focus on CW issues, partly from rereading last night Elizabeth Sigmund's *Rage Against the Dying* — a fascinating account, which she wrote in 1980, but looking back to the period of the late sixties and early seventies.[4] … And I think that that was something which British public opinion was becoming aware of. British public opinion was at least as exercised about chemical as about biological.

What began to change was the need for an international treaty at the time. Significant for me was a briefing that a committee I was on received from the Director of the Microbiological Research Establishment at Porton Down, Dr C E Gordon Smith — who went on to become head of the U.K.'s public health laboratory service a few years later.

Dr Gordon Smith was extremely eloquent on the theme of how particularly vulnerable the U.K. was to biological warfare, and to a particular form of attack (known as the Large Area Concept). Particularly the mass area attack because of the meteorology, because of the population density, because of all sorts of features peculiar to the United Kingdom. We were particularly vulnerable and therefore it was in our interest not to have biological weapons and to make sure that nobody else has biological weapons.

How do you do that? You enter into a treaty. It just seemed common sense to me and nearly 50 years later it still seems common sense to me that that is the basic reason both for why a biological weapons convention was needed and for why the U.K. had a particular interest in taking the lead to the extent that we did. ... So there were relatively few NGOs going against the grain in supporting the U.K. government, and I think they did so because of briefings like those of Dr Gordon Smith to that particular committee in 1969.

Brian Balmer Nicholas, have you got particular NGOs in mind?

Nicholas Sims Elizabeth Sigmund says of the U.K. Foreign Office: "For the British Foreign Office to bring the struggle for an international ban on biological warfare to a successful conclusion, such publicity was necessary." And the publicity that she is talking about is extremely critical or confrontational: citizen disclosures of the campaign against chemical and biological warfare.

The contribution of NGOs that I was involved in was rather different, and it was essentially supportive of the government initiative and didn't have a problem with putting BW first. And thinking of this set of supportive NGOs, I was involved with four in 1969 and through to 1972: two religious and two secular. The two religious ones were a Quaker committee and the British Council of Churches' working group on defense and disarmament. And the secular ones were the Fabian Society arms control study group and the United Nations Association disarmament committee. I think the last of those was particularly significant because it was chaired by Sir Michael Wright who had been the U.K. disarmament ambassador in Geneva (1958–1963), and the vice chair was Sir Harold Beeley who had also held that office (1965–1967).

So they were recently retired ambassadors who were particularly concerned with Foreign Office things like saving the Arms Control and Disarmament Research Unit (ACDRU) when it was under threat of termination in 1969. And there was a good scattering of MPs of different political parties on that committee too. There were long-term disarmers like Philip Noel-Baker and Dame Kathleen Courtney, and then there were young people like myself in academic life. So it was a good mixture of people and I think that that was probably the most significant of those four NGOs.

Having said that, the British Council of Churches working group on defense and disarmament was particularly significant for its contacts with successive heads of the FCO disarmament department, both Ronald Hope-Jones who was head from 1968–1970 and David Summerhayes who was head from 1970–1974, by which time it had become the Arms Control and Disarmament Department. They met with that working group, attended its meetings, and drafted some of its report. And I happily drafted the bit on BWC as it was going to be, this was in 1970–1971, with David Summerhayes, and a few years later I had the honour of serving under his ambassadorship in his delegation to the first BWC review conference.

So Ronald Hope-Jones and David Summerhayes had these particular links with the British Council of Churches working group on defense and disarmament, which met from 1969–1972 and produced a report called *The Search for Security* and was extremely positive about the U.K. initiative.[5] But so were the Quaker committee, and, on the secular side, the United Nations Association disarmament committee.

Jeanne Guillemin One of the things that happened in the 1960s with the American press had to do with the Vietnam War — which had a lot of secrecy surrounding what was going on — and a series of efforts by very intrepid journalists to reveal what was going on, particularly from photographers who would give us the images of Vietnam which were initially suppressed. When they came out, they had an enormous impact on public opinion … So you have the beginning of something going on with the press in the 1960s which makes it much more open. And out of that you get people like Seymour Hersh for example, an investigative journalist, who would get inside government in ways that were preliminaries to the "Deep Throat" reporting on Nixon that would come later.

So what's important about that for CBWs? Well, most people didn't know the difference between CBWs, they only knew that horrible things were going on out there in Southeast Asia and the environment was being threatened, which was a huge deal, and that civilians were dying in the war … And once that came forth as a message, it made it easier to talk about biological and chemical weapons and to understand that there would be a negative public reaction. If you think you're going to go forward with this, you'd better be careful because in fact that's not what people want. So when in 1970, Matthew and his colleagues did research on herbicides in Vietnam they made a very clever move when they returned: they tipped off the Nixon White House … And then a few days later Meselson and his team talked publicly about it at a big science meeting. So that was a position that was very sensitive to what the American public thought about the destruction of the environment because they were looking at themselves, identifying with the victims …

The other thing I want to say … the good thing about the Biological Weapons Convention was that it was presented just at a time when there was just enough disorder in the federal government that you could get this sort of thing through. And the Congress was not in a position to start looking isolationist. Nixon had resigned, Ford was in, who knew for how long. When the Biological Weapons Convention was proposed, the U.S. was heading towards ending the Vietnam War. So it was just very, very good timing in terms of the Biological Weapons Convention, and then also the ratification in 1975.

Matthew Meselson … I want to confine myself to where I

was directly involved. There were at least two such occasions that I can remember. A young man who was a Vietnamese student in some other department, not one of the sciences, came to my office at Harvard with a stack of newspapers from Saigon that I guess his friends and family had sent to him, all showing pictures of deformed children and blaming it on herbicides. And I thought, "Well, it doesn't have any scientific substance to it." And then a graduate student in our department had a girlfriend who worked for Ralph Nader and she had got hold of a purloined copy of a study funded by the government of the mutagenic, teratogenic and carcinogenic characteristics of a large variety of pesticides, herbicides and fungicides. And in this big study, it was about that thick, there was only one thing that did anything to guinea pigs and that was 2,4,5-T, one of the ingredients of Agent Orange. It was reported to cause abnormalities in these animals.

So I could see the repercussions if these two things were put together, and because there was strong feelings about Agent Orange by then, I went down to Washington to see Lee DuBridge, President Nixon's science advisor. He had been the president of Caltech, so I knew him well because I was from Caltech. I showed him this stuff and to my amazement right then he picked up the telephone and called David Packard, who was number two at Defense at the time, and they agreed to restrict Agent Orange, just like that. So what I'm getting at is where there is a kind of threat that the government will be shown to be in some way not on top of things, then you can get a decision. Now of course there were two other herbicides, Agent White and Agent Blue, so it didn't mean we couldn't still spray things, but it was the beginning of the end of Agent Orange. It took a while before it really took effect but that was an astonishing thing on the phone, just like that! Not even consulting the President.

The second case was the one Jeanne mentioned. After we'd come back from Vietnam we had a lot of very impressive pictures, particularly from the mangrove forests there, which are particularly sensitive to phenoxyacetic herbicides, much more than the inland forest hardwood trees, and you could see the total wipe-out of all the mangroves. They were very impressive pictures. And I took them over to the White House and gave a briefing there, and then went to the annual meeting in Chicago of the American Association for the Advancement of Science. They had asked me to design a study of the ecological and health effects of herbicides in Vietnam. I decided to conduct a pilot study there and I was in Vietnam doing this for 6 weeks in 1970. And while we were presenting, as I remember, it was December, 29, news came that President Nixon had announced that there would be rapid yet orderly phase out of all herbicide operations. Also, he had a recommendation from the U.S. Ambassador and the U.S. military commander in Vietnam, very critical of the herbicide program. I imagine that in this situation the people around the President didn't want him to be blindsided by this and that in any case he decided to take charge of the situation.

Brian Balmer We've touched on question three — which was: How important and influential do you think NGOs or individuals such as scientists were? — but did any of you have anything you wanted to add?

Nicholas Sims Yes, just that Ronald Hope-Jones, whom I mentioned before who headed the FCO disarmament department from 1968–1970, always saw that the BWC should be credited to one person above anyone else and that was Solly Zuckerman, the government's science advisor. And Solly Zuckerman had been Chief Scientific Adviser to the Ministry of Defense (1960–1966) but from 1964 he'd become Chief Scientific Adviser to the Prime Minister and the cabinet as a whole (1964–1971).

According to Ronald Hope-Jones, Solly Zuckerman had played a crucial role in a cabinet subcommittee which at last brought the MOD on board in support of the U.K. initiative, which up to then had been an FCO initiative with the MOD, under Denis Healey, having some reservations about it. Solly Zuckerman managed to persuade the MOD representatives in his cabinet subcommittee that they should support it. According to Ronald Hope-Jones, he made some dramatic gesture towards the lake in St. James' Park and the point was what a very small quantity of Botulinum toxin could do. This was all to do with verifiability and up to then the MOD had said, "No, it will be an absolutely disastrous precedent if you put forward a treaty of any kind on arms control and disarmament which does not have verification as conventionally understood." But Ronald himself saw it as a great virtue of the BWC that it did not have verification as conventionally understood, it had lots of other things, well it would have had lots of other things instead — what I would call "functional substitutes for verification", though I don't think that phrase was in use at the time.

Matthew Meselson I can tell you one other story — all these are just individual stories. I got to know Philip Noel-Baker in London and we knew the Swedish resolution (of December 16, 1969 by which the UN General Assembly affirmed the scope of the 1925 Geneva Protocol as including tear gas and other harassing agents within its CW prohibition) was going to come up for a vote. So we agreed that he would write a letter to the *New York Times* saying he was in Geneva in 1925 and he knew what Lord Cecil had in mind, he listened to all the discussions, and clearly it prohibited lachrymatory agents. I would get this letter and contact a friend of mine who ran the letters page of the *New York Times* and she would print the letter on the morning of the scheduled vote before the General Assembly and Alva Myrdal, the Swedish representative to the UN would talk to all of the delegates at the UN who she knew, and many of them could vote without instructions from their capital — like the representative from Malta, he could vote whatever way he wanted. So when the vote finally came, that morning the *New York Times* had Philip's article saying, "I was there, I know what the protocol means, this is what it means." ... And the vote, as you said, was 89 to three with

30 abstentions. The three were the United States, Portugal and I forget who else.

Jeanne Guillemin Australia.

Matthew Meselson Oh, Australia, that's right, because they were using it with us. It didn't change U.S. policy but it went into the brief that was subsequently written by the legal advisor at State saying that it's going to be a tough argument to say that we can ratify without entering a formal reservation ...

And then I decided to try to prevent a Senate vote on the Geneva Protocol. I remember arguing this with some of my friends who said, "You might lose the whole thing if you don't get it to the vote now. The President is in favour of it." Nixon was in favour of it, he'd sent it back to the Senate. This was one of the first things that Julian and I worked on together. We had the view that a damaged protocol was maybe even worse than no protocol. In any case, I worked hard to prevent a vote by talking to Senator Fulbright and his assistant, Richard Moose, and others, so that it wouldn't come up to the floor until after we basically were out of Vietnam.

Then President Gerald Ford had lunch with Senator Fulbright and agreed on the executive order, which allows only five, almost trivial, uses. One of those for example is to use riot-control agents to help rescue downed pilots. If there are guys with pitchforks trying to kill you, you are the pilot, and they lower a rope from a helicopter and you're blinded by the CS, where's the rope? The obvious thing is if guys with pitchforks are trying to prevent me from being rescued I want the helicopter to shoot them. (Laughter) It makes no sense.

Nicholas Sims The Canadian ambassador, George Ignatieff, said in his memoirs how greatly influenced he was by Joshua Lederberg when Lederberg came to Geneva and addressed the CCD on the need for the BWC.[6] And that is particularly significant because although Canada was one of the very first backers of the U.K. initiative — I've got it in a scrapbook I was keeping (Reads): "Canadian support, July 16 1968: Canadian support for

ENDC that the U.K. had put forward." — but George Ignatieff himself, the Canadian ambassador who subsequently became Chancellor of the University of Toronto, was personally very doubtful about separating chemical from biological. He felt that there was really a case for continuing to pursue the two together and to try to get — as many states originally thought was the right goal — a convention on chemical and biological weapons at the same time.

Matthew Meselson Josh (Lederberg) was passionate on this long before the British initiative. He ran a regular column in the *Washington Post* and he devoted many issues to warning about the danger of using disease as a weapon.

Brian Balmer What was your reaction, or the reaction of those you worked with, when CW and BW did become separate issues in Geneva?

Julian Perry Robinson Well we certainly worried at the time when the separation of BW and CW happened, because the Geneva Protocol — on which everything else rested — treated them together. So to separate them was to impugn the authority of the Geneva Protocol. That's an argument which I think in retrospect is not particularly strong …

Matthew Meselson Would it give a green light to chemical weapons?

Brian Balmer But it was a worry at the time?

Julian Perry Robinson Oh yes.

Brian Balmer Before opening up for audience questions, are there other things that you think important that we should touch on about this period?

Nicholas Sims: I want to comment on the role of scientists. I was dimly aware of the role of Matthew Meselson and Martin Kaplan at the time, and I've since become a great admirer of both and of the great contributions they made, without which I don't think we would have a BWC.

My impression is there were also quite a number of significant scientists on the U.K. side, and in particular Dr John Humphrey comes to mind. I always think of Dr John

Humphrey, later of the Royal Postgraduate Medical School in University of London, as being the biological equivalent of Joseph Rotblat on the nuclear side, also University of London, that they were pushing the scientific case for biological disarmament and for nuclear disarmament respectively. I didn't know John Humphrey personally, though I did correspond with him. I'd be very interested to know about his role and that of the Bernal Peace Library meeting in early 1968 (see Chapter 12, Interview by Rose & Lentzos), and also the British Society for Social Responsibility in Science (BSSRS), of which I must confess I was a member though just a rank and file member, I didn't hold office in BSSRS at all. I think that Steven and Hilary Rose did.

And nobody's mentioned John Cookson and Judith Nottingham. These were two University of Newcastle-Upon-Tyne students who from 1965 through to 1968 did an enormous study that eventually became a huge book: *A Survey of Chemical and Biological Warfare.*[7] And it came out in 1969 just in time to take account of the U.K. initiative of which it was critical. They were critical of the U.K. initiative not because it was separating BW from CW for prior treatment, but because it lacked verification, or what they saw as deterrence. And they were writing in 1969, not in September 1971 when the FCO line I received was, "Yes, we have had to compromise an enormous amount; yes it is enormously diluted; yes we have had to compromise to the maximum possible," which was the Ambassador's statement in Geneva, "but we've got Article VII." What is now Article VII of the Convention was seen at the time as the major deterrent to anybody using BW so it didn't matter so much that other things had been lost, but as I argued in 1971, I objected to Britain's new posture because Britain was settling for a BWC without the explicit ban on use, which had always been Article I of the successive draft conventions.[8]

Brian Balmer We are going to shift to a question and answer session, and open for questions and comments from the floor. John.

John Walker (Author of *Britain and Disarmament: The U.K. and Nuclear, Biological and Chemical Arms Control and Programmes 1956–1975*) There's a lot in the first part of the panel that was very absorbing and chimed with my own rummaging through the archives, but I've got a few points to pick up …

On the point that Nicholas raised about the peculiar vulnerabilities of the United Kingdom to BW and the briefing you got from Gordon Smith, the Director of the Microbiological Research Establishment (MRE) at Porton Down. Smith was on Zuckerman's working party that led to the review of the proposal to have a convention, but I could find absolutely no connection between the technical appraisal that emerged from MRE's work and goes back to studies in the early 1960s, and the proposal for a separate BWC.

… I also wanted to comment a bit about Zuckerman's role. … He chaired the working party as Chief Scientific Advisor to the government. Of course he was loathed in the Ministry of Defense by this time; absolutely detested because of his views on nuclear weapons issues …

And a bit about verification. Zuckerman of course was involved heavily in advising the government as Chief Scientific Adviser on the comprehensive nuclear test ban issue and he had come across some new scientific developments in the mid-1960s which he thought would solve the problem of verification of the treaty — what's called the black box, basically remote seismic detectors — which, in his view, would remove the need for on-site inspection. Because until that time the USSR was adamantly opposed to on-site inspections of any shape … So Zuckerman was always on the lookout for something which would avoid the need for verification, and the BWC could go ahead without it.

Nicholas Sims Was there discussion of proliferation at this point?

Susan Martin (Department of War Studies and Centre for Science and Security Studies, King's College London) You certainly see it in the U.S. documents. I've just been reading

House Committee hearings from 1969 where there is concern about proliferation and the argument is being made that the U.S. shouldn't get out ahead and develop these weapons, since they would benefit other countries more than they would the U.S.

Robert Bud (Department of Research and Public History, the Science Museum) I had a separate question about public attitudes in the 1960s, and there were two points about public attitudes both in the U.K. and the U.S. In the U.K. we haven't talked about the Porton Down affair of 1967–1968 when Porton, under public pressure, had to be opened up to public visits. So Porton as a biological warfare place had a high visibility.

The other aspect I was thinking about was the attitude of young people in the U.S., which was very practical in that you could be called up, you had a number ... And also for people not going to work for chemical companies. I was a student in 1970 and the big question was: Would you go and, as a bright chemist, would you work for DuPont or Dow, particularly Dow, which made Agent Orange. So that in particular critical areas surely the public attitudes to chemical warfare, to chemical agents, really mattered.

Jeanne Guillemin If you're talking about the anti-war movement and the universal draft, you're absolutely right. That was at a time when anybody, if your number came up, unless you were in medical school or you had a family with children, your number came up and you went. And that created a very different atmosphere ...

The other thing that's interesting to note is that, in terms of funding, the Vietnam War overall increased the level of funding in the Department of Defense and auxiliary institutions, so all boats rose with the tide. And if you look at the budget for Fort Detrick at that time you will see that it also goes up, so although there may have been pressure in the U.K. to get rid of biological weapons, it was very different in the United States because Detrick was moving much more into strategic areas and getting more and more proficient with large area attack, and also attacks on crops, rice crops in particular. So the BW program didn't necessarily go there but its officers were looking to go there, and again they had the funding.

Stephen Twigge (U.K. National Archives) How much was Porton in the consciousness at that point?

Julian Perry Robinson Well, insofar as it was in the public eye, it was in the public eye as an offshoot of the Vietnam War, which was of course influencing absolutely everything then. And the CS question and herbicides and all these things impinged.

Ulf Schmidt (School of History, University of Kent, and principal investigator of the Porton Down Project on the history of chemical warfare research during the Cold War) When you look at the documentary record there is considerable publicity from early in the 1960s also around CND campaigns. They have protests, there are arrests being made, some of the issues are not particularly well managed by Porton and that's been recognized by Whitehall officials, so they recognize at some point they need a slightly different, slightly more subtle strategy in dealing with public relations and I think the open days are a response to that.

Brian Balmer Nicholas, do you want to say more about the public?

Nicholas Sims The one very well-known point of intersection between government and non-government groups is the February 2, 1970 controversy when the U.K. government announced it interpreted the 1925 Geneva Protocol as excluding CS tear gas … One of the reasons why the British Council of Churches, Quakers and the United Nations Association reacted as they did with a joint pamphlet was because they had been so supportive of the FCO for the previous year, and they felt the FCO was being defeated by the MOD and they wanted the FCO to retain the traditional reading of the Geneva Protocol. It was disappointment and it was also the feeling that this was possibly damaging through its political repercussions in Geneva to the chances of the BWC.

Jeanne Guillemin The other thing I wanted to point out … is that there was also a change in our Congress in terms of it becoming more investigative. … through Richard 'Max' McCarthy in the 1960s, the Senate becomes an investigative agent that is going to push agendas forward, and the Congress is the means by which you do that … If you go back to the 1960s, you see Max McCarthy and you see Congressional action to reveal to the public what the problem is and then say, "And now your government must act on this." So Congress acted as an investigator but also as an agent in the whole process.

Alex Mankoo (PhD student, Department of Science and Technology Studies, University College London) How did, in terms of splitting CW and BW, there manifest in the media a feeling that CW was different from BW, and did that lead to the split as well?

Jeanne Guillemin The question is pretty much, if I understood it, about tear gas, which I think is a really good case. From the American point of view thinking of Northern Ireland and the use of tear gas in Northern Ireland simply wasn't of much interest and we didn't resonate to it, but I think here in the U.K. it certainly was important and I think it changed public opinion in ways that, again, I don't think happened in the United States.

Julian Perry Robinson How about Berkeley? …

Jeanne Guillemin I was a student at that time and there was a film going around, an unbelievable film, where they showed the Berkeley riots and one of the voiceovers was about these brave students and look how they are being terribly hurt by their own government.

And then there was another voiceover for the same film being circulated, telling us, look at these horrible communists and how they are a threat to the United States. It's quite true: "A threat to the United States" and look how much your government is doing to try and control them.

But it was the shootings at Kent State, not the use of

tear gas at Berkeley that turned it all around. It was the deaths, and the brutality of the deaths. And they were your kids, you see, they were your kids being attacked. But at Berkeley, those were communists.

Nicholas Sims I think some of the crucial consciousness-raising events in the U.K. had occurred in 1968 before the first use of CS gas in Northern Ireland. And one of them that hasn't been mentioned yet, was the television program 'A Plague on Your Children.'

Another was the work by Nigel Calder, *Unless Peace Comes*, which was looking at all the terrors that could come from scientific warfare.[9] And although that wasn't exclusively about BW, I think it had quite an important biological element in it. Nigel Calder was a very distinguished science writer.

The third thing that I suppose wasn't specifically BW was the treatment of Tam Dalyell MP, who was reprimanded very disgracefully by the House of Commons over the science and technology committee visit to Porton Down. There was a disagreement between him and the committee over the status of the report which found its way into *The Observer*, and he was castigated and reprimanded very formally for that as a breach of the privileges of the House of Commons ...[10] But that isn't as specifically BW as 'A Plague on Your Children' or the strong BW element of Nigel Calder's *Unless Peace Comes*. But all three things were in 1968.

Julian Perry Robinson When was Leonard Beaton's book?

Nicholas Sims Thank you for reminding me. Leonard Beaton was the naval correspondent for *The Times* and then the defense correspondent at *The Guardian*. He was a young Canadian who had been very influential in the early years of the Institute for Strategic Studies, now the IISS in London, and he was a very early supporter of the BWC,[11] which he said must have a serious administration ... Again, he was someone who was associated with that British Council of Churches working party from its very beginning, in 1969.

Leonard started his book, *The Reform of Power*, in 1965 and rewrote it in 1970. He signed it off in March 1971, shortly before he died, and the book was published soon afterwards.[12] It was very supportive of the British initiative.

Jeanne Guillemin There were also demonstrations, I think it was in 1968, at Fort Detrick. The best-known one was by a group of Quakers and there was at least some theory at the time that because Nixon had been raised as a Quaker that he perhaps noticed that event. But there were lots of other events going on too.

Caitríona McLeish (Science Policy Research Unit, University of Sussex, and co-director of the Harvard Sussex Program) I have three questions. I'd be interested to know what was perceived at that time about the Soviet Union's program.

Second, what other countries, particularly for the U.K., would have been important in the context of the BWC negotiations?

And my third question, Jeanne you talked about the passion of Joshua Lederberg, and I'd be really interested to know your views on why it was he was so successful in communicating the message and particularly, Nicholas, at the CCD.

Jeanne Guillemin Just let me say a few words about Josh Lederberg. First of all he had impeccable credentials: He was a Nobel Laureate. He worked very well with the National Academy of Sciences and I think people forget that he made that his base. Some people say, "Well, he was once president of Rockefeller University," but that really was not his power base at all ... It was the National Academy of Sciences that was the political base for him and I think he was just a fascinating person and absolutely brilliant. I think Josh organized almost every meeting so that he would be the smartest person in the room. (Laughter)

He also had a very strong notion, which he spoke to for years, which we could as a civilization, as a species, be overcome by infectious diseases. You have to understand his generation. He lived through the time when many children under five died of infectious diseases.

Nicholas Sims I'll just add that I think he was speaking at a time when microbiologists were organizing to say, I know it sounds like a cheap slogan but, "we should all be making war on germs not with germs." And the 10th International Congress for Microbiology in Mexico City, around the same time as Joshua Lederberg addressed the CCD in August 1970, was listing the dangers and also the possibilities of turning things to good use, the beneficent uses of microbiology, which then became a theme of Article X of the BWC, including the prevention of disease, most importantly.

... And in answer to Caitríona's other question about how other countries got on board: Well, Sweden certainly did not. Alva Myrdal became, along with Kroum Christov of Bulgaria, the most severe critic of the U.K. in the CCD.

Caitríona McLeish Other than the United States, were there countries that the U.K. would pay attention to?

John Walker I can address that last point. The NATO disarmament experts group was a key coordinating forum on disarmament policy, and the U.K. did go and brief what their position was, tried to get support for it because it was important to be able to go into these multilateral negotiations knowing that the NATO allies were supportive. And if you just go back a little bit into the NPT negotiations, Germany was of course very important — West Germany was not a member of the ENDC/CCD at that time but it exerted a disproportionate influence on the positions both of the U.K. and of the U.S. But generally the group tended to happily go along with the U.K. and be supportive. One country that the U.K. of course, paid acute attention to was Sweden. They had technical expertise and it was the Swedes who really came on board to the idea of a separate convention, and saying "You ought to include toxins too." Of course the U.S. made the same point. The U.K. was quite happy to go along with that and amend their draft convention.

The point I wanted to make originally was that in the U.K., the CW and BW programs were never avowed, they were secret. ... So that had an impact. Not long after the BWC entered into force, the U.K. made a statement in the UN to the effect that we never had an offensive BW program. Of course we did, but diplomats and even MOD policy staff had no way of knowing the existence or details of the wartime offensive BW program ... Now looking back into the decision in 1968, it was not evident at the discussions that people knew there was an offensive program in the 1940s and there was certainly no evidence that people were worried about a Soviet program. ... And you don't see a correlation over concerns about a Soviet program and a reason for the British decision.

The final point I want to make is disarmament was important for the Labour party in the 1960s, particularly given the fact that the party had gone into the 1964 election on the platform that it would renegotiate the Polaris sales agreement, and get rid of nuclear weapons. Wilson and Healey wanted to keep the program and there was an inter-governmental review in 1968 about whether Britain should keep nuclear weapons and the departments split along predictable lines. ... Doing something on disarmament was important for the Labour party at that particular time, and that was the main impetus: what more can we do on disarmament post the NPT?

The final point I want to make about that is that CBW disarmament has been strongly bipartisan. ... You basically see no difference whether it's Conservatives sitting in Number 10 or Labour; they are all strongly supportive of CB disarmament and arms control.

Robert Bud The point I was going to raise was actually about the role of *New Scientist*. *New Scientist* at this time had got as editor the microbiologist, Bernard Dixon, and Bernard, with all the focus on the nuclear field, is very interested in biology as an area where *New Scientist* can play a role.

Jeanne Guillemin Yes, we talk about the news and newspapers, but there are these very powerful journals: *New Scientist*, *Science* itself, *Nature* — which do have a political component, expressing more than just great forward-looking science articles. ... *Scientific American* would be another one. They had very high credibility in terms of science reporting, but also with their Op Ed pages and their points of view.

Brian Balmer It's been an absolutely intriguing afternoon. A warm thank you to the panel, and of course the audience too. (Applause)

Notes

1 Tansey T (2007) 'Witnessing the witnesses' in Doel, R *et al.* (Eds.) *The Historiography of Contemporary Science, Technology and Medicine.* London: Routledge.

2 AHRC grant AH/K003496/1 'Understanding Biological Disarmament: The Historical Context of the Biological Weapons Convention.' With thanks to Alex Mankoo for editorial assistance, Alberto Aparicio for recording, and Debra Gee for transcription.

3 SIPRI. *The Problem of Chemical and Biological Warfare.* Six volumes published during 1971–1975. London: Humanities Press.

4 Sigmund E (1980) *Rage Against the Dying: Campaign Against Chemical and Biological Warfare.* London: Pluto Press.

5 British Council of Churches and Conference of British Missionary Societies (1973) *The Search for Security: A Christian Appraisal.* London: SCM Press. Report of a working party on defense and disarmament, chaired by Edward Rogers.

6 Ignatieff G (1985) *Memoirs of a Peacemonger.* Toronto: University of Toronto Press.

7 Cookson J and Nottingham J (1969) *A Survey of Chemical and Biological Warfare.* Sheed and Ward.

8 Sims N (1971) 'Biological Disarmament: Britain's New Posture,' *New Scientist* Vol. 52: 18–20, December 2, 1971. The article was written in September but *New Scientist* could not publish it — or anything else — through October and November 1971 because their printers were on strike.

9 Calder N (Ed.) (1968) *Unless Peace Comes: A Scientific Forecast of New Weapons.* Allen Lane: The Penguin Press; New York: Viking Press.

10 See Balmer B (2012) *Secrecy and Science: A Historical Sociology of Biological and Chemical Warfare.* Farnham: Ashgate, pp. 93–96.

11 See, for instance, Beaton L (1970) 'A ban on germs,' *Survival* Vol. 12: 17–18.

12 Beaton L (1972) *The Reform of Power.* Chatto and Windus.

Interview

Unconventional Weapons and Activist Scientists

Steven Rose & Filippa Lentzos

Editor's note Steven Rose has had a long and distinguished career as Professor of Biology and Director of the Brain and Behaviour Research Group at the Open University. He has also been politically engaged throughout his career. In the 1960s, he was instrumental in rallying scientists and sounding the alarm about military misuse of the life sciences. During that time, he took part in numerous protests against CBW and was banned from Porton Down, the principal military research facility in Britain. Together with Tam Dalyell, a Labour MP equally determined to penetrate the secrecy at Porton, he revealed the tear and nerve gas experiments going on there and exposed the university researchers collaborating with the military research facility — all of which led to Dalyell being formally reprimanded in Parliament for leaking classified information.[1] Rose also edited *CBW: Chemical and Biological Warfare,* a hugely influential volume written by scientists for non-scientists and translated into dozens of languages.[2] The volume was the first of its kind to describe CBWs, and in addition to covering the nature, development and use of these weapons, it considered legal and moral aspects, and became the handbook for academic opposition to CBW. A later book, *No Fire, No Thunder*, written by Rose with two coauthors, followed a few years after. I interviewed Steven Rose about the role of scientists in the movement against CBWs in early June 2015 at his Islington home in London.

Filippa Lentzos In *No Fire, No Thunder* you talked about building an unstoppable movement against CBWs. Why and how did biologists like yourself become politically engaged in the 1960s and 1970s?

Steven Rose This goes back to the Vietnam War and to my, and many other colleagues', moral and political opposition to it. What triggered my interest in unconventional weapons was a series of articles in *Science Magazine*, the U.S. journal, written by Elinor Langer, in which she documented the use of defoliants in Vietnam and also the use of CS (tear) gas. I was outraged by what I saw as the abuse of my science. CS was a British product, invented in Porton. It was manufactured largely in the States, but also in this country. It is now, of course, universally manufactured. The CS used against Turkish protesters in Istanbul last year, for instance, was largely manufactured in Brazil; another prime manufacturer is, of course, Israel. So I was concerned about the abuse of my science.

I was also concerned about claims that you could have "non-lethal" weapons of this sort. Many American scientists were similarly outraged.
In particular, a plant physiologist, Arthur Galston, who had been one of the key figures in the development of the plant hormones used in the defoliant campaign. So it seemed to me, and to others at the time, that we as scientists had a particular role to play in the campaign against the Vietnam War.

Filippa Lentzos Was it part of the rise of counter-culture?

Steven Rose Counter-culture had nothing to do with this at all. Counter-culture was about hippies, love, power, the Beatles, tune-in drop-out. My political engagement has been about the abuses of science, whether they are abuses in relationship to the uses of CBWs, or to the other things I've been involved with such as the IQ debate. My engagement has to do with scientific, moral and political opposition to particular developments.

Filippa Lentzos How did your involvement in the movement against CBWs begin?

Steven Rose In 1967, there was a series of meetings at the Roundhouse in London organized by the Angry Arts against the War. So we organized a comparable, but a one-day, event in February 1968 called Angry Science against the abuse of science. That meeting was held in the Conway Hall, just round the corner from here. I, and others, invited a group of prominent scientists including two Nobel laureates, Maurice Wilkins and Dorothy Hodgkin, to speak at the meeting.

This was at a time when the university campuses across Britain and the whole of Europe, and the United States, were exploding, not just with campaigns against the Vietnam War, but with the authoritarianism of the universities and so on. There were mass occupations going on.
A meeting by the student Chemical Society at Essex University was due to be addressed by a speaker from Porton. The students occupied and invited me and two or three others to come down and to speak at the occupation against the use of chemical weapons.[3]
It was also the starting point for a group of us to initiate the formation of the British Society for Social Responsibility in Science (BSSRS).

We also organized a major conference about CBW in general and its use in Vietnam in particular. We were supported by the Bernal Peace Library, which had been established to foster research on peace and which was housed just down the road here in Clerkenwell, as well as by the publishers as an advance on the book which was going to be edited from the conference, which became *CBW: Chemical and biological warfare* and went into many translations.

Speakers came from the U.S. including Matt Meselson and Elinor Langer, from Europe, and elsewhere. We showed a film from North Vietnam showing the effects of the defoliants not just on the plants, but also the teratogenic effects — the dead fish in the water, the birth deformities and physiological abnormalities that were appearing, and so on. One American participant walked out during the viewing. He said it was Vietnamese propaganda and refused to accept it. In fact, it was not until the U.S. veterans came back from the war in the 1970s and began to show similar signs that the Americans began to take the toxic effects of the defoliants seriously. Until then it was Vietnamese propaganda.

Alastair Hay, who wrote *No Fire, No Thunder* with me — along with Seán Murphy a research fellow working with me at the Open University — played a huge part in bringing into the open the effects of the defoliants on the Viet vets in the United States. He gave evidence there many times and really became a key figure in that issue.

Filippa Lentzos Were the Vietnam veterans and the use of defoliants the principal shapers of public opinion about unconventional weapons in the late 1960s, early 1970s?

Steven Rose Yes, they probably were. The Americans said defoliants aren't chemical weapons because they're not, after all, aimed at people. I went to Vietnam with my wife Hilary Rose (A renowned British sociologist of science and social policy) in 1970–1971 to look at the effects of the chemical defoliants. Hilary did a survey of the effects on refugees from South Vietnam who we interviewed in the hospitals in Hanoi. She wrote it up as a publication for *Science*. Some referees originally rejected it on the grounds that you couldn't believe the testimony of the Vietnamese. It wasn't until Hilary protested about this being a racist objection that *Science* finally published the paper, and this became the first published report of the effects of chemical sprays on humans.

This of course fed into the debate about non-lethals. CS gas is a non-lethal weapon and there was a huge debate in this country about whether you could have a chemical agent which was a non-lethal agent — and this debate has gone on ever since. They're now referred to as 'less lethal' agents. One of the things Hilary and I were concerned to demonstrate was that the way CS was being used in Vietnam was anything but non-lethal because it was used specifically to flush the guerrilla fighters out of the tunnels and to put them into the line of fire.

When the British used CS against Irish republicans in Derry a few years later, Hilary went to Derry to interview people who had been gassed, and again published the results, which sufficiently worried the government that it established a special committee under Harold Himsworth to report.

Filippa Lentzos All weapons are horrible, but some say CBWs are particularly horrible because they are the only truly discriminate weapons: they are far more likely to kill civilians than the military, the weak than the strong, the ill than the healthy, the pregnant than the non-pregnant, the young and the old rather than those in their prime. Is that why those weapons stood out for you?

Steven Rose That's an interesting question. There's always been a moral revulsion against biological weapons, particularly because they affect the civilian population and they're uncontrollable once an epidemic starts — and this is despite their early historical use such as the smallpox infected blankets and the allegations, which are still unclear to me, about the use of biological weapons in the Korean War.

Chemical weapons seemed to me at the time to be yet another extension of the armoury of weapons, but they were particularly significant to us because they derived from the work that I and others did in the laboratory. It was *our* work that was being abused. So it was really a moral thing about how could it be that we are working to acquire scientific knowledge, ideally in a biomedical context for the benefit of humanity, and this is turned into a weapon. And that was also Art Galston's point.

So I suppose the revulsion was very similar to the one the physicists felt about the development of the atomic bomb. And which is why physicists developed the Atoms for Peace program and all the campaigns around that, trying to dissociate the military uses of nuclear knowledge from the potential peaceful uses. In fact, of course, they're indivisible.

One of the things that came up as a result of studying what was going on in the development of CBWs was the network of university contracts, particularly in the United States, with the American Department of Defense, with U.S. Defense Advanced Research Projects Agency (DARPA), but also the comparable set of Ministry of Defense contracts that existed here in this country, which angered the students and angered university academics. These were the semi-secret contracts which Eisenhower famously called the industrial–military complex, and which was now developing into an industrial–military–university complex. Of course none of that seems shocking now because of the way the universities have developed anyhow, particularly in the life sciences in the aftermath of the genetic revolution, which began not so much in 1953 with the discovery of the structure of DNA but certainly by the 1980s with the development of biotechnology and genetic manipulation. What shocked us then seems perfectly normal and the way universities operate now.

The Brain and Behaviour Research Group that I directed became fairly politically involved in opposition to this developing industrial–military–university complex. The group worked as a collective. It was at a stage when we were all young, the researchers were radical in a way it is not possible to conceive of now in a research group, and we wanted to do things that were not just in our own terrain, in our own laboratory practice, but also in terms of the outside world. So we initiated, from the Research Group, an appeal to all members of the International Society for Neurochemistry not to accept NATO research grants and to support campaigns against CBWs. We were similarly involved in work on IQ and genetics at that stage as well.

The pledge in the book, which you mentioned earlier, about building an unstoppable movement against CBWs, and which seems wildly romantic and rhetorical now, was prepared I think in relation to the debate that Ritchie Calder (A science writer, socialist and peace activist) wanted to initiate in the House of Lords. Richie had been involved from a very early stage in the campaigns against CBWs; he wrote the foreword to the CBW book and had been instrumental in organizing and helping set up the Conway Hall and Bernal Library meetings.

Filippa Lentzos What were your main concerns at the time about the military development of biology?

Steven Rose That these are primarily weapons to be used by a highly technologically advanced state against liberation movements or against guerrilla movements. You can see that in Syria at the moment, with the barrel bombs and chlorine bombs. So they are agents with particular military functions in wars of colonialism or imperialism, designed to support the interests of imperial powers against struggling national liberation movements, or struggling democratic movements as you see in the case of the very complex fights that are going on in Syria — at least that's what Syria was at the beginning, whatever it is now, which is just a complete bloody mess, is something different.

Filippa Lentzos How important and influential do you think individual scientists and NGOs were in the 1960s–1970s international disarmament efforts? What sort of contributions did they make?

Steven Rose Since the 1960s and right up until today there's been a fairly loose collective of people in Britain who've all been involved in these discussions: Alastair Hay, Julian Perry Robinson, Pat Wall, professor of anatomy at University College, myself, Malcolm Dando at a later stage. We are all familiar with one another, but we all do slightly different things.

I think we have all played a part in framing the debate and how these things have been discussed, but, personally, I was less interested in the international negotiations. I took the position then, which was naïve and probably a bit hard line, and I wouldn't take now, that the only thing that would drive prohibition would be social movements, or forces on the ground. The negotiators could go on negotiating for as long as they liked, but unless there was a pressure from below nothing would actually happen.

So I was more interested in the actual use of unconventional weapons and the development of the scientific–military complex which generated those uses; and chemical weapons were my main focus. Of course I could see that you needed to take the whole issue of CBWs together as a group, because that was the way they were conceived, and that's why the Bernal Library meeting and the book were about both CBWs.

Most of the people involved in the negotiations on CBW were people whose professional lives were about disarmament negotiation, like Julian or Malcolm. I have always been a working neuroscientist and my primary community is not the NGOs but my fellow neuroscientists.

Filippa Lentzos If you thought nothing would budge on the negotiations without a social movement, were you surprised when there was a treaty and in such a relatively short time on the biological side?

Steven Rose I was pleased. I think I always recognized that it would be much easier to get a BW treaty because the military was not very enthusiastic about the use of biological weapons. They didn't think that BW was a useful weapon. So military scepticism about the use of biological weapons was hugely significant in this. The military distaste for certain weapons was also important — this goes right the way back to the Geneva Conventions where gas was seen as an unsporty way to fight — so that was certainly part of it too and has remained part of it.

Filippa Lentzos Did you think a Chemical Weapons Convention was feasible?

Steven Rose I always thought it would be extraordinarily difficult, because of the problem of the upstream chemicals and defining what comprised industrial chemicals. Once you got to the binaries, which we were very concerned with back then and was the main focus of *No Fire, No Thunder*, then the possibility of getting an effective treaty were significantly diminished.

I became involved, once again, in the issue of chemical weapons with Halabja, and with the Iraqi use against the Iranians in the 1980s. Hilary and I worked for a little time with the Kurds, and Alastair and I went to the Cromwell Hospital to interview the Kurds who had been airlifted to Britain for treatment. I have been interested in the issues whenever there has been a field report of the use of chemical weapons — reports of use in Angola, claims that the Israelis had used some sort of gas against Lebanese fighters and Palestinians during the Israeli invasion of the Lebanon.

I went with a medical team to Beirut, just after the massacres at Sabra and Shatila. Our primary concern was to look at the health status of the Palestinians in the camps, but also to try to see if we could verify any allegations about the use of mysterious gases. And of course you can't. You know all sorts of things get alleged in any of these conflicts and to get verifiable data is quite hard, and I decided in the end that that was yet another of these wild rumours that circulated. Just as there was a rumour that gas was used in the recent Israeli massacres in Gaza. There was a brief reference to gas being used but that hasn't been verified either. And I would doubt it. I mean there are quite enough weapons in the Israeli armoury to not need that. What they do use are the non-lethals, so what I've been particularly interested in are the development of the non-lethals and the developments in neuroscience which are leading to new generations of agents.

Filippa Lentzos What are your concerns there?

Steven Rose Apart from BZ, earlier generations of chemical weapons did not affect the brain, they were peripheral — they burned or paralysed neuromuscular junctions — but now we're developing a whole set of agents which have potential effects directly on brain processes and these include not just chemicals but the use of transcranial magnetic stimulation and long range use of microwave radiation. DARPA, for instance, is particularly interested in these things and we wrote a bit about that in a Nuffield report on novel neurotechnologies last year.[4]

So I've become more interested, not so much in just the chemicals, or just the biologicals, but the whole range of the novel neuro-technologies that can be used in civil conflicts and asymmetric warfare for surveillance, for coercion, for mind-manipulation.

The range of technologies from the biochemical to the electro-magnetic promise new methods of surveillance and intelligence gathering, not just in traditional war zones abroad but also in controlling an unruly citizenry at home. And the line once drawn between the military and the police is being redrawn as wars abroad return in the form of urban terrorism and riot to haunt the heartlands of the old imperial powers. Most of the developments are veiled in secrecy of course, but that doesn't mean we should not persevere in bringing them to light and into open discussion.[5,6]

Filippa Lentzos Fifty years on from the Conway Hall meeting, how do you think the political role of scientists has changed in Britain and in the life sciences?

Steven Rose I think it has changed profoundly. The life sciences were separated from direct engagement with either the military or industry in the time when I first became a working scientist. What's happened in that half century is the transformation of what were the small sciences of biochemistry, neuroscience and genetics into the vast mega industrial techno-sciences that you see today, and with that the position of scientists themselves have changed in my terrain to become patent-holders, entrepreneurs and shareholders.

Contrast the refusal of César Milstein to patent monoclonal antibodies back when they were first developed in the 1980s, so they became a free technology for the world, or the refusal in this country to patent penicillin, with today's pressures to patent, to start up companies, to become locked in with the biotech industry. That inevitably transforms the role of scientists.

To refer to yourself as a disinterested scientist these days is an oxymoron, and of course the reason why journals are so concerned with reproducibility, with competition, with patent infringement, with declaration of financial interest. Now there's no going back. A romantic view of how science was in the 1930s, or the 1950s, or the 1980s, is anyhow overly idealistic. But the scale has changed enormously.

Filippa Lentzos Did we lose something in that transition? Did we lose a collectivity of politically engaged scientists?

Steven Rose I don't think there is the same sense of political collectivity that there was back then. If you look at the batch of Nobel Prize winners who signed up to that pledge document, or the conferences we were running at the time, you couldn't get that today. I think that has changed.

Notes

[1] See Balmer B (2012) *Secrecy and Science: A Historical Sociology of Biological and Chemical Warfare.* Farnham: Ashgate, pp. 93–96.

[2] Rose S (Ed.) (1968) *CBW: Chemical and Biological Warfare.* London: Beacon Press.

[3] See Balmer B (2012) *Secrecy and Science: A Historical Sociology of Biological and Chemical Warfare.* Farnham: Ashgate, pp. 96–100.

[4] Nuffield Council on Bioethics (2014) *Novel Neurotechnologies: Intervening in the Brain.*

[5] Rose S 'How the military Want to Control our Brains,' *The Guardian* June 1, 2012.

[6] Rose, Hilary and Steven Rose (2012) *Genes, Cells and Brains: Bioscience's Promethean Promises.* London: Verso.

Point of View

Responsible Science: Strategies for Engaging Key Stakeholders

Jo L. Husbands

The accumulation of treaties, national and international laws, and regulations provide the foundation for bioweapons nonproliferation. Building on the legal foundation to implement these agreements requires engaging a range of stakeholders from a growing number of sectors and parts of the world. Policymakers continue to struggle with questions about the most effective ways to undertake that engagement. What is the best way to begin? Is it better to emphasize legal obligations or broader notions of personal and social responsibility when attempting to engage scientists? As someone who has spent over a decade in the trenches of scientist engagement, initially as part of the staff for the Fink committee and then working with other international scientific organizations to promote the acceptance and implementation of its core ideas, the choice of framing strikes me as one of the most important questions going forward for biological non-proliferation.

Scientists matter because continuing advances in the life sciences, which increasingly involve collaboration with other scientific and technical fields, are combined with the continuing spread of research and industrial capacity throughout the world. These trends offer the hope of addressing global challenges ranging from improving health to preserving the environment and promoting sustainable economic development. But the same trends also complicate non-proliferation efforts as more countries, groups and even individuals are gaining access to capabilities that have the potential to be misused for biological weapons or bioterrorism. The challenge is particularly acute for so-called "dual-use" research that, although carried out for beneficial purposes, could produce knowledge, tools or techniques with the potential to be misused.[1]

For understandable reasons, the natural inclination of many of those involved in bio-weapons non-proliferation is to base their engagement strategies on the legal obligations with which individuals and institutions must comply. This is the world in which they live and operate and a substantial number of policy-makers and diplomats are lawyers, or have backgrounds in the military and law enforcement. This is reflected in documents such as those from the review conferences of the Biological Weapons Convention. The final report from the 6th Review Conference in 2006, for example, urged:

> ... the inclusion in medical, scientific and military educational materials and programmes of information on the Convention and the 1925 Geneva Protocol. The Conference urges States Parties to promote the development of training and education programmes for those granted access to biological agents and toxins relevant to the Convention and for those with the knowledge or capacity to modify such agents and toxins, in order to raise awareness of the risks, as well as of the obligations of States Parties under the Convention.[2]

This emphasis on *requirements* can be challenged on a number of grounds. One is effectiveness: as we learned from the early Cooperative Threat Reduction Programs in the former Soviet Union (see Chapter 12, Interview by Smith & Lentzos; Point of View by Finley & Gaudioso), without active support from the leaders of institutions, rules and procedures have limited effect. This is reflected in the current interest in concepts of "safety and security culture," which draw on broader lessons from organization studies to avoid a "check box" mentality of compliance.[3] Another is relevance: If researchers genuinely believe that their work is intended for beneficial purposes, what meaning do the BWC or UNSCR 1540 or even national regulations have for them?[4] Moreover, they may quite naturally resent the suggestion that they or their research should be considered threatening, a sentiment echoed in statements such as "the vast majority of scientists are law-abiding, ethical individuals who are unlikely to cause harm deliberately" (Imperiale and Casadevall 2015: 3).[5] This does not make the legal requirements less important, but it does suggest the need to consider other ways to open the door, especially if those approaches can provide the foundation for discussions of potential security risks and the non-proliferation regime intended to address them.

Personal and social responsibility

One opportunity for a different framing for scientist engagement comes from the growing discussion across the international scientific community about what constitutes responsible conduct of science. The discussion is another reflection of the increasingly international nature of the scientific enterprise and the recognition that common standards and practices are needed to facilitate collaboration. Scandal has also played a role, as a number of high-profile retractions of papers and issues related to the difficulty of reproducing experiments, have pointed to the need to devote more attention to professional ethics.[6] In 2012, the heads of national science and engineering funding bodies from around 50 countries created a virtual organization called the Global Research Council. The group includes promoting research integrity among its principles.[7]

Discussions of responsible conduct of research are part of the larger question of the social responsibilities of science, which puts an emphasis on what scientists "should" do, rather than what they "must." Increasingly, scientists are considered responsible for more than simply doing the very best science. As noted in the 2012 report

Responsible Conduct in the Global Research Enterprise from the InterAcademy Council (IAC) and IAP — The Global Network of Science Academies:

Because of the increasing importance of research in the broader society, scientists and other scholars bear a responsibility for how research is conducted and how the results of research are used. They cannot assume that they work in a domain isolated from the needs and concerns of the broader world.[8]

Moreover, changing social attitudes have significant effects on how science is carried out, which shape the standards and norms for what constitutes professional conduct.[9] How scientists do their work may be shaped as much, if not more, by these professional norms as by legal requirements. One of the most important recent developments is a growing acknowledgement that the fundamental principles of freedom in the conduct of science are accompanied by responsibilities and the need to maintain public trust. Names do matter and a striking example comes from the International Council for Science, one of the staunchest advocates for the primacy of scientific freedom:

To address and promote both aspects [freedom and responsibility], ICSU established the Committee on Freedom and Responsibility in the conduct of Science (CFRS) in 2006. This Committee differs significantly from its predecessors that, since 1963, had focused on scientific freedom, in that it is explicitly charged with also emphasizing scientific responsibilities.[10]

In addition to the growing number of high-level statements that address fundamental social responsibility, a number explicitly address security. In 2005, as a contribution to the BWC intersessional discussions of the "content, promulgation, and adoption of codes of conduct for scientists," IAP produced a *Statement on Biosecurity*.[11] The Statement provides a set of principles that IAP member academies believe should be addressed by science bodies as part of developing codes. This also reflects a view that codes will be most effective if developed closer to where they would be applied, to encourage a greater sense of ownership and commitment. More recently the 2012 IAC–IAP report included a discussion of the risks of misuse, explicitly addressing biosecurity and dual-use research. The report concludes that "researchers should bear in mind the possible consequences of their work, including harmful consequences, in planning research projects," a statement with direct implications for non-proliferation policies.[12]

Another example, from the 2014 edition of ICSU's booklet on *Freedom, Responsibility, and Universality of Science*, cited the fundamental issues raised by the response to emerging infectious diseases, including:

> For individual scientists, there are important issues relating to biosafety and access to, or sharing of, materials and data. For example, tissue samples and scientific data may variously be considered as essential public health tools, dangerous precursors of biological weapons, demonstrations of scientific prowess or levers for political influence.[13]

Engaging scientists in security

Scientific organizations and science policy groups that work on engaging scientists in bioweapons non-proliferation point to these examples to argue for framing the initial engagement in the context of "Responsible Science." They argue this enables them to draw on longstanding norms of self-governance in the life sciences, as well as the norms and practices of biosafety and a range of guidelines and other "soft law" measures. Responsible Science thus becomes a foundation on which to build, and opens the door for the focused attention on security and regulation required in biosafety and biosecurity training. By emphasizing that responding to security challenges is part of a scientist's professional responsibilities, it also has the distinct advantage of making scientists part of the solution, not part of the problem. This underscores that the two approaches to framing scientist engagement — requirements and responsibilities — are not mutually exclusive. Many laws reflect social norms and the BWC is the international legal embodiment of a powerful norm against the use of disease as a weapon.

There are signs that the argument for Responsible Science is gaining acceptance.

A number of organisations engaged in biosecurity education have found that concepts from the social responsibility of science provide a framework that makes it far easier to introduce scientists to dual-use issues and biosecurity.[14] On the policy side, "Reduce proliferation risks through the advancement and promotion of safe and responsible conduct in the biological sciences" became one of five deliverables for Biological Security sub Working Group of the Global Partnership Program.[15] In October 2013, the U.K. government chose "Responsible Science" as the theme for one of the Global Partnership meetings under its presidency, and added a public session on the topic held at the Royal Society.[16] And the report of 2013 BWC's Meeting of States Parties concluded that "In order to further efforts on education and awareness-raising about risks and benefits of life sciences and biotechnology, States Parties agreed on the value of using science responsibly as an overarching theme to enable parallel outreach efforts across inter-related scientific disciplines."[17] Finally, given the increasing attention to the convergence of biology and chemistry in key areas relevant to the BWC and the Chemical Weapons Convention, it is worth noting that the Director-General of the Organization for the Prohibition of Chemical Weapons (OPCW) used the opportunity of his speech accepting the Nobel Peace Prize to state that "Our aim is to contribute to efforts towards fostering a culture of responsible science. This will ensure that current and future generations of scientists understand — and respect — the impact that their work can have on security."[18]

The signs of acceptance from both the scientific and policy side suggest that taking a less traditional approach to engaging a key sector in bioweapons non-proliferation efforts could pay significant dividends.

Notes

1. National Research Council (2004) *Biotechnology Research in an Age of Terrorism.* Washington, DC: National Academies Press.
2. Biological Weapons Convention (2006) *Sixth Review Conference*

of the States Parties to the Biological and Toxin Weapons Convention: Final Document. BWC/CONF. VI/6. Geneva: Biological Weapons Convention.

[3] See, for example, the Fall 2014 special issue of the journal *1540 Compass* on "Comprehensive CBRN Security Culture." See http://cits.uga.edu/uploads/1540compass/1540PDFs/Compass_Magazine_7-web.pdf (accessed May 3, 2015).

[4] For an account of the lessons learned by Malcolm Dando and Brian Rappert in the course of their international efforts to raise awareness of the potential misuse of life sciences research, see Rappert B (2008). "The Benefits, Risks, and Threats of Biotechnology", *Science & Public Policy* 35(1): 37–44.

[5] Imperiale MJ and Casadevall A (2015) "A New Synthesis for Dual Use Research of Concern", *PLoS Med.* Epub ahead of print April 14, 2015. DOI:10.1371/journal.pmed.1001813.

[6] See, for example, the cover story in *The Economist* October 19, 2013 entitled 'How Science Goes Wrong'. (http://www.economist.com/news/leaders/21588069-scientific-research-has-changed-world-now-it-needs-change-itself-how-science-goes-wrong).

[7] More information may be found at http://www.globalresearchcouncil.org/.

[8] Inter Academy Council and IAP — The Global Network of Science Academies (2012) *Responsible Conduct in the Global Research Enterprise: A Policy Report.* Amsterdam,The Netherlands: InterAcademy Council, p. x.

[9] The changes in standards for the treatment of human subjects in experiments, which developed over time, particularly during the 20th century in response to egregious abuses by researchers, is one of the clearest examples. The standards for the treatment of laboratory animals have continued to evolve as well.

[10] International Council for Science (2014) *Freedom, Responsibility and Universality of Science.* Paris: International Council for Science, p. 3.

[11] IAP — The Global Network of Science Academies. *Statement on Biosecurity* (2005), http://www.interacademies.net/CMS/About/3143.aspx (accessed May 3, 2015).

[12] InterAcademy Council and IAP — The Global Network of Science Academies (2012), as per note 8, p. 16.

[13] International Council for Science (2014), as per note 10, p. 12.

[14] Examples of such activities were presented at a side event during the August 2014 Meeting of States Parties to the Biological

Weapons Convention; copies of the presentations may be found under the "side events" heading at http://www.unog.ch/80256EE600585943/(httpPages)/F837B6E7A401A21CC1257A150050CB2A?OpenDocument.

15 U.S. Department of State (2012) *G8 Global Partnership Agrees to Biosecurity Deliverables Document.* Fact Sheet. See http://www.state.gov/t/isn/gp2013/rls/docs/196021.htm (accessed May 3, 2015).

16 UK Foreign and Commonwealth Office (2013) *Global Partnership Against Weapons and Materials of Mass Destruction: President's Report for 2013.* London: Foreign and Commonwealth Office.

17 Biological Weapons Convention (2013) *Report of the Meeting of States Parties.* BWC/MSP/2013/5. December 23, Geneva: Biological Weapons Convention, p. 8.

18 Organization for the Prohibition of Chemical Weapons (2013) "Nobel Peace Prize Lecture: Working together for a world free of chemical weapons, and beyond", *OPCW Today* 2(5): 11.

Interview

International Security and Counter-Terrorism

Trevor Smith & Filippa Lentzos

Editor's note International security featured heavily at the first G8 summit taking place after 9/11 in June 2002 in Kananaskis, Canada. Coming out of that meeting, the seven major industrial countries plus Russia outlined a new initiative entitled the "Global Partnership Against the Spread of Weapons and Materials of Mass Destruction." It committed the G8 to raise up to $20 billion over 10 years to help initially Russia, but also other nations, destroy their stockpiles of nuclear, chemical and biological weapons, dismantle production facilities, reemploy former weapons scientists, and fund projects to prevent terorrists and other proliferators from acquiring WMDs. Over the years the Global Partnership expanded its membership and its reach, and in 2011 the program was extended. I interviewed Trevor Smith, the senior program manager in biological and chemical security for Canada's Global Partnership Program, on the margins of the Partnership's coordination meeting of its biological threat redution programs at the Canadian Mission to the United Nations in Geneva in December 2013. We spoke about the Partnership's first 10 years, changing threat perceptions and evolving responses, and how biology is different to other unconventional weapons.

Filippa Lentzos How was the biological weapons threat generally perceived when you first started out in biological arms control in the early 2000s?

Trevor Smith The focus was very much on state programs. At the time, we were still coming to terms with the magnitude of the Soviet program. There had been the initial revelations by President Yeltsin and others, and of course the confidence-building declaration submitted by the Russian Federation confirming the program, but there was still a lot of confusion about what that program had looked like, how far it may have seeped, what the brain drain threats were, where some of the Soviet weapons scientists had gone.

It's not that people were oblivious to bioterrorism. Bioterrorism has been a concern for a very long time, but I think it's fair to say that at that time the main emphasis within the biological threat spectrum was more leaning towards putting in place a traditional arms control regime than dealing with non-traditional threats.

Filippa Lentzos How did that threat perception change?

Trevor Smith It happened in an instant. It's that simple. Our U.S. friends very often say that 9/11 changed the world. It changed the American view on the world, no doubt, and the American view has incredible influence on the world. 9/11 did cause a major rethink of the WMD threat, and the rumblings, rumours and chatter over the years about bioterrorism were not something we could afford to ignore any more. Some of the evidence that was gathered in subsequent years, alongside the anthrax letters, forced the international community to realize that this is not an academic threat; bioterrorism is not something that is beyond the realm of possibility.

There were some, at the time, who overreacted; who felt that the end was nigh, that 9/11 would immediately be followed by devastating WMD attacks again and again. For many of those who were on the ground, dealing with these issues, including through the Global Partnership, that was not the perception. We never tried to overplay the threat. It was very much a matter of trying to strike a balance, because the pendulum had swung too far. It went from "this isn't an issue" to "this is the greatest issue of our times," and the reality is probably somewhere in the middle. That bioterrorism is a very considerable threat, but that it's one of these low likelihood, unimaginable consequence type events — and not just in casualty terms; so much of terrorism is about economy. You saw that with 9/11.

The fatalities on that day were terrible, but they were less than an average day in either the First or Second World War when you look at the number of deaths — several thousand. In the World Wars, there were days when tens of thousands, hundreds of thousands died, so it's not like the world hadn't seen that type of carnage before. We've seen it all too often.

What the terrorists succeeded in doing with 9/11 was scaring the bejesus out of people; terror is their objective. And the damage done to the economy was staggering. Just the clean up cost of the anthrax letters was somewhere north of $700 million, just to decontaminate the post offices. That's nearly equivalent to Canada's entire Global Partnership budget for its first 10 years.

Filippa Lentzos How did the evolving threat perception impact on the Global Partnership?

Trevor Smith Back in the early 2000s, you'd turn on the television and pundit after pundit on CNN and other news channels would be misrepresenting the threat of bioterrorism, nuclear terrorism and chemical terrorism. I don't think the threat was ever what was publicly presented and publicly feared. I think it is far more subtle. And the type of attacks that we think could be most devastating now are attacks that go undetected; they're not about somebody putting anthrax in an envelope and sending it to a senator announcing you now have anthrax.

The Global Partnership, as a program, has evolved over the

years, and starting with the Canadian G8 presidency in 2010, when we identified biosecurity as a major priority, we started focusing more on things like disease surveillance, early detection and rapid response.

If you look at things like foot and mouth disease, which cost the U.K. economy tens of billions of dollars, that is an incredibly powerful incentive for a terrorist group that has a real hate for a country, or for a society or an institution, to be able to cripple a country's economy and bring it to its knees.

That doesn't have to be your al-Qaeda who wants to make the public statement. There are many kinds of terrorism, and there are many types of terrorists, and I think our understanding and our view of the terrorist threat has changed dramatically. There are many evil people in the world, and there is not just one terrorist mentality.

So what's changed is that we're trying to deal with a whole range of terrorism threats, from the obvious to the very discreet, from the people who want the headlines to the people who never want to be noticed.

Filippa Lentzos You mentioned 9/11 and the anthrax letters. Those two events were very much linked in our minds and in political minds at the time. We didn't know who were behind the attacks, and Amerithrax focused minds very much on bioterrorism, as opposed to any other kind of terrorism. Looking back, if we had known at the time that 9/11 and Amerithrax were carried out by very different groups with very different goals — that the anthrax letters had been sent by somebody inside a U.S. government lab, a military lab — do you think that would have changed the way in which the U.S. and the international community responded to those events?

Trevor Smith Of course it is impossible to say. Even if it was clear at the time that A and B were separate, they're still linked. There wasn't a coincidence of timing. Having come from a history background, the question is always is it the man or the woman, or is it the time? In this case I think it was the time: The time was right for that to happen. Unfortunately.

Would the letters have been put in the mail had 9/11 not happened? You could say maybe. Personally, I would say unlikely. It wouldn't have had the same impact. The world was nervous; the United States was petrified — it was vulnerable in a way it had never been vulnerable before.

These things have happened before. They'll happen again. They'll never happen in that context again. 9/11 and Amerithrax focused people's attention. Even before the anthrax letters, people were thinking about the WMD nexus. Just two weeks after 9/11, we were hosting the annual plenary of the Missile Technology and Control regime in Ottawa. The issue of WMD terrorism was present in that meeting in a way it had never been before, and that was before the anthrax letters. Likewise, in the Australia Group meeting that was taking place in early October 2001, we were right in the midst of the anthrax saga and the whole issue of quantities and size became really important for export controls. It wasn't just about whether we should add crop dusters to the list, it was about the particular sizes of fermenters. Were 10-liter fermenters less of a risk than 100-liter fermenters? We were acutely aware we were only focused on the state threat, and that we needed a serious rethink. And that was happening not just because of the anthrax letters, it was happening because of the increased appreciation that the terrorism threat was more pressing than we thought, and more damaging than we had ever expected it to be.

Filippa Lentzos We've talked a little about how political thinking about biological threats in general changed over the last decade from a primary focus on states to a primary focus on terrorists. Could you say something about how you think perceptions of biological terrorism itself have evolved and changed?

Trevor Smith In the early years of the Global Partnership, and in the early years of my own experience dealing with biothreats, the primary focus was on the al-Qaedas of the world — the terrorist groups that are of considerable concern. It was looking at the big bang approach to terrorism. From a terrorist point of view, 9/11 was such a success; it was the grand slam in what they were able to accomplish. It captured the world's attention. It changed governments. It caused wars. It was really a remarkable event. From the point of view of the terrorist, it really achieved an enormous amount.

This large-scale, big bang al-Qaeda threat hasn't gone away. That's very clear. New terrorist groups are coming in too, the Al-Shabaabs of the world, and Boko Haram (and, since the interview, IS). These are groups that you cannot afford to ignore. They are frightening, and they will haunt us for a very long time, but they're not the only ones out there.

There are other types of terrorism we need to pay attention to too. Economic terrorism, for instance, and bringing a country to its knees by paralysing its agriculture. In Canada, in 2003, we had a single case of BSE — mad cow disease — and foreign borders were closed to Canadian beef exports. Billions and billions and billions of dollars were lost. It devastated our farming economy. I grew up in a farming family so I was very aware of this. The ability to have that type of impact, and to do it completely unnoticed — throwing an infected sample of something into a pig trough and no one's the wiser — that's a threat.

So that's why we at the Global Partnership started to think our responses can't just be about prevention; we simply can't stop everything, you can't get into the mind of every single person — especially on bio. When you look at the chemical and nuclear side, the materials are controlled in a way that is simply not possible on the biological side. Not that they are inaccessible. The recent theft of the radiological materials in Mexico is a prime example of that, and concerns about the Syrian CW arsenal certainly continue to be a problem. Industrial chemicals, blowing up chlorine tankers: These things will always be out there, no doubt about it. But the sheer availability of biological agents in every country in the world, the prevalence of disease, it's very, very different.

And there is a built-in discretion in disease, because it is naturally occurring. If you attack someone with sarin you know you've been attacked because sarin is not naturally occurring. It can't have been an accident. If you, all of a sudden, have foot and mouth disease occur in your animal population when you haven't had it before, you've got to scratch your head. That's a bad day; it's really unfortunate that I've had a naturally occurring outbreak of foot and mouth disease in my livestock. And it probably was. But it doesn't have to have been. So that's the type of incidents that, over the years, we've realized we can't afford not to be aware. We don't want to overreact, because it is one of these threats that is unlikely, but it's not impossible.

So then you have to do the risk consequence analysis. You have to start looking at things and ask: Are we prepared to take the risk of not doing something? Or is the risk significant enough that we need to establish some type of insurance policy — that insurance policy being the Global Partnership.

We can't stop everything, but we can certainly make a very significant contribution to mitigating the threat — not just at the front end, but also at the back end — by preparing first responders to give better diagnosis; improving surveillance, personal protective equipment, transportation of dangerous materials training; developing field diagnostic kits and field training; ensuring biosafety cabinet certification; all of these different things. It's about building up, not so much the infrastructure, but the capacity so that no matter what the cause of the disease, we'll have people all around the world who are equipped to respond to it — quickly, capably and effectively.

Filippa Lentzos Is that how you would characterize the Global Partnership's response to the bioterrorism threat over the last decade or so?

Trevor Smith Yes, we went from a "we have to prevent" to a "we must prevent, prepare and respond" approach. The Partnership was always very clear: It was first and foremost about prevention. It's the very first line of the Global Partnership statement issued by the G8 leaders at the Kananaskis meeting: "We commit ourselves to prevent terrorists, or those that harbour them, from acquiring or developing weapons of mass destruction."

In the early years of the Partnership, our focus was almost exclusively on securing the 40,000 tons of chemical weapons and various radiological and nuclear sources in Russia. We were in a lockdown mentality: We had to get a hold of them and secure them. And we did. We locked down a lot of these things and we destroyed as much as we could. But there was still a whole whack of security threats out there, the biologicals in particular, for which the gun, gates and guards mentality didn't work. In the bio field you can't just say "we'll lock it up, we'll put guards out there, and we can forget about it." The threat doesn't go away.

The lack of a destruction option on bio is what the Global Partnership struggled with for the first few years, and it is one of the key reasons that there wasn't as much subscription on the bio side as there was in the other areas. It was not as gratifying, not as definitive, not as sexy. You couldn't say we've destroyed 5,600 metric tons of nerve agent as we did at Shchuch'ye in Russia.

In the biological field, we can't eradicate stocks like you can in the chemical or nuclear fields. So we have to do something different. And it took us a long time, as an international community, to figure out what that new thing was. It really wasn't until 2010, during our G8 presidency, that we came up with the strategy for strengthening global biological security. This was not an easy process; it was very, very difficult. And it was part of the evolution of the Partnership and the move away from Russia and the former Soviet Union. But that strategy now forms the basis for all of the activities that the Global Partnership does in the biological sector. It is not a set of marching orders, but it is deliberately a very broad framework and includes work at the health security interface. And some have, I think very mistakenly, concluded that we've been "healthified."

Many talk about the securitization of health. Well, there's

a flipside to that, which is the healthification of security. And I dispute that, because it is not. It takes a more nuanced understanding of the work that we do and the objectives that we're trying to achieve to really understand how what we are doing, and what we have done, is 100 percent rooted in what the Global Partnership is fundamentally about: Counter-terrorism.

I can't tell you the number of initiatives that we look at and say, no, we can't do it, because this has nothing to do with us. We've never seen a terrorist yet who's interested in tuberculosis or HIV; both are horrible diseases, and sufferers have our full sympathy, but we have no business investing in these areas because they don't have a military or a terrorist application. Of course we've seen HIV used as a weapon — it happens in every country, where you have people who have deliberate sexual contact with someone in order to infect them — but that's a criminal act, not a terrorist act.

Things like tuberculosis and HIV are often the primary concerns of some of our partners. We actually just had this happen in one of our partner regions. Our public health agency brought in a project proposal saying this organization is in desperate need of enhanced capacity to deal with tuberculosis. We said, well, they've come to the wrong place, but, if they don't have the capacity to deal with tuberculosis what would they do in this region — which sees a lot of international traffic, a lot of traffic from Canadians, and a lot of high profile mass gatherings — if there was a suspicious outbreak of an emerging or infectious disease that *is* of terrorism concern? Well, they wouldn't have a response capacity. And all of a sudden there is a role for the Global Partnership.

It's not that we're not securing any more, we're still doing that in places like Kyrgyzstan, Russia and Kazakhstan, where you actually go in and say, you used to develop biological weapons here, that's not good, we need to do something about that, so we're going to lock this stuff down. But in places that don't have a bioweapons program legacy, our focus in on giving them the capability to tackle a disease outbreak. If a bioterrorism attack arrives at their door, they'll know how to handle it and they can do it safely and securely, and don't have to call the Centers for Disease Control and Prevention (CDC) or the Winnipeg Lab or Porton Down, or one of these other places. They will have an indigenous capability, because the initial hours are so important, and if you're putting something on a military aircraft to send it somewhere else, you're losing those hours, and the disease is getting ahead of you.

So that's the way we're looking at it now. 99.9 percent of the time our partner countries won't be using Global Partnership funded biological capacities for counter-terrorism purposes, and we have no problem with that, because that 0.1 percent of the time will repay our investments in spades. God help us that they ever need it. We hope that they don't. But if there is a sophisticated bioterrorism attack, and if we haven't given them the capacity to respond to it, if we haven't worked with them to be prepared for this, they'll never know what hit them, and the rest of us will feel the impact.

Filippa Lentzos You talked about this guns, gates and guards approach, and the focus on securing labs with locks and developing lists of pathogens that are particularly dangerous, etc. How has the Global Partnership dealt with intangible technology — the people, the know-how?

Trevor Smith Well, that is something we've been dealing with already since before 9/11. If you look at the International Science and Technology Centre, and the Science and Technology Centre Ukraine, they were all about the intangible technologies. They were about tens of thousands of people, who had been employed in the Soviet military complex, developing weapons of mass destruction, all of a sudden being un- or under-employed. It was not what they had in the labs as much as what they had in their heads that was the primary concern. And one of the priorities for the Global Partnership from the very beginning was reemployment of former weapons scientists. So that was the case with a lot of the work done in the early days. There was a preoccupation with the former Soviet Union — and it was a deserved preoccupation, because the threat was so unique — but every country in every part of the world has intangible technology threats.

So how can you control what's in someone's head, what they do with it? Well, you can't. I'm not talking about dual use research of concern. That's a separate battle altogether, and an extremely complex one. I'm talking about the people who actually have intent to do something wrong — not the people who are doing cutting-edge research that might cross a line, unknowingly or unwittingly. Now, if dealing with pathogens is hard, dealing with the intangibles side is exponentially harder. It's a Herculean task, or actually more of a Sisyphean task: The rock will always roll back over you, because as hard as you try there will never been a complete solution.

Dealing with the bioterrorism threat will always be measured, I hope, in best efforts and in the sincerity of the commitment made. It is not possible to put some type of impermeable net over the problem. *But*, and it's a big but, I look back at all of the prognostications that have been made over the years, by very educated, very well-informed people, from all around the world, that there will be bioterrorism attacks — including the 2008 World at Risk report predicting there will be a large-scale terrorist attack by the end of 2013, and it will likely be a biological attack — and none of it has happened. Why not?

Well, there are many ways to look at it, but there are two easy ways to put it. Either the threat isn't real and it has been exaggerated. Or the efforts that have been made by many different groups, including the Global Partnership, have paid dividends, and the results that were feared and expected have not come to pass because we put sufficient obstacles in the way to prevent them. Impossible to prove of course — you can't prove a negative — but we do know that some of the work that we've done has helped to prevent very bad things from happening.

I can give you an example we have cited before. We don't publicize it aggressively, but in 2010 there was civil unrest in the Kyrgyz Republic. In 2009, we had done security upgrades at an anti-plague station in Osh, in the southern part of the country. That anti-plague station was attacked during the uprising, and the people couldn't get in, because we had secured the facility. Why were they attacking the facility? Were there bioterrorists in the crowd trying to acquire the pathogens? We don't know that. And personally, I would say probably not. But opportunism is an unknown; it is very difficult to measure. What do you do when you acquire something? Especially in a region like the Fergana Valley which is a home base for so many different types of terrorist organizations. So you don't know. But what we do know is that this facility was not accessible because of work that was done by the Global Partnership. And there are other similar examples. There are anecdotal stories we have from scientists who say they have been approached, but didn't go because of the support they've received. And I think it's fair to conclude that if you take all of those things, in their collective, and if you take all the risks that we don't know, but can fairly assume, I think the value of programs like the Global Partnership, and the investments we've made in biosecurity, globally, has paid incredible dividends.

Filippa Lentzos Final question: Do you think biological weapons are more abhorrent than other weapons?

Trevor Smith Yes I do, and I say that as somebody who's worked across the nuclear, biological and chemical fields. Chemical weapons have a special place in the hearts of Canadians, because it was against Canadian troops that they were first used, in the First World War, in the second battle of Ypres. But I have yet to see someone who has died of naturally occurring sarin.

Everybody fears disease, whatever it is. You're a parent. I'm a parent. Just the thought of your kids getting sick puts fear in your heart. And to think we, as a civilized society, as civilized humanity, have worked so hard as a collective over the years to stop this, and someone would do it on purpose?

It is not to say that killing someone with a machine gun is better. It is still wrong. But in my own mind, and this is very personal, disease crosses yet another line, especially if you're talking about a contagious virus, because it's so indiscriminate. Nuclear weapons and chemical weapons are indiscriminate in a targeted fashion, in an isolated fashion, whereas the global implications of an infectious disease outbreak, it's really hard to imagine, and so that's why, in my own mind, it is one step further across the pale.

Point of View

The Front Lines of Biological Weapons Non-Proliferation

Melissa Finley & Jennifer Gaudioso

Building CTR programs

The intentional release of *Bacillus anthracis* through the United States Postal System in 2001 validated concerns that bioterrorism was in fact a real and achievable threat. With the simultaneous rapid expansion of the bioscience industry globally, beneficial technologies and breakthroughs are now viewed as dual-use in nature and their use, highly scrutinized. This emerging threat prompted the release of *The National Strategy for Countering Biological Threats*, which proposed seven objectives to help U.S. Government Agencies and international partners better mitigate the threat of bioterrorism in the U.S. and abroad.[1] This strategy has not only helped solidify the value of the (CTR) programs, but has also led to more consistent and comprehensive implementation of biological threat reduction programs globally.

To create outcomes that will last beyond U.S. government funding, CTR programs pursue a multifaceted approach that entails establishing priority targets in the form of a region or country; building sustainable partnerships with these countries' governments; and engaging the scientific and biomedical communities to build a comprehensive biosecurity program led by the host nation. Establishing sustainable programs requires flexibility and adaption to mitigate the evolving threat in diverse environments, and cannot be implemented using a "one-size-fits-all" approach.

The two U.S. bio-focused CTR programs (Department of State's Biosecurity Engagement Program and Department of Defense's Cooperative Biological Engagement Program) use three pillars to structure their international engagement programs: (1) Biosafety and Biosecurity; (2) Disease Detection and Control; (3) and Scientist Engagement. Although seemingly distinct, these pillars can be intricately linked to create comprehensive biological threat reduction programs that can be tiered in most countries to adapt to variations in infrastructure, funding and intellectual capital. In this section, we provide examples of work on the frontline of biological CTR to demonstrate the diversity and complexity of CTR programs and highlight countries or situations with the following challenges: (1) Few laboratories with limited capabilities and widespread uncontrolled endemic infectious diseases; (2) vaccine production in low-resource environments; (3) and an overview of challenges that are found with high frequency.

The Afghanistan example: Few laboratories with limited capabilities and widespread uncontrolled infectious diseases

Incriminating documents recovered at Tarnak Farms suggested al-Qaeda's interest in producing and deploying biological weapons and highlighted the biological threat in Afghanistan. Because of the ongoing battle with the Taliban, the active insurgency, and the possibility that biological weapons had been pursued, the CTR programs put a priority on mitigating the biological threat. Afghanistan had a dilapidated laboratory system to diagnose infectious diseases, almost no active bioscience research, a lack of astute biomedical professionals, and a country not only ravaged by war but also infectious diseases.

Because security is an ongoing problem in Afghanistan, the laboratory directors embraced enhancement of physical security and adoption of new security practices. The components of biosecurity were implemented in a stepwise fashion, starting with physical security, followed by raising awareness of personnel reliability, information security, and material control and accountability and finally the introduction of inventory systems. Biosafety training was also provided to address the existing safety concerns, with an emphasis on practices that can be sustained with limited resources. This reduces the risk of accidental release without significantly increasing the proliferation risk. Alternate laboratory techniques were also introduced (pathology, histopathology and molecular biology) to improve the laboratories ability to diagnose diseases while also reducing their reliance on conventional techniques that require amplification of pathogens. Once completed, the status of the laboratories' activities remained the same, and therefore, only moderate yearly engagement was required to maintain the systems and personnel use of the system. These engagements demonstrated that even in the most challenging situations, biorisk management improvements can be sustained if there's appropriate consideration of resources and the desired end state from the beginning of the project.

With persistent funding and active risk mitigation strategies in place at priority laboratories, the State CTR program began to focus on reducing the opportunity that dangerous pathogens could be obtained from a naturally occurring outbreak. Veterinary professionals lacked clinical and applied training to support early detection programs, early detection systems were absent and comprehensive control strategies were sorely needed. Additionally, the country lacked functional and secure transportation systems to deliver clinical samples to the central laboratories from remote locations to confirm the cause of infectious disease outbreaks — a challenging baseline to begin cooperative efforts to improve control of infectious diseases in livestock. With limited resources and the proliferation risk posed by the animal health sector being the greatest challenge, the State CTR program worked to develop national policy on disease detection and control, train clinical veterinary professionals to detect and prevent infectious diseases and veterinary colleges and engaged non-governmental organizations to sustain and enhance clinical veterinary training.

Because of the ongoing conflict, Afghanistan served as an excellent example of a program with long-term, but limited, funding and a situation where programs were developed to address the biological threat posed by the laboratories and naturally occurring infectious disease outbreaks. The work in Afghanistan is ongoing, and has become much easier because relationships have been established and reliable partners identified.

Vaccine development and production in low-resource environments

Vaccine development and production in low-resource environments presents a significant challenge to non-proliferation programs. Most countries value indigenous vaccine production to develop immunizations with indigenous pathogen strains, to demonstrate independence from the global market and to provide veterinary professionals with low-priced vaccine.

In most cases, the vaccine is produced in less than optimal conditions, with little technical knowledge of antigen development, and lacks the necessary efficacy and safety testing required to enter competitive markets. Because of funding limitations, most of these facilities do not have modern production equipment including fermenters, dryers and high volume mixers, and as a result, export controls have little value in monitoring the proliferation potential and/or preventing large-scale production capabilities in a given country.

Vaccine producers without sophisticated production tools are extremely resourceful and utilize available equipment to produce significant quantities of vaccine rather than using export controlled equipment. In many cases, these producers grow large volumes of bacterial vaccine strains using multiple

10-liter flasks in small rooms with floor heaters, and viral vaccine strains using large flasks, cell culture systems developed from animal tissues and small incubators. As a result, these technical staff can produce large volumes of vaccine strains using relatively common tools and minimal infrastructure. An even more significant risk, most technical personnel are underpaid, and, as a result, are constantly seeking alternate employment to support their families making them more vulnerable to coercion.

Technical experts have proposed various programs to reduce dual-use capabilities, enhance working conditions, and/or redirect the facility to alternate business operations. Potential programs include reducing dual-use capabilities through a:

(1) "For further manufacturing" program. Such a program would require the company to acquire proven antigen in bulk from reputable producers and then bottle and distribute vaccine as if it were from the facility. This accomplishes many objectives: (1) reduces dual-use production practices; (2) provides the country with safe and efficacious vaccine to prevent infectious diseases; (3) provides jobs that require little skill; (4) and helps the company build a better business model to increase income, and ideally, increase staff salaries.

(2) Facility redirection to pharmaceutical production. Pharmaceuticals can be used without providing dual-use equipment in a low resource environment. Pharmaceutical production reduces the proliferation risk by: (1) minimizing work with infectious agents; (2) reducing dual-use work; (3) and providing earning power to increase staff salaries and improve working conditions. The nature of the work can be simple to complex, and keeps technical staff engaged.

Vaccine production facilities are commonly encountered in resource-deprived regions where the proliferation risk is high. These staff members have skills that would benefit clandestine biological programs with limited access to export controlled equipment. Such facilities should be a priority for engagement.

Field challenges that impede non-proliferation programs

CTR-based non-proliferation program development and implementation requires tremendous flexibility and innovation to address challenges in the field that may result from infrastructure deficits, lack of human capital, funding insufficiencies, capacity building by programs not affiliated with CTR and an inability to prevent facilities from working with pathogens that pose a proliferation risk. In this section, we highlight some of these challenges and provide examples of solutions provided.

Many resource challenged countries struggle with transporting samples from the field to a diagnostic laboratory for testing. In many cases, laboratory capacity building is a priority for CTR-based programs, but unfortunately, these laboratories will go unused if there is not a reliable method to move samples from the field to the laboratory. Creating sample transportation systems is challenging and requires substantial commitment in the form of resources and time. Technical implementers of CTR programs have developed mathematical modeling to evaluate and optimize sample transportation using existing infrastructure. Such models helped improve the timely, safe and secure delivery of clinical samples to laboratories for Ebola testing in West Africa.

Diagnostic laboratories on the forefront of detecting infectious disease outbreaks often have limited staff to improve laboratory biorisk management. In many cases, to be successful, the CTR programs must provide creative modifications and incentives to encourage staff to engage and participate in these activities. As a result, the CTR programs have developed adaptable curricula that can be applied to a range of staffing limitations to create appropriate biorisk management programs. Even with these adaptations, overworked staff members are less inclined to take on additional responsibilities to an already demanding workload, so engaging the leadership of key institutes is fundamental to making sustainable changes. In additional to adaptable curricula, program incentives must be included. Some of these incentives include: (1) provision of a twinning program that enables technical staff to engage with a mentor on a routine basis to provide unique skills and training; (2) participation in mentored activity that results in a publication or an opportunity to present an abstract; (3) and making staff aware of the fundamental risks to themselves and the community if biorisk management is not a priority.

A number of governmental, non-governmental, and international aid organizations work to build laboratory capacity to improve a country's ability to detect and diagnose infectious diseases. Many of these agencies focus on their programmatic priorities and do not consider the risk posed by inserting these capabilities into laboratories without critical biorisk management programs in place. For example, when highly pathogenic avian influenza (HPAI) spread to countries lacking the infrastructure to detect the virus in the poultry population, international donors helped laboratories with the necessary tools and training to isolate HPAI in remote laboratories. Often these donors provided assistance without implementing associated biosafety and biosecurity measures. As a result, remote laboratories produced and stored large quantities of HPAI, which is a zoonosis with high mortality in both animal and human populations. Similarly, we know of a program to enhance Brucellosis testing in resource deprived environments that have provided at least one laboratory with the training to isolate *Brucella sp.* without adequate biorisk management measures.

The above mentioned scenarios highlight a few of the challenges encountered in building sustainable CTR programs. The CTR programs must rise to address the continually evolving infectious disease threats through the development of innovative strategies and flexible programs.

Conclusion

This contribution has showcased a few examples of proliferation risk encountered and mitigated through CTR activities. Although implementation of biorisk management programs and disease surveillance and control are mainstays to CTR, the evolving risk and challenges in the field continue to lead to new capabilities and insights. As the risk evolves, CTR programs must remain flexible, innovative and persistent to enhance global security.

Notes

[1] National Academies of Science (2009) *Global Security Engagement: A New Model for Cooperative Threat Reduction*. Washington DC: National Academies Press.

Roundtable

The Future of Biothreat Governance

Iris Hunger, Jez Littlewood, Caitriona McLeish, Piers Millett & Ralf Trapp

Wilton Park, September 2014

Editor's note In late September 2014, deep in the Sussex countryside, a group of government officials and bioweapons experts gathered for 3 days for the foreign policy dialogue and quiet discussion that Wilton Park has become renowned since it was first established, 60-odd years ago, by Sir Winston Churchill. On the margins of the meeting, Amy Smithson and I spoke to some of today's foremost experts on biological disarmament and non-proliferation to learn how they view the threat of biological weapons and how we can best respond to it. What follows is an edited transcript of our discussion.

Amy Smithson When it comes to the biological weapons threat, what do you worry about?

Jez Littlewood Black Swans! The outlier and the surprise when you put the whole collective issue together: dual-use knowledge and capabilities; a history at least within science where you get people making very unusual breakthroughs which have large implications for legitimate purposes; a constant low level of interest in bioweapons amongst certain states; system *indications* that various non-state actors are at least interested in or attracted to the idea of bioweapons, even though very few have ever achieved workable weapons.

But I don't think you can ever sleep safely at night thinking no one's ever done it and no one's going to do it within the next few years. I'm not worried about states, but I *am* concerned about potential outliers, you can never rule them out. The threat is incredibly hard to quantify; it's incredibly hard to qualify. But that's the one thing that I worry about: who is out there or what is out there that I cannot anticipate in the next year, 2 years, 3 years.

Iris Hunger Bioweapons don't actually keep me awake at night at all. I don't believe there is an immediate threat. I'm not saying that there might not be an attack. There might well be, and there might even be 10, 20, 50 people getting ill or even dying, but I don't believe in mass casualties and mass deaths from bioweapons. I don't see bioweapons as an existential threat in Western states.

My thinking is partly based on a fairly large-scale bioterrorism exercise we ran last year in Germany. We had about 20,000 people supposedly infected and there was no sign whatsoever that the German public health system wouldn't be able to deal with this number. I don't think that it would be much different in any of the other Western states, though as we're currently seeing with Ebola, it can be completely different in other areas of the world. But, for me personally as a Westerner with a good public health system and health insurance, I don't lose any sleep over this.

Amy Smithson Is there anybody losing sleep here?

Piers Millett It's not losing sleep, but one of the things not represented in that particular world view is the very good OECD data that indicates developed countries are getting much better at dealing with complex emergencies. The fatality rate is dropping phenomenally. But just as the death rate is dropping the cost of those emergencies is escalating exponentially. So whilst people might not die in Germany or the U.K. or the U.S., the cost of dealing with that situation might be exactly the opposite and there are broader societal implications to those costs.

Amy Smithson Did I miss it or did you just boil this down to actuarial tables?

Piers Millett No, the OECD did that.

Jez Littlewood I don't think anyone's losing any sleep. Most of us who've looked at this would say the sophisticated bioweapons threat from violent non-state actors is low. We see that historically, and there's nothing in the public domain indicating that it's going to change. It's the same from states. So I don't think any of us will lose sleep over bioweapons. But I do think all of us worry in our day jobs that this is a long-standing problem that's existed historically, that has new dimensions contemporaneously and in the future, and no one can turn away from the bioweapons problem. Yet in reality so few people have a sophisticated level of knowledge about the full gamut of the bioweapons problem, and that's the problem. Take Ebola for example, what happens if Ebola arrives in Canada? Well, it's very clear the Canadian public health system will deal with it and has protocols in place to do so, but that's not news. That's not what galvanizes parliamentary questions. Fear and hyperbole and ignorance are the real problem.

Ralf Trapp For me there are three different levels here. First, there is the level of actual, immediate and current biological threats — they tend not to be associated with deliberate releases, but with unexpected disease outbreaks like Ebola, etc. By making public health threats a security concern we're actually diverting resources from where they are needed today: fighting diseases in countries that can't cope with them.

The second one is the state issue. We know that some countries continue to look at bioweapons, either in the context of defense programs with an option of going offensive if there were an opportunity to do so, or by just playing on the margins of what the Biological Weapons Convention (BWC) allows them to do. That means that if something comes around the corner that we're not aware of, if an opportunity is created that we didn't foresee, there might well be a willingness to use biological weapons. States may or may not decide to revert to biological warfare, we don't know what the decision would be, but the question could boil down to whether the legal prohibition is strong enough to keep that willingness at bay.

The third issue is terrorism. The question for me here is not so much the threat in terms of causalities, but in terms of societal impact. If a bioterrorism attack happens, I think the psychological impact would far outweigh the actual casualty rates.

Amy Smithson As a citizen of the Washington DC metropolitan area I assure you, you cannot underestimate the psychological impacts. Amerithrax was so much worse than 9/11 itself in a certain sense because people didn't understand it nearly as well. Caitriona, do you want to chime in here?

Caitriona McLeish I'm not losing sleep either but I am a bit concerned about how the problem is being framed and, so by extension, how the solutions are being framed. The way that the biothreat problem is currently framed tends to highlight certain aspects and attributes of biological weapons over others. The focus is often on the cutting edge, the lethal, the high impact and high consequence events. Well, what about biological weapons developed or used that don't kill or kill very few, we shouldn't worry about them? I also don't hear a lot about animals and plants, and that worries me too because we're concentrating our resources — for very understandable reasons, both historical and impact-wise, don't get me wrong — on preventing human deaths. You don't get human body bags with animals or with plants, but that doesn't mean a deliberate disease outbreak targeted at plants or animals wouldn't have an impact on humans, on society — yet we don't seem to be paying equivalent attention to them, coming out with countermeasures. If I'm to be worried, I'd worry about being blindsided.

Amy Smithson So you're back at Black Swans, which is a reasonable place to be. Let me get you to roll out the plant and animal part of this equation a bit more. Are we focusing too much on the threat to humans and not enough on the threat to livestock and animals, or is this something that states and non-state actors are not as interested in?

Caitriona McLeish I think it's dangerous to try to get inside the head of what a state or non-state actor with this intention might or might not do. The historical record shows us that we ought to be cognizant of deliberate use of plant and animal diseases, especially animal, but that doesn't change the current policy frame. Do we emphasize human disease? Yes. Do our biodefense-specific countermeasures emphasize human diseases? Yes. Now, it might be that in animal and agricultural services they have a different perception on disease management and disease security such that perhaps there are measures in place which would be sufficient if there was a deliberate outbreak. If that's the case, I would like to hear more about them.

Amy Smithson Our tendency is to fall back on catch phrases like low frequency, high consequence, do you have any other ways you would like for this threat to be characterized? How should we be characterizing this threat if not with phrases like that?

Jez Littlewood It's a persistent low level risk.

Piers Millett It's something you're going to have to live with. It's not one that's going to go away. There's a need for a broader societal discussion about living with certain levels of risk. The increasing access to or reliance on the benefits of biotechnology and life science applications comes with a degree of risk. How we're prepared to live with that risk is part of the discussion.

Ralf Trapp Because we're talking about biological weapons, we tend to phrase discussions in terms that come from a military context: casualties meaning dead bodies, high probability — high impact, versus low probability — low impact. But what we are really measuring in the case of biological weapons and biological factors could be health impact, it could be long term effects such as sickness and disability, not necessarily lethality. So that's one of the things we need to qualify when we talk about the effect of bioweapons. We're not necessarily just talking about dead people — mostly not, actually.

Iris Hunger I actually like the focus on people because for me that's the most important negative effect. Human life has no price tag — no monetary value can be attached to it. We would do everything to save a human life. There is no compromise and it is not the same with animals and certainly not with plants. So I think it's right to focus on ill people or dead people.

Ralf Trapp I think you should separate these issues. They're all legitimate concerns albeit for different reasons. Anti-crop and anti-livestock weapons have a strong economic component. They also have a component of social stability and sustainability. But it's a different thing to killing or making a large number of people sick.

Iris Hunger In terms of the prohibition and the norm against biological weapons it is essential to include plants and animals. If we focus too much on humans, a side effect might be the weakening of the norm against anti-crop and anti-livestock weapons. But in terms of response I think it is right to focus predominantly on humans.

Jez Littlewood Ultimately, it comes down to a framing issue: How do you grab people's attention and convince them to do something about it? Disease outbreaks in animals don't resonate with the media or with politicians. Dead pigs don't count. The foot and mouth disease outbreak in the United Kingdom is a very good indication of the potential economic cost of anti-livestock weapons, but they're not attractive to the vast majority of terrorist groups for good reasons as far as we understand terrorist groups.

For state use of anti-livestock weapons we're getting

into strategic calculations, not tactical use, and our scenarios would enter a whole different ballgame in which everything as we understand it now is off the table. The strategic use of biological weapons is a very different world to the one we have lived in for the last 45 years.

Piers Millett I have two issues on this. Firstly, the preparations and response capacity for animal and plant diseases are orders of magnitude below human diseases, so just the resilience of the system is not the same. And if you move into societies where the boundary between starvation and discomfort is not quite the same as it is in Europe or North America then you end up in a very different security dynamic. Secondly, if you believe that biotechnology could be a major manufacturing platform for the future, then the scope of current discussions is radically altered. If we rely on biological production facilities to make things, we open up a new vulnerability and then the security dynamic in which body bags are the metric changes.

Amy Smithson Why haven't there been more bioterrorism attacks?

Piers Millett Because it's hard!

Iris Hunger I agree. For most biological agents if you get the temperature wrong, or the broth that they're growing in wrong, they're just not going to work — unlike with ricin, for example, where there are very primitive ways of producing it and it doesn't matter if you add a bit more from one thing into the mixture, there will still be ricin coming out at the end. So I would also say it's not that easy, especially for smaller groups.

I must say quite frankly I don't understand it. It's not easy in the sense that everybody can do it, but there are enough people who are able to do it. Why those have never been recruited by a terrorist organization really puzzles me.

Jez Littlewood I'm a big subscriber to the work of people like Kathleen Vogel and Sonia Ben Ouagrham-Gormley on tacit knowledge and its importance for developing biological weapons. So just because cutting edge research on something like synthetic biology is published in *Science* or *Nature* it doesn't mean everyone can now go off and produce polio virus from scratch. Vogel's work makes it quite clear they can't do that. It is not a simple recipe you follow. It's not simple replication. There is a whole set of understandings and experience.

Put simply, the idea of terrorists trying to become scientists is a risk we can live with because we have a sense of the likely outcomes of that. The problem of scientists becoming radicalized to violence is a more complicated and more worrying issue.

Ralf Trapp I agree with that, but at the same time, a scientist turned terrorist is not yet a weaponeer. There're still a number of steps to go from being even a brilliant scientist knowing exactly how to do biology, to having something at the end that you can actually use as a weapon.

Caitriona McLeish I agree with everything that has been said, it really isn't as easy as sometimes it is made out to be and Ralf points to that really important stage between having something and actually being able to use it. That is such an important stage.

Amy Smithson Has the focus on terrorist level issues over the past 15–20 years short-changed the state level threat?

Piers Millett Yes. If you believe having access to all the bits to make a biological weapon equals making a biological weapon, then that framing becomes very difficult in a terrorist setting. Because with inherently dual-use technology, in an environment where arguably a degree of tacit knowledge has been eroded in the weaponization process, and a significant number of steps have been simplified through technological advances, then the capacity, theoretically, to produce a weapon is easier. And so the focus on terrorists being able to do that comes to the fore when the capacity to deliver that in a reasonably reliable and systematic manner probably still requires a degree of resources not easily accessible in many non-state settings. Therefore, if you were going to apply the sorts of things that are generally considered to be elevating risk in the contemporary risk environment, in my view, a state would be more likely to put them together in a way that would change the risk environment than a non-state actor.

Amy Smithson Then explain to me why states aren't at the forefront of the discussion of biological threats?

Piers Millett Because terrorists are nice low hanging fruit ...

Iris Hunger There's no clear indication that states are interested in bioweapons. When you look at the evidence it's all "may" or "could" or "has an interest" or "has the capability"; it's not clear evidence that they have state programs except probably in one or two cases. When the State Department compliance lists started coming out there used to be half a dozen or a dozen states on it with bioweapon programs, but the list got shorter and shorter after 1989 and I don't know if anyone is even still on their list except probably Iran and North Korea.

Amy Smithson Is anyone on your own list?

Iris Hunger North Korea, not that I have any proof, but simply because it's a country where I believe they would do everything nasty they can. But that doesn't mean other countries couldn't if they wanted to.

Ralf Trapp I believe that what you have to think about is why and under what circumstances countries may decide to move back into an offensive program. You mentioned North Korea, I don't know whether they have a program or not, but it's possible. It's also possible that they are just at an R&D stage.

There are a number of countries that have capabilities in certain areas but I don't believe any of those countries have an actual active bioweapons acquisition program at this point in time. The question is what circumstances would prompt them to change their policy and breech the Convention to move back into offensive programs if they thought that was to their advantage.

So I'm interested in how offensive bioweapon programs emerge in the state context. What are the motivations states may or may not have to open a BW program? Science and technology is an important enabler, it's got to be there, but that hasn't changed to the degree that I can see something so fundamentally new today that all of a sudden everybody's turned to bioweapons, that hasn't happened yet.

Caitriona McLeish It's really important to have utility calculations, potential drivers, etc. at the heart of our thinking if what we're trying to do is ensure our norm remains strong. We might not talk about these things publically but I'm sure we all think about them in private.

Amy Smithson What would change that calculus for a state? You alluded to certain factors that would change decisions on whether or not to go in this direction.

Ralf Trapp Well, it's a complicated political calculus to break out of an international treaty and a system you are part of. What would be the perceived benefit from that, and would it be different for different countries?

And a country may not do it openly. It may well be part of the slippery slope of monitoring what happens in science and technology and finding something that a state perceives as creating an advantage, but that by itself doesn't necessarily change policy. You still need to have a context within which it makes sense to change government policy and develop a biological weapons acquisition program.

Amy Smithson I'm going to float this around to a question that I think needs to be asked and I think it deserves an answer. Why has Russia not opened its military facilities? There're so many facilities that were opened under CTR. There are some that remain closed. What explanations do you have for that?

Iris Hunger As far as I know, it was all the military facilities that stayed closed. All the non-military ones are accessible; the military ones not. So an explanation could simply be that it was a general decision that military facilities stay closed to their former biggest enemy. If it was just one that remained closed I would be much more suspicious, but because none of the military facilities opened up, I don't think it necessarily implies the state is trying to hide something.

Caitriona McLeish Answering your question with a question Amy, and playing Devil's Advocate: Why should they, what do they gain?

Jez Littlewood It's the classic problem of changing people's world views. It can take a preponderance of evidence to change someone's mind. If you are of the view that the Soviet Union had an offensive bioweapons program ready to go — and pointing to the evidence I'm aware of in the public domain written by experts I would go along with that — which Russia inherited and has been less than ideally transparent in confirming its continuing existence or not, then there's always going to be suspicion over the Russian program.

From the Russian perspective, there's always going to be suspicion over the U.S. biodefense program, and revelations immediately prior to 9/11 from Judith Miller and others supported those suspicions. So even if you don't agree with the Russians you can at least understand where they are coming from. I certainly know that some of the U.S.' closest allies were raising their eyebrows and asking what was going on in the U.S. biodefense program. So it's a perception issue and a world view issue. I could reel off two, three, four countries I might have personal concerns about without having any evidence. It's a world view; it's a perception of how they are, how they react in the international community, which influences that. It's not based on any evidence of what they are doing in this realm of potential military uses of biotechnology.

Filippa Lentzos Do you think it likely that Russia still has an active bioweapons program?

Jez Littlewood I'd view it in the same way that I viewed the revelations from 2001 on the U.S. biodefense program. It's the "so what" question.

So, say someone is playing around with this. They go to senior people and say, "do you know what guys, we can do X, Y, Z, this has potential for major contribution to operations, this is a game changer." At some point in time somebody has to make a political decision saying "we're on board." The move from potential to capability, the move from potential to incorporation into doctrine that takes a very hard political decision and I think many people when you begin to cross that line would say, "hold on a second, what are we actually gaining here? Outside a survival scenario we are potentially not making our military situation or our political situation better." So I think this is where the norm plays in. This is where the taboo plays in. This is where the various elements against bioweapons play in, in ways that we cannot easily quantify or qualify.

Amy Smithson How then do you explain what we now know to be a Soviet biological weapons program? Because there were obvious political decisions taken to go after something that big, that diversified, that quantity, that designed to kill in large scales.

Jez Littlewood But in a "just in time if we need a creative capability", not in a "let's have it ready to go in missiles" capability.

Iris Hunger I think you need to make a difference between deciding to start a program and deciding to continue a program.

The 1970s, when the big decision was made in the Soviet Union, was at a time when big bioweapons programs had been taking place for decades, not just in Russia, but in the U.S. particularly, so it was just a continuation.

Now, I think pretty much even the Russians must know that the U.S. doesn't have a big bioweapons program any longer. They might be suspicious about certain activities, but I think even most of the Russians know that no one has rockets ready to go. So it would be a completely different thing to make that decision today.

Ralf Trapp That takes you back to the question of the role of transparency in one sense, and also why the Russians look at this differently from other people. The Russians would say "does it matter if we open up everything in the past; is it not more important that there is no program today and that we stick to the regime as everybody else does." There is a tendency in the Russian way of looking at things to say, okay, this is the past, now let's deal with the future. Let's deal with what we actually have today and what we're doing in the future. Why on earth dig into things that don't do any good today?

Jez Littlewood The most appropriate analogy is in a sense to the U.S. Let's say the U.S. government decides to open up the facilities involved in its biodefense program. Lots of people may look at the evidence and be convinced that this is legitimate defense. But there will be a segment of society within the United States and there will be a segment of society within the international community that will take what they see and say "see, we told you so, they are doing this, they are covering up offensive bioweapons activities." So this is where your world view and dissonance issues come in.

We saw it in our earlier discussion today too. The U.K. archives clearly indicate that at some point in 1956 there was a Cabinet level decision to abandon our offensive chemical weapons program. There's a papertrail that tells us that. Yet if someone came in and said "give me the piece of paperwork that tells me the U.K. abandoned the bioweapons offensive program" we'd have a hard time. The person with the closest knowledge of that history and with access to that documentation cannot find a single piece of paper saying that. So if you wish to believe the U.K. is continuing an offensive bioweapons program the evidence is there before you: You abandoned chemical weapons formally, here's the decision at cabinet level. There is no comparative decision at cabinet level within the U.K. for a bioweapons program, therefore, ergo, you must have continued.

Of course, I have zero concerns about the U.K., my

point is you need a preponderance of evidence to convince and change your mind. We know the Soviet Union had an offensive bioweapons program. We have concerns about Russian transparency in terms of their various facilities which leads us to believe there is potentially a Russian program, and it will take a lot of evidence to change our minds.

Amy Smithson Let me take you back to Asilomar and the early days of recombinant DNA technology when there was such public concern about the technology that the scientists who were conducting this work decided to suspend what they were doing and get together to discuss what they could do to make the public feel comfortable with their science. It was really one of those situations where you have to take your hat off to scientists for recognizing that public concerns quite frankly could shut them down.

Today there is again controversy about life science research — whether it's mousepox or H5N1 or gain of function in other ways — but it doesn't appear that the science community is taking the same proactive approach. Can life scientists govern themselves? Do we have a science governance problem?

Jez Littlewood The very few incidents involving the deliberate use of biological weapons and the vast increase in the number of scientists with the potential knowledge base and access to technology which could be misused suggest that they *can* govern themselves, but there are probably other issues like norms and responsible science that are more important. Can we ever offer a guarantee that no scientist will go down this route for personal profit or personal political agendas? Of course, we can't.

Iris Hunger I don't want them governing themselves. I'd like a pretty strong legal framework. We don't let teachers or doctors govern themselves. They have the Hippocratic Oath, sure, and that's very important, but there are rules and regulations and laws and prisons if they don't follow those. So I think we need the same thing for scientists.

Filippa Lentzos For all scientists or only scientists who are working with certain pathogens or doing particular kinds of research?

Iris Hunger Of course, it cannot be the same regulation for all types of work and we have that to a certain degree already in place. We just need to make sure that it's sufficient. Scientists are governed by laws and regulations on certain types of activities. It's as if we're still under the impression that scientists work under the famous freedom of science credo. Of course, it's an important credo and I support it with all my heart, but there are limits to scientific freedom; scientists are not allowed to do whatever they want to. They have to work within the law.

Amy Smithson What credo do you think life scientists should live by in today's life science environment?

Iris Hunger Do no wrong to the best of your knowledge and abilities. It is a basic rule that any person should live according to.

Caitriona McLeish I'd add be modest about what you know, respectful towards what you're studying and be transparent about, and accountable for, all of your actions.

Ralf Trapp It's what you *do*, not what you *are* that matters in terms of regulation. You do certain things that are regulated so that brings you under the regulations, not whether you're a scientist or technician or something else, or whether you are somebody who has happened to acquire the knowledge through traditional means. That's not the point. The point is what you're actually doing. So if you look at safety, that is, what you do in a safety regulation. I don't care if somebody is a chemist or a biologist, if he does certain things there are regulations for what one can do and how to do it.

Piers Millett What I'd like to get at is the starting line of what's allowed. Iris, in Germany, is the starting line for regulation everything's permitted or everything's prohibited unless you have permission?

Iris Hunger The starting point is, everything is allowed unless it's prohibited or you need a license. There'll be certain biological agents and certain kinds of work like genetic modification that needs some kind of license. Facilities get licensed, and people and projects get licensed.

Piers Millett The U.S. oversight system is very Institutional Biosafety Committee (IBC) dominated. What if I was in a setting that didn't require an IBC, say if I was doing this at home with private funding that wasn't NIH driven, would I need to go through any of those steps? No. But would I need to do that in Germany?

Iris Hunger Yes, you would. Whenever you take, for example, Ebola in your hands you have to do certain things independently of who you are and where you do it.

Amy Smithson Are there certain risks to life scientists if they don't become more proactive in terms of self-governance? If something happens that is perhaps understandable from a life science perspective, but very scary from a lay public perspective, are there certain risks they're taking by not being more proactive in self-governance?

Iris Hunger I always like to believe that there is an international scientific community and that scientists in general, most of them, try to do good things. And I think for the vast majority of them that holds true. Also from my personal experience with the biocommunity in Germany I think most are shocked when they learn that there are security issues associated with their work, and that they have a true interest in preventing something bad coming out of their very exciting work.

In general, we have seen that science has woken up to the fact that they have a larger responsibility to society — it's not just the life sciences and it's not just security related issues. It's science in general, because science is so advanced now that it can create serious risks for society. We see that scientific institutions have become much more active in public outreach and in their PR work. At least what I can see in Germany has become much more open and public orientated. So there are public events and open days and kids days and this kind of stuff which actually explains to the public what you are doing, particularly the positive sides. It's not just about telling them what the negative sides are or could be or how to prevent them. It's also about telling them why we need to do certain things and I find that a very encouraging development. If you can just fit the security issue in there I think that would be the best way, rather than dealing with it as something particularly difficult or bad or complicated.

Caitriona McLeish I've had the same experience with the U.K. science community.

Jez Littlewood Play this scenario with me. The U.S. is playing around with potentially offensive biological weapons. Then what happens? Even if senior decision makers say "we can change the nature of warfare" or "we can have a significant implication for operations," somebody at a senior level has to say "ok we'll introduce this" and somebody at a more senior level still i.e. presidents and principals have to decide that "yes, we're going to do this." They're highly unlikely to do that.

In biowarfare, this is a no win situation. There's an incredibly strong norm against it. There's a public revulsion against it. Only under the most extreme set of circumstances of an existential threat — which we will deal with through our nuclear weapons anyway — does the notion of senior level decision makers signing off on an offensive bioweapons program in Western countries come into play. So we can worry about biodefense quite legitimately, but we equally have to be cold-hearted in realizing this is only one part of an overall process of how a weapon gets integrated into operational use.

Now this might well not be the same in other countries. I have zero understanding of how it works in China. I have zero understanding of how it works south of the Mediterranean. I have no idea about those cultures. I have no idea about the power of civil society, political structures, military people. What I would immediately draw from is the nuclear weapons proliferation literature which makes it very clear that coupling science and technology with ambitious military objectives leads you to proliferation.

Amy Smithson There have been so many phenomenal breakthroughs in the area of arms control and disarmament in the last 30–40 year, but in the area of biological non-proliferation and disarmament we've literally had nothing to crow about for coming up on 35 years, why is this the case?

Jez Littlewood I'm not sure I agree with your premise. The BWC does something fundamental. We can put a diplomat who knows nothing about the subject but is responsible for it in this room and in a couple of hours I can probably explain to them, if they're relatively open-minded, why it's important, how it operates and what he or she needs to do over the next 3–5 years of their diplomatic career.

The BWC also offers lots of flexibility without closing too many doors. Do we have nothing to crow about? We have nothing to crow about as we measure it in traditional arms control literature. We do not have an international organization. We do not have a structure of verification. What you have, however, is the dissemination and enrichment of a norm within broader society and multiple layers of activity. And should the BWC collapse in 2016, the UNSCR 1540 wouldn't fall with it, the UN Secretary General's investigation mechanism would not fall with it.

So there are weaknesses within a disaggregated multilayered structure. There are also inherent strengths to it. I feel more confident about the survival of the BWC as a disaggregated structure that is more likely to survive than a single monolithic international treaty like the CWC.

Iris Hunger I think it has to do with what we are controlling. Bioweapons are different to chemical or nuclear weapons. There are many more possible scenarios. There are so many different agents that can be used, and they all work differently. We cannot ban them because they are naturally occurring. Anthrax is a normal occurrence in a lot of the world. But it's not here in Europe.

And that brings me back to the point about the game changer. You said it's about the number of people affected and no one's ever been affected by anthrax. I think that's an important point. It's the rare diseases, the diseases that we don't know, that scare us. I don't think anthrax letters in South Africa would have been such a game changer. The salmonella on salad bars in the U.S. in '84 wasn't a game changer, not even afterwards when it was recognized as a bioterrorism attack.

Biology is fundamentally different. It's also that we still don't know very well how disease works in our bodies. There are a lot of open questions and it's difficult to decide what we want to limit, regulate, even prohibit. We don't agree on that and I'm not sure whether we even can agree on that. So it's also the underlying science that's making it difficult to coordinate steps.

Ralf Trapp I'm coming from a different angle. My focus is on institutional mechanisms and states as bureaucracies. States need to decide on policies and implement policies because they're bureaucratic organizations. So when you have a bunch of states who have agreed to a treaty like the BWC, they can either all implement it themselves, or you could have a degree of institutionalization and formalized bureaucratic processes at the international level. For the larger countries that doesn't really matter that much, but it matters for the smaller ones. It gives them reassurance. It gives them a certain ability to control the process, and, of course, it also makes it possible for them to outsource certain things.

The level of institutional structure that we currently have in the biological field is simply not adequate in the long run. I'm not suggesting anything like an Organization for the Prohibition of Chemical Weapons (OPCW) in the BW field unless you know what you want to do with it, but there are certain things that I think even today we could agree need to be done at the international level, that need structured support and input and some degree of management which simply cannot be achieved with the existing structure we have today. So it's a very mechanical and bureaucratic argument, but without it you're not going to get beyond the stage where there is no international system at all; you just have states agreeing on something and then they go and do what they think is right.

Caitriona McLeish As much as we can probably all become annoyed and frustrated by the constructive ambiguity of the four pages of the BWC treaty text, when you're projecting that 25 years forward, that constructive ambiguity can be quite advantageous. I don't recall right now how many hundreds of pages the CWC treaty text is, but words lock you in, and potentially they can become aged. The CWC is magnificent for very many reasons and it's really written very nicely but you're already seeing that there are aged principles or aged concepts within it that 25 years from now will only become more aged. So, all right, the BWC's four pages cause a huge amount of problems of which you've just illustrated one about the institutional support, but I defend the BWC's brevity on that basis.

Having said that, I want to say this about us using the word non-proliferation. The BWC is a disarmament treaty so what is proliferating?

Proliferation means something very specific: because the word is closely associated with the study of cancer cells it carries this implicit idea of an automatic process that once started can't stop; a process of multiplying and spreading that will inevitably overwhelm the system unless some form of drastic external action is taken. When you transfer that idea onto bio-technologies, you're saying the spread is automatic and that we are on this deterministic path, where bio-technologies will end up as biological weapons. That is not true. I know what you mean of course, but this is not a non-proliferation problem.

If you're talking about dual-use technology spreading, we're past it. I'd say we're post proliferation. It's already spread. You can't stop it. You can't rewind it. You can't turn it back, nor should you, and nor is it correct or right for you to try to do that. So you manage and that involves a different set of mechanisms and processes and thoughts and considerations and audiences and participants than needed if the spread of technology is seen as this inevitable pathway whereby anybody who possesses the relevant technology is going to create weapons.

Piers Millett But that's not what we do. That's not arms control and disarmament. Risk management is not arms control and disarmament.

Amy Smithson But is that what it should be in this domain?

Jez Littlewood That is what we understand as arms control and disarmament because arms control and disarmament is a very old war-orientated structured understanding. One of the biggest problems we have here is getting over the notion that control of potentially dangerous weapons requires us to be in this frame of mind and adopt these kinds of structures. Like Ralf, I agree there should be a fundamental international legally-binding base and foundation to this.

Amy Smithson But is it a risk management game, not a disarmament and non-proliferation game?

Jez Littlewood We have disarmed, therefore we are in the management of disarmament. We are in the post disarmament world where we are managing dual-use risks.

Piers Millett Can we ever get to zero risk?

Ralf Trapp Of course not. This reminds me of the discussion we had on safety risk assessments, where we went from risk assessment to recognizing actually, it's risk management we need, not just assessment. Assessments change, conditions change. What we do is actually managing the risks and then communicating them, making sure we get the actors together who deal with these things. Here we're doing exactly the same.

Jez Littlewood This is where framing comes back. Look

around this table: we have an individual who negotiated a treaty, two individuals who worked on a failed set of negotiations, an individual who's worked on those negotiations, and so on. None of us have worked for states but we have a fairly complex understanding of the real world. The problem is the way this is framed out there in the other world where it is portrayed as simple as: legally-binding multilateral structure good, anything else bad; biological weapons capabilities, technological determinism bad, nuance is far too complicated. There are these simplistic binary versions of the world of good and bad, black and white.

This is about the management of complex risk issues for which we cannot foresee the future. We need flexibility, but fundamental foundations matter. If I was going to urge anybody to do something in the next 10–15 years I would need to find Iris's counterpart from China, Ralf's counterpart from India, Caitriona's counterpart from Pakistan, Piers's counterpart from Nigeria — because unless those people are around this table, who are knowledgeable, experienced, have practical experience of this problem, at numerous levels, and fundamentally are sensible, our hopes of dealing with this in the future are significantly diminished.

Amy Smithson What can be done either through the formal structure, as it now exists, of the BWC, or through some other mechanism to reduce biological weapons proliferation risks?

Jez Littlewood Everyone in this room has been to Wilton Park before. We all know each other. But if I was going to plan this out I would say, okay, over the next 25 years I need to build a network. In 25 year's time, I want the kind of multinational community experienced and knowledgeable about this issue that I can bring together at a certain point in time to deal and advise and comment on these problems. So it's a very soft, not very tangible, not really quantifiable, approach.

But I would say organizations like Wilton Park or Stanley Foundation in the U.S. need to say, okay, in 5 year's time who are the up and coming people we want at the 9th Review Conference. And then I want them to start thinking about, okay, who in Africa, Asia, Eurasia, everywhere else, do they need to start bringing into this conversation where they can facilitate their expertise, where they can take advantage of their tacit knowledge. Where I can understand and they can communicate some key fundamental issues in a sensible way that resonates with sensible people who have an input in the policy-making structure.

Amy Smithson I know that the right people need to be in the room, that the knowledge level needs to be there. I'm asking you what we need to *do*; what are the actions that need to be taken either in the BWC arena or outside of it?

Jez Littlewood In the BWC arena, I would say that the States Parties who are broadly forces for good need to continue to embrace and to make use of people who are not representatives or representing those States Parties. So I need to be able to have an honest conversation at numerous levels with various people who work in western democracies and have an influence on policy making. I have that position at this point in time by virtue of my past.

What I need or what I would advise is you need to ensure that in 15 year's time, in 10 year's time, there is somebody who is much smarter, much more dynamic than me who is advising the same people or their equivalents saying you don't want to talk to Jez Littlewood anymore because he is so 1990s. You need to talk to me. And you can only do that by giving people practical experience. No amount of book learning can replicate lessons from practical involvement in complex policy issues. I learnt more working with Iris, talking to Ralf, working with Piers in the past, or talking to Caitriona. I learnt more in a practical conversation than any amount of book learning could ever give me and there is no substitute. The single greatest strength for me as a scholar is I have experience of doing it; no book on BW arms control proliferation would ever give me that.

Amy Smithson Iris, what do we need to do to better our condition?

Iris Hunger I would like to see changes in the science community. I would like to see many more meaningful, long term exchanges with scientists in these particularly interesting facilities, not necessarily the military ones because that would be difficult, but the Ebola research at CDC, Ebola research in Germany, Ebola research in South Africa. Exchanges where its not "you come to us to learn how to do it," which is still very often the case, but that they have projects that they're working on together and the people involved are rotating between the facilities. That way they are there long enough, not just a week, to get a feel for the place. Actually working with people is one of the best ways to get to intent. Of course, you still have the military facilities that remain closed, but at least for research where certain kinds of biological agents are involved. And you can think about doing it for certain types of activities also, certain types of gain-of-function activity for example, as long as it is meaningful for both sides. So it can't be the "I educate you" approach.

I would also like to see it becoming more normal to address social issues at international life science conferences. I don't want scientists turning away and getting their coffee while 'social' sessions are on. I want them integrated in a way that makes it exciting for them so that they actually stay. This speaks to developing a culture of responsibility, but that's a hard job to do and it would take a long time.

Amy Smithson What's the minimum time of a science exchange where you're in somebody else's laboratory where you think you get a real idea of what they're up to?

Iris Hunger I would say half a year. A year would be better. After a year you know your way around.

Caitriona McLeish You brought up the norms of science Iris. In my ideal world scenario, I would like scientists to talk to scientists more irrespective of what their working environment is. I don't see why there should be an issue with military scientists and civilian scientists talking to each other, it's been done before, forums created I mean. Why have they got to be cut off and judged separately? Surely scientists are scientists. Like Iris, I would like a degree of normalizing certain things.

Amy Smithson Give me your top three things for biological risk management in terms of deliberate threats?

Caitriona McLeish In terms of managing, a clear framing of "what is the risk(s)" with all the discussion that entails which then allows for identification of what is it that you're wanting to manage, who are your participant players? Mapping and identification of the participant players of the risk that you want to manage is second. And three, a more participatory management process at all levels but increased expert participation in international environments, the Science and Technology (S&T) discussions at the annual meetings as an example.

Ralf Trapp Number one: an attempt amongst states of the BWC to actually talk about compliance amongst themselves, and not just bilaterally or within themselves, in order to identify what it is that they are concerned about and what can be done to alleviate these concerns.

Number two: an attempt to create at least a *general* agreement and then from there develop a broader participation in creating the basic norms at the national level that need to be complied with.

And number three relates to engagement within the scientific community. As a scientist you have a problem, a problem's pointed out to you, or you have it and you try to fix it. You come up with a solution to the problem either in the form of a regulation or in the form of a norm or whatever and that's it. What you really need is long-term engagement on these issues, but that's something that takes time, effort, engagement and most of the scientists are actually doing their science rather than engaging in regulation or self-regulation. So you need to find a way of keeping this discussion alive in the scientific community as an issue that you continue to discuss and where concerns can be dealt with.

Filippa Lentzos Any final thoughts?

Jez Littlewood One of the central aspects of bioweapon controls at whatever level is a requirement for individuals to understand the issues — plural — and care about the norm. That cannot be left to states alone or international civil servants. For a long time there has been the epistemic community around chemical and biological disarmament issues. If we accept that science has globalized and that we are managing dual-use risks related to knowledge, materials and technology it should be clear that the epistemic community needs to flourish and expand. Our collective efforts should include expanding that epistemic community so it is representative of all parts of the globe and all cultures.

Caitriona McLeish Following on from that: for this treaty to remain relevant, to make sure the norm remains strong, requires a lot of work. Some of that work is visible, and maybe we do some of it, but a lot of the work is invisible by which I mean we don't know about it or won't get to know about it until much later on. But whether it is visible work or invisible work, I don't think any of us can afford to get too comfortable. We've all got our role to play so just need to keep tending to that treaty, keep caring about the norm as Jez puts it.

Filippa Lentzos A very warm thank-you to all of you for participating and sharing your terrific insights.

Index

D

H

I

O

P

T

U

V

www.ingramcontent.com/pod-product-compliance
Lightning Source LLC
Chambersburg PA
CBHW050524300426
44113CB00012B/1940